THE BRITISH CHANNEL ISLANDS
UNDER GERMAN OCCUPATION
1940–1945

Maurice Gould attempted to escape from Jersey with two teenage friends in a small boat in May 1942. Aged only 17, he was caught and imprisoned in Jersey, then moved to Fresne prison near Paris before being transferred to SS Special Camp Hinzert. Brutally mistreated, Maurice Gould died in the arms of his co-escapee Peter Hassall in October 1943. Initially buried in a German cemetery surrounded by SS graves, his remains were repatriated to Jersey through the efforts of the Royal British Legion in 1997, were he was reinterred with full honours.

THE BRITISH
CHANNEL ISLANDS
UNDER GERMAN
OCCUPATION
1940–1945

Paul Sanders

SOCIETE JERSIAISE

JERSEY HERITAGE TRUST

First published 2005
by Jersey Heritage Trust and Société Jersiaise

Copyright © 2005 Paul Sanders

ISBN 0-9538858-3-6

Printed in Great Britain by Biddles Ltd., King's Lynn

SUBSCRIBERS

The Jersey Heritage Trust and the Société Jersiaise are most grateful to the following for supporting the Subscribers' Edition.

Contents

Expert panel list   v

List of sponsors   v

List of subscribers   vi

Foreword by Sir Philip Bailhache, Bailiff of Jersey   ix

Preface by Francis Corbet   xi

Acknowledgements   xiii

Introduction by Paul Sanders   xv

Chronology   xix

  I   *Occupation Economics*   I

  II *Collaboration? What Collaboration?*   57

  III *Resistance, Repression and Persecution*   99

  IV *The Culture of Survival*   147

  V *The Visitors*   173

  VI *The Practice of Modern Slave Labour*   191

  VII *Epilogue: The Disposal of Occupation*   231

  VIII *Conclusion*   255

Sources   261

Bibliography   267

Index   275

Foreword

OCCUPATION IS A suffocating and destructive experience. The suffocating intensity of the Nazi occupation of the Channel Islands is illustrated by the fact that in Guernsey in 1942 there were nearly as many Germans as local people; even in Jersey there were more Germans per square mile than were to be found in Germany. The small size of the islands meant that there was no escape from the physical presence of the occupier. The destructive nature of the Occupation is exemplified by the undermining of the economy, the distortion of law, justice and morality, and of the suppression of freedom in all its forms.

Small wonder therefore that, in the aftermath of the ecstatic joy of liberation, most islanders were inclined to bury their memories and to seek to put behind them the experiences of humiliation and deprivation which they had endured for five years. Some memoirs were published, and an important work by Dr Charles Cruickshank emerged to mark the 30th anniversary of the Liberation in 1975. But, taken in the round, it was not until the 50th anniversary of the Liberation that the desire to record overcame the desire to forget. Since 1995 a small torrent of books and memoirs have been published and, even more importantly, a huge amount of archive material has been released both in the Islands and in England, France and Germany.

Some of that archive material has regrettably been abused so as to justify selective reporting and sensational analysis. The tide has however begun to turn. Some important monographs have been published, including a seminal work by this author entitled *The Ultimate Sacrifice*. In the foreword to that work, which I was privileged to write, I expressed the subliminal hope that it would lead to 'more detailed and objective study of documentation now available than has yet seen the light of day.'

That hope has been fulfilled and this book is the latest attempt to record the facts and to analyse the complex nature of the occupation of the British Channel Islands between 1940 and 1945. The author is well qualified to conduct this analysis. He is a polyglot historian who has been able to study all the relevant archive material in its original language. He is also an historian who has written other important studies on the Second World War including the *Histoire du marché noir*, an account of the black market in occupied France. Paul Sanders has written a book of impressive scope and scholarship. It is an historical account of aspects of the Occupation and an examination of the chemistry of relationships between the occupier and the occupied. Both are equally stimulating.

This book is no whitewash. From an insular perspective it does not always make comfortable reading. No one could however reasonably describe the author's rigorous and principled examination of the actions of the islands' authorities, from the Bailiffs downwards, as being anything other than legitimate. Yet those actions are always placed in their proper context. What does 'collaboration' really mean against a background of overwhelmed and isolated small communities largely denuded of young men of fighting age? With a small number of dishonourable exceptions, collaboration in the Channel Islands was something quite different from collaboration in the rest of occupied Europe. What does 'resistance' mean in small territories where there is no strategic purpose in armed insurrection and where melting into a remote hinterland is impossible? In fact the many recorded instances of different forms of passive resistance and, more significantly, sheltering forced and slave workers who had escaped their masters, testify to the considerable courage of many local people.

The author lays bare the moral dilemmas which pervaded the lives of islanders subjected to enemy rule. A number of tales of heroism emerge from these pages; so do instances of less admirable conduct. The vast majority of people however concentrated on the business of surviving until the day of liberation came. Channel Islanders have waited a long time for a fair and balanced account of this troubled period of their history. Paul Sanders has provided such an account. This book is an important addition to the historiography of the German occupation of the Channel Islands.

Sir Philip Bailhache
Bailiff of Jersey

Preface

THOSE OF US who lived through the years of German occupation in our islands, even as children, have indelible impressions of the privations which we suffered and of the spirit of optimism which prevailed. Dr Paul Sanders has taken this, perhaps the last, opportunity to listen to the anecdotal evidence of innumerable survivors, including an 'expert panel' of Jerseymen who have enjoyed the privilege of working with him. He has concluded that Occupation was a unique experience for each individual and, similarly, for each of the islands.

Dr Sanders is a polyglot, equally fluent in the English, French and German languages and having a working knowledge of Russian. This facility has enabled him to explore the official war records in London, Paris and Berlin, including many documents which have only recently been released, as well as numerous contemporary accounts by English, French, German and Russian witnesses, to a degree which no previous author has achieved. It has also provided him with an acute awareness of the nuances of meaning which a word such as collaboration can convey. A whole chapter is devoted to 'collaboration', and the analysis of the many shades of grey which the word can convey is masterly. Readers may be surprised on occasions by analogies, such as that to the Greek islands in classical times, but on reading on will appreciate the aptness of the comparison.

The high academic standard which Dr Sanders brings to his work is evident in his meticulous and extensive reference to his sources, in the depth of the reasoning behind his conclusions and in the original analysis displayed in much of his writing. The chapters on Occupation Economics and on the Occupation of Alderney are particular examples of this skill.

I am convinced that the quality of the research and the well-balanced conclusions which the author advances amply justify the faith which the Société Jersiaise, the Heritage Trust and, indeed, the States of Jersey have reposed in him. Dr Sanders has produced a work which will be consulted and referred to by scholars for many generations to come.

Francis L. M. Corbet
President of the Société Jersiaise

Acknowledgements

A NUMBER OF individuals and organisations have been involved in the production of this new study of the Channel Islands occupation. At a time when the squeeze is on in academia, the first word of thanks must go to the sponsors who funded this one-year project. In this respect my particular gratitude goes to Sir Philip Bailhache, the Bailiff of Jersey, who took the lead and supported the project in every possible way. Francis Corbet as President of the Société Jersiaise enthusiastically supported the project from the beginning and acted as proofreading coordinator. The wise men of the Expert Panel were unflinchingly enthusiastic about the venture and wired me to reality in a way only veterans of the Occupation can do. Our regular, often very animated and amusing discussions were certainly the most fun part of the job. I entirely empathise with Andrew Roberts who once wondered why he got on so well with people of the wartime generation and will happily plead guilty to the charge of being somewhat old-fashioned. Jon Carter, Freddie Cohen, Doug Ford, Sue Groves and Linda Myers of the Jersey Heritage Trust were there at every step, enhancing the project with elementary inputs, and taking on an array of organisational challenges. Terry Neale acted as a proofreader working at great speed to meet the very short time constraints. Roger Long of the Société Jersiaise also ably assisted with checking the text again working a great speed. John Saunders designed and produced the book. Sue Lightfoot created the index. The staff at the Jersey Archive and the Jersey Museum made my research a pleasant task, with Bronwen Garth-Thornton providing unfailing logistical assistance. The short duration of the project made it necessary to rely on a number of research assistants: my colleague Silke Struck in Berlin, Andrew Hargreaves in London and Peter Steinkamp in Freiburg. My Sekundant in Jersey was William Millow who spent many hours ploughing through source materials and who drew up the first part of the timeline. Of the many archivists, researchers and other individuals who gave of their time I would like to mention in particular Stephen Walton at the Imperial War Museum (Duxford), PhD candidate Michelle Irving in Bristol, Frank Le Blancq at the Jersey Met Office, William Bell in Guernsey, Ronald Meentz at the Bundesarchiv (Aachen), Dieter Ballauf in Frankfurt and the prosecutor's office at the Landgericht Hamburg. The Société Jersiaise, the

Jersey Archive and the Channel Islands occupation Society generously made available their photo archives. The final acknowledgment must go to my wife who rescued me from burning up valuable time by translating a number of texts from the Russian.

Jersey, April 2005

Introduction

THE GERMAN OCCUPATION of the British Channel Islands in World War Two was unlike any of Hitler's other conquests. So unique, in fact, that it is extremely hard to put into words. To say that the situation was complex would be an understatement, for this same complexity has been the undoing of many an author who attempted to beat sense into the subject matter. Their job was not made easier by a general approach lacking in subtlety, and which all too often overlooked the impact of insularity and the cultural peculiarities of these small, vulnerable, but proud communities. Negative news has a far greater impact here than in larger societies and one has to tread that little bit more carefully in unravelling the past. A further point worth remembering is the need to draw a line between the specifics of Jersey, Guernsey, Sark and Alderney. Geography, allegiance to the Crown of England since 1204 coupled with a constitutional relationship giving the islands' parliaments and institutions an autonomy unrivalled anywhere else in the British realm, are, arguably, the only major elements the 'Channel Islands' genuinely share. The rest mostly derives from these constituents and really is quite open to discussion. The fact that these micro-states all have their individual stories certainly does not make things any easier for the historian who has to start summarising and building a narrative somewhere; but, however hard the job, this can still be no justification for amalgamations or short-cuts. This is not the only difficulty. The most formidable challenge to Channel Islands occupation historiography is the fact that the memory of the Channel Islands occupation is situated in a highly sensitive zone: between the celebration of the victor nation, with its own taboos, and the soul searching of other formerly occupied nations of Europe. How influential a factor this has been over the last sixty years cannot be stressed strongly enough.

Additional challenges are derived from the antiquated nature of the islands' governments at the time of the Occupation. Administrative practice still relied heavily on honorary appointments, with professional civil servants being few and far between. This is not a criticism or an attempt to blame the islands for not having modernized earlier, but a simple statement of fact. The system, much of which continues to survive to this very day on the parish level, also has its civic fortes. The absence of a professionalised civil service means that although the

Channel Islands shared (and share) many of the attributes of nation states, the quality and consistency of their archives were not on the same level. Until after the war it was extremely rare to see comprehensive studies, statistical surveys or analytical reports produced or commissioned by these island governments on par with the United Kingdom. The collection and upkeep of archives was down to the initiative of individual administrators: while for example the archives of the Crown Officers of Jersey are complete, the same is not the case for many of the departments and committees. This imbalance may be disappointing, but it is hardly surprising, considering the enormous material and immaterial resources required by archives policy. As a result of these various factors, the overall documentation available from the Channel Islands side is often anecdotal, patchy or downright confusing. All this is nothing new and can also be inferred from Charles Cruickshank's official history of the Channel Islands occupation (1975). It requires the historian to place some reliance on oral sources, which poses problems all of its own.

The world has changed significantly since the publication of Dr Cruickshank's official history and many new materials have been declassified during the intervening period. In addition to public archives, a growing number of private diaries and papers are available today. This new study is characterised by a return to the roots of the documentary basis, in an attempt to broaden the prevailing resistance-collaboration binary and to propose in its stead a reconfiguration of the old, with an injection of new blood. The concepts the reader will meet are 'dilemmas', 'contradictions' and 'deconstruction of myth'.

Important impulses were given by the new wealth in research literature. As I noted in *The Ultimate Sacrifice* (Jersey Museums Service, 1998), the uneasiness of the past decades has given way to a new interest and openness. This development is demonstrated through a number of highly original initiatives launched in recent years, all of which cast light on a growing number of new aspects.[1] Once subordinate to military history and condemned to footnotes, the social and economic history of the Occupation has established itself as a discipline in its own right. The focus has shifted from a bird's eye view to a grassroots perspective; an approach interested in the civilian face of the occupation and impacted by the memoir writing of many an islander. The text pays due credit to this shift. New efforts needed to be expended toward the description of the protagonists, be they British, German or foreign. The occupation provides a powerful foil for Anglo-German relations, profiling more closely some important paradigms which have shaped relations between the two countries. As a historical context the interaction of Germans and British in the occupied Channel Islands, on a basic human level, and not through the spectre of military conflict, diplomacy or

---

[1] One of the most recent initiatives is the Channel Islands Occupation Birth Cohort Study, a three-year medical research project conducted at the University of London.

international relations, is a rather unique opportunity to probe mutual perceptions and examine this quintessential *Hassliebe* (hate-love) relationship. Many
publications of the past also failed in providing a critical, but fair portrayal of the
ethical choices of the islands authorities. The description of resistance, already
pre-configured in *The Ultimate Sacrifice* is an important stepping-stone in the
historical rehabilitation of the islands' record. Many of the acts of resistance, or
defiance, that occurred during the occupation may seem trivial at first glance.
But the supposed triviality did not save many Channel Islanders from being sent
to prisons or, worse, concentration camps for their acts. Furthermore, the idea
that petty resistance was 'petty' constitutes an *ex post facto* extrapolation which
takes little account of the pressures created by a totalitarian regime. A majority
of historians now accept the view that the myriad of minor manifestations of
disapproval or defiance in occupied Europe are indeed significant if taken as a
whole.

   The importance of this historical event is particularly pronounced in the
changing memory – and this lies at the heart of the topic's imminent interest not
only to Channel Islanders, but also to mainlanders. The Channel Islands have
gone from a post-war myth, vaguely reminiscent of the Gaullist myth in 1950s
and 1960s France, to a situation where the wartime record of the entire island
'race' has been considered suspect by large sections of mainland public opinion.
Even more astounding is the almost perfect unanimity of view between Left,
Centre and Rightist press when it comes to the interpretation of the Channel
Islands occupation. My thesis is that the current 'over-focus' on collaboration in
the islands is not merely a reaction to the comfortable myths of the past, but that
it bears a relation with the current political context. Human societies receive the
traditions of the past from their forebears, but they also take an active part in
remoulding them in line with their own preoccupations and challenges. Thus
the way the topic is handled today has as much to do with the Occupation 'as it
really was' as with Britain's uncertain position within a wider (and enlarging)
Europe and, as a consequence, UK concerns about loss of sovereignty. The
memory of the Occupation – just as the memory of the Second World War – is
a 'sword' in the ongoing present-day political debate, and it is passed to the
public through the press.

   It would be unrealistic (and irresponsible) to purport that the documentary
basis warrants any major shifts (apart from false shifts). That memory is the
single most powerful parameter is attested through the realisation that – with
some notable exceptions – the discussion of the period still revolves around
virtually the same pillars as it did sixty years ago. And yet the way not only
islanders, but, more importantly, outsiders perceive the occupation has undergone several seismic shifts. The conclusion must be that these different appreciations of one and the same event owe their existence to perception rather than

physical realities. That this is an appropriate analysis is compounded by the fact that the Channel Islands are not closed societies; information circulates freely. We may compare this situation with that of the former Soviet Union, where large swathes of history were – and still are – total blanks, where historical memory was eradicated with a totalitarian vigour and violence non-existent in the Channel Islands.

The future of the debate is characterised by graduations rather than giant leaps in our understanding, with the real issue being interpretation, and not facts.

Chronology

1940

10 June Major General J.M.R. Harrison, the Lieutenant-Governor of Jersey, writes to Charles Markbreiter at the Home Office, enquiring about the defence situation and suggesting evacuation is United Kingdom's responsibility.

11 June The Chiefs of Staff decide to send troops to the islands and evacuate women, children and men of military age.

12 June The decision to send two battalions and evacuate certain people is abandoned by the UK government. Refugees from France begin to arrive in Alderney.

14 June Harrison and Alexander Coutanche, Bailiff of Jersey, phone the Home Office to discover that no final decisions have been made.

15 June The two Lieutenant-Governors are informed that airfields will be protected while needed but 'thereafter the policy of demilitarisation will rule.'

16 June British troops begin to evacuate from Alderney (continuing until 18 June 1940).

17 June Ships from Jersey help with evacuation of troops from St. Malo.

18 June Jurat Edgar Dorey (Jersey) meets Home Office officials in England. It is decided to evacuate women, children and men of military age.

19 June Lieutenant-Governor of Jersey is informed of UK decision to demilitarise the islands.

Major General A.P.D. Telfer-Smollet, Lieutenant-Governor of Guernsey, gives Brigadier F.G. French, Judge of Alderney, 'discretion to do whatever seems necessary.'

Announcement in islands' presses of evacuation of women, children, men of military age and others, if possible.

20 June Last troops evacuate from Guernsey and Jersey. Jersey's Island Defence Force disbands.

Long queues for registration in Guernsey. Registration order worded that many suppose it is obligatory, some panic ensues.

23,000 people register for evacuation in Jersey.

Jurat Dorey tells the States of Jersey of his 'disgust' at prospect of local people ('who should be rooted to the soil') leaving.

Coutanche and Judge Pinel speak to crowd in Royal Square, St. Helier. They urge people to keep calm. Coutanche announces he will never leave.

Ambrose Sherwill, Guernsey's Attorney General, addresses Royal Court, saying '[I]t is improbable that any more people [after children, mothers and men of military age] will be evacuated.'

'Official' evacuation boats begin to leave.

Admiral Karl-Georg Schuster (Commanding Admiral, France) informed by Berlin that 'the occupation of the Channel Islands [is] urgent and important.'

21 June Both Lieutenant-Governors leave. Following Home Office plans, Coutanche and Victor Carey, Bailiff of Guernsey, remain and take over the civil responsibilities of the departed Lieutenant-Governors.

Jurat Reverend John Leale tells States of Guernsey: 'I met the local doctors this morning, and they assured me – I asked them the question – that we can maintain health on milk and vegetables.'

Following Leale's proposition, Controlling Committee set up in Guernsey with Sherwill as President establishing cabinet-style government.

Carey announces: 'It is impracticable for others [i.e. those not covered by the special classes] to hope to be evacuated.' Guernsey authorities begin running anti-evacuation campaign.

German reconnaissance of the islands begins.

22 June Farmers in Guernsey and other essential workers 'begged to remain at their posts as a patriotic duty.'

Press release from the Home Office announcing demilitarisation is prepared but withheld.

Judge French addresses Alderney's population and decision is made to leave.

23 June Guernsey doctors tell Sherwill evacuation is necessary. Sherwill tells Home Office total evacuation is desirable, a view supported by Leale.

'Official' evacuation boats cease to run. Ultimately, 6,600 (out of 50,000) leave Jersey, 17,000 (out of 42,000) leave Guernsey. 471 people remain in Sark (out of 600).

Alderney is evacuated leaving behind 20 people.

24 June Carey and Coutanche receive message from the King regarding withdrawal of Armed Forces.

Staffs of Guernsey's Methodist churches meet to discuss situation; suggestion that complete evacuation should be urged upon Home Office. Leale says this points in the 'direction of desertion from duty.' He says that if any spoke of relinquishing his post he would obtain from HM Procureur [Sherwill] an Order restraining such.

First meeting of Superior Council in Jersey with Coutanche as President mirroring Guernsey's cabinet-style government.

25 June Volunteers from Guernsey arrive in Alderney to salvage food and livestock.

26 June Chiefs of Staff consider whether Foreign Office should inform German government about demilitarisation.

28 June German air raids on the islands (33 killed in Guernsey, 11 in Jersey).

BBC announces demilitarisation of the islands on nine o'clock news.

29 June News of air raids released officially by UK government

30 June Foreign Office asks Joseph Kennedy, US Ambassador in London, to transmit notification of demilitarisation to German government.

Hauptmann Liebe-Pieteritz lands in Guernsey.

1 July Major Albrecht Lanz, first Military Commander of Channel Islands, arrives in Guernsey. He meets Carey and then proceeds to the Royal Hotel.

Ultimatum dropped in Jersey. It declares 'liberty of peaceful inhabitants [is] solemnly guaranteed.' Arrival of troops in Jersey under command of Captain Gussek. First units in occupation of the islands are detachments from Infantry Division 216.

2 July Alderney occupied.

Churchill minutes General Ismay: '[P]lans should be studied to land secretly by night on the islands and kill or capture the invaders.' Plan eventually develops code-name: Anger / Ambassador.

4 July Sark occupied.

7 July Second Lieutenant Hubert Nicolle lands in Guernsey to gather information.

8 July Proclamation issued in Jersey indicating regulations concerning governance, prices, sales and entertainment.

10 July Second Lieutenant Philip Martel and Second Lieutenant Desmond Mulholland land in Guernsey. Nicolle picked up.

15 July British attempt to land three parties totalling 140 men in Guernsey fails. Martel and Mulholland stranded in Guernsey.

Sherwill is ordered to make a thorough search in case some of the raiders are still at large. In passing this on to the police he observes: 'I can foresee all sorts of trouble if people land here clandestinely…however detestable the duty of reporting the presence in our midst of such strangers may be, in the present circumstances I can see no way of avoiding it.'

18 July Sherwill drafts a letter for Markbreiter: 'I do not know what the object of the landing was but to us it seems senseless.' The letter is not sent.

25 July Small party of Guernsey men travel to work in Alderney. Working parties proceed to travel to Alderney on a regular basis.

28 July After hiding with family members, Martel and Mulholland give themselves up, wearing uniforms procured by Sherwill. They are sent to France as prisoners of war. Sherwill finds himself in awkward position, playing a double game forced upon him by circumstances. He tries to decontaminate the situation by driving home a personal policy of cordial relations with German decision makers. This policy eventually fails because he is not aware of the Byzantine nature of the German system.

August The islands' Purchasing Commission begins its undertakings in France. Guernsey representative is Raymond Falla; Jersey representative is Jean Louis Jouault.

1 August With the intention of reassuring islanders evacuated to Britain over the well-being of their compatriots, Sherwill agrees to a speech broadcast on Radio Bremen which is exploited by German propaganda.

3 August Stanley Ferbrache lands in Guernsey to find Martel and Mulholland. He is picked up on 6 August 1940.

9 August The civil affairs unit, Feldkommandantur 515, arrives in Jersey under the command of Colonel Schumacher. Nebenstelle set up in Guernsey and Aussenstelle in Alderney. While technically subordinate to the military governor in France, FK515 yields considerably more autonomy than other FKs in the area of occupied France. In the ranks of the German military administration in France the British Channel Islands are known and treated as a 'special case'.

10 August The Census of Jersey reveals the population as 41,101.

4 September Hubert Nicolle and Second Lieutenant James Symes land in Guernsey to reconnoitre the size and activities of the German garrison and hints as to preparations for the invasion of England. A plan to land Robert Le Masurier in Jersey is abandoned.

6 September The rendezvous to pick up Nicolle and Symes and take them back to England fails. The two agents are marooned and will stay with family and friends over the next five weeks.

17 September Communal meals for children begin in Jersey.

19 September Gussek leaves Jersey. His military responsibilities are assumed by Prinz von und zu Waldeck, his civil duties by Feldkommandantur 515.

26 September Oberst Rudolf Graf von Schmettow appointed Military Commander of the Channel Islands

27 September Captain John Parker lands in Guernsey to gather information for operation 'Tomato', a British assault on the islands. He is captured immediately and, after interrogation, sent to a prisoner-of-war camp.

October The Germans suspect the continuing presence of British personnel among the local population. Major Bandelow, a German commanding officer arrived in Guernsey on 18 September 1940, promises Sherwill an amnesty: in case of surrender all British personnel in the islands will be treated as prisoners of war. The offer is accompanied by a threat of reprisals, including the taking of hostages, in case of the discovery of non-observance and continued sheltering by the civilian population after expiry of the amnesty deadline. Sherwill is aware of the presence in the island of Nicolle and Symes and urges them to give themselves up in order to avoid reprisals.

21 October Nicolle and Symes give themselves up, five minutes before the end of the amnesty deadline announced in the press. Contrary to Bandelow's promise (Bandelow was in no position to give such assurances) 13 friends and family (including Sherwill) are arrested and sent to Cherche Midi Prison in Paris, where Symes's father commits suicide.

First Order against the Jews registered in Jersey.

23 October First Order against the Jews registered in Guernsey.

11 November German order in Jersey for the confiscation of wireless sets due to 'cases of espionage.'

December Red Cross messages begin to arrive in the islands.

30 December The islanders arrested during the Nicolle-Symes affair are released from Cherche Midi prison. The death sentence pronounced against Nicolle and Symes for spying is commuted and the two men are sent to a PoW camp. Sherwill is no longer allowed to hold office. Leale becomes President of Controlling Committee, with Jurat Sir Abraham Lainé as Vice-President.

1941

January Building of Lager Nordeney in Alderney commences. Lagers Sylt, Helgoland and Borkum to follow.

15 March Bailiff's News and Enquiry Office opens in Jersey to deal with Red Cross messages.

May Fortress Engineer officers carry out 'preliminary surveys' in the islands.

June Infantry Division 319 relieves Infantry Division 216 in the islands. Commander of 319, Major General Erich Müller, replaces von Schmettow as Military Commander. Von Schmettow remains in command in Jersey.

2 June Hitler asks to see maps of the islands' defences.

13 June Hitler orders reinforcement of the islands. The German fortification consists of two fortification projects running parallel: on the one hand improvement of field-type concrete constructions, on the other hand preparations for fortress-type construction.

25 June Rule of the road in the Channel Islands changes to the right.

July 'V for Victory' signs begin to appear in the islands following British radio campaign.

8 July Carey offers £25 reward for information on people marking V-signs.

August After rationing has been extended to practically all basic necessities and food items, finally bread is rationed. Vegetables and fruits, available in season, constitute the only flexible food reserve.

3 September Dr. Wilhelm Casper becomes Chief Administrator at Feldkommandantur 515.

12 September Britain puts into process her intention to intern German agents and citizens working in Iran against the Allied cause. Hitler is outraged by this act and orders the German Foreign Ministry to consider reprisals, suggesting that 10 Channels Islanders be deported to the Pripet Marshes for every Iranian hostage.

October Prompted by Hitler's deportation order, the Germans start to take an interest in the make-up of the Islands' population. They order lists of diverse categories of people, among them all mainland-born islanders, British officers and reserve officers. All religious communities are being investigated as to their political orientations. Mysteriously, Hiter's deportation order of September 1941 is not carried out in the end.

The Organisation Todt (OT) ordered to islands. OT worker numbers in the islands will finally peak at 16,000.

Fuel rationing begins in Jersey.

21 September 22-year old Jerseyman Denis Vibert makes his way to England in an 8-foot boat.

4 October Schumacher resigns due to ill health and is succeeded by Colonel Knackfuss.

20 October Hitler issues personal order regarding fortification: large scale attack unlikely, but he wants to deny Allies propaganda victory. He orders submission of monthly reports.

November Dr. Fritz Todt, head of the OT, personally visits the islands

1942

17 March Frenchman François Scornet shot at St. Ouen's Manor (Jersey) for trying to escape from France to England. This is clearly destined to send out a measure of deterrence, as no islander will ever be executed in the islands.

7 April German military counter-intelligence (Abwehr) in France indicates the measures it deems necessary to ensure the security of the islands' fortresses. The suggestions include a ban on all wireless sets owned by the civilian population.

21 April Three foreign single Jewish women are deported from Guernsey to France. In July 1942 they are sent on to Auschwitz where they will perish.

May Trial of 17 Guernsey policemen for stealing from German stores. The sentences are severe and the Guernsey police force is put under direct German supervision.

3 May Dennis Audrain, Peter Hassall and Maurice Gould attempt to escape from Jersey. Audrain drowns, Hassall and Gould are sent to Germany, where Gould dies in 1943. Hassall survives the war and later emigrates to Canada.

30 May Knackfuss informed about decision to confiscate civilian population's wireless sets on basis of Article 53 of Hague Convention.

6 June Bailiff of Jersey informed of confiscation of wirelesses.

8 June Carey writes to Feldkommandant: 'Nothing has occurred to warrant this' confiscation.

JEP carries notice of confiscation.

9 June Carey writes to tell Coutanche about the protest he is making in case Coutanche wishes to take this information on board.

W Gladden, a Jersey businessman and supporter of resistance activities, writes to Coutanche: 'Many are saying that they would be prepared to go to jail rather than comply with the order.'

13 June Wireless sets are confiscated indefinitely. In Jersey this amounts to a total of 10,050.

Coutanche writes to Carey: 'We […] were assured that military reasons made any withdrawal or modification of the Order impossible.'

15 June Bulletin No. 1 of the British Patriots is produced in Jersey: 'Article 53 of the Hague Convention quite definitely does not give the German Authorities the right to confiscate cycles, wireless sets or any other form of personal property […] the German Authorities have neither legal nor moral right to confiscate our wireless sets.'

20 June Ten hostages are taken in Jersey in response to the distribution of the bulletin. The authors, the Gallichan brothers, give themselves up and receive prison sentences.

22 July Hitler talks about the future of the islands: '[W]e have now firmly established ourselves [in the islands], and with the fortifications we have constructed and the permanent garrison of a whole division, we have ensured against the possibility of the islands ever falling again into the hands of the British. After the war they can be handed over to Ley. For, with their wonderful climate, they constitute a marvellous health resort for the Strength through Joy organisation.'

13 August Over 1,000 foreign workers arrive in Jersey. Many locals are struck by their appearance as they march from St Helier to the west.

September Allied Operation Dryad: Prisoners taken from Casquets Lighthouse.

Swiss Government enquires of German government whether Channel Islanders might be repatriated to the UK as part of an exchange for seriously-wounded PoWs. Hitler discovers that his original deportation order of September 1941, concerning civilians from the Channel Islanders, was not carried out and the order is re-issued.

15 September Coutanche learns of deportation order and protests to Knackfuss: '[I]n view of what [is] proposed I and any other member of the Island Government […] would be entitled to resign.' Knackfuss counters with argument that it is better for islanders if their government stayed.

Coutanche ensures Constables do not select deportees: their 'role must be limited to showing cause why the persons selected should not be evacuated.'

Guernsey authorities learn of order. Told by Brosch there is 'no hope' in trying to alter its course. They accept evacuation as inevitable adopting 'soften the blow' as the motto. Decision to provide clothes and food for the journey.

16 September Jersey Superior Council decides island government will provide 'food, clothing, footwear, toys, books, education material, sewing machines and other articles.'

280 deportees leave Jersey.

18 September 346 deportees leave Jersey.

22 September Superior Council decide not to protest against discrimination against British-born residents for fear that 'such a Protest might, by enlarging the field of choice, encourage the German Authorities to take a larger number.' A protest on basis of the Richthofen surrender document (01/07/40), guaranteeing the inviolability of the lives, well-being and property of Channel Islanders in case of peaceful surrender, is handed to von Aufsess. The deportation is a profound shock for the islands authorities who now realise to what purposes the 'statistical lists' required of them in 1941 are being put, triggering a scaling down of their administrative involvement.

26 September First contingent of deportees leaves Guernsey. Von Schmettow travels to Guernsey to ensure operation runs smoothly.

9 people deported from Sark. Two others commit suicide rather than leave.

28 September Second contingent leaves Guernsey.

825 people leave Guernsey in total. Deportees taken either to Dorsten or Biberach.

29 September 560 deportees leave Jersey (making 1186 people in total from Jersey).

3 October Allied 'Operation Basalt', a small-scale commando raid on Sark: 4 Germans killed, 1 German taken prisoner.

23 October Decision not to use Dorsten as Internment Camp. Single men (over 16) from Dorsten and Biberach transferred to Laufen. Married couples with children from both camps [Dorsten and Biberach] go to Wurzach. All others sent to Biberach.

31 October Schloss Wurzach holds 618 Channel Islands internees

December Red Cross parcels arrive at Internment Camps.

18 December Ominous 'Order for the Protection of the Occupying Authorities' issued in the Channel Islands, making it an offence not to report an infraction of German orders.

27 December Following the Sark raid, the Germans suspect that the previous deportations have not removed all 'unreliable elements'. Some of the categories suggested for removal are very specific: Jews, high-ranking Freemasons, officers and reserve officers, clergy, persons with previous convictions, plus all Sark inhabitants not engaged in agricultural work; others categories are very wide and open to interpretation: 'leading public figures and wealthy people susceptible to exert anti-German influence', 'politically suspect' and young men without 'useful employment'. The first number of deportees cited is around 1000 (not counting family members).

1943

January Red Cross counts 1011 internees in Biberach. Only 20 are not Islanders.

28 January New deportees also to include ex-officers and families of imprisoned policemen; justification: 'for military reasons.'

February In total, 201 deportees are removed from the islands.

March SS Baubrigade I arrives with 1,000 prisoners from Germany, to take over Lager Sylt in Alderney.

3 March First arrest in St Saviour Wireless Case in Jersey: Joseph Tierney. Finally eighteen people will be charged with an offence.

The Germans are intent on requisitioning labour on the basis of Hague Convention. An argument between the Feldkommandantur and the islands authorities ensues about the circumscription of the type of work islanders can be expected to do. International law excludes all work having a connection with operations against the motherland. The authorities provide no nominal lists, leaving the job to the Germans to make their own pickings.

April 319th Infantry Division requests the dissolution of Feldkommandantur 515 and transfer of its duties to the division. Request denied by Military governor in France and OB West who realise that it is preferable to interpose a civil affairs unit between the combat troops and the population to avoid a deterioration in relations.

9 April The St Saviour Wireless Case trial takes place. The sentences for the ringleaders are harsher than habitual sentences for wireless offenders. Four are eventually taken to the Continent, including Canon Clifford Cohu who dies at the SS 'work education camp' in Zöschen, in September 1944.

27 April Coutanche writes to W Renouf of St Clement: 'I have been informed that the intention to return sets to their owners when the 'military reasons leading to their withdrawal cease to exist' will probably be over-ruled by the (German) Superior Authority.'

May After heavy Allied raids on shipping in the Channel Islands, OB West decides to reduce the food rations to British nationals. Following representations from both islands governments, including a first attempt to appeal to the International Red Cross and the Swiss Embassy in Berlin, the cut is moderated. To avoid the impression that this was a reprisal, the Germans extend the measure to other nationalities present in the islands. Ration levels are re-established at their pre-May level in August 1943.

Whilst investigating a robbery, Jersey police are informed that James Davey and Frederick Page are in possession of wireless sets. The December 1942 'Order for the Protection of the Occupying Authorities' places the authorities in a dilemma. After protracted agonizing over the ethical implications, they inform the Germans about the find. Page ends up being transported to a German prison where he dies in 1945.

4,000 workers present in Alderney, the majority forced or slave workers.

Wehrmacht strength in islands reaches 26,800 (13,000 in Guernsey, 10,000 in Jersey and 2,850 in Alderney).

4 September Müller leaves the islands and is replaced by von Schmettow who moves to Guernsey. Colonel Hoine replaces von Schmettow in Jersey.

November Beginning of withdrawal of large numbers of OT workers to fortification work in France.

16 November Baron von Aufsess replaces Dr Casper as chief administrator in the Channel Islands; Casper joins staff of Reich plenipotentiary Dr Werner Best in Copenhagen.

15 December The occupation mark, Reich Credit Currency Notes (Reichskreditkassenscheine), withdrawn from circulation in France. Many holders of this now useless currency try to deploy it in the Channel Islands where it remains legal tender.

1944

January By this date, 484,000 cubic metres of reinforced concrete spent on the fortification of the islands, one twelfth of the total of 6.1m cubic metres available for the Atlantic Wall. German fortifications in the islands boast 11 heavy batteries with 38 strongpoints, more than along the 600 mile stretch of French coastline from Dieppe to Saint Nazaire.

2 March Feldkommandant Knackfuss leaves Jersey, to face trial over 'defeatist remarks'.

early May Under the strain of Allied attacks, French exports to the islands – much reduced since the beginning of the year – practically cease.

19 May Feldkommandantur 515 is renamed Platzkommandantur, in anticipation of an Allied landing, resulting in a reduction of its staff who are drafted into combat units and a diminution of its status and level of autonomy vis-à-vis the Wehrmacht commanders in the islands. Baron von Aufsess becomes principal German administrator.

June The Allied landing in Normandy raises hopes in the Channel Islands of a speedy delivery. In anticipation of an impending attack, the German garrison is put on high alert.

30 June One of the last convoys of civilian prisoners from the Channel Islanders, among them Jersey islanders Louisa Gould and Harold Le Druillenec, reaches St Malo, together with slave workers from Alderney.

22 July In view of the intention of the garrison to draw upon civilian food reserves in the Channel Islands, the German military governor in France contemplates the evacuation (to the UK) of all islanders not active in food production and essential infrastructure, or an approach to the International Red Cross for relief measures.

August After the fall of St Malo to the Allied forces the last link with mainland France is cut. Islanders and German garrison are set to survive on the limited islands resources alone. The bottlenecks are severe in food; but they are even more severe as concerns fuel and coal necessary to maintain public utilities. A complete breakdown of island life beckons. However, optimism reigns supreme with regard to the arrival of food relief.

31 August Coutanche sends a memo to the occupying authorities outlining the position of insular supplies, urging an approach to the Protecting Power and expressing concern at the German suggestion that they can hold out until late January 1945.

The Allies mount a psychological warfare operation aiming at obtaining an early German surrender. This begins with the dropping of leaflets.

1 September Two letters on SHAEF notepaper are dropped in the Channel Islands for the attention of von Schmettow.

September German High Command orders the reduction of food distribution to the civilian population to the absolute minimum, or evacuation.

Gas supply ceases in Jersey.

22 September Von Schmettow refuses to confer with Allied envoys off the coast of Guernsey. The Allied operation to obtain an early surrender fails.

27 September The British Cabinet is informed by the Swiss government of the food situation in the Channel Islands, and German preparedness to accept evacuation of the civilians or relief through the Red Cross. The Chiefs of Staff voice a preference for sending relief, but buckle under pressure from Churchill who prefers to induce the Germans into surrendering if they cannot meet their obligations towards the islanders.

October The German occupiers wash their hands of the islanders refusing to accept any responsibility. Leale, Carey and Coutanche launch protests with von Schmettow, branding the requisitions as a violation of the Hague Convention. Von Schmettow refutes these out of hand, pointing to 'military necessity'.

The Germans launch a massive campaign of islands-wide searches for food hoards, registering and blocking stocks.

The evacuation plan of July is revived by the Germans, but then discarded as problematic, for fear of loss of labour resources and leakages of military intelligence. Hitler orders negotiations for civilian food supplies with the British government, via the Protecting Power.

The first requisition of twenty tons of potatoes at the end of the month in Guernsey marks a 'desperate watershed', according to John Leale.

30 October The Superior Council of Jersey approves the draft of a communication to the Protecting Power which is handed to von Aufsess. Parallel action is undertaken in Guernsey.

31 October In Guernsey the shortage of catgut leads to the decision that surgical operations are to be limited to life and death cases.

The Germans report a good harvest which will assure the survival of the German garrison until May 1945. However, no provision is made by the occupier for supply of basic food provisions to the civilian population beyond January 1945.

November Massive German requisitions of food continue. The situation becomes critical. From both islands various reports on the desperate supply situation – some of them from official sources – are relayed to the British government via islanders escaping to France.

Electricity fails in Guernsey.

Medical services in both islands grind to a standstill. Insulin is running low. After much agonising, doctors in Jersey reach the decision to apportion the scarce supplies equally among the patients. While some patients die, others survive by adopting a special regimen.

7 November After facing Cabinet pressure, Churchill changes his position: fears about 'feeding the garrison' are now allayed by the analogy that the garrison constitutes a virtual PoW camp and bears no further threat. The decision to send relief to the Channel Islands is finalised.

19 November Internees at Würzach witness the arrival, from Bergen-Belsen, of 'exchange' Jews of various nationalities, all of whom are in a pitiful state.

December Gas supply in Guernsey ceases.

The Red Cross vessel 'Vega' leaves Lisbon on 20 December for her first of several trips to the Channel Islands, docking at Guernsey on 27 December and at Jersey on 30 December. *Vega* carries 750 tons of supplies saving the population from starvation.

Jersey prison is overflowing with 'offenders against the occupying authorities', escapes are occurring on an almost daily basis. A waiting list is drawn up with prisoners taking their turns as soon as a 'place' is vacant.

1945

January Electricity ceases in Jersey.

Signs of malnutrition among the German garrison. On the other hand, selected German troops on extra rations are undergoing commando training for raids on the French coast.

27 February After a long campaign to undermine Major General von Schmettow, the latter is replaced by Vice Admiral Hüffmeier, one-time commander of the *Scharnhorst*, as head of overall command of the Channel Islands. Von Schmettow returns to Germany in March. Hüffmeier is a hard-liner who intends to make sure that orders from Berlin are obeyed.

A battle over potato and milk supplies ensues in Jersey between Coutanche and the German authorities.

7 March An explosion rocks the Palace Hotel in Jersey, a training school for officers. The reasons for this explosion are still controversial.

9 March A small-scale German raid on Granville, staged from the Channel Islands, catches the Allies unawares. This raid is followed by further spring raids, including the Malzan demolition party, on the Cotentin peninsula.

20 April Hüffmeier shows no sign of weakening resolve in his speech on Hitler's birthday

30 April Hitler commits suicide in his Berlin bunker. The situation in the Channel Islands remains uncertain.

8 May VE Day. Negotiations off the Channel Islands coast continue. Meanwhile islanders are allowed to listen to Churchill's radio broadcast.

9 May German forces in the Channel Islands finally surrender. The islands are liberated by Force 135 under Brigadier Snow.

I

Occupation Economics

IN HER PhD thesis on perceptions of insularity in Classical Greece, Christy Constantakopoulou describes the concept of insularity demarcated by two main aspects: interaction and connectivity; or isolation.[1] From the first emerges the topos of communication, trade, worldliness and sophistication. Isolation can be the point of convergence of a number of varied topoi such as utopia (Sir Thomas More's *Utopia* is set on an island), refuge, paradise, but also the prison island. It is a well-established fact that what an island becomes in the end is rather more dependent on the force of representation and auto-perception than geographic determinism.[2]

The Channel Islands buck the trend of the majority of the world's islands and microstates, where isolation and backwardness still is the predominant feature (as it was in 1940); they are affluent places. This wealth does not spring from natural resources or strategic position – the islands' only unlimited resource is their access to the sea. But these seas bear as much potential for isolation as for connectivity, as they are difficult and dangerous to navigate. In common with other peoples whose situation presented them with no particular advantage – one could also cite Switzerland as an example – their wealth derives from human ingenuity. This attains expression in the skill developed to navigate these waters and the ability to make the most of the limited economic potential through a small number of specialised value-adding activities. It is easy to see that this predisposition carries in it a heightened sensitivity to upheaval and vulnerability. Crisis brings out the negative features of islands dependent on overseas communications and without the potential for self-sufficiency, quickly turning the 'paradise island' into a 'devil's island'. In the case of the Channel Islands this risk of vulnerability is particularly pronounced, because of the high population density that adds a component of claustrophobia.

[1] Christy Constantakopoulou, 'The Dance of the Islands: Perceptions of Insularity in Classical Greece', D.Phil. thesis, Oxford, 2002.

[2] Lucien Febvre, *A geographical introduction to history. An introduction to human geography*, London, 1999 (reprint), 201–25.

The German invasion of 1940 placed the islands in an unprecedented and extremely problematic situation, and it is hardly imaginable what would have happened had one-third of the population not evacuated in June of that year. The pre-war prosperity of the islands depended on trade, and trade depends on communications. This was the first problem as military government brought a string of regulations, licences and permits which had a definite impact. Travelling from the islands to France, or even between the islands, required German authorisations. The problem attained nightmarish proportions in 1942 when the Germans reacted to a security scare scenario by stepping up control and putting an ever tighter grip on communications. Communications were not only impeded by German interference, but perhaps even more by the increasing scarcity of transport. And the fortress building programme was driven forward with such speed that the priority almost invariably went to military over civilian supplies. When these hurdles could be overcome, perhaps the most formidable obstacle of all was that they were cut off from their usual sources of procurement. As did the Breton islanders of Sein, Ouessant or Belle Île, the Channel Islanders went to the French mainland for their supplies. There was, however, one fundamental difference in the fact that for the latter France was a foreign country with which, despite its geographical proximity, there had been practically no commercial ties before the war. Even under peacetime conditions switching markets, on such a massive scale, was an unenviable and seldom attempted job. In this adverse business climate, and with no financial and material resources to offer in exchange, it was virtually impossible. Prosperity was now strictly the lot of a happy few: some privileged Germans who turned their posting to the Channel Islands into the time of their lives; and those Channel Islanders who partook in their parties and games, or who seized the unique profit making opportunities. For the others the question of prosperity no longer posed itself; the Occupation was a definite down-grade from their former existence, with scores of once thriving shops converting to the only legal business left – the second-hand trade – selling articles that became more and more tatty as the Occupation wore on. Most were living on their margins or, more appropriately, on the abyss, continually threatened in their livelihood.

Conversion, improvisation and economic control

While working for the UK Treasury during the Second World War, John Maynard Keynes found that war economies had to cope with three important challenges: the reorientation of means of production towards an unproductive use, war; the ensuing creation of scarcity and the spectre of inflation. Less supply for civilian needs, meaning a decrease in possibilities of consumption, is opposed to tendencies increasing global purchasing power, such as full employment and wage rises owing to the increased demand for labour.[3] Far-fetched as it may seem, Keynes's abstract framework is as relevant for the Channel Islands' Occupation as it is for the larger warfaring nations. Occupation placed an additional burden on war economies: any occupier, however benevolent, was to represent an additional drain on already limited resources. More importantly, however, asking people to tighten their belts and endorse restrictions requires credibility and legitimacy which administrations working under foreign occupation simply do not have. Non-compliance and the dodging of regulations, always a temptation, now took on an additional patriotic aura.

The islands' pre-war prosperity was based on several sources of income: the intensive cultivation and export of luxury crops (tomatoes, flowers and fruit in Guernsey, early potatoes in Jersey), tourism, investments abroad and the pensions and remittances of wealthy retirees and settlers who had made the islands their home. The focus on the specialised crop trade meant that with a few exceptions, such as milk, all other food had to be imported, as did most consumer items. June 1940 presented them with a 'double whammy': not only were they deprived of all their sources of income, but they were also cut off from their source of commodities supply. Imports ceased and conditions in France, the only realistic option for procuring replacement, were chaotic to the point that the first Purchasing Commission sent over in July 1940 met with limited success.[4] Islanders lived off the stock accumulated in private and public depots, which were also a target for the appetites of the rather insatiable German visitors who had often never seen products of comparable quality. When these stocks ran out – one year into the Occupation – there was practically nothing to patch up the situation. Several sources, among them the diaries of the Reverend Ord, in Guernsey, confirm a rising death rate during the ensuing period, especially among the elderly. Rudimentary supplies were trickling in from France, but this did not start to make any significant difference before 1942. The conversion of island agriculture had not yet borne fruit, and the unforeseen and huge influx of German troops and foreign workers in the autumn of 1941 was an additional and important drain on resources. People were being turned out of their houses with no notice given and many simply seem to have lost the will to live. For all these reasons there is some suggestion that – the last siege winter excepted – the winter of 1941–1942 was the hardest of the Occupation.

---

[3] Keynes, 'How to pay for the war', in: Moggridge (ed.), *The collected writings of John Maynard Keynes. Activities 1939–1945 – Internal war finance*, 40–49.

[4] In an interview Raymond Falla, the Guernsey representative on the Channel Islands Purchasing Commission, stated that he was left entirely alone during the first three months of his task in France. He also said that he felt 'depressed', as British propaganda was still in its infancy then, see IWM Misc. 2826 189/2 (Tapes 4415 to 4416). Interview with Raymond Falla, n.d. Conditions in France did not normalise before August-September 1940.

The financial position of the islands demonstrates the onus on feeding and supplying the civilian population with essential commodities. The slump in revenue from 1940 was mainly due to the loss of earnings through impôts (excise) and income tax. Although every year saw an increase in income tax, or surtax, the overall effect on public finances was modest, as the following UK Treasury figures[5] show for Guernsey:

GUERNSEY	1938	1939	1940	1941	1942	1943	1944	1945
Revenue	443,308	463,007	362,456	260,390	267,624	276,228	301,773	392,857
Expenditure	465,792	566,501	908,946	1,603,061	2,243,156	2,920,774	2,721,999	2,070,807

In Jersey the loss of revenue from impôts, entry dues and other sources of income was even more pronounced than in Guernsey. Revenue basically did not pick up again; even though tax collection rose continually during the Occupation and even though, by 1944–45, pre-war tax collection figures had more than doubled.

JERSEY	1938/39	1939/40	1940/41	1941/42	1942/43	1943/44	1944/45	1945/46
Revenue	515,546	512,758	361,781	284,187	236,839	235,444	321,777	300,580

One of the immediate economic impacts of occupation was to drive up costs for the islands which, having lost their sources of wealth, now lived way beyond their means. Although this may seem counter-intuitive, the bulk of the extraordinary expenditure did not go into direct payments to the Germans or billeting costs – at least not until 1944.[6] As the following figures demonstrate, the bulk of the extraordinary expenditure during this period went towards the Channel Islands Purchasing Commission in France.

Extraordinary expenditure (Guernsey)

	1940	1941	1942	1943	1944	1945
Occupation	108,266	188,575	337,476	276,323	1,236,274	995,722
GUB[7]	175,381	395,673	241,743	261,432	113,737	nil
Potato Board	25,962	50,314	62,700	70,346	112,275	73,000
Unemployment	25,669	61,679	6,097	nil	nil	nil
Purchasing Commission	87,801	441,581	1,195,819	1,887,081	855,637	142,621
Other	77,757	102,377	81,081	134,869	76,702	122,338
Total	498,836	1,240,199	1,924,916	2,630,051	2,394,625	1,333,681

[5] PRO WO 32/13750. Treasury document 'The Islands Budgets', 1945–46. 1945 figures in the following three tables were partly estimated. The Guernsey figures are being used for reasons of clarity.

[6] After having risen during the first two years, Occupation payments actually dropped in Guernsey in 1943.

[7] Guernsey Glasshouse Utilisation Board

These extraordinary expenses represented the additional costs to Guernsey of the difference between increased production or purchasing costs and the prices the States were asking from the end consumer. In other words: indirect subsidies to keep prices at the controlled levels and hedge against the social disruption which would have occurred had the authorities decided to pass the additional cost occasioned by occupation onto the consumer. Another interesting point is the progressive elimination of unemployment in Guernsey; unemployment payments disappeared after 1942. Jersey, in contrast, continued to dedicate substantial funds to relief measures:

Extraordinary expenditure (Jersey)

	1940/41	1941/42	1942/43	1943/44	1944/45	1945/46[8]
Relief	80,523	153,182	111,898	100,242	112,789	112,814

The production of certain items received direct subsidies. The most prominent item standing out in Jersey's 1945 accounts was the £90,000 flour subsidy, which stabilised the price of bread.[9] According to a German report of 1942 this was the third highest expenditure item (after the Purchasing Commission and Occupation costs) in the Jersey accounts. Other subsidies went toward the provision of wood, peat and fuel, the upkeep of roads, as well as food control expenses.

Early on it was decided that the islands needed to become self-sufficient in the staple food item, bread, and produce their own flour. Accordingly, the area under cultivation for luxury crops had to be converted to wheat. The second overriding principle of agricultural production in both islands, to maintain herds at their previous strength, was informed by the recommendations of doctors and nutritionists who insisted on the vital effects of the distribution of full milk, especially to children. This very successful policy was carried out throughout the five years of Occupation and under extreme conditions, in particular during the last six months of the Occupation when the pressure was on to begin with the slaughter of the herds.

The conversion to an austerity basis was also felt with regard to mechanisation. The blockade of Europe by the Royal Navy made fuel a prime strategic factor. Much of the fuel needed to feed the German war machine came from the oilfields of Ploesti, in Romania, and the Germans were also experimenting with the production of synthetic fuel. Naturally, civilian consumption was curbed to the absolute minimum to release the maximum to the German military machine. Enacted practically from the day the Germans set foot in the Channel Islands, these communities went from one of the highest concentrations

---

[8] ibid.
[9] AN AJ 40/821A. Militärbefehlshaber in Frankreich, Abt. Wi V/2 Währung, Kredit, Versicherung, Note, 17 Jul 1942.

of automobiles in Europe to next to nothing in a matter of days. In order to lower diesel consumption the Germans built a coal-fired electricity plant in Jersey.[10] The end of mechanisation also meant that manual mowing and threshing machines, as well as horse-drawn vehicles, were brought out from the backs of sheds. Farmers had to hone long-forgotten skills of the pre-mechanical days, such as stack-making, and diesel machines were adapted to run on a gas fuel. 'Living off the land' also entailed making better use of home base resources. Jersey put her ancient mills back into operation. Her sister island ran a salt and a brine plant, a forestry and a peat undertaking and experimented with the production of a substitute for cod liver oil, on the basis of the livers of coarse fish, such as the dog fish and blue shark.[11]

Jersey had a clear advantage in attaining self-sufficiency, as it had been a grower of crops in pre-mechanical days. There was still a sizeable population of octogenarians and septuagenarians who could be brought out of retirement to teach forgotten skills. Geographically the island also had an advantage as it slopes towards the sun and its soil is suitable for the growing of wheat, even though the yields are smaller than in France or England.

Guernsey was not so fortunate: it had no innate expertise with crop culture, it slopes to the north and its soil is not suited for the growing of wheat. Guernsey also suffered more from German interference and a garrison that weighed twice as heavy on island resources than was the case in Jersey. The much heavier scale of fortification and the requisition of farmland cut deeply into the total surface of available agricultural land. Guernsey's particular problem was what to do with its main asset, ironically also the source of its pre-war wealth, which in this situation was more of a liability: the glasshouses. These represented a massive investment, but owing to their use of precious diesel for the water pumps, they were very difficult to operate under the new conditions. Clearly, only the low-lying glasshouses could be operated. But once they were up and running again, what were they to grow? Surely not the easily perishable tomato or flowers? As a matter of principle all glasshouses of growers unwilling to continue were requisitioned by the Guernsey Glasshouse Utilisation Board (GUB) in 1940. The foundation of this body made eminent sense and was scheduled to make sure that growers pulled in one direction and produced food for the population. When two Jersey Deputies visited Guernsey in the spring of 1941 the experiment with the glasshouse production of vegetables, fruits and potatoes had begun in earnest. The two men found that besides potatoes and tomatoes the GUB was also cultivating cattle feed, such as lucerne, mangold-wurzel and maize, in

[10] AN AJ 40/547. FK 515. Survey 'Verwaltungsüberblick über die Kanalinseln' by Dr Casper, June 1943.

[11] JAS B/A/W/4513. Bailiff's War files. Report on a visit to Guernsey by Deputies Philip Le Feuvre of St Mary and John Le Marquand of St Helier, Apr 29 to May 1, 1941.

addition to parsnips, carrots, cabbage and turnips, as well as small amounts of French beans and peas.[12] Another rationale for the operation of the GUB was to hide unemployment. As the States carried the burden of the wages of the surplus labour, it made huge losses during its first two years of operation. This ineffective use of resources may have been the reason why the Germans eventually favoured the idea that growers retake control, a suggestion which the GUB refused. This position continued for some time until, in March 1942, the Germans transferred eighty acres to Timmer Ltd and, in October 1942, by refusing to agree to the GUB budget, forced the return of the majority to the owners. This left the GUB with those glasshouses belonging to evacuees.[13] In 1943 yet another U-turn occurred, when the Germans demanded that 50 per cent of all glasshouse properties be cropped with tomatoes again which were exported to France and Germany in 1943.[14] That year the GUB made its first profit, of £43,000, but although the German higher authorities in France insisted that this export trade continue, the cropping plan for the following year, 1944, foresaw a cut in tomato production to ten per cent, possibly on the instigation of the local Feldkommandantur who favoured self-sufficiency.[15] In view of the transport difficulties this was a reasonable choice.

Whether the GUB system worked satisfactorily is contested: while some islanders criticised the scheme for not making efficient use of resources, including labour, and thought that they were best run by the owners themselves, others defended it as the only way forward in ensuring that glasshouses were put to the use of the community. The other explanation is that the GUB was founded in order to limit German interference in the industry and for the avoidance of their cropping plan. The indication is that the Germans were under the misapprehension that the glasshouses could be turned into vegetable or crops 'factories' which could produce all year round. While at first amused by these amateurs – who had never seen a glasshouse before – giving advice to the president of the GUB, Jurat Dorey, a man who had spent a lifetime in the industry, John Leale soon found it 'extremely irritating' to be told by soldiers what was good for the island. Arguments that the glasshouses had been designed to meet the unique needs of a high-class export trade received the typical response that 'nothing was impossible', which resulted in unnecessary work.

[12] ibid
[13] IWM JRD.09. Force 135, I (b), report 'Civil administration in Guernsey during the Occupation', 20 May 1945; PRO HO 144 22834. Memo 'Guernsey', by J T D Hubert, August 1943.
[14] PRO HO 144/22834. Memo 'Guernsey', by J T D Hubert, August 1943.
[15] PRO WO 32/13750. Treasury document 'The Islands Budgets', 1945–46.

	1940	1941	1942	1943
GUB expenditure				
Wages	159,000	329,000	177,000	51,000
Total expenditure	175,000	395,000	241,000	261,000

John Leale described interference in the GUB as a typical example of needless self-assertion which made the Germans either 'dangerous' or 'meddlesome'. The fear of losing face made them unwilling to learn, adopting opposition for the sake of doing so.[16] In any case what this succession of events betrays is incoherence, indicating that agricultural conversion in Guernsey was not as straightforward an affair as it was in Jersey. The inability to make an entirely 'fresh start' continued to dog Guernsey throughout the Occupation. It is inconceivable why otherwise the population of Guernsey would have had to queue for potato peelings in the spring of 1942, while only a year later tomatoes were being exported with a profit to France and Germany. Such a dramatic change of direction points to a worrying lack of long-term strategy. The reason may be that too much focus was being placed on the glasshouses and that the interests of this industry overrode other feasible options, such as the increased utilisation of the otherwise available agricultural land. It is perhaps indicative of the fact that Guernsey had no Board of Agriculture such as the one that existed in Jersey. But even if refocusing had occurred, it is doubtful whether, in the little time available, Guernsey could have acquired the expertise necessary to become an even halfway adequate grower of corn. For one thing no agricultural equipment, such as threshing machines, would have existed that could be brought out of sheds and put into a workable condition, as there were in Jersey. Nor was there much in terms of purchasing potential for such machinery in France or anywhere else for that matter. Still, by 1943 the islands had attained self-sufficiency with regard to potatoes, vegetables and fruits. Jersey extended its area under cultivation to grow enough wheat to meet ten months' worth of civilian flour consumption, while Guernsey's small wheat production would only last their population for one and a half months.[17] According to the Feldkommandantur the main bottlenecks remained meat, fertilisers and all consumer items.[18]

It was not sufficient, however, merely to convert and manage agriculture. In a situation of systemic scarcity the market system could not be trusted to provide a just allocation of resources and the economy therefore also required controls that would ensure that the benefits of conversion were imparted to the community. In both islands the rationing scheme was extended in September 1940 and the most heavily rationed items were bread, meat, sugar, tea, butter,

[16] PRO. HO 45/22424. Report of the President of the Controlling Committee of the States of Guernsey on the activities of the Committee during the five years of German Occupation, 23 May 1945.

[17] AN AJ 40/898. FK 515 an Chef des Militärverwaltungsbezirks A, Anbauplan 1943/44 für Kanalinseln, 29 Oct 1943.

[18] AN AJ 40/547. FK 515. Survey 'Verwaltungsüberblick über die Kanalinseln' by Dr Casper, June 1943.

milk and fats.[19] There were, however, also some food items that were never rationed: carrots, swedes, turnips, beans, peas, fruits and lettuce. The snag, of course, was that they were seasonal. Therefore the toughest months for food were always the spring months when supplies were running low and the new harvest was not yet available. Rationing was complemented by the supervision of the production, quality and distribution of a variety of services and goods: food, gas, fuel, electricity, milk, tobacco, clothing and footwear. Essential Commodities bodies, seconded by other departments or sub-departments, such as Agriculture or Transport, were created to implement and oversee the new body of economic regulations.[20]

Equally essential was the fixing and control of prices. In both islands orders setting maximum retail prices for bread or fresh eggs, or for controlling the price and quantity of coal, were passed in the Royal Courts. Price control is more intricate and a trickier exercise than rationing or quality and distribution control. The entire body of economic theory is based on the concept of 'demand and supply'. Scarcity – the notion that there is never enough of one commodity to go around for everyone – is a direct spin-off of this central tenet. Price is the device which negotiates scarcity, the mechanism which establishes an equilibrium between supply and demand and allows markets to clear. During the Occupation the discrepancy between supply and demand was particularly large: the islands were cut off from all import sources and scarcity was accentuated by the combined effects of civilian freak purchases and the sprees of the army of invaders in the Channel Islands' shops. Both phenomena hit the Channel Islands within one week of the arrival of the German force. The invaders were particularly interested in woollens and silk, but also in gold rings and brooches. Diarist R Fletcher wrote that windows soon emptied and even ready-made suits disappeared. When the public realised what was going on, namely that there would be no new supplies, they panicked, laying siege to shops. Long queues formed, customers only being admitted two at a time, after which the doors were locked behind them. Similar developments took place with regard to foodstuffs,

[19] Butter, sugar, meat, bacon already were rationed in June 1940, see JAS L/D25/M410. States of Guernsey, Committee for the Control of Essential Commodities: Report on Essential Supplies and Services during the Occupation of Guernsey by German Forces and the Work of the Committee, 1945.

[20] In Jersey control of agriculture, horticulture and livestock fell to the Department of Agriculture; the distribution of hydrocarbon oils was the responsibility of the Department of Transport and Communications; food was channelled through the hands of the Food Control Office. Identical or similar arrangements are found in Guernsey: the Farm Produce Board was set up for the purchase and distribution of cereals and seeds bought in France; the Potato Board bought up potatoes and vegetables at controlled prices, before distributing them to the trade; the Guernsey Glasshouse Utilisation Board oversaw use of this mainstay of the local specialised food production, see JAS B/A/W/4110. The Solicitor General to the Bailiff of Jersey, 23 May 1941.

in particular tinned foods. Again, Germans seen carrying off large parcels did not send out the right kind of message. Finally, on 7 July 1940, all shopkeepers were ordered not to supply German soldiers with more than 50 cigarettes or 25 cigars, one bottle of wine or two bottles of beer for their own consumption, three shirts, collars and ties. Only one suit length of cloth and a small quantity of silk was allowed for each man. No foodstuffs other than fruit, biscuits and confectionery were to be bought by soldiers. But there was a *quod licet Iovi not licet bovi*[21] dimension to this, as a February 1941 case was to bring forth. At a Jersey flower shop a German officer fancied some purple orchids – which were prepaid and had been set aside to decorate a funeral wreath – for his local lady friend. Naturally, flowers were at an absolute premium at this time of the year and, in particular, under military occupation. Refused twice by the assistant, he phoned the Kommandant and then told the assistant that her choice was between giving in to his demand or a one-week closure (this had happened with another shop). The result was obvious and shows that for some, often highly placed Germans, orders were there for the breaking.[22] Before the end of the first summer of the Occupation shops were practically empty. If, for the same liquidities in the market, there are fewer and fewer goods to go around, one is faced with excess purchasing power which drives up the prices of still available quantities of goods and then also spills over onto substitution goods. The effects of such price hikes are particularly damaging to society if they concern basic necessities such as food, clothes or medicine. The only way of cancelling out such price rises is to establish price ceilings and attempt to drain off excess liquidity through the emission of war bonds, forced saving or other devices.

While the need for price fixing is quite clear, its implementation creates problems which lead back to the mind boggling task of replacing the sophistication of myriads of market transactions per day with government-decreed rules and regulations. First there is the issue of the level at which prices should be fixed. An oft-adopted procedure was to freeze prices at free market rates on a precise historical date, but this was inadequate in an economy undergoing vast mutations. As it is, prices not only serve as the mechanism at which markets clear, but also have a signal function to producers as to what, and in which quantities, they should produce. They thus play a vital role in the distribution and use of production factors. Interested in seeing potato cultivation partially replaced by corn production, the public bodies of the Channel Islands needed to give a price incentive to farmers to convert to corn. Accordingly, the price of potatoes should have been set lower than the price of corn. This principle points to the more complex option of price fixing, which is to base prices on their mutual values of substitution. These are some of the most typical problems: if the

[21] 'What is allowed to Jupiter is not allowed to the cattle'
[22] IWM. R E H Fletcher diary.

legislator regiments the price for milk, but fails to do so for other dairy products such as cheese or butter, then farmers will be inclined to convert their dairy production and no fresh milk will arrive on the market; an outcome contrary to the original intention, which was to provide reasonably priced milk in sufficient quantities. Price fixing one item also requires fixing all products that can serve as substitutes. One good example is honey and sugar: if sugar is price-controlled, honey will also need to be price-controlled, otherwise too little, or even no sugar at all, may be produced. Substitution effects are the reason why price fixing often spreads like a bushfire, until no products – except for *objets d'art*, collectors' items, antiques or luxury products – remain uncontrolled. The disappearance of items from shop windows the moment they are price fixed and their almost simultaneous reappearance in black market channels is another possible unwanted side effect.[23] Again this can happen in total contrast to the original intention, which was to provide a more equitable distribution of resources. There are two possible reasons for this: first the official price may not offer the same profit-making potential as the freely fluctuating market price. In a rising market there is also a tendency to hold back commodities in the hope of being able to realise an even higher profit later. The second possibility for the disappearance of a price-fixed product from the official market is that it may no longer guarantee a fair recompense. If farmers are unable to recoup the rising cost of cattle feed or fertiliser through the ulterior sale at controlled prices of their livestock or crops, official sales will cease and the production will be diverted to the black market. Therefore, if the public bodies want to see continued production of cattle and crops, they need to fix the price of feed and fertiliser at a level that will guarantee a fair recompense. What this means in an environment where feed and fertiliser may be scarce is that the public bodies need to ensure that sufficient quantities are available, and they need to back this up with repression in order to avoid speculative hoarding. Too ambitious a scheme was almost a recipe for failure. In many situations it would have made better sense to restrict price control and rationing to foodstuffs, the production and distribution of which were genuinely controllable. Too much state rigour in substituting private initiative and insufficient allowance for realities was not a recipe for success.[24]

The lesson across Western Europe was that price-fixing was most successful in high volume raw material sectors such as coal, steel, iron, gas, and in services – telecommunications, utilities, rent and transportation. Electricity production and consumption left practically no leeway for under-reporting or dissimulation.

[23] The Revered Mylne noted the disappearance of articles from the market the moment price fixing was introduced in Jersey. Authorities did not go all the way and control producers, see JAS L/C/2007. 'Under the Crooked Cross. Jersey 1940–1945. 2. Domestic Life', by the Reverend Mylne, post-occupation.

[24] See also Memo 'Le Marché Noir', étude par Hubert Mansion, Vichy, 20 Septembre 1941, in: AN F/60 1009. Commission Interministerielle pour la répression du marché noir.

Heavy industry was an equally unsuitable ground for fraud, as the amount of coal and raw material allocations determined the amount of re-expeditions.[25] The more complex or essential the product, and the more intermediary steps between producer and end market (such as when production of an article is spread out over several firms), the higher the likelihood of price rises or dissipation into the black market. This is borne out by the situation in the Channel Islands: although the cost of gas, coal and diesel bought in France had risen four-fold and six-fold respectively, the additional cost of gas was not passed on to the consumer and the cost of electricity merely doubled.[26]

Overall, price control was most inadequate in food markets. This is best reflected in the price index for rationed basic food and consumer items. In Belgium – perhaps a better case for comparison than France – this rose from 150 to 400 between May 1940 and August 1944.[27] The progression of black market prices for the latter was even more substantial, from 400 to 2,000. Depending on the measure in which they supplemented their supply through black market procurement, by the end of the Occupation the average Belgian family could end up spending between two and four times the amount paid for the same basket of food as before the war.[28] The situation in the Channel Islands was rather comparable.

Price control offers a particularly pertinent typical illustration of the adage that a law is only as effective as its implementation. The main institutions exercising penal jurisdiction over contraventions were the Royal Courts of Jersey and Guernsey. Prosecutions were instituted by the Attorneys General, at the request of government departments, the police or 'verified complaints' of members of the public.[29] The activities of the Royal Courts have been much criticised for the severity of their judgments. Typical punishments in Jersey were imprisonment with or without hard labour and fines of up to £500.[30] The prime objective of these punishments was prevention, as the entire architecture depended on people sticking to the rules. Severity was a vital part of the architecture of deterrence. The difficulty was that even with economic control the Channel Islands could never provide as equitable and sufficient a distribution of resources as wartime Britain. But then Britain was not an occupied

[25] In the view of Jean-Claude Hazéra and Renaud de Rochebrunne it was above all the small textile and shoe manufacturers who were most successful in fraud, see Jean-Claude Hazéra, Renaud de Rochebrunne, *Les Patrons sous l'occupation*, Paris, 1995, 173.

[26] PRO HO 144/22834. Memo 'Guernsey', by J T D Hubert, August 1943.

[27] BA-MA RW 36/257. Militärbefehlshaber in Belgien und Nordfrankreich. Abschlussbericht Abteilung Wirtschaftslenkung und Wirtschaftskontrolle, 1944–45.

[28] Warmbrunn, *The German Occupation of Belgium 1940–1944*, 246/47; Meisterhans, 'Die öffentlichen Finanzen Belgiens', 74 pp.

[29] JAS. B/A/W/41 10. The Solicitor General to the Bailiff of Jersey, 23 May 1941.

[30] ibid.

country. Economic control was merely the lesser of two evils: with it at least the little that was available could be distributed evenly; without it there would have been chaos, public disorder and possibly worse.

It didn't help that the administrative capacity within the Channel Islands' control bodies (which also pre-dated the Occupation) were no match for the challenge they were about to face. The part of the police – already widely overstretched – in keeping economic control on track is obvious. They were seconded by inspectors employed in the departments; in Jersey, a mere three inspectors at the Department of Agriculture, detailed not only to checking the quality of potatoes and tomatoes offered for sale, but also the prices. The Department of Essential Commodities also had three inspectors who checked the prices and grading of meat, vegetables and fruit and controlled the grocery trade. In addition, one markets inspector supervised the public markets and exercised control over the stall-holders.[31] This was certainly no adequate base to keep track of the thousands of transactions taking place even in a small island. However, as the experience of most occupied countries with economic control shows, it is questionable whether the results would have been any better had there been a much larger administrative base.

Although the primary rationale was not to assist the Germans, but to make the most of limited resources, it was commonly believed that controls were merely another German method to get hold of resources. This was inaccurate: firstly, economic control in the Channel Islands pre-dated the Occupation and was instituted as early as September 1939. The only real change in June 1940 was the hand-over of economic control from the Defence Committee to various new departments. Secondly, the German Occupation of the Channel Islands was run on the back of France, from whence the Germans imported most of what they needed. Jerseyman R E H Fletcher described the billeting of new German arrivals in his vicinity in July 1941. Insight into their quartermaster's store – practically opposite his own house – provided a glimpse of copious provisions stocked with food of all descriptions: French cheese and wine, dates, sweets, freshly ground coffee, beans, meat joints, sugar, but also tobacco, cigarettes and cigars, all at the time already luxuries for Channel Islanders. The men were generous and sold Fletcher some of this plenty at prices much lower than on offer in local shops.[32] Sometimes the provisions brought over from France were so copious that individual Germans took them back to Germany or Holland where they were sold to relatives or friends for currency. In 1942–43 one such enterprising German stationed in Jersey had created a small business venture sending members of his unit to the Continent, on forged travel documents, where

[31] ibid
[32] IWM R E H Fletcher diary.

they would supply a number of people.[33] There were, of course, exceptions where the Germans would also draw on island resources – potatoes, fruits and vegetables – but serious competition between islanders and Germans over the scarce food resources in the Channel Islands only began in earnest in 1944. Otherwise the invaders in the islands were more into hunting for antiques, sterling, gold and all other valuables the islands could muster and this only changed in 1944 when the Germans began to build up a comprehensive picture of agricultural resources. What the occupier did achieve, however, was to give an example which discredited the local control effort: when the smuggling of French butter, cigarettes and tobacco into Jersey was brought to his attention in February 1941, the Feldkommandant decided that local Customs be authorised to carry out controls. Except for items of 'personal consumption' all goods were to be confiscated and offered for sale at the import office. The only snag, however, was that citizens of the German Reich were to be exempt.[34] Nor did it help that almost everyone relied on the black market. And 'everyone' included members of the island elites; it was of particular piquancy that members of the Royal Courts were not immune to the allure of the black market. As a result of moral ambiguity, offenders were able to pass themselves off as economic resisters and economic control became ineffective. Successful economic control requires, above all, popular endorsement. Not surprisingly the only successful experiments with economic control took place in the unoccupied countries: Germany, Britain, Sweden or Switzerland. In Germany this success was founded on a mix of draconian penalties, including capital punishment, and the suction of resources from across Europe into Germany; in Britain and in other countries on unprecedented government intervention such as forced saving and consensual politics.

Wages are a direct function of prices. The entire architecture of economic control depended on preventing the setting in motion of an inflationary price–wage spiral. This meant that wages were controlled in equal measure as prices. Unfortunately, the implementation of wage control was much better than the implementation of price control; and wages soon began to lag behind price levels, meaning that an honest day's work no longer sufficed to guarantee an adequate livelihood. In both islands work schemes were created in order to limit islanders' temptation to take up employment with the Germans. Workers under States' authority would engage in logging, clearing streams, road works and other public utility projects. The snag, however, was that the occupier enforced a low level of wages on which physical survival in an environment of scarcity and constantly rising prices became extremely difficult. Although the islands'

---

[33] Island Archives. FK 13/4. Feldkriegsgericht des Kommandeurs der 13. Flakdivision. Feldurteil in der Strafsache gegen den Oberleutnant Otto Feld, 29 Sept 1943.

[34] JAS B/A/W/50 11. FK 515 to Bailiff of Jersey betr. Lebensmittelschmuggel, 12 Feb 1941; Feldkommandant Schumacher to Bailiff of Jersey betr. Lebensmittelschmuggel, 20 Feb 1941.

authorities attempted to counter this move by instituting subsidies on major articles of consumption, efficiency bonuses, children's allowances and free milk distribution, conditions were such that the lure of higher pay and better food available through German work was often too much to resist. While the average weekly salary was between £1.10s and £2.10s, the Germans offered salaries of £5, sometimes rising to £12 and higher. This gives some idea of the magnitude of the temptation; and one also has to factor in the rise in commodities prices.[35] Nevertheless the Germans also tried the direct route to requisition labour. The first attempt, in 1941, failed.[36] Matters rested there for the time being, but starting in about 1942 the Germans attempted to drive people from their 'redundant' professions in order to 'liberate' labour for their own purposes. One particularly revealing German letter, written by Knackfuss himself, set the target of closing down as many firms, shops and offices as possible and then to syphon off labour by the means of labour requisitions under the Hague Convention.[37] Then, in March 1943, Knackfuss informed Coutanche and Leale that more specialist workers were needed and that he would draft them, if necessary, from the body of men engaged in 'non-essential occupations'. On this occasion, 150 workers were required in Jersey alone. The authorities were given a choice to co-operate, but the German authorities were uncharacteristically coy in conceding that the Channel Islands' administrations would only need to 'name to the FK the groups of persons to whom such a requisition would apply'. In all appearance the Channel Islands were conceded the right to enlarge the lists and make detailed nominal allocations by examination of their registries, but no pressure was exerted.[38] After what we have seen about German targets of closing down 'unproductive' or 'non-essential' enterprises, the bait set for the islands' authorities was obviously to get them to name individual enterprises which they may have considered dispensable or to let the Germans do the job themselves. The episode bears some interest as it demonstrates the dependence of the Germans on the local administration. As a British intelligence report stated, the Guernsey Labour Bureau was a 'labour exchange' which kept an employment card index of all persons over sixteen. This bureau also dealt with requisitions and was ordered to provide patrols on the occasion of the V-sign campaign. The report continued that it was never approached by the Germans for recruiting labour on a large scale, as better pay and rations were enough to attract a sufficient workforce.[39] The story of the labour draft continued all through May 1943 and it

[35] 'A Worker for the Germans states his Case', *Evening Post*, Jersey, 15 Jun 1945.
[36] See JAS B/A/W/54 7.
[37] Island Archives. FK 29–6. Letter of Feldkommandantur to Nebenstelle Guernsey, 1 Apr 1943.
[38] JAS B/A/W/40 163. Correspondence of FK 515 with the Jersey Department of Labour, 3 Mar 1943.
[39] IWM JRD.09. Force 135, I (b), report 'Civil administration in Guernsey during the Occupation', 20 May 1945.

looks as though both islands did put up some institutional resistance.[40] John Leale enquired of the Germans what they meant by the term 'war work' and whether any of the men would be required to engage in activities which were not in accordance with the Hague Convention which outlaws compelling civilians to partake in operations against their own country, including construction of entrenchments and fortifications.[41] The Germans then determined that the draftees would principally be employed as gardeners, kitchen helpers, transport and depot workers, and on other non-military tasks.[42] Leale remained persistent, launching another letter in August 1943 in which he stated that many of the non-military tasks allocated to Channel Islanders qualified as indirect and thus undue assistance to the enemy and that, strictly speaking, under the Convention these workers could only be employed on a very small number of tasks such as road repair work, bridge building, emergency work, clearing up of wrecked districts and extinguishing fires.[43] In Jersey Deputy Le Quesne asked individual employers to 'listen around' and see whether any of their men were prepared to enlist as volunteers. After that he declined to oblige any further and the Germans finally decided to pick up people from the streets and check their employment records. They did this rather reluctantly as they themselves were unsure which businesses could or could not be closed down without disrupting economic life too much. Finally, in 1944, they reverted to the method of drafting entire year groups of civilians, such as those of 1920 and 1921.

Purchasing in fair France

The conversion of the island economies to self-sufficiency and the institution of a framework of economic control was one part of absorbing the shocks generated by the Occupation. Now a substitute source had to be found for the import shortfall in vital commodities usually procured from the UK or the international markets. Despite a lack of pre-war trade contacts, France was the obvious choice. Purchasing in France depended on factors that were precarious at the best of times. The effort included not only procurement, but also assemblage and shipping.[44] German goodwill and support was necessary for the provision of

[40] See JAS B/A/W/40 164.

[41] FK 29–6. Letter of the president of the Controlling Committee of the States of Guernsey to the FK Nebenstelle, 27 Mar 1943.

[42] FK 29–6. Letter of the FK Nebenstelle to Feldkommandantur 515, 5 Apr 1943; response of Feldkommandantur to the FK Nebenstelle, 18 Apr 1943.

[43] FK 29–6. Letter of the president of the Controlling Committee of the States of Guernsey to the FK Nebenstelle, 24 Aug 1943.

[44] PRO WO 32/13750. Treasury document 'The Islands Budgets – The Occupation Period', 1945–46.

facilities in an exceedingly difficult business environment, and Allied air raids and the rarity of transport further complicated the job.

The Channel Islands' Purchasing Commission was dispatched to Granville as early as August 1940. The Purchasing Commission was headed by two able men, Falla, the representative for Guernsey, and Jouault, the representative for Jersey. Falla later stated that one of the most pressing needs at the time was sulphate of aluminium which was necessary for the maintenance of clean water. Initially the commission stayed in Granville for a few days before making their next moves. The plan was to 'make friends' in Granville before moving further afield. With regard to the reception by the French, Falla says that the latter were 'rather resentful' at first and that it took many a 'sob story' of the islanders' plight to soften hearts. Apparently, Jouault had more talent in this regard than Falla. The description given by Falla of life in France during this period is full of detail: conditions in the country were still good, but the towns were already seen to be suffering from shortages. If restaurateurs did not know a face, it was often difficult to obtain even a simple meal and Falla would pay his way for hotel rooms and other expenditure with butter. Most of the purchases seem to have taken place in Normandy, but sometimes they could travel as far as Nantes or Paris, as in the cash-in-hand purchase of 3,000 tons of flour from the *Grand Moulin de Paris*. Coal and fuel purchases were also done in Paris, with the oil being shipped from as far as Ploiesti, Romania.[45]

Although important from the onset, food purchasing did not really take off until the following year. Prompted by an adverse local public health report submitted to the Germans in 1941, Feldkommandantur 722 in St Lô was instructed to lend a hand.[46] In a meeting, on 19 March 1941 in St Lô, attended by representatives of the FK 515, FK 722, the Intendance de la Manche and the islands, it was decided that the latter were to be directly attached to the Département de la Manche from the point of view of food allocation (*ravitaillement*). *Prima facie* the islanders were now on a par with the French population, but practice was different: no allowances were made for losses in transit, which were extremely heavy, especially through pilferage. Also no allowance was made for rationed and controlled goods which had gone bad or been damaged in transit. This was inevitable because of the delays in shipping.[47] A continuing headache was the rise in prices which doubled year by year.[48] The price of foodstuffs

[45] JAS L/D/25/L/17. Channel Islands Occupation Society. Raymond Falla speaking to the CIOS, 30 Mar 1978.

[46] See JAS B/A/W/661.

[47] JAS L/D25/M410. States of Guernsey, Committee for the Control of Essential Commodities: Report on Essential Supplies and Services during the Occupation of Guernsey by German Forces and the Work of the Committee, 1945.

[48] JAS B/A/W/4110. The Sollicitor General to the Bailiff of Jersey, 23 May 1941; JAS B/A/W92/2. Summary of price increases as of 28 Apr 1942.

imported from France and sold in the Channel Islands catapulted almost immediately in 1940. To pick out but a few examples: from June 1940 to June 1941 the price of imported flour shot up from over £11 to over £18 per ton, the differential of over £7 being granted as a subsidy; barley rose from over £8 to £18 per ton and oats from over £7 to over £18. Clothes prices were even worse: the price of boots and shoes rose three-fold during this short period, the price of stockings and socks five-fold.[49] And this was only the beginning of what was to become a spiral out of control. By 1943 premium items such as bicycle tyres weren't even available from France; they could only be procured on the black market. [50] Naturally, the colossal price increases magnified the difficulties of the Purchasing Commission who had to tread carefully in a foreign land. However, when the official allocation system was no longer able to meet the need, the Channel Islands' Purchasing Commission found themselves doing what everyone else was doing at the time, shopping on the French black market.[51]

Worse than the price rises, however, according to Raymond Falla, was getting the necessary shipping space.[52] The 18 months from 1941 to the autumn of 1942 were probably the best period with regard to transport. Dr Casper wrote that in 1941 the Feldkommandantur still had at its disposition a fleet of eight vessels which could be used for transport. After this period it often had to be shared with OT (Organization Todt) and Wehrmacht whose demands could be extravagant.[53] It is no secret that progressively the Germans became less scrupulous about their observance of the Hague Convention, exploiting the situation of the islands by intermingling civilian with military supplies. Other bottlenecks were created by the scarcity of packing materials which often had to be sent back to the factories or farms before a new delivery could be made.

Although myth would have it that what came across from France was smelly Camembert, in an often putrefied condition, reality was different. Although paid at often exorbitant prices, the supplies procured in France provided a vital complement to the island resources. The Guernsey Committee for the Control of Essential Commodities reported in 1945 that in terms of volume the Purchasing Commission imports from July 1940 to August 1944 procured, per head of the population, an average of just under one pound of food per day; this compares quite favourably with the pre-war average of two and a quarter pounds per

---

[49] JAS B/A/W/41 10. The President of the Department of Essential Commodities (Jersey) to the Bailiff of Jersey. Information with regard to prices of foodstuffs etc., 14 Jun 1941.

[50] JAS B/A/W/63 39. States of Jersey, Motor Traffic Office, report 'Supply of Tyres to the Channel Islands', 29 Jan 1944.

[51] This is confirmed in the statements of Mr Butterworth, the manager of 'Boots' in Guernsey and Raymond Falla, the member for Guernsey on the Channel Islands purchasing commission.

[52] IWM Misc. 2826 189/2 (Tapes 4415 to 4416). Interview with Raymond Falla, n.d.

[53] AN AJ 40/547. FK 515. Survey 'Verwaltungsüberblick über die Kanalinseln' by Dr Casper, June 1943.

day.[54] While it is true that the flow of some products ran practically dry – no meat and poultry, and practically no fish were ever imported – the Guernsey imports of macaroni, salt, potatoes, flour and, surprisingly, coffee and cocoa (!) were in keeping with pre-war imports and the reduced size of the population.[55] The largest import volumes however were not food. In 1942, probably the most successful year of the Purchasing Commission, diesel oil (£134,000), coal and coke (£122,000) and clothing (£65,000) figured at the top of French purchases.[56] Only then followed flour, footwear, meat, tobacco, and also leather, seeds, artificial manures, agricultural machinery, medical supplies and chemists' and druggists' sundries.[57] In his post-war report the manager of Boots in Guernsey, a Mr Butterworth, described how he would place orders for insulin, baby food, heavy drugs, chemicals and other Boots' staples through Raymond Falla, the States buyer, with Jean Langlois & Co in Rennes. Later, as some of the Langlois merchandise was a write-off, he switched his orders to Rhône Poulenc in Paris. He also met a German who put him in touch with a Hamburg-based firm supplying them with other pharmaceutical products required by doctors, dentists, hospitals and the general public. What is interesting is that items from France were often bought at black market prices and no two consignments were the same price, whereas the price of the goods supplied by Krause never changed.[58] Early in 1944 the activities of the Purchasing Commission slumped, but this had more complex reasons than simple transport problems occasioned by Allied raids. For one thing, beginning in mid-1943, the French authorities – with some German prompting – stepped up their drive to combat illegal markets, and this moved the Granville Purchasing Commission into the sights of the local economic control bodies. On 23 October 1943, Hall, one of the Jersey purchasers, informed the island authorities that the French authorities were moving 'against all so-called "illicit" deals and it is of course well known that we are obliged to pay more than the official price if we wish to obtain goods which are not definitely allocated to us'.[59] Hall's letter to the Jersey authorities was motivated by two visits of the controllers of the Service du contrôle économique

---

[54] JAS L/D25/M410. States of Guernsey, Committee for the Control of Essential Commodities: Report on Essential Supplies and Services during the Occupation of Guernsey by German Forces and the Work of the Committee, 1945.

[55] JAS L/D25/M410. Official report on Essential Supplies, Guernsey, post-occupation.

[56] PRO WO 32/13750. Treasury document 'The Islands Budgets – The Occupation Period', 1945–46. Whether the figures relate to the purchasing price in France or the controlled sales price in the Channel Islands is not entirely clear.

[57] PRO HO 45/22399. Bailiff of Jersey, memorandum to Home Office, 3 Jul 1945; also Boots report.

[58] PRO HO 144/22176. Final report on the activity of Boots & Co Guernsey during the Occupation, 1945.

[59] JAS D/Z/5323. Etats de Jersey, département du ravitaillement, O L Hall, Granville, for the attention of the Attorney General and Solicitor General, 20 Oct 1943.

to Mr Pannier, of Donville, the accredited buyer of cider, in September and October. During the examination of his books they had come across discrepancies which proved that Pannier had paid for cider at production prices about 60 per cent higher than the official rate.[60] Another letter of the Purchasing Commission explained that the procedure in the purchase of cider had been followed for over twelve months. At first Jouault had approached Pannier for help in obtaining the names of farmers in the vicinity of Granville who were willing to sell. According to standard procedures these names were then submitted to the appropriate French authority, the Intendance Générale at St Lô, who issued requisition permits for cider at controlled prices which was shipped to Jersey. A short while later he was approached by the local trade about the possibility of increasing cider purchases and told that price was not an obstacle, providing he could vouch for the quality. When he informed Mr Pannier, the latter said 'that if he was strictly restricted to controlled prices no supply could be obtained as farmers would not deliver even on requisition order from the Intendance'.[61] This was a new situation, as Hall stated that they should get prepared for 'similar cases in respect of other purchases here by the States or States nominees'.[62] Although in the end no action was taken against Pannier or the States of Jersey, and although one French official intimated to the Purchasing Commission that no notice would be taken of black market activities, Hall urged that caution be exercised in the interim.[63] No documentary evidence is available to ascertain whether the Purchasing Commission was able to continue with illegal purchases, but it is highly unlikely.

Some elements of the purchasing programme never took off. Theoretically the skins of the cattle bought in the neighbouring département La Manche and slaughtered for the islands in Granville were to be sent to tanneries and then used to supply the islands with leather. In reality, judging from the extreme scarcity of the material and the fabulous premiums paid for shoes and other items on the French black market, chances are that this leather never crossed the Channel. A similar fate seems to have fallen upon a soap factory intended to produce for the islands, also in Granville. It is unrealistic for the French economy to have relinquished products that were as scarce there as they were in the Channel Islands. An equal flop was the 'encouragement of pork production'

---

[60] Pannier had offered wholesalers' prices to producers: ffrs4.65 instead of ffrs 2.78 (per litre), see JAS. D/Z/H/5323. Service du contrôle économique, Coutances, Procès verbal, aff. Maurice Pannier, 18 Oct 1943.

[61] JAS. D/Z/H/5323. Jouault to the President of the Essential Commodities Department, 27 Oct 1943.

[62] JAS. D/Z/H/5323. Etats de Jersey, département du ravitaillement, J-L Jouault, Granville, for the attention of the Attorney General and Solicitor General, 20 Oct 1943.

[63] JAS. D/Z/H/5323. Etats de Jersey, département du ravitaillement, O L Hall, Granville, for the attention of the Attorney General and Solicitor General, 11 and 13 Nov 1943.

in the islands; in all likelihood owing to the low prices paid for pork in the official market this was only available from the black market. This was little different from the situation in France where the cost of buying a piglet and feeding it up into a decent-size porker often exceeded the actual fetching price at market.[64]

Procurement of the large amounts of currency required to finance the Purchasing Commission is another extraordinary story. In the beginning the Channel Islands – and especially Jersey – were rather short of liquidities for the Purchasing Commission. There were occasions in 1941 when the Guernsey purchaser was instructed to loan cash to his Jersey counterpart who had run out. The Germans first tried to induce the Jersey authorities to open credits in francs with the Paris branch of Lloyds, but they were unwilling to run up additional debt which ultimately would have to be honoured by the British government.[65] Some relief was at first provided through the sale of motor cars to the Germans. Then an entirely different procedure was adopted: this authorised the Purchasing Commission to recycle the 'occupation marks' disbursed by the Germans in the Channel Islands which landed in the bank vaults. They were then shipped to Granville where they were converted into francs and credited to an account at the Société Générale. These 'dud' marks were not identical to the marks in use in the Reich (Reichsmarks). Labelled 'Reich credit cashier bills' (*Reichskreditkassenscheine* – RKK), they were for exclusive use in the occupied territories. The particular variety in circulation in the Channel Islands was emitted by the Reich credit cashier in Paris and debited to the French Occupation account. Conversely, the actual Reichsmark was not legal tender in the occupied territories. What all this meant in practical terms was that the French were now also financing the provision of food and other commodities to the islanders. This came on top of the fact that the French state was, effectively, already financing the bulk of the Channel Islands' Occupation: the troops themselves, the cost of troop deployment and 75 per cent of the billeting cost in the Channel Islands. Although this made perfect sense from the German point of view who – for the purposes of finance – were simply treating the Channel Islands as a part of the area of the military governor in France, and thus as a part of French territory, the French government protested against this additional burden. Therefore, as early as spring 1942, the military administration was probing the possibility of establishing a clearing between the islands and France which would transit through the French branch of Barclays. This agreement was signed into effect by the German and French governments on 13 October 1942 and in November the manager of Barclays in Jersey was ordered to Paris to

---

[64] 'Making the Channel Islands Self-Supporting. Co-operation of German and Island Authorities'. Interview with KVR Pelz (FK), *Evening Post*, Jersey, 7 Jan. 1941.
[65] See JAS B/A/W/426

meet officials of the military administration and the French government. He was advised that a clearing system was to be operated through the French clearing office, the Office des Changes, and that no more RKKs were to be physically transported from the islands to France.[66] The introduction of the clearing agreement would now have implied a double debt for the Channel Islands: first the RKKs ending up in the bank vaults would no longer be put to any constructive use and could be mopped up by the Germans as 'occupation costs'; on the other hand a substantial debit would accrue for French imports, at the Office des Changes in Paris, which would need to be repaid at some point.[67] Finally the intended use of the clearing mechanism was aborted. The finance of French exports to the islands was to continue as before, with a mere technical difference that the RKKs were now to be transferred through the central clearing system at the Office des Changes before being converted into francs. How exactly this came about is unclear and one can only surmise that once more the 'special status' of the islands, a fact well appreciated among German administrators in the area of the military governor in France, had a bearing. This was a rather astounding development, as it implied an overruling of the decision of the German military administration in France and the usually rather influential German delegation to the joint Armistice Commission, under Hans-Richard Hemmen, which had brokered the deal with the French government. The military in the Channel Islands knew how to make the most of the fact that they were in charge of an operational area of particular significance to Hitler. The Channel Islands' administrations also seem to have played no mean part in bringing about this reversal. On 19 November 1942 John Leale wrote a particularly perplexed letter to the Feldkommandantur, demanding that, if the RKKs accumulated in the island could no longer be used for purchases in France, islanders be paid in francs. This followed up on earlier correspondence in July in which he had demonstrated the effects of the proposed measure: if the RKKs could no longer be exported to France and converted into francs, the States would be faced with a level of debt which was impossible to shoulder. On the other hand, if the States refused to buy up the RKKs, this would lead to a flight from currency into durables, a break-down of trade and an extension of the black market. For the grower and milk producer RKKs would no longer represent any value and this would lead to a reduction in output.[68] This could

---

[66] 'Banking in Jersey under German Occupation', *Journal of the Institute of Bankers*, October 1946, pp 208.

[67] Jersey had accumulated a credit of £233,413; Guernsey a credit of £545,000, see PRO T 231/334. Treasury to French Financial Attache, M Calvet, 27 Sept 1945.

[68] JAS B/A/W/4263. The Controlling Committee of the States of Guernsey to Feldkommandantur 515, Nebenstelle, 19 November 1942; The Controlling Committee of the States of Guernsey to Feldkommandantur 515, Nebenstelle, 2 July 1942. The letter of 2 July requests 'permission for a delegation to visit Jersey to confer with the local Administration'

have had an impact, as the Germans were interested in Guernsey resuming its tomato export in 1943. That the Guernsey authorities were quite capable of making this point was demonstrated when Bailiff Carey asked the rhetorical question, one year later, why they should export tomatoes, if no sufficient provision was being made to feed the population. Resistance was also coming from other quarters. In February 1943 the management of Barclays in St Helier corresponded with the Commissary Administrator of Enemy Banks in Paris, stating that his bank was reluctant to play its assigned part in the clearing system. They advanced that conditions were such that they were liable to run considerable losses as a result. According to their information French subjects with large interests in France, but no confidence in the future value of the franc, were intending to use the clearing machinery to transfer funds to the Channel Islands; in some cases sums representing the whole of their capital or at least the accumulated interest for several years past. The reference to the bank's unwillingness to launder tainted money was obvious.[69] Barclays also pointed to the RKKs worth RM 200,000 that were being imported illegally into Jersey every week; the bank seemed to suggest that if the Germans were unable to stop this unchecked accumulation, then the Channel Islands should at least be given the chance to get rid of them through their purchases in France.[70]

The outcome seems to allow the conclusion that economic and financial argument did not fall on deaf ears and that, in the interest of maintaining halfway normal conditions in the islands, the Germans were willing to concede. Throughout 1943 the finance side of purchasing in France continued as before, with the rather significant difference that in the perpetually rising French market great losses were now being incurred. Guernsey was ploughing into the Purchasing Commission cash obtained for its resumed tomato exports to France and Germany.[71] But even though 1943 was the peak expenditure year it is likely to have delivered less in goods than the preceding year. This would suggest that islanders had to rely more and more on their home base for survival. Still the

because the interests of both islands were involved. Whether such a delegation visited or not cannot be ascertained but, in view of the final outcome, it is rather likely that Jersey took a similar view of the affair. In any case copies of Leale's correspondence with the Nebenstelle found their way into the Bailiff of Jersey's wartime archives.

[69] AN AJ 40/821A. Barclays Bank, St Helier to the Commissary Administrator of Enemy Banks in Paris re. letter of 29 Jan 1943, 6 Feb 1943.

[70] AN AJ 40/821A. Barclays Bank, St Helier to the Commissary Administrator of Enemy Banks in Paris, report on RKK accumulation in Jersey, 8 Feb 43. The rate of RM 200,000 per week seems to have been something of a constant: in the eleven weeks from late November 1943 to mid-February 1944 the position of illegally imported RKK notes in Jersey banks increased by over RM 2.29m and then by another estimated RM1m until late April see JAS B/A/W/4261. Bailiff's War files. Letter of the Jersey Treasury to FK 515, 18 Feb 1944; letter of the Jersey Treasury to FK 515, 28 Apr 1944.

[71] PRO HO 144/22834. Memo 'Guernsey', by J T D Hubert, August 1943.

islands had obtained some valuable breathing space. Without this the islands would have incurred huge additional debt to the French; they may have also been starving as early 1943, instead of autumn 1944.[72] Islands' purchases with RKKs only decreased when these were withdrawn altogether from circulation in France, in December 1943 and became useless. Consequently, island income, expenditure of the Purchasing Commission and, consequently, imports declined by this reduction in liquidities. Only then did RKK redemption start to become a real problem for the Channel Islands. The surplus RKKs which landed in the bank vaults now had to be paid out to the Germans in the islands as occupation costs. In Guernsey the expenditure for the Occupation account shot up by over £1m, from under £200,000 in 1943 to over £1.2m in 1944.[73]

The new situation now brought out the other feature associated with RKKs: speculation. The official rate of exchange between mark and sterling was mostly stationary during the Occupation. During the first few months the mark was definitely overvalued – a standard procedure of exploitation – and the lowest rate was five marks to the pound, less than half the pre-war rate of 12.17.[74] After some fluctuation, the rate was set at 9.6, on 3 September 1940; two years later the rate was changed again, to 9.36.[75] Although much closer to the pre-war rate, there was still a significant difference between this official rate and the black market rate with its typical variations of between RM30–40.[76] With islanders still keeping their books in sterling, despite the physical disappearance of the notes, and their replacement by RKKs, there definitely was a potential to be exploited. Jersey Treasury figures suggest that the amount of sterling both in island banks and with the general public when the Germans invaded was £450,000, of which over £312,000 was still deposited in the banks. [77] This is a

---

[72] PRO WO 32/13750. 'Report on the Financial and Economic Position of the States of Guernsey', 10 Jun 1945.

[73] ibid. The figures of Occupation payments in Guernsey are remarkable:

Year	Sum (£)
1940	107,966
1941	171,722
1942	243,755
1943	182,608
1944	1,219,272

[74] 12.17 is the 1938 rate, see *One hundred years of Economic Statistics: United Kingdom, United States of America, Australia, Canada, France, Germany, Italy, Japan, Sweden*, compiled and written by Thelma Liesner, The Economist Publications, 1989, 54–5.

[75] 'Banking in Jersey under German Occupation', *Journal of the Institute of Bankers*, October 1946, 208.

[76] IWM Misc. 2826 189/2 (Tapes 4394 O/L and 4396 O/L). Interview with John Blampied, n.d.

[77] The scope for illegal transactions may have been even greater in Guernsey, as a great deal more local currency, i.e. Guernsey pound, seems to have been circulating there. On Liberation money circulation in Guernsey still was: £600,000 in RM, £450,000 in local currency; Jersey:

very conservative estimate. One must remember that these were the days when fortunes could still be kept hidden in stockings, in barns, rooftop lofts or other treasure troves. By September 1942 bank deposits had decreased by £230,000, a large proportion of which had been sold on the black market and exported (as had, by inference, other private hoards that were not known to the authorities).[78] In Guernsey the drop in public trust went even further. A 1941 report by the Guernsey Controlling Committee to the Nebenstelle noted: 'In days like these some people prefer to have their own property under their own care […] The Banks [*sic*], in fact, play a less important role in our economy than hitherto.' [79] This tendency definitely showed in the figure of British and local sterling notes holdings which decreased from a little under £80,000 to £44,000 between December 1940 and late July 1941, despite injections of extra cash by the States to the tune of £29,000 during the same period.[80] Six months later the position was down to a little under £34,000.[81]

While most of these notes would have paid for illegal food imports, Channel Islanders who changed pounds into Reichsmarks at the 'real rate', and then took the gamble of sitting it out until they were honoured on Liberation, had the key to making a killing. Other significant points of attraction were gold holdings, jewellery or other valuables. The Bailiff of Jersey himself said before the war that there probably were large amounts of gold in the island.[82] As long as conditions existed which facilitated the exchange of RKKs into francs, the purchase of scarce items for export to the islands and the subsequent extraction of real value from the islands, profit-making opportunities were almost boundless.

If things in Nazi Germany had always been done 'by the book', RKKs never could have become the standard black market tender in occupied Europe. Unfortunately an immense abyss existed between image and a reality which was based, principally, on racist principles; namely that corruption was a Jewish or foreign problem, but that the honest Fritz or Hans was more or less immune. So much trust in the solid nature of the Aryan warrior led to fund distribution

£1.475m in RM, £60,000 in local currency, see PRO T 161/1197. Civil Affairs Unit, Force 135 to Hampshire (WO), 20 June 1945.

[78] JAS B/A/W/4261. Bailiff's War files, Letter of Jersey Treasury to FK 515, 28 Apr 1944. The remainder of the bank balances of £82,000 was blocked in 1943 and finally withdrawn by the Germans, in exchange for worthless RKK bills.

[79] JAS B/A/W/9222. Bailiff's War files. Report of the Controlling Committee of the States of Guernsey (A J Lainé) to FK 515, 1 Aug 1941.

[80] Report of the Controlling Committee of the States of Guernsey (A J Lainé) to FK 515, 1 Aug 1941.

[81] Report of the Controlling Committee of the States of Guernsey (John Leale) to FK 515, 21 Jan 1942.

[82] The Bailiff said this in a meeting in London on 4 May 1939, see JAS L/D25/A/55. 'Banking in Jersey – 1939/40' by Colin Powell, n.d.

within the military in occupied Europe being virtually unaccountable. Anyone with a large enough power base could lay claim to funds, on the flimsiest of grounds, with often inadequate or even no documentation at all. Such was the danger of getting caught that the real professionals didn't even shy away from issuing blanket cheques or outright forgeries to get their hands on cash. By the look of it corruption was not the exception to the rule, but rather endemic. The higher one climbed, the more putrid the smell. At first almost imperceptible, RKK expenditure in France became a particular problem from the summer of 1943. This followed a decision of the German authorities finally to put tabs on the rather too liberal assignment of the French francs provided by the Vichy government to pay for occupation. The new measures, which included the stepping up of repression, were designed to curb the practice of organised black marketering and make better use of existing resources in France through official channels. It also meant the onset of austerity for the Germans in France who, up until then, had lived like the proverbial 'gods in France'.[83]

Trafficking and black marketeering now fell back onto RKKs which were still legal tender. Combined with a lack of cross-border controls for Germans, this 'funny money' could take account of price differentials and be deployed in higher yield territories. Practically useless in eastern and south-eastern Europe, where scarcity had caused the return to a barter economy, they were transferred to countries where the supply situation was still relatively good and confidence in currency was maintained, such as France, Hungary, Romania and Italy. Most were used for illegal purchases of food and this is the reason why there was no additional influx into the Channel Islands, at least not before they were withdrawn in France. When this occurred, however, many people found themselves, overnight, with useless currency on their hands and the temptation was great now to transfer this to the Channel Islands where it was still being used in daily transactions. As a result, a definite surge in illegally imported RKKs took place which Channel Islands' residents were trying to place in bank accounts. The FK reported to St Germain in March 1944 that RKKs worth RM106,000 had been blocked and confiscated in the islands. The notes had been smuggled over on the barges sailing across from France and then handed to Channel Islanders who had tried to acquire sterling or real estate.[84] One such case concerning RM 70,535 consigned to Mr A R Riches by an Advocate Monnier of Caen was blocked at Lloyds Bank, Jersey, in February 1944.[85] This and similar discoveries were the result of instructions of the Treasurer of the

---

[83] 'Leben wie Gott in Frankreich' (to live like God in France) is an idiom which encapsulates the idea of unheard of abundance, similar to 'vivre au pays de Cocagne' or 'living in Cocagne'.

[84] AJ 40/821A. FK 515 to Chef Militärverwaltungsbezirk A (Mbf) betr. Währungsfragen auf den Kanalinseln, 7 Mar. 1944.

[85] JAS B/A/W/4261. Bailiff's War files. Letter of the Jersey Treasury to FK 515, 18 Feb 1944.

States to bank managers, in January 1944, to report and block questionable funds.[86]

While there is some indication that the High Street banks enforced due diligence procedures, a lot of Channel Islands middlemen seem to have been able to place funds in Post Office Savings accounts during this later period of the Occupation. In Guernsey about 2,000 and in Jersey 3,422 new Post Office accounts were opened during the Occupation. The Guernsey figures show two periods when deposits rose: while the first eighteen months were quiet, the first substantial increases occurred after the end of 1941 until March 1943 – amounts deposited almost tripled between March 1942 and March 1943 alone – then one quiet year again, and then another fifty per cent surge in deposits between March 1944 and March 1945. The large amounts deposited until March 1943 would point to people who made money smuggling or bartering and selling goods on the black and grey markets, a practice which, as we already know, became increasingly difficult after that date; the amounts deposited from March 1944 are certainly funds placed in the trust of Channel Islands middlemen by French, Germans or others. Withdrawals show almost equally interesting movements: negligible until March 1943, they become more important after this date, but are still dwarfed by deposits. Obviously the great majority trusted that the post-war government would honour these funds which continued to elude the authorities – even when investigations were launched – as the authorities were merely on the look-out for 'enemy accounts'.[87]

The banking sector was perhaps one of the professions which put up the most resistance to German demands. Not only was Barclays reluctant to play its allotted part in the clearing mechanism in 1942 and not only did the banks signal suspicious accounts to authorities, but in 1942 they also attempted, to the best of their ability, to 'defend' customers whose nationality they had been called

---

[86] Société Jersiaise. Occupation collection, box 10, item 10: Wartime banking, diary kept by Mr Phillips of Les Près, Grouville, letter of the Treasurer of the States to bank managers, 31 Jan 1944. This letter makes express reference to 'French nationals [...] trying to purchase properties [...] by sending very large sums in Reichsmarks to a local resident acting as an intermediary.'

[87] PRO NSC 21/295. Report of the Guernsey Post Office to Force 135, 20 Civil Affairs Unit, 16 May 1945.

Guernsey Post Office savings accounts (figures in £ sterling)

	Deposits	Withdrawals
July 1940 – March 1941	406	5651
1941 – 1942	16,558	4413
1942 – 1943	48,086	7502
1943 – 1944	49,083	13,619
1944 – 1945	74,211	19,202

The figures for Jersey are even more substantial, see NSC 21/295. Reports concerning the continuance of Savings Bank business in the Channel Islands during the German occupation, 1945.

upon to disclose. This was the first real attempt at interference. Only once before, in February 1941, had two visiting officers called enquiring on organisational issues and securities, and inspecting the strong-rooms. The new move, however, was more serious and had the aim of identifying holdings of evacuees and others residing in enemy territory. This could be a preliminary for sequestration. After having received the visit of the administrator of enemy banks in Paris, Hans-Joachim Caesar, of the Reichsbank, in January of that year, the banks replied that they did not enquire about nationality when opening accounts, but respectability. Finally, a compromise was agreed, according to which customer balances were grouped in 'believed to be British', 'believed to be French' etc. Similar tongue-in-cheek defiance would emerge when companies in Jersey were requested to provide information on shareholders out of the island. They also rejected the 'double-think' potential presented by the term 'enemy property'. The Financial & Trust Company Ltd, in Royal Square, Jersey, on its own initiative, employed the term 'holdings of shares in the names of persons out of the island' (instead of 'enemy property') and ended the list of the few names given with the cheeky comment: 'All the above shareholders are of British Nationality. There are no enemy holders of shares in Jersey.' The secretary of the company put 'BRITISH' [sic] behind her signature. There were also questionnaires which all firms in the island had to fill in according to the decree for the registration of Enemy Property. A good example of how this was taken up by Channel Islands' companies is Boots the Chemist who gave practically no information, except for the most obvious such as name and address of the local branch, turnover in the three preceding years 1939–1941 and the number of employees; but none with regard to capital, number of shares or shareholders, claiming that this information was at head office. It is well known that Boots did not limit themselves to stock in trade, but in their stock declaration they did claim that all they held was 'stock in trade at Queen St.' Some firms were more timid and gave a little more information with regard to company ownership. Obviously a large British registered and controlled company with its head office in the UK could get away with a lot more than a Channel Islands company. Significantly, none of the companies responded to question no. seven: 'Are any shareholders Jewish?' The absence of information was particularly amusing in the declaration of the Singer Sewing Machines Ltd branch in Jersey, at 32 Queen Street, which merely gave its turnover for 1941: £551.[88]

For the banks the next interference did not occur until June 1943, when all bank managers, together with Jersey Treasury officials, were ordered to the Feldkommandantur to receive instructions on the examination of securities,

[88] AN AJ 40/990. Declaration of Enemy Property, April 1942.

deed boxes and other deposits. In July, German officers of the German currency protection squad (Deutsches Devisenschutzkommando-DSK) in Paris visited the banks and blocked all valuables, in the main household silver and jewellery, but also currency, certificates and bearer bonds.[89] On orders from Paris, the FK blocked all British pound notes in the Channel Islands' banks on 28 November 1943. Two months later, on 20 January 1944, sterling holdings worth £82,000 were taken from Jersey alone and paid with marks. The bank managers protested through the Bailiff and the Treasury, stating that confiscation was not permitted under the Hague Convention, on the grounds that the funds in question were not the 'property of the State', but then weakened.[90] In May 1944 more officers arrived and removed from the island banks all remaining gold coin and currency. This included sovereigns purchased on behalf of the Bank of England in June 1940 and which could not be sent away. The officers also brought with them signed instructions from various French customers resident in France relating to gold and currency held by the banks on their behalf, and which were taken by Germans and deposited in France.[91] The managers of the six branches in the islands were required to attend at the Feldkommandantur in Jersey where they were compelled to sign receipts; again the Bailiff of Jersey protested, on 19 May, that this was irregular procedure under international law.[92]

Trade and commerce

Three types of trade existed: the trade of the privileged few, based on distributing the Purchasing Commission imports. The more significant trade, however, was that done in the second-hand shops; but these were the sign of a society on its knees, as they merely served to redistribute resources already in the islands. From late 1942 to early 1943 all other trade was subject to the growing impact of restrictions. Securities trading was another of these 'useless' trades which came to a standstill during the Occupation. All securities had been transferred to

[89] These items were taken from the Westminster Bank Guernsey, National Provincial Bank Guernsey, Barclays Jersey, National Provincial Bank Jersey, Westminster Bank Jersey, Midland Bank Jersey, see AN AJ 40/1105. DSK Paris. Ouverture de coffres à Jersey et Guernesey, 5–12 Jul 1943.

[90] JAS B/A/W/4261. Bailiff's War files. E Benest to the Treasurer of the States of Jersey, 21 Jan 1944.

[91] 'Banking in Jersey under German Occupation', *Journal of the Institute of Bankers*, October 1946, pp 208

[92] In both islands small amounts of Bank of England notes were destroyed after recording their numbers, for example £1,720 in Guernsey, see PRO T 161/1197. States Supervisor (Guernsey), H E Maynard to The Chief Accountant, Bank of England, 11 Jun 1945.

England and thereafter only one or two local stockbrokers remained in operation; from 1943 this class of business was further restricted. Mr Woodall, the owner of a Jersey haberdashery, complained in a diary entry in November 1942 that trading was becoming more and more regimented and that people were no longer allowed to sell what they sold before. Licences were needed for everything.[93] This echoed developments on the Continent where the Germans were moving fast to liquidate the bulk of production for the civilian sector and divert these resources, including labour, to their war effort. They were now closing down many trade establishments, artisans' workshops and small businesses which had become redundant as there were no raw materials to convert and nothing to sell. Apart from this the only other trade was the black market trade.

Like so many other omissions it is curious how *the* two core realities of economic life in occupied Europe – the black market and the barter trade – could have been overlooked for so long. The reason is probably that the black market has been perceived as a mere distasteful expression of avarice and that the barter trade (the 'grey market') is too close a sibling for people to be able to see the difference. What is conveniently forgotten is that in most cases black market activity was more a phenomenon of necessity than of real choice, and that its formation was determined, in the main, by economic conditions.

What is a 'black market'? First of all the black market was one among several possibilities for the deployment of surplus funds. The other was to simply hoard money, to deposit it in a savings account – in the hope that after the war the exchange rate would be honoured – or it could be ploughed into real estate or the stock market. Very often government intervention set limits to this deployment, but there were other 'opportunities' that could not be controlled as easily, such as the sales of valuables, gold and jewellery, or antiques, collectors' items and *objets d'art*. Throughout Europe, auction sales – which under these conditions were little more than legal black market sales – thrived, and the Channel Islands were no exception. Another tried and tested method to deploy funds was to buy life insurance several years or decades in advance; that is if one could find an insurance agent who was either corruptible or unable to see through the stratagem.

A black market principally denotes an 'illegal' or a 'parallel' market.[94] The correlation between black market, scarcity and economic control will have emerged from an earlier section. Black market formation is encouraged whenever there is a particular imbalance between scarcity and excess purchasing

---

[93] IWM Woodall diary, 11 Nov 1942.

[94] The author is aware of the issue of political correctness emerging from the use of the term 'black' in this context; unfortunately no terminological alternatives exist at the present time which captivate reality in a similarly poignant way as the subdivision in black, grey and white markets.

power. This is a necessary but not a sufficient condition. The operation of black markets would not make sense in a genuinely free market economy where the price mechanism is the tool to accommodate supply and demand. Thus black market formation also requires a situation where legal or official markets are unable to satisfy demand and where state intervention has undertaken to restrict or suspend market forces through rationing, price control and other devices.[95]

The 'black market' bears similarities with the discussion of 'collaboration': there is a marked tendency to view the phenomenon in Manichean terms. Some people, such as the Very Reverend Matthew Le Marinel, the Rector of St Helier, made a point of never using the black market.[96] The results were obvious in Le Marinel's considerable weight loss. According to Jerseyman Bob Le Sueur, after some months his dog collar started to hang very loosely around his neck, as he had lost half his body weight. This position was not very realistic, perhaps even foolish. While Le Marinel probably could not afford to by-pass the black market, the Bailiff of Jersey – who later also wrote that he never used the black market – probably had enough pre-war substance to live on during the Occupation and could limit himself to barter transactions which saw no money changing hands.[97] That a Manichean view is inadequate was already noted by Jersey chronicler Leslie Sinel who saw a need for distinctions between, on the one hand, hoarders with the intent of profiteering and, on the other, what the French aptly described as 'le marché noir familial'.[98] Another Jersey resident, G Attenborough, wrote in his diary that the population would have suffered more without the black market than they did with it. He also believed that if it had not existed, the rations would not have been any higher, as this gain would have benefited the occupier.[99] One does not have to go that far to realise that the population faced, once more, a typical Catch-22 situation: had people followed all the rules, they would not have survived; not following the rules, however, meant taking the risk of punishment. In the end the vast majority took their chances. In this particular case the problem was not really the people, but the outdated norms. Although it was patently clear that the black market was a fact of life, the pretence was maintained – during and after the war – that shopping on the black market was a naughty thing to do. This bred double standards. One Jersey advocate defending a Jersey resident charged with an economic offence was courageous enough to say the obvious, i.e. that 98 per cent of those

[95] G. Reimann, *The black market, inevitable child of statism*, Hindsdale, 1948.

[96] A similarly rigorous, legalistic position is the tenor of Charles Cruickshank's treatment of the topic in his official history of the Channel Islands Occupation.

[97] That Coutanche still lost weight can easily be determined by comparing photos of him at the arrival of the Germans in 1940 and at the conference with Bailiff Carey in Guernsey in December 1944.

[98] IWM Misc. 2826 189/2 (Tape 23 4399 O/L). Interview with Leslie Sinel, n.d.

[99] IWM 02/17/1. Diary of Mr and Mrs G Attenborough.

present in the courtroom had probably used the black market, indicating that
the rules of the game were in need of revision.[100] The remark points at the
inevitable generalisation of the black market trade which was not only encouraged by the depletion of official markets, but also by the fact that for those
without acquired pre-war wealth, buying 'on the black' predisposed getting
active on the sales side first.[101] Many islanders were said to have bartered rather
than consumed the food they received from Germans billeted on them. That the
'98 percent mark' is not as far-fetched as it may seem, and that there was a
serious dissolution of pre-war morals, is also confirmed by a case recorded in the
memoirs of Jersey concentration camp survivor Peter Hassall. Forced to assist in
his mother's black market business, he was particularly ashamed when he had to
serve two customers he probably hadn't expected: a cleric and a judge, both
well-known in the island; the latter because he had tried a great many cases
involving offences against economic regulations.[102] Another excellent indicator
that the black market had, in fact, become economic normality, is given in an
official report on the malfeasance of George Moyse, acting district manager of
the Pearl Assurance Co Ltd in Jersey. This report, drafted by the Committee of
Management of the Associated Life Offices Central Fund, a pool of the
insurance industry, stated that the man had been suspect for some time because
of his heavy drinking, his contacts with Germans – among them the dreaded
Wölfle of the Secret Field Police – and the fact that he was living beyond his
means, but that nothing was done 'because it was well known that he had close
connection [*sic*] with the Black Market trade, and it might well have been that
he had some personal gain from this source'. Moyse was only found out as a
consequence of persistent rumours that the rot ran deeper and that the
Committee had better take a look. His main offence was not the connection to
the black market, or the fact that he may have sold insurance policies in order to
help people deploy black market profits. Examination of the books in November
1944, after Moyse had been asked to resign from the Committee, found that he
had consistently misappropriated exorbitant sums of money, either through the
redirection of money destined for staff assistance or by the means of fictitious
claims.[103] Further enquiry after the Occupation found that he had, in fact,
pocketed a total of over £15,000.[104]

[100] ibid.

[101] BA-MA. RW 36/257. Militärbefehlshaber in Belgien und Nordfrankreich. Abschlussbericht
Abteilung Wirtschaftslenkung und Wirtschaftskontrolle, 1944–45.

[102] Peter Hassall, 'Night and Fog Prisoners' (memoirs of Peter Hassall), 55, published at
<www.occupationmemorial.com>

[103] JAS D/Z/H/5444. Report of the Committee of Management of the directors of the Pearl
Assurance Co. Ltd., n.d. (probably end 1944).

[104] JAS D/Z/H5/444. Law Officer's department, the Solicitor General to the Lieutenant
Governor of Jersey, 7 Sept 1946.

That not all illegal business activities were always 'bad' or detrimental to the civilian population is demonstrated nowhere better than by the case of Raphael Bogrand, an entrepreneur born into a family of merchants from Saint-Brieuc. Bogrand had learnt his trade in the import-export business and by the late 1930s he had established a small network of department stores in Brittany. Bogrand was an Anglophile and during the 1939–40 *drôle de guerre* he served as liaisons officer with the British Army in Le Mans where he came into contact with a Major Reginald Oates. When Oates was debriefed on his return to England in June 1940 he testified to Bogrand's pro-British leanings and gave his name as one of two potential intelligence sources in France. A short time later Bogrand was approached by agents who recruited him to survey troop movements in the Breton ports. All the while he was continuing his business activities. In order to lift the requisition of one of his stores, he agreed to open three German sections in already extant retail stores in Granville, Morlaix and Rennes. Later he also opened *Soldatenkaufhaus* branches in the Channel Islands, on the premises of Woolworth's. Although this seems to suggest that Bogrand fitted the archetype of the economic collaborator, the man also knew how to pinpoint the weakness of the allocation system and work it to his advantage; and that of the civilian population. After the war it was found that although the sales were supposed to have been made to Germans only, Bogrand, in fact, diverted considerable supplies.[105] Several hundred Channel Islanders signed a petition attesting that they had gained possession of articles – soap, textile products, ham and butter – carrying the *Soldatenkaufhaus* stamp, at very reasonable prices.[106] His activities were particularly successful in the domain of textile points, a majority of which were made available to civilian buyers in France and in the Channel Islands. Unsurprisingly, Bogrand did not have an easy stand in post-war France where he was put into jail and investigated. His case defied perceptions of resistance workers as 'whiter than white' heroes as he was rather close to what French historians today describe under the term *résistant-collaborateur or collaborateur-résistant*. It is hard to say which was the dominating of Bogrand's instincts; his case seems to suggest, however, that good business instinct was not necessarily incompatible with patriotism.

Total avoidance of the black market was not only unreasonable because of the physical degradation it entailed, but also the fact that it was inevitable. This was also the diagnosis of John Leale who correctly addressed money accumulation as the principal culprit of black market formation: salary recipients had no other wish than to get rid of their RKKs 'as soon as possible without asking

[105] PRO FO 371/161158. Case file 'Raphael Bogrand vs Attorney General of Jersey', Feb 1961.
[106] Paul Sanders, *Histoire du marché noir 1940–46*, Paris, 2001, 302–7.

questions about prices'.[107] The black market exemplified one of the negative features of insularity. Sealed off from the outside, with no hinterland that could be explored on foraging trips it was a lot more difficult to alleviate shortages and counter the imbalance between goods and liquidities. Without exaggeration the islands were the perfect breeding ground for scarcity and the black market. Items smuggled into this 'desert' received a very high premium, especially highly sought after consumer and food products. Islander John Blampied described them as a 'smugglers paradise', confirming Leale's findings that the money people earned did not mean very much. The main thing was to turn it over as quickly as possible and get hold of barter goods which could be converted into other stable value items.[108] Cruickshank writes in his history that the exhibits in the second-hand shops were not to be had for money, but barter, and that many of these goods were treated as an investment passing from one shop to the next without being consumed.[109] Toward the end, the situation in Guernsey became so depleted and prices so high that even the black market in certain products 'dried up': Guernsey-made cigarettes fetched RM40, Jersey grown tobacco up to RM250 and wheat from Jersey was sold at RM20 per lb.[110] Extra milk and fish outside the rationing system was only available on a barter basis.[111] In Alderney the partial repeal of a money economy arrived even earlier. This was due to a level of depletion that was worse than in the other islands and also to the fact that practically all goods had to be shipped in from Cherbourg. Apart from the meagre supplements available in the canteens, the substantial amounts of currency going around there – troops were being paid in French francs – could not be deployed in goods.[112] Similar to the situation in post-war Germany, cigarettes became the main currency.

Talking of *a* black market is in itself a simplification. The fact is that there were several types: one based on goods smuggled across from the Continent on the barges; another in locally produced agricultural products; there was the barter trade that went on with practically anything people could dispense with; then there was currency speculation; and finally a black market animated by the Germans themselves. Mr Attenborough recorded that black market growth in Jersey was slow and insidious. Two of the first articles to become short in

---

[107] PRO HO 45/22424. Report of the President of the Controlling Committee of the States of Guernsey on the activities of the Committee during the five years of German Occupation, 23 May 1945.

[108] IWM. Misc. 2826 189/2 (Tapes 4394 O/L and 4396 O/L). Interview with John Blampied, n.d.

[109] Cruickshank, 144–45.

[110] IWM JRD.09. Force 135, I (b). Document signed W Einart (GFP Guernsey), 20 May 1945.

[111] PRO HO 144/22834. MI19/1742. Report 'Channel Islands Guernsey – Interrogation of two escapees from Guernsey', Aug 1943.

[112] JAS L/D25/A/4. 'The Alderney Story', by Colonel B E Arnold, n.d.

supply, in 1941, were cheese and cigarettes, but shortfalls were evened out by the smuggling on the barges, initially at quite reasonable prices. Then, during 1941, tobacco, alcohol and meat became scarce, and sugar was replaced by saccharine. Later, when food ran very short, potatoes, grain and flour were added to the list of black market items as were boots and clothing. Some of the products sold on the black market, such as cognac, cigarettes and saccharine, came from France or Germany, whereas meat, butter and eggs were local. Another local product which came to the fore during the last two years of the Occupation was Jersey Calvados – which 'smelled worse than it tasted' – sold at £5 a bottle.

The stages in the development of the black market mirrored price developments. Upward trends in prices were inevitable, even in the official market. As the Table 1.1 shows, the difference between pre-war and official Occupation prices is significant.[113]

One reason for these substantial rises was the inexorable rise of costs. Before the war the islands had operated within the bounds of international trade, purchasing essentials such as cattle fodder, flour and artificial manure in the cheapest markets. With the onset of the Occupation the same items had to be purchased in France where prices had risen significantly.[114] More intriguingly, however, production costs for home-grown produce also increased, a fact that was little understood by the local population and fed rumours of widespread graft. The Bailiff of Jersey explained the principle to the Home Office in 1945, in response to criticism pointing to the substantial difference between wartime prices in Jersey and in the UK. Coutanche responded that it was 'absurd to compare [...] the price of breakfast meal produced and sold in huge quantities with the price of breakfast meal made from oats grown in Jersey and milled under primitive conditions in old water-power mills. Transport costs alone, in the later stages of the Occupation, by horse-drawn trolleys, were very considerable.'[115]

Black market prices typically constituted multiples of the already rather significant official prices. The worst months were without doubt the last 11 months of the Occupation (see Table 1.2).

Of the prohibition of the sale of spirits in pubs, Attenborough wrote that this was one of the German orders which was liberally disregarded. Generally

---

[113] PRO HO 144/22834. MI19/1742. Report 'Channel Islands Guernsey – Interrogation of two escapees from Guernsey', Aug 1943.

[114] 'Making the Channel Islands Self-Supporting. Co-operation of German and Island Authorities'. Interview with KVR Pelz (FK), *Evening Post*, Jersey, 7 Jan. 1941.

[115] PRO HO 45/22399. Note, Bailiff of Jersey to HO re. memorandum and re. petition to HM, 3 July 1945.

TABLE 1.1. *Prices for diverse products in Guernsey*

Product	Pre-war price	Official price during occupation
Rationed food		
Meat (8 ozs.)	10d.	1s.
Butter (4 ozs.)	5d.	9d.
Sugar (3 ozs.)	½d.	1½d.
Cooking fats (2 ozs)	5d.	9d.
Potatoes (5 lbs)	5d	1s.8d.
Bread (2 lbs.)	4½d.	4½d.
Skimmed milk (pint) – for adults	1d	3d
Full cream milk (pint) – reserved for children	4d	4d
Unrationed food (per 2 lbs.)		
Spinach	2d.	9d.
Parsnips	2d.	7d.
Carrots	1½d.	12d.
Onions	4d.	2s.
Cabbage	1d.	9d.
Turnips	1½d.	7d.
Clothing		
Coat	£3	£10
Suit	£2.10s.	£12
Shirt	8s	£3
Socks	1s.11d.	11s.3d.
Shoes (pair)	10s.	£2
Miscellaneous		
Cigarettes (20)	7d.	1s.9½d.
Matches	2½d (12 boxes)	1½d. (1 box)

alcohol could be obtained with a doctor's certificate from a wine merchant at 25s a bottle, but larger quantities came from the Germans themselves, at 32s in the beginning and £10 at the end of the Occupation.[116] Pubs provide an interesting case, as they, together with barber and hairdressers' shops, were the main exchanges for a substantial amount of the black market trade in the islands. The trade in the latter establishments was no secret to the authorities and on 18 February 1942 a notice appeared, signed by the Bailiff of Jersey,

[116] IWM 02/17/1. Diary of Mr and Mrs G Attenborough.

TABLE 1.2. *Selection of black market prices*[117]

	1943–44[118]	**1944–45**[119]
Butter (lb)	£1.5s	£3.10s
Boots/Shoes (pair)	£7.10s	£10–15
Soap (tablet)		£2–5
Suit	£10	£25
Tea (lb)	£12	£18–50
Potatoes (cwt)[120]	£3	£5
Grain (cwt)		£20
Tinned fruit (tin)		£2.10s
Teats for babies' bottle		£3.5s
Cigarettes (20)	£1.1s	£2.2s.6d
Tobacco (lb)	£1.2s.8d	£8.10s
Sugar (lb)	18s.8d	£2.10s
Whiskey (bottle)		£10.10s
Christmas Turkey		£15.18s
Eggs (dz.)		£20

forbidding entry to foreign OT (Organization Todt) workers.[121] Much of the rest of the trade seems to have been conducted under the counter, with legal business activities serving as a front. As in most other occupied territories the black market also operated from within the legal market. German policeman Einart testified to British investigators that in 1943–44 Guernsey grocers had actual tariffs with fluctuating prices according to the supply of pilfered or smuggled goods.[122] These tariffs operated in parallel to the official prices and it was the ability to pay the unofficial prices which determined whether a grocer was or was not 'out' of a certain product. Most customers knew that availability depended on the size of one's purse or some other factor such as status or influence. Some grocers also did deals with German units. Theoretically, all

[117] 12 pence = 1 shilling; 20 shillings = £1; 240 pence =£1.

[118] IWM P338. Le Cocq diary; PRO HO 144 22834. MI19/1742. Report 'Channel Islands Guernsey – Interrogation of two escapees from Guernsey', Aug 1943; PRO HO 144 22176. Final report on the activity of Boots & Co Guernsey during the occupation, 1945.

[119] IWM P338. Le Cocq diary; PRO HO/144 22237. MI19/2507. Report 'Guernsey Side Lights on Island Affairs' and 'Excerpts from private letter of 'Guernsey Commission Agent' brought over by informant 2503/2503A', 20 Nov 1944; IWM 02/17/1. Diary of Mr and Mrs G Attenborough; PRO PREM 3 87. Information and Records Branch. Report based on 227 extracts from letters from the Channel Islands dated November and December 1944, 15 Feb 1945.

[120] 1 hundredweight (cwt) = 50.8 kilograms

[121] JAS D/Z/H/5137. Notice of Bailiff forbidding foreign OT workers to enter hairdressing establishments, 18 Feb 1942.

[122] IWM JRD.09. Force 135, I (b), document signed W Einart (GFP Guernsey), 20 May 1945.

military units were supposed to receive their food supplies through their quarter-master, but some units also purchased goods destined for the civilian population. In one such case in Guernsey in January 1942, official allocations of potatoes and vegetables were sold to a German unit which supplemented tobacco, cigarettes, flour and other rare items to the bill. The entitled among the population were then told for up to three weeks by the grocer in question that he had simply not received his allocation. With ready access to sugar, tobacco and cigarettes, Wehrmacht members were also mopping up a substantial part of the goods offered in the St Peter Port barter shops opened for the exclusive use of the civilian population.[123]

The 'other' black market was more organised and relied on imports from France, with the complicity of certain German units or services. The harbour police in Jersey were tied in with Emma C. who was running operations out of the photographic depot of Edmund Hassall, her common-law husband. The OT had their own thriving black market operation which was run from their food stores, no doubt products they had either brought over on their barges or food they were snatching off the rations allocated to their workers. Some of the most active German black marketeers were the German policemen. When the British searched the headquarters of the Secret Field Police in Guernsey in May 1945 they were shocked to find a number of Red Cross parcels.[124] The infamous Karl-Heinz Wölfle ('Wolf of the Gestapo') was said to have been 'up to the neck' in illegal business with his local partner, a Jersey butcher by the name of Cornish who was also referred to as 'king of the black market'.[125] There were at least half a dozen people contesting this title, among them a North African PoW. The black market in the islands was also supplied by the individual Germans who imported shoes, leather goods, jewellery, wines, Cognac, tobacco and cigarettes. A good profit could also be made by reselling purchases made in the German canteens which, naturally, were not accessible to civilians[126]:

Prices in RM (Nov 1943)

	German canteen	Paid by civilians
Butter (lb)	4	18
Meat (lb)	6	12
Tobacco (100gr)	2.5	6

[123] Island Archives. FK 4/8. GFP Gru 131, Aussenkommando Steinberger. Bericht über Straftaten/Eigentumsvergehen, die in den Monaten Oktober 41 bis Januar 1942 zur Anzeige kamen, und in denen als Täter deutsche Wehrmachtsangehörige genannt wurden, 18 Jan 1942.

[124] IWM JRD.09. Force 135, I (b). Report 'GFP in Guernsey', May 1945.

[125] IWM JRD.09. Force 135, I (b). Document signed W Einart (GFP Guernsey), 20 May 1945; IWM JRD10. Captain Dening's Intelligence note books, 1944–45; PRO. WO 106/3004. MI12. Extracts from postal and telegraph censorship, 1944–45.

[126] PRO WO 199/3303. Interrogation of Gefreiter Peters captured near Caen on 18 Jul 1944 – Situation Report on Guernsey (Nov 1943), 23 Aug 1944.

German involvement may seem somewhat contradictory, but it was a variation on a theme being played out on the Continent. Since the very beginning of the occupation of Western Europe resources were escaping into the black market which the Germans were bent on extracting for their own purposes. To this effect they set up a commercial infrastructure of competing firms whose task was to drain all illegal supplies still available in France, Belgium and the Netherlands. For this they used a growing proportion of the occupation payments levied off the occupied countries as well as the existing clearing channels. After some initial success in 1940–41, the secret scheme, by 1942 carried out on an industrial scale, led to a speculative bubble and unequalled corruption. In 1943 all German black market purchasing was finally banned, in favour of full collaboration which promised a more economical use of resources.[127] The scheme itself had no influence on the situation in the Channel Islands, as the islands, in their utter state of depletion, offered the exact opposite picture to France or Belgium: they had no secret food or raw material caches of interest to the German war economy. In this respect the Germans were running more of a damage limitation strategy; had they decreed black market exploitation as in France, the result would have been total *tabula rasa* and, ultimately, damage to the interests of the occupier. What did spill over from France, however, was the attitude and the corruption. For a long time the Germans turned a blind eye and the only indication of a sterner attitude coincides with the 1943 black market ban in France and Belgium. Thus one MI5 informant stated that the black market was tolerated until spring 1943, but then black-marketeers were suddenly treated as 'scoundrels of the worst kind'.[128] In May 1943 both Bailiffs had to register orders prohibiting price rises.[129] What was also quite obvious was the penchant of individual Germans for speculating in currency, gold or jewellery.

The agricultural black market was supplied through under-reporting or dissimulations. Tom Mansell, a farmer in Guernsey, said that after threshing there was always some corn left which went to the black market at £100 a hundredweight.[130] Most of the meat trade on this market was of local origin: pork and veal mainly, sometimes beef, rarely goat. Black market pork and cattle came from unregistered animals. As one can imagine, slaughtering is quite noisy: the animal's muzzle has to be tied, sometimes the animal was electrocuted and also chloroform is said to have been used.[131] Many court cases came about as a result of denunciations, but farmers were also fined after visits from

127 Paul Sanders, *Histoire du marché noir 1940–1946*, Paris, 2001.

128 PRO KV 41/78. Consolidated report: 'The I(b) Reports on the Channel Islands', by Major J.R. Stopford, 8 Aug. 1945.

129 JAS B/A/W/30127. Knackfuss to Bailiffs of Jersey and Guernsey re Order of 20 May 1943 prohibiting price rises.

130 IWM Misc. 2826 189/2 (Tape 4425). Interview with Tom Mansell, farmer, Guernsey, n.d.

131 IWM 02/17/1. Diary of Mr and Mrs G Attenborough.

inspectors, and these fines became progressively draconian as the Occupation wore on. Unfortunately the most common result of these fines was to increase the risk premium and thus drive up the price of black market meat.

That farmers, through their black market sales, were the greatest beneficiaries of the Occupation is one of the 'accepted truths' throughout Europe. This claim, however, owes more to the post-war search for an ideal scapegoat than reality. There were about as many farmers who made a fortune as there were farmers who lost out or who lived on their pre-war wealth during the Occupation. And even those who did get involved in the black market did not always start out as callous black marketeers. G Attenborough wrote in his Occupation diary that in the beginning agricultural producers in Jersey were quite well disposed towards the 'townies'. Butter rations, for example, left a surplus in the island and many farmers were willing to sell to relatives and friends at prices which were by no means excessive. This in turn animated a lively barter trade in town. As long as these products remained among locals things were fine. Prices started to rise when the Germans muscled their way into this market and when island courts fell in line with the Germans demanding prosecution. After the first cases had been heard in court, the farmers saw where the game was going: with rising risks, prices now also started to increase, thus reflecting the risk premium.[132] Some farmers reoriented their sales towards Germans. Again the situation was more of a dilemma than commonly imagined. There probably were cases where farmers said 'no' to begin with, but it is easy to see why this attitude would not have had much future: they were definitely sitting at the end of the barrel. The other reason was that the Germans would protect their providers from ending up in the island courts. What has gone unchallenged is that there were professions and classes of people whose business risk was much lower and where profit-making opportunities were even better. This was also the opinion of an anonymous letter writer signed 'Countryman' in Guernsey's *Daily Sketch* in 1946. The writer opined that while black marketeers or farmers who sold at high prices were 'criminals', they were by no means the worst racketeers. He seems to have had a point in condemning the numerous sales of gold and jewellery which eventually ended up in the hands of the enemy.[133] The problem was rather more endemic, as gold sales had occurred across the board. One German veteran recalled acquiring gold required for a tooth replacement at Boots in Guernsey.[134]

One has to realise that agricultural produce was not the only type of rarity with high premiums. Other big earners were the importers, both legal and illegal, of consumer items other than food products which had now became luxuries. These middlemen played an important part in the liquidation of island

---

[132] ibid.

[133] PRO HO 45/25845. 'Letter to the editor', *Daily Sketch*, 10 Jun 1946.

[134] Author's interview with Herr Ballauf's son Dieter, 25 Sept 2004.

wealth. Many an item removed from the houses of evacuees or carted away from depots where they had been deposited for safe keeping seems to have ended up in the barter trade. Other culprits were the auction houses. One of the most prominent victims of looting was the former Lieutenant-Governor of Guernsey, Major General J R Minshull-Ford, who had left behind in 1940, at Government House, antiques, furniture and paintings, among the latter a portrait of King Charles I by Van Dyke worth £500. After the war none of these items remained where they had been left and the Channel Islands' authorities had definitely had a hand in this. In their drive to procure funds for the operation of the Purchasing Commission in France, some of the Lieutenant-Governor's possessions had been 'auctioned off': his carpets and rugs (pre-war value: £310) for £2, a mere fraction of what these items would have been worth under these conditions.[135] Islanders who returned to intact properties often didn't know how lucky they were. The 3,500[136] properties of Channel Islanders who evacuated in 1940 came under the category 'enemy property' and if procedures adopted in other occupied territories had been followed they would have come under temporary administration which would have set certain limits to wildcat or spontaneous looting. Not so in the Channel Islands where a large number of billets were required and these properties provided an unheard of potential for looting. Over the years much of the furniture and other effects from the requisitioned properties was shipped to the Continent or shifted around the islands, some as far as Alderney. Suzanne Malherbe and Lucie Schwob, two French artists imprisoned in Jersey for resistance activities since November 1944, spent the first weeks after their release from the Jersey prison chasing up what was left of their belongings. Other looting was the work of Channel Islanders themselves, or forced workers. Shocking as it is, It would have been rather surprising had there been no looting under such conditions. One Guernsey escapee admitted that petty thieving was the order of the day. Under the impact of requisitioning and confiscation not much importance was attached to property any more and the island had become a 'den of thieves'. With great reluctance and shame he recounted how, driven by his and others' need for food, he had stolen 200 to 300 tins of cooked ham from a German store. He was also honest enough to add that the pillaging of German stores was not a sign of resistance but evidence of how far the shortages were driving people. According to his interrogators, this showed 'that respect for the law was still 'intact'.[137]

---

[135] See PRO HO 144/23219; PRO. T 161/1286, correspondence of Lieutenant Governor of Guernsey, Major General J R Minshull-Ford and his wife with Home Office and Treasury, 1945–46.

[136] AN AJ 40/899 (11). Versorgung und Evakuierung der Zivilbevölkerung 1944. Lagebericht für die Zeit vom 1.4. bis 30.6.1943 – Feindvermögen, 6 Jul 1943.

[137] PRO MI19/2144. 'Report Channel Islands Guernsey'. Further interrogation of informants 2132, 2136 and 2141 (information as of 1 Dec 1943), 24 Apr 1944.

What was left in ownerless property at the end of the Occupation was collected and people were invited to make claims. It is unlikely that a Van Dyke would have survived among this *bric à brac*. From similar operations elsewhere in Europe it is known that publicity was often the main problem and that not everyone was aware that they could reclaim belongings. After expiry of a certain period 66,000 items of furniture which had not been claimed back were assembled for one large display and then put up for auction.[138]

Do the right thing?

After the Occupation the two main criticisms of the Channel Islands' authorities from among the local population were their alleged co-operation in the deportation of the non-natives in 1942 and their inability to stamp out the black market. Considering that they started from the lowest points one could imagine, this appears hardly adequate. One particular criticism was that rather than keeping prices at acceptable levels, the authorities' price control effort helped to increase prices or led to the disappearance of food items such as meat.

While non-regulation of meat would have probably brought more meat into the shops, albeit at very high prices, the type of problem itself was by no means restricted to the Channel Islands. As to the severity of repression, one should note that as a general rule this was the only way forward in ensuring that at least the little that was available received the most equitable distribution possible. Severe penalties were also a function of the desperately inadequate staff situation. Jersey chronicler Leslie Sinel said that black market meat was expensive because it involved such high risks[139], an opinion echoed by diarist Mr G Attenborough who regretted that the administration did not adopt a 'Nelson' attitude, instructing inspectors to turn a blind eye to the black meat market. Attenborough believed that without interference the meat would have been cheaper and there would have been more of it.[140] While nothing could be less certain, anecdotal evidence suggests that the authorities targeted trade intermediaries, such as black market butchers, rather than agricultural producers whom severe repression might persuade to not produce at all.[141] There is also an indication that in the cases of end consumers the local authorities tried to drag their feet, especially during the siege. The 1944 price surveillance reports for

[138] IWM Misc. 2826 189/2 (Tape 4423). Interview with Vernon Le Maitre, Billeting officer, n.d.

[139] IWM Misc. 2826 189/2 (Tape 23 4399 O/L). Interview with Leslie Sinel.

[140] IWM 02/17/1. Diary of Mr and Mrs G Attenborough. Despite his criticism, Mr Attenborough believed that this was one of the areas where the Jersey authorities did best; for him policing and the maintenance of order was the core problem of Occupation government.

[141] IWM P338. Le Cocq war diary, Jersey.

Jersey give a few very unimpressive samples of cases taken further by the local authorities.[142] If their efforts against trade intermediaries were not always what they should have been, some credit must also go to the Germans who protected black marketeers working for their side against prosecution by the authorities. This practice only ceased in 1943–44 when the Germans finally outlawed their own black market and the islands' authorities were allowed to take further a number of cases of people who had worked for or with the Germans. The main blot on this record was that, as ever, some were more equal than others. Another reproach one can make is perhaps the lack of imagination and the over-zealous behaviour of some public servants who had little idea of where the common good actually lay; a problem one still confronts 60 years on. Some moments of bureaucratic insanity need mentioning. In November 1944 a second-hand suit was being sent to the Textile and Footwear Control Office for valuation. As a result a detailed description of what was wrong with it and why it was not worth the RM 200 it had been sold for, but a mere four guineas, was established. What is most harrowing about this case is that administrative resources were being wasted which could have been spent more wisely in order to determine the facts on this relatively trivial affair. It involved a lengthy correspondence which went right up to the Attorney General, Duret Aubin.[143] The important thing – from the historian's point of view – is that these cases involving not only tatty suits, but also half pigs or mares, were brought to the attention of the authorities through anonymous letters, also called 'notes'. This perhaps explains why they followed up these cases at all, rather than being exposed to criticism of the Germans that they weren't doing their job properly. Without these tip-offs there may never have been any inquiries. One incident in the spring of 1945 – again requiring the attention of the ubiquitous Attorney General – proves that they were capable of judging cases on their individual merits. Throughout the Occupation milk samples were being sent to the Official Analyst's Lab in Halkett Place, where water and fat content would be compared in order to establish any tampering attempts. In one case, concerning a Trinity farmer, a complaint was received from the Victoria Dairy and the milk was found to be deficient. When the island authorities went further into the case they found that German soldiers had been stealing milk from this farm every night of the month of March 1945 and replacing it with water. The farmer found out about this on 20 March and now faced a catch-22 situation. If he didn't submit his quota he would be punished; if he delivered the milk that had been tampered with he would also be punished. Which involved the least risk? The German soldiers were finally apprehended and tried in their own court and when the proceedings established that no

---

[142] JAS B/A/W/4110. FK 515. Preisüberwachung – Monatsberichte Jersey, 1944.
[143] JAS D/Z/H/5396. Law Officer's Department, 1944.

complicity had been involved the Attorney General decided that prosecution against the farmer should be abandoned.[144]

On the other hand the overall success of the Purchasing Commission in France was an achievement for such small and vulnerable communities. A post-war UK Treasury assessment was quite impressed, as state trading on this level had been unknown in the Channel Islands and everything had to be improvised from absolute scratch.[145] The purchasing activity not only brought a comple-ment of essential goods to the islands, but had the added benefit of limiting money accumulation. Improving the overall resource basis while also neutral-ising idle liquidities diminished both the impact of scarcity and the black market. The arrangement also meant that a large part of the cost of Occupation was transferred to France. How well the system had worked to the advantage of the Channel Islands was that, paradoxically, at the end of the war both islands had a positive clearing balance with France, despite their occupation trade deficit with France. This was only possible because they had been able to turn the RKK importation into purchases in France and by-pass clearing arrange-ments.[146] Only in 1944 did the combination of clearing and occupation costs really start draining the economic life blood of the islands. The UK Treasury opined that, had this procedure been adopted already in 1940, the Guernsey debt to the banks would have been £8m rather than the eventual £3.5m.[147] It would also have entailed incurring huge additional debt for the French exports to the islands, without which the island would have been starving as early 1943.[148] The islands, it seemed, had enjoyed the best of both worlds.

Financial savoir faire was also displayed in other areas. For one thing the authorities limited their emission of new sterling notes to small denominations that were necessary to replace small silver and copper coinage which was disappearing fast in 1941. In Guernsey this position had decreased from about £17,500 in July 1940 to as low as £2,200 one year later. That year Jersey issued £15,000 and Guernsey £10,000 in small denominations. In 1942 Jersey issued a further £35,000 in ten-shilling notes and other smaller denominations, whereas

---

[144] JAS. D/Z/H/5444. Law Officer's Department, 1945.

[145] PRO WO 32/13750. UK treasury document 'The Islands Budgets', 1945–46.

[146] Jersey accumulated a credit of £233,413 and Guernsey a credit of £545,000, see PRO T231/334. UK Treasury to French Financial Attache, M Calvet, 27 Sept 1945.

[147] PRO WO 32/13750. UK Treasury document 'The Islands Budgets', 1945–46.

[148] PRO WO 32/13750. Report on the Financial and Economic Position of the States of Guernsey, 10 Jun 1945. The figures of Occupation payments in Guernsey are remarkable:

Year	Sum (£)
1940	107,966
1941	171,722
1942	243,755
1943	182,608
1944	1,219,272

Guernsey now reverted to marks and pfennigs.[149] While the catalogue of causes for the disappearance of sterling notes and coins is rather complex – hoarding and changes in commercial habits are often cited – the main one was that sterling was being used for speculation. In conjunction with the commercial banks, the authorities prevented the deployment of questionable foreign funds in the Channel Islands. They also refused to place British notes in the hands of the enemy: when a request was made in Jersey to collect British notes from the public, for exchange into French currency, they refused. They equally turned down offers of oranges from Spain and tobacco from Bulgaria, probably made by Nazi-controlled purchasing organisations such as the notorious SOFINDUS, against payment of sterling.[150] Denying access to convertible currency demonstrated a laudable awareness of the realities of war finance.

Naturally, all this autonomy of action came at the price of a formidable blackmail potential.

The spoils of Occupation

Planning for the financial rehabilitation, but also the confiscation of war profits preceded Liberation by many months. What emerges quite clearly is the little concern for financial or economic cleansing and the concentration on the normalisation of economic life. This normalisation was to progress along the following stages. During the early part of reoccupation trade was not permitted on ordinary commercial lines, but through official channels only. This was to be followed by the reopening of the mail service, resumption of control by Channel Islanders over property in the UK (and vice versa), and only then restoration of normal trade.[151] As early as April 1944 the Treasury did not consider depriving collaborators of the 'wages of sin' a matter for them. The prediction was that there would be no 'cleansing' as it was impossible to freeze the money of suspected persons and put in limbo economic normalisation by waiting until 'the local gossip (was) sifted'.[152] The usual lack of agreement on definitions and a

[149] See JAS B/A/W/9223. In November 1941 Jersey applied for an issue of a total of £100,000 in pieces of 1s, 2s, 10s and £1 notes, a request which was not granted by the Germans who believed that this would increase inflation. In the summer 1942 even the introduction of French francs was proposed by the Feldkommandant, as many Wehrmacht soldiers were importing francs to the islands which they could not spend. This solution was then discarded by the Germans in September, for political reasons.

[150] JAS B/A/W/4261. Bailiff's War files, Jersey Treasury to FK 515, 28 Apr 1944.

[151] PRO T 161/1196. Trading with the Enemy Department. Memorandum on action to be taken on reoccupation of the Channel Islands, 29 Jan 1944.

[152] PRO WO 32/13750. Mynors (Treasury) on Channel Islands Currency on Liberation, 30 Mar 1944.

distaste for 'experiments' and 'unknown paths' characterised the debate. In a rather typical exchange of opinion between the Home Office and the War Office the suggestion was advanced to base enquiries for questionable funds on whether someone had been a collaborator. Markbreiter (Home Office) then wrote to Brigadier French (War Office) that the UK government were not interested in having to find a definition which they considered beyond them, as they admitted not being 'sure where to draw the line'. They suggested that for the purpose of freezing accounts it was better to adopt the formula of a RM credit balance substantially in excess of what could be expected given the conditions and with regard to pre-war balances.[153] At this point there was still a consensus that problematic accounts should be frozen and investigated, but this would be abandoned soon afterwards. In October the situation was still unclear as the Channel Islands' Financial Directive contained nothing whereas the Financial Plan seemed to make provision.[154] On 19 October 1944 the Home Office wrote to the Treasury saying that they saw a need to make adjustments 'in the light of recent experience in Europe', but also because of information they received through Channel Islands' escapees who were now pouring in at a steady rate. They now knew that some people had made considerable sums on the black market and there was also a suggestion that many profiteers had invested in real estate. One particular escapee told the Home Office that the population trusted that the accumulated RM would be valueless on Liberation. The Home Office now also feared that if sterling was exchanged against RM without discrimination this would arouse 'public feeling' and that 'undeserving people' would benefit. Finally, in November, the Channel Islands' Civil Affairs Directive was modified to take account of the possibility of black market profits or gross inflation. According to this new regulation the exchange was to begin with limited fixed amounts, but in those cases where large profits had been made the RM would not fully be changed into sterling until after necessary investigation. The issue on how measures should be designed which selectively penalised profiteers without prejudicing people not under suspicion was deferred until later.[155] On the insistence of the War Office it was agreed that the island authorities should shoulder as much responsibility as possible. Although it was conceded that there was no certainty about how much they would be capable of bearing, the principle was established that Force 135 and the island authorities should establish a close working relationship and that they would require one another to get their jobs done.[156]

[153] PRO WO32/13750. Markbreiter (HO) to French (WO), 4 Apr 1944.

[154] PRO T 161/1196. Markbreiter (HO) to Mynors (Treasury), 19 Oct 1944

[155] BoE Archives. OV 173/5. General Liberation Channel Islands. Mr Lithiby's Personal File. Treasury to Howard (HO), 24 Nov 1944.

[156] BoE Archives. OV 173/5. General Liberation Channel Islands. Mr Lithiby's Personal File. Hampshire (WO) to Mynors (Treasury), 9 Dec 1944; Mynors to Hampshire, 11 Dec 1944.

The withdrawal of German currency was implemented under different conditions in both islands; Guernsey had laid plans for currency exchange well in advance. Since September 1944 a supply of Guernsey paper had been deposited at the branch of Midland Bank. Already, on 2 May, distribution was made to the other banks and as soon as the Germans communicated their intention to capitulate, on 8 May, all banks closed their doors. During the next three days, between 9 and 11 May, all RM notes were withdrawn. This exchange was limited to £25 in cash to Guernsey ID card holders, the rest being cashable on and after 25 May. In Jersey, affairs were different. Here, local currency to the tune of some £64,000 had been issued during the Occupation and the island government had made no preparations for withdrawing RM. Therefore, the exchange proceeded along the lines of the Finance Plan. withdrawal did not take place before 16 May and lasted a week, until 23 May, with a lower withdrawal limit of £5 cash.[157] The total amount of currency exchanged – including holdings in banks – was RM 5.77m (approx. £ 0.6m) in Guernsey and RM 13.8m (£ 1.47m) in Jersey.[158] These were not excessive sums, a fact acknowledged by Force 135 who saw no reason to interfere in the exchange.[159] The focus clearly was on the liberalisation of economic exchange as soon as possible, for an order raising the ban on the importation of notes from the Channel Islands came into force on 23 May 1945. This followed the Financial Directives of Force 135 which stipulated that while there should be no interference with book transfers between the islands and the UK, the restrictions on transfers and movements of currency between the islands and places other than the UK were maintained.[160] This was a damage limitation strategy designed to prevent an influx of RM from Continental Europe. The blocking and confiscation of war profits was then deferred until the passing of war profits levies modelled on the UK Excess Profits Tax. Under this scheme, businesses

[157] PRO WO 32/11409. Preliminary report on the financial position of the Channel Islands and Appendix A. The RM exchange in Guernsey was conducted at the lower rate of RM10 for every £1; in Jersey the rate was 9.36:1. The slower pace of the RM exchange in Jersey was credited to the following factors: computation with a broken sum rate, larger population, the fact that only the six branch banks were involved whereas in Guernsey the exchange was carried out in many outstation depots. Interestingly, the author also mentioned the 'overall tightness of outlook' and, as a result, the large amount of red tape in Jersey. Here the exchange had produced a pile of declarations. Author feared that this would simply be waste paper. In Jersey people are accustomed to take a very strict and rigid view of all monetary transactions.

[158] PRO T 161/1197. Civil Affairs Unit (Force 135), to Hampshire (WO), 20 June 1945. The Guernsey figures are not entirely conclusive as two different rates were in operation during the exchange: one for the civilian population, another for the banks.

[159] PRO T 231/333 to 335. Extract from report on working of 20 Civil Affairs Unit, 9 May to 27 May 1945, 28 May 1945; PRO WO 32/11409. Money circulation on liberation; PRO WO 32/11409. RM Exchange – Jersey and Guernsey.

[160] PRO WO 32/13750. Channel Islands Financial Directives 1944.

were taxed 60 per cent of the excess of the profits for the years 1940–44 over the pre-war standard profit; transactions at 80 per cent of the excess of the aggregate profits during the Occupation; transactions on currency operations at 100 percent. [161] It may have not even come to this, had the British government not insisted that the willingness of the Treasury to provide for the shortfall in mending Channel Islands' budget holes was dependent on islanders helping themselves through profits levies. The War Profits Levy (Jersey) Law was passed by the States in October 1945, received Royal Sanction on 18 December 1945 and was registered the following March. That year a similar law was also passed in Guernsey. The most obvious shortcoming with the war profits levies was that they introduced a drastic, but rather academic distinction between 'legitimate' and 'illegitimate' profits that did not exist in their UK equivalent.[162] Also, they did not address 'off-the-book' transactions or barter deals. Rather prophetically a Home Office correspondence with the War Office in April 1944 had already stated that if someone has been 'sailing near the wind to obtain financial gain, he will probably have farmed out his gains in such a way that we wont be able normally to spot him through his bank balances'.[163] A widely cited example of a currency transaction which was taxable under the law was not something a gifted speculator would have bothered with. Some people had exchanged British Treasury notes for a higher Reichsmark rate and then inscribed these into bank accounts where they were credited as sterling. This was small game. The Attorney General of Jersey, Duret Aubin, also commented in late 1945 that a share of the ill-gotten gains had probably already been expatriated through the mail services. It is feasible that some funds could have returned in the form of company or property investment which reached the islands during the post-war boom. Too much depended on the authorities' power to obtain information and here the picture didn't look particularly brilliant either. In Jersey the measure was implemented with the resources of income tax, with an honorary board of referees set up to deal with appeals. Whereas in other countries the confiscation of war profits was a long and unwieldy process based on the war profits levy, in the Channel Islands it was a matter of a couple of ledger entries. Nothing in terms of documentation survives today and it is impossible to say how much revenue was actually levied. It is possible that the £100 penalty for failure to give notice of liability may have scared off the smaller fish, but it would have had little or no effect on the larger operators. Eventually, the Jersey War Profits Levy petered out. Asking for a ruling on whether he should proceed with the collection of certain cases already assessed, the Comptroller of income tax was told by

---

[161] Attorney General to the Lieutenant Governor of Jersey, 27 Oct 1945.

[162] HO 45/25853. The Attorney General of Jersey to Markbreiter (HO), Nov 1945; The Solicitor General of England and Wales to the Secretary of State, 11 Dec 1945.

[163] PRO WO 32/13750. Markbreiter to French, 4 Apr 1944.

the Finance Committee on 6 December 1946 that the procedure to be adopted was left to his discretion.[164]

In Guernsey the operation of a similar law was impaired by the absence of administrative staff; as late as November 1946 there were still many cases to be assessed. Such delay was contrary to the very spirit of the measure which should have relied on the element of surprise. Out of fear that some persons may transfer their assets, supplementary legislation prohibiting movements to and from specified bank accounts in Guernsey was contemplated.[165] An internal Bank of England note, of 1 November 1946, commented on this Guernsey proposal to block accounts for six months in order to impose the levy as 'fantastic'. Rather scathingly it commented that the 'one or two big fish' which the Guernsey authorities hoped to net were not sufficient reasons to inconvenience the entire community: 'Surely if the Guernsey Authorities [sic] who are in London were to discuss their problem with our Exchange Control (Gestapo Branch) [sic], some better solution could be found.'[166] The chief cashier only responded that on the Continent account blocking had been used for de-monetisation and as a tool against inflation, associated maybe with war profits, but in no case for this last reason alone. He had no suggestion to make, other than that the clearing banks, whose head offices had been contacted for their view on the opportunity of additional legislation, had indicated that the measure should be pursued through the ordinary machinery of the law and civil courts.[167] The move finished in a dead end. On 21 December 1946 the States Office of Guernsey reported back to the Home Office that in view of the banks' attitude they had decided to waive all controls and to inform the banks. Responsibility was shifted to the Income Tax Department and it was hoped that not too much money would be lost through lack of control of the export of sterling to the UK.[168] Further opposition was fermenting at the grassroots. A petition against the War Profits Levy was sent by 11 States Members to Bailiff Sherwill In November 1946. It maintained that it was impossible to tax profits made in an unpatriotic way and that the law was doomed to failure, imposing additional hardship on 'honest people who remained in Guernsey and did their utmost to maintain economic life'. The petitioners may have had a point, though, in stressing that most of the money made during the Occupation was spent owing to the tremendous cost of living and that nothing had been set aside for a levy which was introduced retrospectively. Other criticism pertained to the treatment

---

[164] States Greffe, Jersey. Protocole of 174th meeting of the Finance Committee, 6 Dec 1946.
[165] BoEA C40/100. Home Office (Howard) to Thorley, 1 Nov 1946.
[166] BoEA C40/100. Internal Bank of England note (Hawker) re. Guernsey, 1 Nov 1946.
[167] BoEA C40/100. Reply of chief cashier, 5 Nov 1946.
[168] BoEA C40/100. States Office Guernsey (Guillemette) to Home Office (Howard), 21 Dec 1946.

of so-called profits on property sales. All sums received in excess of 1939 sums were to be taxed, a measure which did not take account of the general increase of values owing to currency depreciation. What was seen as particularly unjust was that owners who did not dispose of property until after the Liberation were unaffected, although they managed to obtain even higher prices.[169]

Who were the profiteers? Marginals, foreigner, or upstarts? Unsurprisingly, no clear answer can be given to this question. One was the mother of Jersey escapee Peter Hassall who – while her son was languishing in German prisons and concentration camps – relocated her black market 'business' to France, early in 1944. Another method of burying war profits was to sink them in company accounts or to invest them in the continuing issues of share capital for extant or new companies.[170] Applications were generally granted on condition that particulars of all issues of capital be reported, especially the names of shareholders and the amount paid in. Also, no transfer of shares was legal without permission. It is doubtful, however, whether the islands would have had sufficient resources to exercise genuine control and a fair number may have simply slipped through the net. There has also been much talk about investment of black market profits into property during the Occupation. However, apart from anecdotal evidence there is nothing to suggest extraordinary variations in the volume of property transactions during the war. In the Channel Islands, property deals are registered in the Royal Courts, a complicated business involving witnesses, and illegal property transaction may be one of those topics blown out of proportion after the war. Naturally a limited number of people could have tried to buy property without the necessary registration. What is spurious, however, is the correlation of Occupation property transactions and the post-war property boom.

Another type of profiteer was Timmer, a Dutch grower and exporter of fruit, flowers and seeds, active in Guernsey since 1928. His company, Timmer Ltd, was incorporated in October 1927, with a share capital of £5,000. Timmer was well integrated, having married the daughter of a Jurat in 1929. When the Germans occupied they approached the States with regard to their supply of vegetables. The Controlling Committee, however, seems to have been reluctant and the occupier then appointed a private contractor, Timmer. Later the States were ordered to hand over a large acreage of glass to the latter. A damaging report, submitted by the Committee for the Control of Essential Commodities, in June 1946, stated that Timmer had hampered island efforts to become

[169] PRO HO 45/25845. Petition against War Profits Levy , 19 Nov 1946.

[170] The detailed study of company records and official documents detailing company creations during and immediately after the Occupation would probably give a better idea of the real war profiteers than the virtually non-existent documentation on the war profits levies themselves. This is beyond the scope of the current project.

self-sufficient. Whereas most growers were regimented, Timmer was given a free hand to grow whatever came to his fancy. Timmer could also export freely and secured large areas of glasshouses whose owners were forced off their properties. In addition Timmer procured extra supplies of vegetables and fruit, inducing other growers to cede them by offering transport facilities and higher rates. Much of the animosity towards Timmer was also due to the fact that while other growers were required by the States to lift their bulbs in order to grow food, Timmer was able to purchase these very cheaply. At the end of the war he owned large stocks while the stocks of all other growers were depleted. It was also said that at one time during the siege Timmer was growing flowers in the greenhouses.[171] Timmer denied that his actions had hampered island supply stating that he had been in constant contact with island officials who had never criticised his activities. On the contrary he alleged that the island authorities considered it in the inhabitants' best interest that a definite area be set aside for the Germans – a possible scenario. Oddly, one claim for the recovery of rent taken by the owner of part of a glasshouse property occupied by Timmer failed in the Royal Court of Guernsey who favoured Timmer. That the case may have been given greater publicity (than would have been the case otherwise) because he was a foreigner could be suggested by the fact that none of the people who had ceded produce to Timmer at black market prices seem to have been inconvenienced in quite the same manner. There is no question that Timmer did not clearly benefit from the Occupation. His bank account balance inflated from a pre-war debt of £340 to a credit of £70,000 and a tax claim against him was satisfied under the War Profits Levy. If he had not been married to a local woman with two children he may have even been deported. What awaited him and his family instead – social and economic ostracism (or 'public vilification' as Timmer stated himself) – was perhaps worse. As a result of the continuing allegations Timmer's solicitors requested a public inquiry, but no agreement was reached with the Attorney General of Guernsey. Finally, Timmer launched a petition to the King, stating that he was anxious to submit to the examination of any tribunal in order to refute the public incrimination of being an active collaborator. This petition was, indeed, submitted, but the Home Office advised against taking it further.[172]

Many letters were written to the editor of the *Daily Sketch* after the publication of the report incriminating Timmer Ltd, during May and June 1946. What is worth noting is that they carried noms de plume, such as Loyal, D.S., DDT, Grower, Queer Justice. It confirms the appreciation of an intelligence source which stated that, in July 1945, the boundaries between 'collaboration' and

[171] PRO HO 45/25845. Note re Timmer, 4 Dec 1947.

[172] PRO HO 45/25845. Gerrit Timmer, Petition to the King, 22 Feb 1949; Note re Timmer, n.d. (probably 1947); Home Office to the Lieutenant Governor of Guernsey, 22 Mar 1949.

'collaborationism' was so undetermined that islanders were generally afraid to come forward with anything for fear of being denounced as collaborators in turn. The most amusing of these was 'Radio Sunshine' a former internee who lived in Lancashire before his repatriation to Guernsey. 'Radio Sunshine' claimed to have met Sir Hartley Shawcross, the Attorney General for England and Wales, in late August 1945, and during this meeting Shawcross is reputed to have said that nothing would come of the investigations unless evidence was forthcoming. Our man pledged to provide this information. 'Radio Sunshine' could not have been more amateurish in his approach: if it is transparency you want from others, you have to lead with a good example. Adopting yet another nom de plume in this world of shadows was entirely counter-productive – and inexplicable. What did he have to fear if he had been deported to Germany since September 1942? 'Radio Sunshine' may have taken himself for a modern-day 'Zorro' for he was also ambitious. The 40 or 50 people he claims had contacted him with 'evidence' on collaboration, black marketering and denunciation were not enough, he wanted more and thus the newspaper interview he gave to the *Daily Sketch*, on 5 June 1946. Pride came before the fall.

Classifications introduced during this period, such as scandalous and non-scandalous behaviour – only blurred the lines further, as much scandalous behaviour could be perfectly legal. In many cases the conspiracy of silence was founded on fear and not premeditation. This is an important factor as post-war observers – and in particular the UK press – often assumed that the silence was the mere result of a sinister design based on too close relations with the Nazis. Characteristically, a former evacuee resident in Vale, Mr Le Brun, called these writers to task in an open letter on 5 June. He described the same phenomenon as did an MI5 agent in July 1945, saying that many had complained to him in person, but had declined to support him on a public platform.

Many people had also expected to be compensated, but the Rehabilitation Committee (which many prospective applicants falsely assumed to be operating on generous funds provided through the settlement with the UK Treasury), was financed by the islands themselves and therefore subjected to austerity principles. This meant that structural grants would be given in cases where a contribution to the economic and social rehabilitation of the islands was proven. An application for the rebuilding of schools or hotels would be considered, whereas private property, which had lost value during the Occupation and which was not considered essential to the reconstruction process of economic life in the islands, had no chance. Also it only covered land and property, but not the contents of houses. These principles were not understood by a great many people and created a lot of bad blood, contributing to rumours that certain people were lining their pockets again, as during the Occupation. Other compensation became available in both islands in 1947, in respect of death or disablement of persons during internment in Germany.[173] In the mid-1960s, after the British government had signed a deal with the Germans for compensation of victims of Nazi persecution, a similar scenario emerged as in the case of the rehabilitation grants. As the term 'Nazi persecution' should have made sufficiently clear, payments were only available for people who had suffered as a result of racial or political persecution, or who had been incarcerated in concentration camps or penal institutions where conditions were comparable. Although the conditions they had endured bore no relation to the privations of a prison or concentration camp, many former internees thought they were eligible. Most did not understand (or did not want to understand) that there was a difference between the privations of war and privations induced by the targeted persecution or annihilation of religious, racial or political minorities or imagined enemies.

Footing the bill

When the Occupation finally ended in May 1945, the islands were bankrupt. Both States' debt to the local banks had grown continually, as had currency in circulation and bank deposits.[174] Both islands faced debts, including debt service and rehabilitation costs, to the tune of £13.75m (Guernsey £6m and Jersey £7.75m), of which £10m was owed to the five clearing banks. This represented many times over the pre-occupation debt of £1,675,000 in Guernsey and £1,339,000 in Jersey. [175] For Guernsey, whose revenue in a normal year was £700,000 and excess of revenue over expenditure a mere £30,000 to £50,000, this was a burden that would take decades to work off.[176] The position in Jersey

---

[173] JAS B/A/W/211. Extra-statutory awards in respect of the death or disablement during internment of persons who were originally resident and gainfully occupied in Jersey and who were removed during the German Occupation, 23 Jan 1947.

[174] 'Finance in the Channel Islands', *Times*, 8 May 1945.

[175] War debt in the Channel Islands (£m)

	Jersey	Guernsey
Billeting costs	0.71	1.07
Levy	1.81	1.29
RM conversion	1.47	0.6
Budget deficit et al.	2.26 (reconstructed)	1.49
Accumulated debt	6.25	4.5

See PRO WO 32/13750. Treasury document 'The Islands Budgets', 1945–46; JAS D/AP/V/511. Notes of conference held at the Home Office on 28 Apr 1946 on the financial position of Jersey and Guernsey.

[176] The cost of funding a £6m debt at 3% over 50 yrs would have been £232,000 p.a., see PRO WO 32/13750. Treasury document 'The Islands Budgets', 1945–46. The excess of revenue figure was given by John Leale, see PRO T 161/1197. Note of Home Office Conference, 13 July 1945.

was very much the same. Where the money was to come from was unclear. In both islands higher income tax, surtax or sales tax rates had been introduced during the Occupation and there was little scope for further tax rises without damaging the core strength of the islands' economy. The mainstay of the islands' economy was specialised intensive cultivation and the export of its agricultural produce. This form of food production was lucrative but it also increased import dependency with regard to other foods, especially as a large immigrant labour force was needed. Also the islanders could not live on the returns from the crop trade alone. Without the invisible exports of returns on investments abroad, tourism and remittances to retirers and settlers who had made the islands their permanent domicile, the trade balance of the islands would remain negative. Low taxation was what drew these spenders to the islands in the first place. Increased taxation, on the other hand, would have required the lowering of imports. This in turn would have resulted in depopulation and threatened the very survival of the islands as distinct communities. The only (false) alternative, the establishment of manufacturing, was not a realistic option for realising the islands' economic potential. The islands could not altogether escape higher taxation as the end of the war had heard calls for welfare provision on a par with the UK. This implied that there was even less scope to finance debt out of the islands' budgets if one did not want to risk reducing the islands to the status of mere peasant or fishing communities. The UK Treasury therefore concluded that both islands together could not be expected to take on more than a total of £5.5m in debt.[177]

Almost immediately the islands turned to the UK for assistance in the liquidation of the Occupation debt and the first steps to remedy the situation were taken as early as June 1945. Over the following months a series of conferences would pave the way to the final agreement in March 1946. At the first of these, on 13 July 1945 – taking place at the Home Office and attended by Coutanche, Leale and both Attorneys General – the Channel Islanders advanced that a large part of the debt, that is the payments for feeding and billeting German troops as well as for the occupation levy, was incurred as an obligation under international law, and should therefore be regarded as an Imperial war debt.[178] The argument was not new and had already been used by the German Ministry of Finance in late 1943, when it was decided to raise the occupation levy to a level which bore no more relation to the financial capabilities of the islands. The five clearing banks whose Channel Islands' branches had taken on the States

---

[177] PRO WO 32/13750. Treasury document 'The Islands Budgets', 1945–46.

[178] PRO T 161/1197. Note of Home Office Conference, 13 July 1945. The president of the Jersey Economics and Finance Committee, Jurat Dorey said that this accounted for over £2.5m of the Jersey debt; reference was also made to the need for social legislation on par with the UK (and thus extra expenditure), to avoid risking an exodus.

Treasury bills had voiced similar sentiments in a memorandum of 13 April 1944, stating that the advances were incurred as a result of the policy decision of the British government to demilitarise the islands and demanding full repayment of their debt.[179] This point did not go entirely uncontested: in February 1946 the Chancellor was to criticise the agreement with the Channel Islands that was being drafted, on the grounds that the banks were the only British businesses in occupied territory who were to be indemnified in full for war losses.[180] By then, however, it was already too late as the entire financial establishment had already settled on the principle that the banks had made a large enough concession by foregoing the interest which had accrued during the war.[181]

Finally, on 28 March 1946, it was announced that Britain would meet the Channel Islands' debt with a gift of £7.5m, apportioned on the basis of £4.2m for Jersey and £3.3m for Guernsey. The British decision took into account the economic utility of a prosperous Channel Islands as an outlet for a UK export trade which had amounted to £6.5m in 1937. The Channel Islands, the preferred place in the sun for British tourists, had also generated a carrying trade of 170,000 passengers a year, in addition to the substantial amount of merchandise transport. Of equal interest were surplus funds remitted by savings banks and Post Office savings banks to the UK.[182] The Channel Islands also had a record of financial stability. Pre-war budgets had been fairly balanced and future earning potential was such that the islands would be able to meet debt repayments. The stipulation was that the gift should be employed for the purpose of reducing the islands' indebtedness to the banks and that the entire process of rehabilitation – which the islands had to finance out of their own pockets – be conducted on austerity principles.[183] The cost of rehabilitation, estimated at £3.2m, was to be raised through a loan issue or States bonds.[184]

---

[179] BoEA C40/100. Memorandum of the five clearing banks, 13 Apr 1944.

[180] BoEA C40/100. The Chancellor of the Exchequer to the Governor of the Bank of England, 25 Feb 1946.

[181] Two weeks after the 13 July 1945 meeting in London, at a conference in St Peter Port, the representatives of both island governments were asked to prepare and submit a firm proposal to the UK government on 11 August. A consensus had been forged on the basis of the discussions of the current and future financial positions, and the island governments were asked to provide figures on the total amount of debt, including rehabilitation cost, the cost of debt service on a 3% basis over 50 yrs and the respective amounts they felt the States and the UK could meet, see PRO WO 32/11711. Minutes of Finance Conference, St Peter Port, 3 Aug 1945.

[182] PRO WO 32/13750. Treasury document 'The Islands Budgets', 1945–46.

[183] The banks also agreed to liquidate the remaining debt of £2.5m by taking on States bonds at 2%.

[184] States Greffe, Jersey. Letters received from the Home Office on the subject of the financial settlement for Jersey, forwarded to the Bailiff by the Lieutenant Governor of Jersey, 30 Mar 1946.

II

Collaboration? What Collaboration?

You say *tə-mä'tō* I say *tə-mā'tō* – Why definition matters

COLLABORATION is a term loaded with controversy and the last ten years was a decade full of revelations about the level of assistance provided to Nazi Germany across Europe and in all areas – military, ideological or economic. Europeans also began to acknowledge their co-responsibility for the Holocaust, which in many ways was being reinterpreted as the defining event of World War Two. As a result collaboration was being increasingly assessed in the light of anti-Jewish or anti-Semitic policy. One of the key book events was the publication of Daniel Jonah Goldhagen's study *Hitler's Willing Executioners: Ordinary Germans and the Holocaust*.[1] In Germany proper detailed studies unravelled the assistance the regime had received from across society: from doctors, artists, lawyers, academics, businessmen and clergymen. The high point of this continuing reassessment was the 1998 'Wehrmacht exhibition' which started in Hamburg and then toured Germany and Austria. This exhibition demonstrated the involvement of the armed forces in Nazi occupation and extermination policy in Eastern Europe, burying with it the myth of a Wehrmacht which had washed its hands in innocence. Studies into collaboration in Eastern Europe led to the realisation that not all locals had been victims and that the Nazis had been able to rely on sufficient numbers to turn on their Jewish neighbours. Occasionally even the Allies could come in for criticism and so a tenacious controversy erupted over the question why the Allies did not bomb the Auschwitz death camp. While it was not suggested that the Allies had collaborated with the Nazis, it was hinted that there was no shortage of anti-Semitism in Britain or the US and that this may have had a hand in preventing any such bombing mission. If in this case the mark may have been overshot, Allied

---

[1] Daniel Jonah Goldhagen, *Hitler's Willing Executioners: Ordinary Germans and the Holocaust*, New York, 1996.

inaction in the face of a human catastrophe of such proportions was at least deeply embarrassing. Nowhere was embarrassment, and occasionally shame, more profound than in the former neutral states. Switzerland was rocked by revelations over its economic relations with Germany, culminating in the resounding 'Nazi gold' debate. In Sweden, film director Ingmar Bergman as well as IKEA founder Ingvar Kamprad came forward and admitted that, in their youth, they had been sympathizers of the Nazi regime. It was not a crime of collaboration to sympathize with a country known mainly from the propaganda the Nazis were feeding abroad, one or two short visits, or, in Kamprad's case, through family ties. However, what most Swedes would have preferred not to be reminded of was that Bergman and Kamprad were far from the only Swedes who had shared such feelings. They only, were brave enough to face the music. Interest in economic collaboration did not stop short of corporations: IBM's links with the SS and the operations of Ford Motors in Germany were scrutinised. It also emerged just how many businesses had profited from the use of slave labour. Albert Speer's laborious myth building, that somehow the technocrats of his ministry for armaments production, as well as German business leaders, had stayed clean, crumbled and collapsed. This list is not intended as a complete one, it merely indicates the scope and complexity of the debate. While the level of genuinely new revelations is probably petering out now, the topic remains charged with emotion.

Nowhere is the passion it arouses stronger than in the Channel Islands where criticism – and in particular criticism from outsiders – is often met with a determined front of rebuttal. 'Collaboration' and 'Channel Islands' have always made an extremely uneasy pair. At most times this is interpreted as denial, but one also has to consider that the foundations of these mini-societies are much easier to upset and damage than those of larger nation states; some of the allergic outbursts to probes into the Channel Islands Occupation as 'off the beaten track' are certainly owed to this fact. The other element is that criticism is only accommodated with some difficulty in small island cultures built on consensus and social conformism. The nightmarish image of the Swastika presiding over this ancient appanage of the Crown has not been an easy one to banish from the collective consciousness. The good fortune of having been able to lock into British wartime history in the post-war era almost eliminated the dissonances, for a while. What has carried the islands over the last sixty years is the powerful myth that, because this was British territory and because the Channel Island's administrations derived their authority from the Crown, there could have been none of the type of collaboration practised on the Continent. Not much of a rational explanation was ever given for this and over the past decade this position has emerged as increasingly untenable. Many of the attempts to redress the imbalance have, in turn, overshot the mark and it has now become almost a matter of good taste to insist that collaboration with the Nazis also reached Britain. Indicative of this trend is Madeleine Bunting's contention – in a *Guardian* article which appeared for Holocaust Day 2004 – that the Channel Islands were 'our part in the Holocaust'.[2] While Bunting has all the right in the world to examine how the Channel Islands – with their particular history as the only British territory to have implemented anti-Jewish legislation during the war – intend to mark the day, the creation of a link between the occupied Channel Islands and wartime Britain seems impertinent, even manipulative. While the Channel Islands may provide an answer as to the resistance of Britishers to anti-Semitism, one cannot but insist on the precedence of fact over fiction, notwith-standing the perhaps greater entertainment value of virtual history. And the fact is that the military and political establishment of Britain did not collapse in June 1940 under the weight of shock and panic – as did France – and got the country back on its feet within a matter of days. Any temptation to pursue an early peace with Nazi Germany was quickly overcome. We do not know what would have happened had Hitler decided to use the window of opportunity at Dunkirk.

In the following pages we will attempt to bring an answer to the question of whether the relationship between German and Channel Islands' authorities can be subsumed under the umbrella term 'collaboration'. This requires some preliminary work of definition and reflection on the use of additional qualifiers. It will involve probing epistemology to decide whether 'collaboration' as a concept can be a valid description of this special context. Or was the situation of the islands such that the term 'collaboration' loses its meaning and relevance?

Collaboration is a phenomenon of great complexity and presents a dilemma rather similar to the 'one man's freedom fighter is another man's terrorist' conundrum. The term originated in Vichy France, and this has not been without consequence. When Marshal Pétain met Hitler at Montoire in 1940 he announced that he was setting off along the 'path of collaboration'. Its precise definition has remained a problem ever since. Franco-American historian Stanley Hoffmann made a first step in the direction of definition in the 1950s, by discriminating between 'involuntary collaboration' and 'voluntary collaboration' on the one hand and '(state) collaboration' and 'collaborationism' on the other.[3] Thus collaboration would apply to assistance motivated by national interest or reasons of state; collab-orationism would apply to assistance for personal gain or to die-hards who drove collaboration beyond the prescribed limits of their own governments or adminis-trations and aligned themselves fully on Nazi ideology. Small wonder, therefore,

---

[2] Madeleine Bunting, 'Our part in the Holocaust: One Channel Island at least is owning up to its wartime shame', *Guardian online*, 24 Jan. 2004 <http://www.guardian.co.uk/comment/story/0,3604,1130153,00.html>

[3] See Julian Jackson, *France – The Dark Years 1940–1945*, Oxford, 2001, 167.

that Peter Davies also calls the collaborationists 'the real collaborators'.[4] Hoffmann's definition of collaboration, clear as it may seem, has thrown up the issue of whether collaboration only occurred in the sphere of politics. Gerhard Hirschfeld, another historian, pleads for a wider definition integrating economic, social and cultural relations.[5] Werner Rings, a journalist, regarded practically all points of contact with the enemy occupier as collaboration.[6] In this sense a newsagent selling a newspaper to a German would be a collaborator, a point of view one does not necessarily have to share. Another contested point is whether collaboration represents a historical category or simply a political slogan. Recent attempts by scholars discussing the application of the concept to contexts other than the Second World War seem to be leading to an emerging consensus that it should cover similar situations throughout the 20th century.[7]

Far from solving problems, standard dictionary definitions rather seem to magnify inherent contradictions. In the *Oxford English Dictionary* two meanings of 'collaboration' are given: 'united labour', 'cooperation'; and 'traitorous co-operation with the enemy'. As in most cases where one and the same word can be used to describe a positive connotation activity as well as its exact opposite the result is very unsatisfactory, and this is no exception. This limitation makes the concept both porous and dangerous to handle, resulting in confusion where polemics reign supreme. The dictionary definition is also inaccurate, as usage in the first meaning has become rather uncommon. Collaboration invariably points to state politics and it refers to frameworks and forms of co-operation that are not *kosher*. The problem with the dictionary definition is easily illustrated through a concrete example: Vichy did not conceive of itself as a traitorous regime. It saw itself rather as the legitimate national government engaged in a repeat match of Bismarckian *Realpolitik*. The majority of its men and women would have subscribed to the view that they were pursuing French interests and in their majority they weren't even particular lovers of Nazi Germany. And yet, their actions were benefiting the Germans more than the French whom they were claiming to defend. Owing to the public trust they enjoyed, the damage done by them was even worse than if they had been common traitors. Therefore defining 'collaboration' as 'collusion with the enemy in a context of occupation' is almost certainly better, although even this allows no space for differentiation or graduation.

---

[4] Peter Davies, *Dangerous Liaisons*, Harlow, 2004, 21.

[5] See Hirschfeld's introduction to *Collaboration in France: Politics and culture during the Nazi occupation, 1940–1944*, edited by Gerhard Hirschfeld and Patrick Marsh, Oxford, 1989.

[6] Werner Rings, *Life with the enemy: collaboration and resistance in Hitler's Europe, 1939–1945*, London, 1982.

[7] see the final report of a colloquium titled 'Fremdherrschaft und Kollaboration: Erscheinungsformen in Nordosteuropa 1900–1950', Nordost-Institut in Lüneburg, Germany, 13–16 Nov. 2003 <www.ikgn.de/veranstaltungen.kollaboration.htm>

In the Channel Islands there is still considerable reluctance to accept 'collaboration' as a concept applicable to their own wartime experience. In the past, the solution has been to lay claim to a special status, founded on the peculiar imbalance of power and scale generated by the island situation and the might of the German Wehrmacht. This has some justification: translating a concept born in the domain of high state politics to these small and vulnerable communities does generate a feeling of unease. Nothing had prepared the islands' authorities for what followed in the summer of 1940: as a result of occupation by Germany they had to shoulder responsibilities surpassing anything they had ever had to grapple with in peacetime. Symbolically this was manifest in the fact that the Bailiffs were sworn in as Lieutenant Governors shortly before the Occupation. Reacting to the new situation was already a genuine challenge for many national administrations; in the case of the Channel Islands the word 'challenge' would be a gross understatement. One could not realistically expect small island administrations reliant on honorary appointments and without the know-how, resources and experience of national governments to be able always to anticipate the future impact of measures and avoid the entrapments of an occupying power of the sophistication of Germany. From this viewpoint the term 'collaboration' appears to be of at least diminished validity.

Unfortunately, it is not these conceptual issues that enter most into the picture when it comes to refuting the term in the Channel Islands. Refutation is not based on an intellectual effort demonstrating its inapplicability. What weighs heavier in the reluctance to adapt to the term are not the material realities, but the associations with collaboration in Britain, the lead culture for Channel Islanders. There collaboration is still seen as a typically French (or Continental) phenomenon. Islanders' allergy to the word is informed by its hefty use in the UK media, where no shades of grey seem to exist and where the only known form of collaboration is 'Vichy-style' cuddling up to the 'New European Order'. Islanders responded to the 'dumbing down' effects through the sanitization of their vocabulary: while the rest of Europe may have collaborated, the Channel Islands 'maintained their administration' or 'co-operated'.

Co-operation ('working together'), seemingly straightforward and value neutral, presents the fundamental problem of credibility. A good word to qualify contacts with the World Health Organisation or the Red Cross, or to describe a working relationship that is balanced, fair and equitable, it does not fit this particular historical bill. Could islanders avoid or ignore the Germans, refuse to have anything to do with them? Were the implementation of measures against the Jews, the pre-emptive £25 reward offered by the Bailiff of Guernsey to islanders prepared to denounce their neighbours, the apprehension of escaped prisoners or the problematic co-operation of the German and Channel Islands police forces something one might choose to describe by the innocuous term 'co-operation'; even if some of these were tactical manoeuvres to deflect German ire? Do we or don't we concede that the Nazi officials manipulated administrations across Europe so that these often ended up doing things they had never envisaged doing to begin with? And did these administrations typically resign or continue in their duties, in the name of the 'greater number', to 'avoid worse' or as the 'lesser of two evils'? Unfortunately the answer is that most, including the administrations of the Channel Islands, continued.

The most important argument against 'co-operation' is the corrosive character of Nazi rule. Officials in occupied countries were not the only ones to believe that the impact of the Nazis could somehow be contained, they were preceded by the appeasers of the 1930s or the German politicians who allowed Hitler's rise to power in 1933 – and they were all proved wrong. 'Beware the beginnings' (*Wehret den Anfängen*) is an oft-cited German slogan and in the failure to have regarded this warning lies the tragedy of many a good man in Germany, France or the Channel Islands. When one has business with Mephistopheles, under whatever arrangement, one cannot expect to come out with an unsullied vest. This is inevitable and quite independent from the level of willingness displayed by the devil's partner. The road to collaboration was a very slippery slope and it proceeded via very short, almost unnoticeable way stations. One Dutch resistance worker interviewed in the landmark documentary 'The World at War' explained that the principle was in function when, early in the Occupation, the Germans took the census of the Dutch population and asked them to fill in questionnaires. These also included a section relating to 'Aryan' origin. He explained that giving an answer to this question was the first imperceptible step on the road to extermination, as it isolated the Jews from the rest of the population.[8] Few recognised this danger and most complied, duly ticking where appropriate, yet they were already doing the devil's work. Similarly many administrations that started out with a pristine record became increasingly tainted as they went along with incessant German demands, trapping themselves into logics which they had not foreseen and which offered no exit. The insidiousness of the methods employed by modern dictatorships brings home the fundamental importance of moral principles, many of which were surrendered rather nonchalantly, for questionable returns. Once a principle was 'out of the window', a host of other demands could be derived from the cave-in. The only way to avoid this kind of entrapment was evasion or early resistance.

The Channel Islands found themselves in a situation which provided particularly inextricable opportunities for blackmail: the islands depended on German help for their supplies from France and pressure could be increased at any time

[8] 'The World at War: occupation', TV documentary narrated by Sir Laurence Olivier, 1974.

by the suggestion of 'evacuation' of islanders to unknown destinations, for reasons of 'military necessity'. All this sent shivers down the spines of every Channel Islander called upon to shoulder administrative duties. The image of the 'slippery slope' applies here as it does to other parts of occupied Europe. One case offering particularly good illustration of its operation in the local context is the case of Frederick Page, a Jerseyman reported to the Germans by the island authorities. While investigating a robbery in late May 1943 the St Saviour's honorary police received information from neighbours that a James Davey had one or more wireless sets at his residence. And indeed, when they followed up this information, they discovered three wireless sets, two of which were the property of a second man, Frederick Page.[9] All wirelesses had been confiscated in June 1942 and wireless retention, as well as all associated activities such as the spreading of BBC news, was considered a serious offence carrying as a typical punishment a long prison sentence in France or Germany from whence by this time few returned. The police now faced the dilemma of either submitting a report which might lead to the prosecution of a fellow islander or running the risk of a denunciation to the Germans that the island police were defying their orders; the likelihood of which was increased by the fact that the police investigations emerged from a neighbour's quarrel and that the discovery of the wireless sets was known and generally talked about. The dilemma was aggravated by the fact that since the passing of an 'Order for the Protection of the Occupying Authorities [*sic*]', on 18 December 1942, the authorities were obliged – under threat of punishment – to signal to the Germans all information which came to their attention bearing a relation to infractions of German orders. In this situation Centenier Garden, the officer in charge, made an informal approach to the Attorney General, Duret Aubin, who later testified that Garden had not taken the matter nonchalantly[10], but 'was gravely disturbed in his own mind as to what action he should take'. Duret Aubin gave him the Salomonic advice that he 'was not disposed to give him an order one way or the other in a matter into which considerations of conscience entered so strongly', and that Garden 'must decide with his own conscience where his duty lay'. He added, however, that if he did receive a formal police report he would have 'no alternative but to forward it to the Occupying [*sic*] authority'. When Garden put the matter to his colleagues at a meeting at the St Saviour police their unanimous opinion was that their duty was to the community rather than to the individual and that he should therefore report.[11] The Attorney General

---

[9] JAS D/Z/1943/19. Police Report. Centenier Garden to Attorney General, 2 June 1943.
[10] A later escapee report stated that Garden was a policeman who was favourably disposed towards resistance, see PRO HO 144/22237. MI19. Report no. 2510. Jersey Siege Conditions. Interrogation of three escapees from Jersey, November 1944.
[11] JAS D/Z/1943/19. Memorandum, Attorney General, 4 Aug. 1945.

received Garden's report on 2 June 1943, which he forwarded to the Germans the following day. Page was tried with the other radio listeners who had gathered at Davey's house and was sentenced to 21 months imprisonment. He died at Naumburg prison, Germany, on 5 January 1945.[12]

While the affair may appear as a simple and straightforward 'greater good' case, there is more to it than that. First of all there is the definition of 'duty to the community' given by the Attorney General in this case, and which appears in the memorandum he submitted to British investigators in 1945. The prevailing consensus was that it was necessary to avoid the suppression and take-over of the police of St Saviour by the Germans in the event of them discovering the facts, a situation, it was said, 'which it had, throughout the Occupation, been the settled policy of the insular administration to avoid'.[13] It is doubtful whether this 'sacred cow' was a goal worth the deliberate sacrifice of individuals. In fact, the slavish adherence to the principle of preventing a German take-over of the whole or parts of the island administrations was one of the main weaknesses of the island governments. The Germans exploited this fear, suggesting that in any event it was better for the local governments to be involved in measures, in order to mitigate their impact. The argument impressed Bailiff Coutanche, Senator Edward Le Quesne and other members of the Superior Council in Jersey who initially gave indication that they were considering resigning over the September 1942 deportation of non-natives, but were persuaded to stay on by the 'buffer argument'.[14] How high this question figured on the authorities' agenda is demonstrated by the fact that this is the first thing exposed by the Bailiff of Jersey in the introductory paragraph of a twenty five-page memo to the Home Office in June 1945.[15] Such firm positioning had a negative impact on the authorities' bargaining power which – considering that Britain was still in the war – should have been much larger. It also stands in stark contrast to the otherwise rather liberal concession-making on other principles. Throughout Europe, clinging to snippets of sovereignty was to damage the legitimacy, and tarnish the record, of many administrations.

Not that the rather abstract scenario of a German take-over was the principal reason for the decision of the St Saviour's honorary police. What is more likely to have happened in the event of a German discovery that the island authorities had not notified them of the case is that Garden and his colleagues would have stood trial, and that similar to the Guernsey policemen tried in spring 1942, they would have been deported to prison in Germany. Ultimately, this was a question

---

[12] Paul Sanders, *The Ultimate Sacrifice*, 39.

[13] JAS D/Z/1943/19. Memorandum, Attorney General, 4 Aug. 1945.

[14] PRO. WO 311/13. In the Matter of War Crimes, Statement by A. Coutanche, Bailiff, 12 June 1945; Edward Le Quesne, *The occupation of Jersey day by day*, entry of 21 Sept 1942, 152.

[15] PRO HO 45/22399. Memorandum, Alec Coutanche to Sir Donald Somervell, 3 July 1945.

of 'us' or 'them'. The situation was not entirely without risk for the Attorney General either. Garden had two possibilities of action: he could either decide to submit a report or not to submit a report. The most unlikely scenario was that he would submit the report and that the Attorney General would then hush up the affair. If the police decided not to submit a report, the Attorney General could have remained silent about his conversation with Garden; but this would have entailed considerable risk for himself, especially if news of the police discovery reached the ears of the German police after all and these decided to interrogate and try Garden and his colleagues. Then all would depend on Garden not revealing his conversation with the Attorney General nor disclosing the conversation to a third party. The other alternative in case of non-submission of a report – probably the most devastating of all – was for the Attorney General to stick to the rules and denounce Garden himself. Failure to do so would have resulted in his being in breach of the law. Thus from his own personal perspective, the adopted solution was the most convenient of four possible scenarios. Interesting as such game theory may be, the 'greater good' argument employed in this affair is not what makes this case so significant; the entire case provides far more powerful illustration of the principle of 'beware the beginnings' and 'slippery slope'. A more important observation is that it need never have come to this. What was disingenuous about the use of the 'greater good' argument in this case was to present it as *force majeure*, passing under a veil of silence the part of the island authorities in turning an activity, which should never have been an offence in the first place, into a punishable offence. Initially, the June 1942, wireless confiscation was met with protest, but this soon subsided into resigned acceptance: instead of an adamant refusal by the authorities to have anything to do with this measure and its implementation, they took on the task of putting the radios in storage. This opened the floodgates, as German action on the wireless issue did not end with mere confiscation. But while the confiscation of the radios in June 1942 was something the island population could be made to accept under the Hague Convention, the prosecution of 'radio offenders' had no basis in international law. Similar to a bad chess player, the authorities had not anticipated the next move and the trap closed in December 1942, when the Germans issued their order compelling the authorities to denounce all offences against German orders. A new crime was born, namely the crime of not reporting offences against German orders, and this placed the knife at the authorities' throat. They thus became an associated party to measures designed to clamp down on 'radio offenders', something they, no doubt, had never intended. It would be too facile to point to their distress without acknowledging that they were partly to blame for this situation. Not only did the authorities not live up to their reputation of 'buffer', but they also failed adequately to assess and foresee the consequences of their action. By the time the Jersey police discovered Davey's radio, the island authorities had already missed their opportunity to put up resistance to the prosecution of 'wireless offences'. The only way to avoid being dragged further into the quagmire of doing the occupier's work would have consisted in resistance from the beginning. This would have entailed risks, but considerations of justice should have led the authorities to take such risks. Clearly in this situation the authorities did not measure up to their reputation as a 'buffer'.

Another Jersey case showing the pernicious workings of the 'slippery slope' occurred on 29 July 1943 when Duret Aubin received a visit from the German Secret Field Police who requested that he hand over all anonymous letters received at his office since July 1942. This he promised for the 31 July, after having checked the matter with the Feldkommandantur. The day after the visit, Duret Aubin, ever the conscientious civil servant, informed Judge Seger, not someone known for a mild disposition, of his apprehension that the procedure seemed 'irregular' and that such a request needed the FK *imprimatur*. Naturally, Seger came to the conclusion that the letters in question were better kept in his own hands and accordingly instructed Duret Aubin who followed up the matter on 4 August.[16] What is remarkable in this case is the Attorney General's rather unquestioning attitude as to the moral implications of transferring denunciation letters to people who might actually make use of them to track down innocent islanders. We do not know whether the letters finally handed over contained any sensitive information or whether Duret Aubin even handed over the complete set of letters he had received. And this seems to be beside the point, for what Duret Aubin never once questioned was whether it was legitimate and appropriate for the island authorities to hand over potentially damaging materials. Due to the failure to take a principled stand, the Germans had created another precedent, namely that letters of denunciation were to be routinely transferred to themselves; it was not known what else could be derived from such administrative cave-ins.

The evidence presented by these and many other similar cases contradicts the claim that the occupation of the Channel Islands resulted in nothing more controversial than a simple 'working together'. Not only does the use of 'co-operation' fail the test of basic facts on the ground; it also fails the test of inherent logic. Reality is never as simple as abstract, ideal-typical dictionary definitions suggest, and one should be resigned to the fact that co-operation and collaboration overlapped a great deal. The practice across Europe shows that voluntary collaboration alternated with involuntary collaboration, as there were cases of collaboration turning into collaborationism over the course of the war. Claiming that the Channel Islands defied the general pattern and that at no

[16] JAS Law Officer's Department. D/Z/H/5309. Duret Aubin, handwritten notes, 29 July to 4 Aug. 1943.

point co-operation turned into collaboration is simply not valid; especially not when a nation such as the Danes – who saved practically their entire Jewish population in an unparalleled rescue effort – can today admit that some of their economic and political ties with Germany amounted to collaboration. Today, in the light of much better research, the insistence on 'co-operation' had become more a liability than an asset. While 'collaboration' – when applied in the absolute – is a dysfunctional and misleading concept and while the occupied Channel Islands certainly have a right not to be put into the same category as other more fully-fledged collaboration regimes, the time has come to cede ground and acknowledge a limited applicability of 'collaboration'. And the solution to making any genuine sense of 'collaboration' in the Channel Islands seems to be to introduce additional qualifiers. Rather than asking 'collaboration or not collaboration?' the question needs to be reconfigured into 'which collaboration?' Rather helpful in this respect is the typology of collaborations established by Werner Rings and Peter Davies which suggests a menu of the following: heart-and-soul collaboration, shield philosophy, conditional collaboration, tactical collaboration, submission on the grounds of superior force and wait-and-see collaboration (*attentisme*).[17]

The parameters of collaboration

The building blocks for additional qualifiers of collaboration can be 'quarried' from the usual factors by which the occupied could influence occupation regimes: from political opportunism and bargaining to ideological proximity or simple lucre. Other factors were outside their control: where they ranked in the Nazi race hierarchy, the size and importance of their country or how badly the Germans needed them or their territory, and for what purpose. This influenced the margins of freedom of the administration in question. Again other factors went even beyond what the occupied or the Germans could influence, they were systemic.

The foundations of the relationship between occupier and occupied in the Channel Islands were unique in Europe. The first pillar was continuity, grounded in the fact that the state of war between Britain and Germany continued, as did the constitutional link between the Channel Islands and the British Crown. The prestige of the, as yet, unconquered enemy stuck to the Channel Islanders and provided something of a virtual screen against abuse. The Germans had to weigh carefully what they did in the Channel Islands, as this could be used against them. Although they had been told by their Führer to

---

[17] Peter Davies, *Dangerous Liaisons*, Harlow, 2004, 23–8.

tread carefully with these British subjects this is not to say that all Germans had the diplomatic sensitivity to appreciate their somewhat special status. Some treated this as just another occupied territory. Still, one of the positive consequences of continuity was the avoidance of split loyalties as experienced by many French citizens. With the signing of the armistice the Vichy French had suspended hostilities until the final signature of peace. Since June 1940 the Vichy government had been persuading the French that the war was over and that they had to bargain for a good place in a new Europe under German rule by making unilateral concessions. Until the time had come to reap the rewards they had stand fast. The rather stringent terms of the French armistice together with the principles of Franco-German collaboration consecrated in October 1940 gave potentially reluctant local administrations in the occupied zone little margin vis-à-vis the Germans who could point to the collaborating government. The capacity to resist was undermined by official policy. By contrast, no such considerations were an issue in the Channel Islands. Michael Ginns, a Jersey youngster during the Occupation, said that nobody he knew ever contemplated Germany winning the war.[18] This was a very significant difference from the point of view of many French people who endorsed Prime Minister Laval's wish, stated in a speech in June 1942, for a German victory to save Europe from Bolshevism. Neither were the French alone in this: across Europe a large number of people in authority had placed their bets on a German victory and these examples were an excellent breeding ground for heart-and-soul collaboration. The Channel Island authorities never tried to persuade their fellow islanders that what they were hearing on the BBC was propaganda. Contrary to Pétain, who elected to stay in France and work with the Germans, the Channel Island governments were instructed by the British government to continue in office. They also could not be compared to the Greek general left in charge of the puppet government in Athens who declared that he would obey the Führer's orders.[19] Despite their oscillating feelings islanders were not prepared to appreciate the 'advantages' of the New Order built on primitive racialist conspiracy theory. In this respect the gap between Channel Islanders and Germans could never be bridged. The little that German propaganda achieved in the islands was quickly undone by the treatment of the slave labourers arriving in 1942.[20] Gaining an ideological foot-hold was not only impeded by islanders' mental set-up, but also the fact that the window of opportunity was far too short. During the first months of the Occupation shock and disorientation drowned out most other signals and did not allow for the emergence of a coherent pattern. The immediate dashing of German hopes of a speedy victory

[18] IWM Misc. 2826 189/2 (Tape 4448 O/L). Interview with Michael Ginns, n.d.
[19] Peter Davies, *Dangerous Liaisons*, op. cit., 20.
[20] Edward Le Quesne, *The occupation of Jersey day by day*, entry of 20 Feb 1943, 182.

over Britain – a drama islanders could see unfolding before their very eyes – plus persistent British resistance convinced many Channel Islanders that the motherland's cause was far from lost. As ever, the financially astute islanders also saw Britain's rising star in the continued strength of sterling, hoarded and traded throughout the Occupation, and well above the nominal exchange rate. The role of continuity was further accentuated by the fact that any break within the allegiance to the Crown would have been entirely 'out of character' and in defiance of over 700 years of the islands' history. Holding on to King and Country was not only dictated by sentiment and tradition, but also by plain common sense: a British victory was the only way to re-establish the islands' cherished autonomy, the essential core of the islands' identity. As islanders could see daily, German rule equalled loss of privilege and position and reduced them to foreigners in their own land and was therefore not in the natural self-interest of the native elite. On the other hand, the long-term historical perspective proper to islanders informed them that the situation in 1940 was not as unprece-dented as may have been suggested: neither was this the first time that the islands were occupied by enemy forces nor that Britain stood alone in Europe under imminent threat of invasion.

The second pillar of the Channel Islands' Occupation was the Hague Convention, at the time the only set of international legal rules governing the relationship between an occupier and a population in occupied territory. This shred of paper was their last link to the world of pre-war civilisation and it emerged as practically the only proxy battleground on which the island authori-ties felt safe. Nobody outlined the principle in operation better than Jurat Leale. In May 1945, he stated that there had been no doubt in his mind that 'the rights and interests as British people were best safeguarded by sticking to International Law [sic] through thick and thin'.[21] This, as well, was not necessarily standard procedure. Across the Channel, in France, an armistice was signed in June 1940 which gave a much closer definition to the principles governing the future Franco-German relationship, soon consolidated into a genuine and comprehen-sive policy of collaboration.

The reliance of the Channel Islands' authorities on international law was a honourable position to take. Eminently defensible after the war, it also demonstrated naïveté with regard to what international law could or could not achieve. The Hague rules were the result of a lukewarm minimum standard that the world powers had been able to agree upon half a century earlier. Although having rules of war was better than having no rules at all, protection of civilians definitely had to take a back seat over issues of governance and property

[21] PRO HO 45/22424. Report of the President of the Controlling Committee of the States of Guernsey on the activities of the Committee during the five years of German occupation, 23 May 1945.

rights.[22] This meant that a large amount of space requiring legal definition was left void. Unfortunately the situation was not rectified until after the Second World War, in the course of which it had become increasingly clear that unprotected civilians were considered a legitimate target of military operations. Legal 'black holes' were of direct benefit to the adherents of the philosophy of 'might is right'. While the Hague rules, for example, advise civilians to abstain from hostile acts against the occupier, the onus is also on the occupier who must not punish the community for the acts of individuals. Naturally multiple combinations or degrees of severity are possible between these two poles. Although one must be realistic and recognise that an occupier will always be considered as an alien body, the occupier himself can choose to look the other way when manifestations of minor discontent occur or react in a benign fashion through trust-building measures. One Guernsey contemporary, interviewed after the war, made the interesting observation that it was easier for a citizen of a neutral country to stick to strict obedience than it was for a population which had reason to understand every act of the occupier as directed against themselves.[23] The inability to operate any differentiation sophisticated enough to account for such variation shows the particular character of German rule. Behind the rhetoric of correct relations and international standards, lurked a rigid interpretation of the Hague rules in their own favour. Although there were notable exceptions, the occupier generally took the dimmest view possible: zero tolerance for disobedience, even if this was often of an extremely trivial nature, coupled with immediate threats of reprisals.

As practising lawyers, at least the Crown officers of Jersey and Guernsey should have shown more awareness of the fact that the international law in which they were placing so much faith had some deplorable deficiencies. Their immutable reliance on the principle of 'the law must be the law' emerges powerfully from the archives they have left behind. Ploughing through these one could almost forget that an enemy occupation had punctuated the administration of the Channel Islands. This continued on very much the same course as before the war: the law – whatever its source – continued to be binding. This failed to acknowledge that the pre-war correlation between 'law' and 'justice' had lost a great deal of its meaning in the legal system under Occupation. The usual gap had widened into a canyon. In addition blind reliance on perennial law when this was being abused by a regime with no real interest in law, was unethical. Paradoxically, to maintain their credibility the officials would have needed to do the unthinkable: something illegal. And this was beyond most. The

---

[22] Greenwood, Christopher, 'International Humanitarian Law (Laws of War)', in: Karlshoven, Fritz (ed.), *The Centennial of the First International Peace Conference – Reports and Conclusions*, The Hague et al., 2000, 252–4.

[23] IWM JRD.04. 'Sabotage and Betrayal', by unknown author (Guernsey), n.d.

insistence of the authorities on doing things 'by the book', even if the Nazis were the principal beneficiary of such correct behaviour, contrasts with the sizeable minority of islanders who proved that they were better pragmatists and found ways of circumnavigating rigid Occupation law that they perceived as unjust, inhuman or simply stupid. They had learnt to draw the right conclusions from the German love of paperwork and administrative absurdities, such as their confiscation of African spears as dangerous weapons from the homes of colonial retirees.

Much of the fixation on the letter of the law has its source in the proud legal traditions of the Channel Islands. The Normans created the most efficient bureaucracy in medieval Europe which they exported to Anglo-Saxon England and to Sicily, and it was based on the strength of their law. This shared experience spans the entire length of the islands' memory as functioning societies. As every visitor will have noticed, the Channel Islands are law-abiding places. They are good and safe to live or do business in, crime rates are low, rates of apprehension almost 100 per cent and one could summarise this as the positive side of communities where the imprint of the law is a strong and powerful shaper of people's existence. But there is also a less pretty side to this story, founded in the proverbial social conformism of small, provincial communities. In times of strife, such as the Occupation, the combination of law abidance and social conformism shows its downside, as illegal – but perhaps legitimate – undertakings are similarly discouraged or even penalised. The Channel Islands were not a good place for conspiratorial activities as these always depend on skills that are somewhere between those of the spy and the criminal. Throughout Europe people interested in serious resistance had to do a number of things carrying an automatic cachet of disrepute in the eyes of 'respectable' social conformists. They had to forge papers, they had to be masters of evasion, they had to find safe houses, procure food on the black market and occasionally they even had to steal, rob or worse. No wonder the 'terrorists' were almost as loathed by the majority of the conforming population as they were by the collaborating police forces and the German occupier himself. A similar position existed in the Channel Islands. Particularly dangerous for those interested in relevant action was the constitution of the timorous, those Channel Islanders unable to overcome fear for their safety and therefore ill-disposed to any type of action likely to provoke the Germans into taking reprisals, as they might resort to the feared weapon of denunciation. Having said this: things between the two segments of the population – the fearful and the audacious – were not decided in advance. This is the conclusion one must draw from the ample help given to escapees, particularly in Jersey, many of them foreigners who were *not* reported and lived among the civilian population. It was for the authorities – for what other meaning is there of the word 'authority' – discreetly to point the way and reconcile rather than widen any emerging cleavages within the population. And it was in this task of building a new consensus, of recasting the parameters of society, that the activities of the island administrations remained unconvincing. Was this a failure of leadership? Or was it simply a question of acting responsibly by being overcautious rather than taking risks that might endanger the population? Naturally, the authorities were also fearful of setting precedents which could lead to an erosion of authority. No doubt, it was sound to give the impression, to the Germans as well as to the population, that German law was to be obeyed. This was particularly important with regard to the destructive elements that exist in every society, interested in hooliganism and anarchy rather than meaningful resistance, as they could be the source of untold tragedy, if encouraged. In view of the extremely precarious supply situation, it was equally impossible to tolerate any non-observance in the area of economic regulation. Many of the harsh sentences passed on islanders were motivated by the consideration of deterring offenders. However, the simple disallowance of feelings of resistance from the population, without putting in its stead anything remotely impressive, revealed many Channel Islands' officials as parochial fathers imbued by their positions in life, but without the necessary imagination or strength to measure up to them. The resistance islanders got from their officials and politicians was the routine shuffling of papers, mixed in with a number of verbal protests.

Making the most of the Hague Convention could not only depend on reliance on the principle that if law prevailed, so would justice. Much was also a function of the relationship and the brokering between occupier and occupied over such contested areas. Equally important were astuteness and cunning, and there is some evidence that the authorities experienced something of a learning curve as the Occupation progressed.

How much margin did the authorities have to begin with? Jersey billeting officer Vernon Le Maistre thought the authorities were sitting on the rough end and were quite exposed, as it was difficult to avail oneself of the intermediation of the protecting power. Confrontations were direct.[24] Raymond Falla, Guernsey member of the Channel Islands' Purchasing Commission, stated that the islands were allowed 'considerable initiative within certain parameters' and 'that no country can occupy every part of another one'. According to Falla there was always room for manoeuvre, if one was clever enough. In particular the German weakness for paperwork, their culture of obedience and the fact that they could not control, but only monitor the moves of the locals, offered scope for exploitation. In Falla's experience once set into black-and-white print, information or figures were practically never double-checked. Interestingly, however, even Falla

---

[24] IWM Misc. 2826 189/2 (Tape 4423). Interview with Vernon Le Maistre.

professed that he did not believe the islanders could have 'got away' with a lot more than they did get away with anyway, even if they had been more astute.[25] Margins of action seem to have been circumscribed by three factors: firstly it was restricted to relatively minor issues; secondly the authorities' leverage was proportionate to the degree to which inputs from the island administration were necessary for the implementation of a measure; thirdly they had to be issues which fitted into the jurisdiction of the Feldkommandantur. One good example of the use of margin was when the islands' authorities stood firm against German threats to Masonic interests in the Channel Islands, in 1941. The greatest impediment to margin of action was the authorities' position within the system of Occupation government. Already not enviable before the summer of 1941, this worsened with the arrival of the bulk of the German force under Major General Müller who, until the summer of 1943, exercised overall operational command in the islands. Müller belonged to a category of German officer whose understanding of the role of civilians in occupied lands was to comply and to provide essential services. Any further deliberations with the local authorities, as was practised under his predecessor, General von Schmettow, could only be a deplorable waste of time. Conveniently enough, orders could be passed on through the mouthpiece of the Feldkommandant.[26] Meanwhile von Schmettow's role was reduced to 'keeping an eye' on the island fortifications and the troops in Jersey. His ADC, von Helldorf, was confined to procuring supplies for the troops in Jersey.[27] There can be no more compelling reference to von Schmettow's temporary fall from grace than the following curious situation which is related in Coutanche's memoirs: in April 1943 Coutanche and Duret Aubin were called for talks with the Feldkommandantur, to discuss the ration cuts demanded by the Oberbefehlshaber West after the Allied sinking of a number of ships en route to the islands. When the two Crown officers emerged from the venue at the end of the talks, they were immediately picked off the road by von Helldorf, von Schmettow's aide, who quizzed them as to the purpose of the meeting.[28] The only inference one can draw from this is that von Schmettow – still island commander of Jersey – was not informed. Even the Feldkommandantur officials, considered second-rate by the rest of the military, failed to notify him of important decisions.

We may conclude that this was not much of a bargaining position which islanders compensated for through strict adherence to the Hague rules on, and avoidance of, anything likely to irk the Germans, the so-called policy of 'correct

[25] IWM Misc. 2826 189/2 (Tapes 4415 and 4416). Interview with Raymond Falla.

[26] IWM Misc 172 Item 2640. Legal Staff, Force 135 to JAG re. descriptions of Brosch, von Aufsess, Knackfuss, 11 Aug 1945. Neither Coutanche nor any other official were able to describe General Müller 'whom they stated they had never seen' to British war crimes investigators.

[27] PRO WO 309/192. Statement of Oberstleutnant Hans W von Helldorf re. Channel Islands, 27 Dec. 1945.

[28] Alexander Coutanche, *Memoirs of a Jerseyman*, op.cit., 33.

relations'. That this never really was the benign 'model occupation' it has been claimed to be, is clear from the simple fact alone that no such thing is possible between a democratic polity and a dictatorship built on nihilism, self-deception and conspiracy theory making it a matter of good education to blame others for one's own misfortunes. Convergence of view on the tenor of international law with such an occupier is practically impossible. The Channel Islands Occupation was only correct and a 'model unto the nations' if one accepted as normal the premise that inhabitants of occupied countries should obey orders and keep their mouths shut. Although no genocidal or murderous excesses occurred, the overall impression is that the islanders were not an equal partner, as a genuine 'model occupation' would have required. This is borne out by the experience of those civilians who dared to claim the legally undefined grey zone of popular affirmation. In areas of real concern to the Germans – such as in the administration of law – the characteristics of the Nazi regime could be well in evidence. The price paid by genuine resisters or slave labourers was not dissimilar to that paid in other parts of occupied Western Europe and substantial numbers of Channel Islanders were sent to prisons and concentration camps. Therefore it would be fallacious to describe the German administration as a consistently benign government.

Collaboration in the Channel Islands came in a rather pure form; it contained none of the political expediency, ideological alignment or bargaining for a better place in the New Europe that characterised the approach elsewhere. From the narrow point of treason, the Channel Islands did not collaborate at all, quite to the contrary: the people of Guernsey sheltered British commandos in 1940, at considerable risk to themselves, in both islands there was none of the defeatism and blame game that can be found in many other occupied countries, islanders said prayers for the king in Church and they turned out in masses to the funerals of Allied servicemen. There is equally little evidence of heart-and-soul or ideological collaboration, despite the doubtless benefits with which the Germans rewarded such dispositions. Again many other countries of occupied Europe allowed hard-core collaborators to accede to government rank – especially in the final year before liberation – and to have defied the trend is already quite something for these small islands. There could hardly be more convincing proof of their general abhorrence of political extremism of all shades and varieties. Robert Paxton, the doyen of Vichy historians, wrote in the introduction to the 2001 edition of his classic study *Vichy France: Old Guard and New Order* that the regime's original sin was to have not limited the 'government's actions under the 1940 Armistice to the maintenance of essential services' and instead to have 'launched partisan initiatives of political revenge and exclusion, the National Revolution.'[29] There was no such hidden political agenda in the Channel

---

[29] Robert Paxton, 'Introduction to the 2001 edition', in: idem, *Vichy France. Old Guard and New Order*, New York, 2001 (reprint), xxix-xxx.

Islands. Although they probably considered their fate uncertain, the islands were tied to a belligerent, Britain, and under these circumstances any pondering with larger visions of a future in a German-dominated Europe would, indeed, have been treason. Islanders did not cross this Rubicon. Although there was a general harshening of the police and law administration, as well as of economic control in the islands, this had more in common with 'maintenance of administration' as practised in Holland or Denmark. Thus, in some respects, we are faced with collaboration that wasn't really collaboration at all; the little there was in 'real' collaboration matched the scale of resistance.

How much bargaining tactics and tactical collaboration occurred is impossible to say with any degree of certainty. If trade-offs there were, they were often, but not exclusively, tied to concrete measures destined to improve the lot of the civilian population. But bargaining tactics also explain the strange and unsettling pro-activity of the island governments on some dossiers, and their resistance on others. Beneficiaries of this arrangement were 'in-groups' such as British army personnel, Freemasons or the established island Jews who were evacuated in 1940; 'out-groups' such as the Jews who stayed behind, foreigners on the run, escaped slave labourers and deviants from the established path had to 'foot the bill'. The adoption of bargaining tactics led to what one German witness described as the constant 'wangling' of the administration, 'with its members looking round to see what they could get'. The post-war investigations saw no reason to contest this view, which was confirmed by other sources.[30] The disposition lay at the heart of a peculiar brand of subservience and gratuitous friendliness on the part of certain officials, who were quite capable of forestalling German demands in order to create a debt. It is as discernible in the implementation of anti-Semitic measures as it is in the authorities' resignation to the 1942–1943 deportations to internment camps. The tendency was also displayed in such a seemingly insignificant act as the surrender to German requests for information on all previous convictions of offenders, up to the late 1920s. Another case where the authorities were clearly bent on ingratiating themselves concerned a dual British-German national by the name of Huyssen. In early 1940 Huyssen, who was English-born, had undertaken steps to volunteer in the British forces, which for the Germans constituted an act of treason. Although it is a principle that the government has no obligation to protect British nationals who are also nationals of another country against the authorities of that country, there was no ruling that officials must support foreign governments in their prosecution of dual nationals. When Huyssen was arrested, he built his defence on denying that he had tried to volunteer, claiming instead that he had received a draft notice. At that time there was no information in the island that could

---

[30] PRO KV 4178. Consolidated report: 'The I(b) Reports on the Channel Islands', by Major J R Stopford, 8 Aug. 1945, 6.

consistently prove or disprove Huyssen's version, apart from the unnecessarily ample information provided by the island authorities. And this information proved that he had, indeed, tried to volunteer.[31] The authorities also covered their flanks by carefully steering around all issues with even the remotest chance of constituting an 'upset potential'. Judging from the nature of totalitarian regimes, the sky was the limit. At times these attempts at anticipating what might cause German ire and catering to their predilections could go too far. This is in evident in an appeal by the medical officer, R N McKinstry, to the Bailiff, in March 1944: by then food conditions in the public prison had become severe enough for McKinstry to recommend that two political prisoners receive TB rations. At that time the diet consisted of coffee, dry bread, swedes, 'soup', potatoes and 'porridge'. McKinstry considered that speedy action was necessary in order to prevent the situation from getting worse. However, for some time things stalled as nobody was prepared to take any action. To be on the safe side the prison governor, after much initial wavering over whether he should consider the recommendation of the medical officer at all, first wrote to the Feldkommandantur for permission to put the men on TB rations. The Germans, in turn, deferred to the Attorney General who 'passed the chip' back to the prison governor, 'asking him for his opinion'. Exasperated by so much trepidation, McKinstry concluded:

> I consider all this delay unnecessary and even the permission of the German Authorities [sic] need not have been sought. Action could have been taken until such time as the German Authorities [sic] saw fit to interfere.[32]

An even better example of 'tactical collaboration' must surely be the business of sanctioning German orders by passing them into the laws of the islands. That this was more than a cosmetic mishap can be seen in the case of the orders instituting measures against the Jews and the ignominious 1942 'Order for the Protection of the Occupying authorities [sic]' which compelled island officials to signal any wrongdoings of civilians to the Germans – a recipe for denunciation. The Germans could have passed orders by decree, but it seems that this was one of those cases where the islands' authorities did not want to spoil their entente cordiale. Unfortunately, this was not a matter of simple symbolism, but had tangible practical implications. The fact that the measures were carried out under the cachet of the Jersey and Guernsey authorities – whom they trusted to defend their interests – was one essential point in persuading Jews in the Channel Islands that they had better comply and register. If this had been pure German law it is unlikely to have had the same effect and many may have

---

[31] For the entire Huyssen affair, see JAS. D/Z/H5/171. Law Officer's Department.

[32] JAS D/Z/H/6. Law Officer's Department. R N McKinstry, Medical Officer of Health to A M Coutanche, Bailiff, 11 Mar 1944.

chosen to not register or go into hiding as a small number of other Jews did. Confusion between German and island regulations had similarly negative effects on economic control, as it cast doubt on the basic fact that most of the legal body was in the interests of islanders. The slightest hint of a suggestion that islanders' material sacrifice, effort and discipline could be of direct benefit to the Germans rather than to the community, could make the extraction of controlled produce from the circuit look like a patriotic duty. Many exploited this disposition in all bad faith.

The authorities in the Channel Islands operated utilitarian doctrines such as 'greater good', 'restraint and influence' and 'differential treatment', in a manner that was not always appropriate. The 'greater number' logic came to the fore in the Page case which we have discussed in a preceding section. It also had some bearing on the measures against the island Jews. The Bailiff of Jersey himself claimed that the seriousness of its implementation was mitigated because 'the number of persons affected was extremely small'.[33] Differential treatment meant that while certain threatened categories of people, such as Freemasons or British officers, received the protection of the islands' authorities, similar aid was denied to others such as Jews, escapees or islanders who had committed offences against the occupying authorities. 'Restraint and influence' is based on the principle that leverage over a given situation grows through positive engagement. Coutanche described the workings of 'restraint and influence' in a post-war memo:

> I almost invariably found it better to hold myself in readiness to make a final appeal to the Germans for mercy when all other means had failed. Constant intervention by me at an early stage would, it always appeared to me, have weakened my ultimate influence for good.[34]

All these principles were problematic, as they required a conscious selection of ground that was to be defended or abandoned. Still, 'restraint and influence' seems to have produced some results, notably in the amply documented commuting of a death sentence, in November 1944, which the Bailiff attributed to his personal intervention.[35] The balance sheet for the greater number doctrine is less certain. As noted in a preceding chapter, operating this principle under genuine duress is not unethical. However, one has to be wary of 'false

---

[33] PRO HO 45 22399. Memorandum, Alec Coutanche to Sir Donald Somervell, 3 July 1945.

[34] ibid.

[35] This would mark out Coutanche as the most astute Jersey politician. The Germans, as a result, maintained a respectful distance. That Coutanche had scruples where other members of his administration put blind obedience to positivistic law is also attested by a good many other events during the Occupation. The ability is also apparent in the run-up to the September 1942 deportations where he can be seen pushing for exemptions with Knackfuss, see JAS B/A/L/331. In the matter of German war crimes and in the matter of Alexander Moncrief Coutanche, statement under oath, 12 June 1945.

dilemmas' which the island authorities may have brought onto themselves through their lack of prior reflection on the consequences of continuing in office while the German occupiers were going ahead with their unacceptable law-making. The Page case determined a fundamental problem – not in the operation of the greater good principle itself – but in the lack of protest against co-operation in the prosecution of 'radio offenders': while the confiscation of radios was justifiable under international law, no clause in the Hague Convention (or in any other body of international law) could be invoked to justify the criminal prosecution of offenders against the wireless order, and especially the clampdown on people spreading the news. This was Nazi law.

Petty bureaucrats, controllers working in economic control services, policemen and members of the legal profession could forget the 'common good' and fall victim to the 'River Kwai' syndrome. The phenomenon was known all over Europe and has served as one of the standard explanations of the friction-less collaboration of bureaucratic machines during the Nazi Occupation. Many officials relished the Occupation as a period of full powers with unparalleled freedom of action. Liberated from the constraints of cumbersome democratic processes they were given a chance to put into practice their schemes, free from the meddlesome politicians and manipulatively obstructive press. This disposi-tion resulted in a heavy-handed bureaucratic approach which drove lack of empathy and a culture of obedience to ever greater heights. In the Channel Islands its effects were magnified further by the parochialism of small communi-ties where people make it their business to stick their noses into other people's business. Policing was the most sensitive area, as discipline invariably suffered from the conflicting sources of power, local authorities and Germans. Picking up all the wrong signals, this vacuum was often filled by arbitrariness. Jersey historian Joe Mière related an incident in which a man who had realised that he would not reach his home in Don Road before the onset of the curfew reported to the police station at St Helier's Town Hall, as he did not wish to be in breach of the law. Having enquired whether a policeman could escort him to his home, he was told that something would be sorted out. Only about twenty minutes later, however, a car pulled up with German military policemen to whom the Jerseyman was handed over. After his name and details had been taken down he was taken to his home and told to report to College House where he was fined ten marks.[36] Attenborough, another well-informed Jersey diarist, also identified policing and the maintenance of order as the core problem of occupation government. He traced the shortcomings to the judicial system, the 'antiquated and clumsy' character of which was powerfully reinforced by the circumstances of the Occupation. The focus of his criticism was the honorary system and the

---

[36] Written information provided by Joe Mière, in author's possession, n.d.

fact that most of the Jurats had no legal training, which resulted in sentences of undue severity.[37] Edward Le Quesne described one such gaffe, more in line with the Salem witch-hunt than a proper trial, in his diary entry of 24 November 1942. That day a Jerseyman accused of falsification of a Relief card was standing trial in the Police court. In total disregard of procedural law the 'judge' devoted his time to a condemnation of the man's private life, sending him straight back to prison, without taking any evidence from the witnesses.[38]

Nowhere, however, is the inability to think 'outside the box' better demonstrated than in the negative test case of the Jersey Aliens Officer, Clifford Orange. It is a well-established fact that Orange exceeded what the Germans demanded of him. This is plainly clear in the fact that some of the people he registered as Jews need not have been registered at all – even under the terms of the German race laws. It is unclear whether his attitude was simply unthinking, unprofessional or downright racist, but its consequence was that people were subjected to discrimination and suffering that they could have been spared. Orange's culture of blind obedience over humanitarianism also came to the fore when he found out that some of his staff had been providing foreigners in the islands with fake documents. Orange declared that he would not tolerate such activity behind his back and put an immediate stop to it. Orange was one of the few officials who relished his task. As for other officials, they seem to have been driven by an appalling lack of imagination rather than zeal. The failure of the top islands' administrators to either emit the right signals to their subordinates or to call to task and restrain bureaucratic zealots must be regarded as one of their greatest failures.

Some officials showed poor judgment in the mutual forms they adopted with the Germans and brought disrepute onto themselves and others. This 'cosmetic' factor was not to be underestimated and it already figured high on the list of Jersey daredevil Dennis Vibert when he reached Britain in October 1941. The trend was continued by his emulators and numerous were the accusations about island officials not keeping the necessary distance and displaying a level of cordiality in their mutual relationships which was inappropriate under the circumstances. British investigators at first interpreted it as a 'needlessly spineless attitude' which they qualified with adjectives such as 'pusillanimous' and 'gratuitous'.[39] Whether this approach really was entirely pointless is a different question. The main criticism was that this was not the right impression to give to the Germans, that it engendered disrespect and encouraged the Germans to pose more outrageous demands. The example of Jean Moulin – the later head

---

[37] IWM 02/17/1. Attenborough diary, L'envoi, 9–11.

[38] Edward Le Quesne, *The occupation of Jersey day by day*, entry of 24 Nov 1942, 164.

[39] PRO KV 41 78. Consolidated report: 'The I(b) Reports on the Channel Islands', by Major J R Stopford, 8 Aug. 1945, 6.

of the French Resistance who served as prefect in Chartres in 1940 – would suggest that showing resistance to German demands did not result in an inevitable transfer to the Gestapo. When the first German Feldkommandant left Chartres in late 1940, he even wrote Moulin a congratulatory and respectful message. No word mentioned the fact that Moulin had attempted to commit suicide while imprisoned in June 1940 rather than sign a defamatory statement incriminating the French army in atrocities against civilians in the vicinity.[40] Moulin obtained respect, but he also realized the unilateral benefit the Germans derived from working with the French administration and did not remain in office beyond 1940. Also, while the Feldkommandant of Chartres was, no doubt, a man open to reason, fully fledged Nazis inspired by Hitler's world view were not able to register such a message when meeting similar resistance. Therefore it would certainly be wrong to pontificate that – at least on the surface – an ability to grant tactical concessions to the Germans when no particular principles were at stake was a bad strategy for smaller communities. The Channel Islands' administrations did not have the depth and resources to fight a steady course of institutional resistance. Rather one had to take advantage of the German propensity for fraternisation and use it for one's own purposes. While certain individuals may have taken these tactics too far, the principle itself does not allow generalisations of the sort professed by the British investigators.

A tale of two islands

That collaboration is not merely a simplistic question of good and evil emerges nowhere more clearly than in a comparison of Jersey and Guernsey. It is one of the open secrets of the Occupation that Guernsey travelled somewhat further down the slope of collaboration than did her sister island. British wartime investigators were to describe the Guernsey authorities as having taken ingratiation tactics with the Germans to greater heights than did their Jersey counterparts and the indication is that this was the result of a number of internal and environmental factors.[41]

On the surface policy in all the islands was identical: non-provocation of the occupier. 'Law is law' and 'greater good' were as valid in one island as the other, as was the preparedness to make trade-offs or bargains in order to increase leverage. Where Jersey and Guernsey differed was in the rhetoric which had a very patronising and disenfranchising undertone in Guernsey. One of the first

---

[40] Daniel Cordier, *Jean Moulin: L'inconnu du Pantheéon*, cited in Jackson, France – The Dark Years 1940–1944, op. cit., 167.

[41] IWM JRD.09. MI5. Captain Dening to Major Stopford, 26 Aug 1945.

steps in eradicating potential resistance occurred even before the Occupation, as early as 21 June 1940, when the Reverend John Leale said in a speech:

> Should the Germans decide to occupy this Island, we must accept the position. There must be no thought of any kind of resistance, we can only expect that the more dire punishment will be meted. I say this, the man who even contemplates resistance should the Germans come is the most dangerous man in the Island and its most bitter enemy. The military have gone. We are civilians.[42]

Was scapegoating the leadership quality that people sought in this situation? And wasn't this heavy-handed policy an unnecessary self-imposed constraint which limited their options? The signals emitted by the Guernsey chiefs left the population in no doubt about how they expected them to behave. While the large majority of the population already understood that hot-headed resistance was not what the situation required, the island authorities continued well beyond, using what looked like demoralising tactics to weaken those who advocated a sterner attitude to the Germans. And by the looks of it there was a fair number of people in the island who wanted their leaders to confront the Germans more openly. One Guernseyman who claimed that he was known as an agitator because he had approached the Bailiff and other officials in a critical spirit, related later that Inspector Sculpher of the island police called on him at the beginning of the Occupation and told him to tone down for the duration.[43] Where exactly Guernsey was heading was demonstrated when Attorney General Sherwill published a short piece in the local press stating that relations with the Germans were not merely 'on a correct basis, they are cordial and friendly'. Although Sherwill's motivation to avoid all unnecessary incidents that could provoke the Germans was understood, many inhabitants were disappointed by this sort of statement and thought it went too far.[44] Four weeks later, at the first States meeting in the presence of the island commandant, Sherwill was to demonstrate to the world his grand scheme of a 'model occupation' The model occupation was put to an almost immediate test when the manager at Le Riche's grocery establishment was reported after he had confronted an assistant who ignored local customers and gave precedence to Germans. Guernsey then passed an ordinance under which islanders could be charged with 'uttering speech likely to bring about a deterioration in the relations between the German Forces [*sic*] and the civilian population'. Naturally it was claimed later that the island authorities had tried to prevent worse from happening to the man by charging him in their courts. What is more likely, however, is that this was

---

[42] IWM JRD.09. Force 135, I(b). Report 'Resistance during the Occupation'.

[43] PRO HO 144/22237. MI19. Report 2507 'Guernsey Side Lights on Island Affairs', 20 Nov 44; 'Excerpts from private letter of Guernsey Commission Agent brought over by informant 2503/2503A'.

[44] IWM JRD.04. Sabotage and Betrayal, Unknown author (Guernsey), n.d.

another case of anticipatory obedience designed to keep Sherwill's 'model occupation' on track.[45] That same month Sherwill recorded a speech for German radio which carried the famous reference that he had no pistol pointing at his head while he was speaking. Motivated by the honourable, but naïve desire to reassure Guernsey evacuees in the UK about the safety of their fellow islanders under German occupation, the exercise backfired as one of the most insidious propaganda coups of the war.[46] The Guernsey authorities still had not an inkling of an idea who they were dealing with and the corrosive presence of Nazi policy soon made itself felt in the extension of the 'most bitter enemy' label to other islanders. The following month eight people escaped to England, as a consequence of which a drastic control of boats was introduced and fishermen were blocked in harbour. That the local population was being deprived of fish certainly was not to be taken with a light heart, but neither did it warrant a hysterical reaction. On 28 September Sherwill wrote in a public letter that those who managed to get away did so at the expense of those left behind and that this amounted to a 'crime against the local population'. The letter reached a particularly ludicrous undertone of paternalism when Sherwill told his readers that the attempt had led to the last minute cancellation, by the German command in the island, of a report telling their superiors how well the civilians were behaving.[47] While one can understand that – with the Damocles sword of reprisals hovering over islanders – Sherwill was in no position to encourage escapes, this pronouncement went in exactly the opposite direction, setting yet another bad example for the people of Guernsey and carrying the seeds for a culture of denunciation. The doctrine of the resister as 'most bitter enemy' of the people was to hold continuing sway. A Guernsey resident who escaped to England in August 1943 stated that many in Guernsey who would consider their escape a 'disgusting and selfish act'; the man also added for good measure that officials in Guernsey would not even close their eyes to instances of passive resistance: 'All they worry about is whether the Germans will turn the screw on them'. That not all Guernseymen shared the same ideas on German behaviour became clear in the fact that while all members of the escape party thought that reprisals against parents and relatives were possible, they raised the point that in the current situation 'Jerry will do some very serious thinking before carrying out any too severe reprisals against British subjects'.[48] In time, the combination of

[45] IWM JRD.04. Sabotage and Betrayal, Unknown author (Guernsey), n.d.; anticipatory obedience was also noted by Lanz who said that after some islanders had been found to not be following the blackout regulations a long article appeared in the Guernsey newspapers reprimanding islanders for not following orders, see IWM JRD.04. Report by Major Lanz, 216 ID, the first German Commandant.

[46] Cruickshank, op.cit., 78–9.

[47] IWM JRD.04. Typed copy of letter to the public in local press in Guernsey, 28 Sept 1940.

[48] PRO HO 144/22834. Memo by Guernsey escapee J T D Hubert, 23 Aug. 1943.

patronising attitude and naïve idealism of the Guernsey authorities clashed with reality: in mid-October 1944, the same 'agitator' who had been instructed to 'tone down' in 1940 was approached again and asked to find reliable fishermen who could take messages across to the UK.[49] An equally good example of inconsequential attitude was Victor Carey's reception of illegal radio news through a network which, if unraveled by the Germans, would have probably had all the makings of a 'bitter enemy of the people'. Thankfully, the man was cautious enough to preclude this eventuality and the authorities were spared another embarrassing situation. After the war he was even commended for his 'good work'.[50]

Verbal lapses of island politicians were to become a mainstay of the Guernsey occupation, although one might add that after the rude shock of repeated visits by British commandos culminating in the Nicolle-Symes 'spy affair' in late 1940, the main motivation would have been to mend fences and avoid an escalation of violence. After a cable sabotage in March 1941 John Leale said, at a meeting of the Controlling Committee, that anyone who had wished to do so could have left the island the year before, adding that two vessels which had left on the Saturday of evacuation week had sailed 'practically empty'; as a result, he concluded, that those who stayed on had accepted the position and would 'act as good citizens'.[51] This episode contained not only a variation on the ominous 'mail boat' reference levelled at critics, but it was also extremely irritating news for those who had been branded 'yellow' or 'rats' during those heady days of evacuation and discouraged from leaving the island. The man who recorded the occurrence clearly felt that too much fuss had been made about this cable which was merely for internal communication and easy to repair. The majority of the population knew that such acts were not worth committing and the author was clearly hinting that the authorities were making a serious mistake by setting German expectations so high.[52] While a few more of these 'cable sabotages' seem to have occurred in 1941, after that date the Germans seem to have grown accustomed to the idea that rather than being the actions of genuine saboteurs, most of these offences were due to a Guernsey cow, the elements or Germans themselves. Even though the Germans may have believed that these occurrences were the work of saboteurs, castigating and putting the civilian population in a

---

49 PRO HO 144/22237. MI19. Report 2507 'Guernsey Side Lights on Island Affairs', 20 Nov 44; 'Excerpts from private letter of Guernsey Commission Agent brought over by informant 2503/2503A'.

50 After liberation Carey voiced his deep appreciation of the risk they had run and that he looked forward 'most eagerly' to the Editors Weekly Survey, see L E Bertrand, *A Record of the Work of the Guernsey Active Secret Press 1940–1945*, published by the Guernsey Star & Gazette Company, December 1945.

51 'Extract from Jurat Leale's speech in the States on March 21', *Guernsey Star*, 22 March 1941.

52 IWM JRD.04. Sabotage and Betrayal, Unknown author (Guernsey), n.d.

state of collective panic each time one of these 'cuttings' occurred did not betray a great deal of statesmanship.[53]

Cable-cutting hysteria never rose to similar heights in Jersey. Presumably the wind and the local breed of cows were just as likely to dislodge cables from time to time, but no threats of reprisals were relayed through the Jersey authorities in the local press. Their communications with the public tended to leave no doubt about the responsibility and authorship of orders. They were clearly worded, matter-of-fact and without the paternalistic undertones used by their Guernsey counterparts. Later in the Occupation the island authorities abandoned the procedure altogether and there were to be no more press notices explaining or warning the population about German orders. One example of what communications in the Jersey press looked like is an *Evening Post* notice of 10 May 1941, titled 'German Proclamations and Official Notices – Warning by the Bailiff'. The notice was passed to warn the population against the removal or destruction of posters containing proclamations and official announcements. Bailiff Coutanche makes clear that the notice was not passed on his own initiative but that he was asked by the Field Commandant to inform the population that such acts constituted sabotage. The only initiative taken by the island authorities in this case was to recommend ninety-nine official posting stations throughout the island. The notice ended with a rather terse 'I desire to warn the population against the serious consequences which may follow upon any further destruction of, or damage to, Official Posters [*sic*]', signed A M Coutanche.[54]

Not only did Jersey have a more realistic and more balanced view of 'correct relations', but this administration also managed to speak with one voice and limit contradictory statements to a minimum. Charles Cruickshank, in his official history of the Occupation, already noted the difference between the two Bailiffs.[55] Cruickshank's judgement is confirmed by the internal appreciations of the German military administration. Here Victor Carey, born in 1871, is described as 'strongly over-aged', a 'mere figure of representation'. Coutanche on the other hand was assessed as a 'versatile, clever administrator who rose to the challenge of his position even under difficult conditions'. Both men were described 'opponents of communism', but whereas the German controllers felt that Carey's sense of belonging to his home turf equalled his loyalty to the Empire, Coutanche came across as an 'English nationalist'.[56] What stands out in

---

[53] One of these 'cable cuttings' is documented in the FK files at the Guernsey Archives. As the ensuing investigation showed, the telephone cables in question had been removed from a hotel by two German soldiers, see Island Archives. FK 1/11. FK 515 Nebenstelle Guernsey Feldgendarmerie an Nebenstelle (Mil. Führung), 26 Jul 1941.

[54] 'German Proclamations and Official Notices – Warning by the Bailiff', *Evening Post*, Jersey, 10 May 1941.

[55] Cruickshank, 330.

[56] Further nuances included: Carey: 'loyal to the German Wehrmacht and military administra-

Coutanche's remarkable career is that he had experience of life outside the islands: called to both the Jersey Bar and by the Middle Temple in 1915, Coutanche was a lawyer in the Claims Commission in France and Belgium from 1917 to 1920, a service for which he received the Belgian Croix de Guerre. After the war he returned to Jersey owing to his father's illness and set up as an advocate. The inference was that, but for his father, he would have contemplated a career at the English Bar. Coutanche was not someone who rose to his position simply because he was a member of the Island establishment. Neither did he begin his States career in 1922 in a non-elected position, but as a deputy of St Helier. His first Crown appointment, solicitor general, followed three years later. By 1935 – when he was in his early forties – he had climbed all the way to the highest position in Jersey, that of Bailiff.[57] Coutanche had a canny ability to navigate the pitfalls which the Occupation presented to a top island politician, halving his peace-time salary of about £3,500 and supplementing his income through funds from a small business venture which turned seaweed into fertiliser, an item of great scarcity.[58] Coutanche, according to his own statements, also never used the black market; another important contrast to other dignitaries. One of these, a judge known for having condemned many people for black market involvement, was a regular customer of Emma C. who was conducting a brisk under-the-counter trade in supplies smuggled across from France to Jersey, at the photographic depot of her common-law husband Edmund Hassall.[59] Having a strong, somewhat 'dictatorial', but also sensible alpha male of the calibre of Coutanche at the helm was more suited to standing united than the dysfunctional Guernsey triumvirate.

Further confirmation of leadership trouble in Guernsey comes from Baron von Aufsess who, in a letter to General von Schmettow in 1944, referred to the Guernsey statesmen as 'weaker characters' and to the Guernsey government as less 'politically sound and stable' than the larger sister island.[60] The only Guernsey public servant who could have perhaps matched Coutanche in this respect was Ambrose Sherwill, but Sherwill did not have the prestige of the Bailiff, nor could he rely on much teamwork. Coutanche, in contrast, was

tion' and 'desiring peace between the two great nations' (Britain and Germany, n.b.); Coutanche: 'prepared for compromise' and 'frictionless cooperation', see AN. AJ 40/543. Description des fonctionnaires. Filing cards for Victor Gosselin Carey, Bailiff of Guernsey and Alexander Moncrieff Coutanche, Bailiff of Jersey.

[57] 'Obituary Lord Coutanche Former Bailiff of Jersey', *The Times*, 19 Dec 1973.

[58] AN AJ/40 821A. Mbf in Frankreich. Abt. Wi V/2 Währung, Kredit, Versicherung, Aktennotiz 'Währungs- und Geldverhaeltnisse auf den Kanalinseln, 17 Jul 42.

[59] Peter Hassall, 'Night and Fog Prisoners' (memoirs of Peter Hassall), 55, published at <www.occupationmemorial.com>

[60] The letter of 14 Sept 1944 is reprinted in his diary, see Max Freiherr von Aufsess, *The von Aufsess occupation diary*, Chichester, 1985, 24.

seconded by Duret Aubin whom he had pushed up as Attorney General over the preceding years. During the Occupation the Jersey authorities staged a rather effective 'good guy, bad guy' routine which von Aufsess described in his diaries: Coutanche, the aloof, curt and arrogant bureaucrat, and Duret Aubin, the jovial confidant. Whereas the Bailiff occupied the high ground, keeping as his trump card the possibility of protests *in extremis*, the Attorney General remained approachable and had to do most of the pleading. The odds are that this set-up contained an element of political gamesmanship to maximise influence with those German officials who had some proclivities towards islanders.

Major Lanz, the first German Commandant, noted that when he arrived in summer 1940 Sherwill, then Procureur (Attorney General), did all the executive business for the Bailiff.[61] Sherwill also became first president of the Controlling Committee, but was replaced by Jurat Leale in December 1940, owing to his incarceration following the Nicolle-Symes affair. Leale, a quiet, restrained and highly respected Methodist minister and member of an established island family was the opposite in character to the outgoing Sherwill. Leale's interpretation of the system the Germans represented was certainly more accurate than that of his predecessor, but one wonders whether such a fundamental change in music, at such a critical juncture, was a good or a bad thing. While up until then the island triumvirate – Carey, Sherwill and Leale – had agreed on the principal course of action, the fact that the top executive man had been dragged away to prison in France sent shock waves through the island polity. It is a fair guess to say that this, inevitably, blew up islanders' propensity to forestall anything susceptible to upset the relationship with the occupier, in order to 'repay their debt'. When Sherwill was released on 30 December 1940 the Germans made clear that they could no longer trust him. After his return from Cherche Midi prison in December 1940 Sherwill was sidelined: he was allowed to take up a public position again only in July 1941[62] and in February 1943 he was deported as an ex-officer. Despite some reservations over his role in the conception of 'model occupation', his courage was never in doubt and he acquitted himself very honourably, and with supreme skill, during the repeated visits of British commandos. His role was acknowledged in a letter from the Home Office sent to Churchill's private secretary in September 1944. This letter was written in response to erroneous information brought to the attention of the Prime Minister according to which two British agents in the Channel Islands had been betrayed by a police constable and shot. The Home Office righted this wrong contention by citing information obtained from Captain Parker according to which a number of islanders went to considerable trouble to see that no harm

---

[61] IWM JRD.04. 'Report by Major Lanz, 216 ID, the first German Commandant'
[62] PRO HO 144/22834. Sherwill, Ilag VII, Lg Laufen to Sir Alexander Maxwell, 6 Jul 44.

came to the officers.[63] Neither was this Sherwill's first act of courage: he was also awarded an MC during the First World War and his rise to prominence from humble beginnings was equally impressive. There was, however, in Sherwill a touch of political naivety to which, according to the authors of *Islands in Danger*, Alan and Mary Seaton Wood, 'exceptionally brave men are often prone'.[64] Sherwill's flamboyance which could be 'over-the-top' emerged again in a letter he sent to Sir Alexander Maxwell at the Home Office, a few weeks after the landing in Normandy, from Laufen internment camp. The purpose of the letter was to communicate to the British government the apprehension of Channel Islanders about the possibility of an impending British attack as well as the effects of a prolonged siege. Clearly, Sherwill was worried about his wife and his two children:

> In so small an area troops and civilians are inextricably mixed up [...] My wife, who is in the midst of one such situation says the officer in charge is very courteous and considerate and the troops are very kind to the children. By the way, lest you should be tempted to misunderstand, I haven't succumbed to propaganda. Please, however, may the situation of the Channel Islanders be given special consideration by His Majesty's Government [...] I hope the flying bomb is not inconveniencing you unduly.[65]

Though a decidedly awkward letter, nobody at the Home Office doubted Sherwill's ulterior good motives. What the recipients could not be so certain about was what they were supposed to do with this 'information' and whether Sherwill was being used for an intoxication. On the assumption that the letter could not have got away without the assistance of the German camp commandant, and probably some much higher officer as well, it was agreed that the reply should be 'extremely non-committal' and the letter was handed to intelligence for critical examination and testing.[66]

Leale claimed in his May 1945 address to the States of Guernsey that the German threat to take twenty hostages during the Nicolle-Symes affair was 'as near to an atrocity as we ever came'. Whether this threat was genuine cannot be said.[67] However, in the jittery atmosphere of 1941 Carey, a figure of representation supposed to have taken a back seat and 'kept in reserve' (similar to the

---

63 PRO TS 26/89. J A R Pimlott (HO) to J M Martin CVC, 18 Sept 1944.

64 Alan Wood and Mary Seaton Woods, *Islands in Danger*, Hodder and Stoughton, 1955, 42.

65 PRO HO 144/22834. Sherwill, Ilag VII, Lg Laufen to Sir Alexander Maxwell, 6 Jul 44.

66 PRO HO 144/22834. French (WO) to Markbreiter (HO), 12 Aug 1944.

67 PRO HO 45/22424. Report of the President of the Controlling Committee of the States of Guernsey on the activities of the Committee during the five years of German occupation, 23 May 1945; whether the Germans had wanted to shoot hostages, as Leale seemed to indicate in his speech, is not uncontested. Leale may have been overreacting, s. William Bell, *The Commando who came home to spy*, Guernsey, 1998, 29.

arrangement between Coutanche and Duret Aubin in Jersey) rose to prominence. There is some indication that Carey's embarrassing interventions in public affairs were also motivated by his resentment of the younger men who had taken over his authority. The first blunder was Carey's personal invitation to take wine on 6 July, sent to the Inselkommandant, his adjutant, Prince Oettingen and Dr Reffler, dated 23 June. Apparently, this invitation got into the 'wrong hands' and was passed on to the British when they returned in 1945. The next, on 8 July 1941, was a literal exhortation of denunciation in the island, by placing a £25 reward for information concerning a 'V sign', posted in the Guernsey *Evening Press*. Finally on 11 August 1941 another notice was published in the Guernsey *Evening Press* reminding the population of the death sentence islanders faced when apprehended in the act of sheltering escaped PoWs or 'enemy forces', by order of the occupying authority. The problem in this case was the terminology; the 'enemy forces' referred to in the Bailiff's notice were not the Germans, but the British. Whatever Freudian lapse occurred here, the British had reason to take offence. In June 1945 Lord Justice du Parq even recommended that the last two notices 'be brought to the attention of the Prime Minister, if not to His Majesty, before any honour was conferred'; he also commented very unfavourably that the 'V sign' order made it virtually impossible to try in the Royal Court of Guernsey any person charged with informing against another as this had been encouraged by their own Bailiff.[68]

The dominating figure for the longer period of the Guernsey occupation was Jurat Leale who succeeded Sherwill as President of the Controlling Committee, an astute and perceptive politician. Leale already demonstrated in his speech of 21 June 1940 that he was a hardliner when it came to stopping in its tracks any attempt at generating resistance towards the Occupation and later statements showed that that he had absolute faith in the law. After the war he stated that 'order was preferable to chaos' and that the authorities had agreed to provide the troops with food and other resources because letting them requisition it themselves meant losing control over how much they were actually getting. According to Leale, practical experience showed that there was nothing to be gained, but much that could be lost by forfeiting any measure of control. The problem, however, was that they were dealing with an occupier who could be very unprincipled. Often the Germans would rely on requisitioning done by the Channel Islanders and, in addition, suck up resources through their extraordinary purchases. Whatever way it was done, the occupier always had the last word, and to this there was really no answer other than playing a 'double game'.

It would be unfair and inequitable to point to the men and forget structural or systemic factors which made the Guernsey occupation a weightier affair than

[68] PRO HO 45/22399. Lord Justice du Parq, Note on complaints against Channel Islands administration by Mr Maugham and Mr Wilson, 14 June 1945.

the more civilian Jersey occupation. Major Lanz, the first German Commandant of the Channel Islands, mentioned in his activity report that from a tactical point of view Guernsey was more important than Jersey.[69] This led to a heavier military imprint, perhaps best demonstrated through the continued presence of the military HQ, the heavier scale of fortification, apparent, for example, in the establishment of the heavy battery Mirrus, and the greater concentration of Germans in the island. In March 1942 Guernsey had to sustain a proportionally far higher number of almost 15,000 German soldiers alone, a figure which was dangerously close to the total number of civilians left in the island. Combined together, soldiers, OT (Organization Todt) workers and slave labourers outnumbered civilians well into 1943.[70] In addition the number of soldiers billeted in private properties (10,800 vs. 6,503) was also higher in Guernsey than in Jersey, where there were more facilities in vacant hotels and boarding houses (4,285 in Jersey as opposed to 1,240 in Guernsey).[71]

Because the civil affairs unit, the Feldkommandantur, was posted in Jersey, the Guernsey officials found themselves on the rougher end of the stick by having to deal with the FK subsidiary, the Nebenstelle, headed by Dr Brosch, a man who could not stand the strain of this exposed position and who was described as 'excitable' by the British. When the non-natives were deported from Guernsey in September 1942 Brosch made such a mess of the situation that his superior, Feldkommandant Colonel Knackfuss, had to come over to Guernsey to take command of the situation. John Leale indicated later that he had direct contacts with the division as even this was preferable to having to deal with the worthless and superfluous Nebenstelle.[72] In his dealings with these pure military men Leale could be told in all earnestness that, owing to Guernsey's frontline position, the doctrine of military necessity cancelled out the provisions of the Hague Convention.[73] The Jersey administration, by comparison, had the considerably easier task of sending Duret Aubin up to College House to deal with more affable civil servants such as Casper or von Aufsess. A further advantage was provided by the presence in Jersey of von Schmettow and von Helldorf. Although their power base was limited, they were not entirely without influence.

[69] IWM JRD.04. 'Report by Major Lanz, 216 ID, the first German Commandant', n.d.

[70] PRO T 161/1196. Treasury files, 'Population distribution in the Channel Islands', n.d.; AN. AJ 40/547. FK 515, 'Verwaltungsüberblick über die Kanalinseln' by Dr Caspar, June 1943.

[71] JAS D/A/U/V/I3. FK St Helier, Vermerk, 5 Mar 1942.

[72] PRO HO 45/22424. Report of the President of the Controlling Committee of the States of Guernsey on the activities of the Committee during the five years of German occupation, 23 May 1945.

[73] PRO HO 45/22424. Report of the President of the Controlling Committee of the States of Guernsey on the activities of the Committee during the five years of German occupation, 23 May 1945.

While the Guernsey politicians deserve criticism for not having found the right balance, one has to be particularly cautious in judging civilians. It is doubtful whether the outlawing of the population, often within their own four walls, reached quite the same proportions in Jersey as it did in Guernsey. Nowhere is this more manifest than in the diaries of the Reverend Ord which document many cases of people being turned out of their houses in a matter of minutes. This was particularly frequent during the terrible winter of 1941–42 which saw a rising death toll especially of older people who could no longer withstand the strain. Many of the people turned out of their houses were often unable to take any but the most rudimentary of their possessions with them. In other cases Germans billeted in the vicinity would simply walk into neighbouring properties and grab whatever took their fancy. When the owners protested, they were abused with platitudes such as 'war is war' or remarks that the Allies had acted no differently during their occupation of Germany after World War One. Ord himself received the visit of a scavenger – a man who claimed to have been a university lecturer – who tried to cajole him into selling his *Cambridge Encyclopedia*. He seems to have attributed his lucky escape – all his neighbours were either stripped of their possessions or they had Germans billeted on them – to having been acquainted with the son of Herman Gunkel, a prominent German theologian, who served as a military judge.[74]

Economically Guernsey was also more vulnerable and this weakness was compounded through lack of experience in crop culture, uncertainty and lack of direction over the glasshouse industry and a flawed export strategy following the pre-war export pattern. The result was a food position which a reliable German witness described as bad, 'about the same as in Germany', but in any case, worse than in Jersey.[75] Insurance clerk Bob Le Sueur visited Guernsey in 1942 and was shocked at the sight of people queuing for potato peelings, something that had not come to his sight in his native Jersey.[76] Visiting the island in late 1944 Baron von Aufsess committed to his diary the observation that Guernsey gave the impression of being 'even more like a sanatorium for the weak and ailing than Jersey. The soldiers look pale and undernourished, the civilians even more so.'[77] In addition, Guernsey was the more difficult place to escape from once it was possible to escape to liberated France in 1944, while its proximity to the UK targeted the island as the principal site for the 1940 commando raids which worsened islanders' leverage over their own situation. While these raids did have military value, some of the blame for the subsequent deterioration in the islands must also fall on the British

---

[74] JAS L/C/144. The Reverend Ord diaries 1940–1945, passim

[75] PRO WO 199/3303. Interrogation of Uschaf Kruse OT, captured at Montfort, 3 Aug 1944.

[76] Information provided by Bob Le Sueur to author during discussion of the Project Advisory Panel, 2 February 2005.

[77] Baron von Aufsess, *The von Aufsess occupation diary*, Chichester, 1985, entry of 17 Dec 1944, 96.

military whose improvised plans failed to return the men to Britain and took little account of the precarious position in which they were placing the population. In particular the Nicolle-Symes affair which led to the arrest of fifteen people in Guernsey who were transported to Paris – where one of them committed suicide – bolstered the camp advocating the view that anything likely to damage the relationship with the Germans should be avoided. The episode certainly did nothing for the next British commandos who came knocking at an islander's door and who would politely be shown the way back to the beach. Military blunders jeopardising the safety of the population reinforced the idea among islanders that they were better off forming an understanding with the more enlightened elements within the German army. Had this early commando action displayed more professionalism in its execution, a greater number of islanders may have also been prepared to defy the recommendations of their own island authorities.

Lastly, the Guernsey police system, centralised since 1920, was a more useful tool in the Germans' hands than the decentralized system in Jersey. And into the hands of the Germans this fruit did fall when 18 of its members, including a deputy inspector, were found guilty of theft, in March 1942. The intelligence officers working in the I(b) section of Force 135, in 1945, certainly had little good to say about the Guernsey police. Informed by the negative impression left by their failure to furnish any detailed information or records which may have assisted the continuing security enquiry, they established a scathing report which stressed the fact that they did not consider it beyond them to take statements with complete impartiality from informers implicating neighbours nor did they shy away from investigating schoolchildren.[78] They seem to have learnt a thing or two from their German counterparts.

Collaboration that wasn't really collaboration

Besides incidents of genuine collaboration, the Channel Islands' Occupation also set the scene for collaboration which was no collaboration at all. Probably one of the first to have described this experience was French philosopher and feminist writer Simone de Beauvoir who stayed on in occupied Paris. She noticed that while she had no sympathies for the German cause and, contrary to a number of Parisian intellectuals, sought no contact with individual Germans, the simple fact of continuing one's existence could be interpreted as collaboration. Many people who, such as de Beauvoir, had been through the experience of enemy occupation felt culpable, without there being any real reason for such culpability.[79] The challenge to their conscience was even worse for officials. In the Channel Islands

[78] IWM JRD.09. Force 135, I (b) section, Report 'Island Police Guernsey', 1945.
[79] Cited in Peter Davies, *Dangerous Liaisons*, 109–11.

there was an additional problem that few people understood what the application of the Hague rules meant in practice. The most unfortunate impression was that following international law could, in fact, look like assisting the enemy. John Leale once stated that when the Germans requisitioned bakers, fishermen and growers, people came to see him and asked whether they had this right under the Convention. Basing his opinion on the available legal commentary, Leale answered in the affirmative which earned him the response from one grower that he was 'not much of a Briton'.[80] Many observers did not understand (or did not want to understand) that under the Hague rules the occupier can demand certain services for the maintenance of the occupation force and that the cost of billeting, labour and other items can be transferred onto the occupied. The occupier also had the right to requisition labour, provided this was used for non-military work and was not directed against the worker's motherland. The core problem with non-military or indirect work, of course, was that ultimately even this had indirect benefits to the German occupier, as it liberated other men for military work. The point that the presence of civilians was beneficial to the Occupation as they carried out tasks which made available Germans or volunteer workers available for other duties emerged every time evacuation of the civilian population was discussed. The most high-ranking German to have defended this point was General Jodl who argued, in 1942, that three-quarters of the population were working directly or indirectly for the Germans and that they would be faced with a desert if the civilian population was evacuated.[81] The concerns of the occupying power and the local population were so inextricably entangled that it would probably be unfair – but not inaccurate – to say that the 25,000 people working in agriculture and the glasshouse industry were 'collaborating'. While they were providing food to the 4,000 Channel Islanders engaged in direct work for the Germans, they were also keeping alive the large number of older people who had remained in the islands.[82] Still the fault for this mess lay not with individual Channel Islanders, but rather with the inadequacy of the law as well as with those officials who, in 1940, had advised them to stay on. Neither would it be fair to assume that all firms or individuals conducting work for the Germans did so voluntarily. Professor Pfeffer who visited the islands in September 1941 was full of contempt for islanders' frequent references to the Hague Conventions and described these attempts as 'impudent'.[83] This point of view was shared by many

[80] PRO HO 45/22424. Report of the President of the Controlling Committee of the States of Guernsey on the activities of the Committee during the five years of German occupation, 23 May 1945.

[81] Cruickshank, 213.

[82] AN AJ 40/547. FK 515. 'Verwaltungsüberblick über die Kanalinseln' by Dr Caspar, Jun 1943.

[83] Island Archives. FK 5–6. 'Bericht über Studienreise nach den britischen Kanalinseln vom 10. bis 25. September 1941', by Professor Karl Heinz Pfeffer.

Germans. Channel Islander Eddie de Sainte Croix ran an electrical firm which wired billets and other constructions, to a specific point acceptable under the Hague Convention. He said that they knew all about the Hague Convention 'because they were given this number to quote', but says that there was not much that could be done against German threats to stop 'this nonsense' or face reprisals.[84]

Similar misunderstandings of the role of the authorities exist with regard to the deportation of non-native Channel Islanders in September 1942. Many post-war public opinion reports stated that the chief bitterness against the island authorities was their 'assistance' in these deportations, in particular the provision of names and addresses of all persons likely to be wanted by the Germans for this purpose.[85] This was accurate and inaccurate at the same time: since the beginning of the Occupation the Germans had demanded dozens of lists of diverse categories of people and not all of these were as obvious as the ones headed 'Jews'. In Jersey the Germans already had been supplied with lists of all nationalities in the island together with the lists of non-natives and retired officers, a good ten months before the first deportation took place.[86] In retrospect it was a mistake to have furnished the Germans with so much information on the population; but to expect the authorities to have anticipated all the eventualities of delayed action is asking too much.

Perhaps the trickiest aspect of this whole complex is the posturing attitude of many islanders. It must be clear that Channel Islanders could not express themselves during the Occupation in the way they may have preferred. One rather controversially discussed example of posturing concerns a conversation between Bailiff Coutanche and a Nazi professor, Karl Heinz Pfeffer, head of the department 'Great Britain' at the Institute for Foreign Affairs in Berlin, during a visit to the Channel Islands in September 1941. Pfeffer had been sent over to cast his view on future German policy towards the Channel Islands and he recorded the conversation in a report. The conversation with the Bailiff had, at first, focused on a discussion of the Jersey Constitution, but soon drifted off to other areas until finally arriving at the topic of Jewish ritual slaughter. How the conversation got there, is unclear, but, to all intents, Coutanche seems to have wanted to use the pre-war exemption for kosher butchers, through a special Jersey law introduced in 1937, to demonstrate how adaptable the island constitution proved:

---

[84] IWM Misc. 2826 189/2 (Tape 4381). Interview with Eddie de Ste Croix, n.d.

[85] PRO KV 4/78. Security Service. The I(b) reports on the Channel Islands, by Major Stopford, 8 Aug 1945; HO 45/22399. 'The Channel Islands under German occupation', 17 Aug 1945.

[86] PRO WO 311/13. Clifford Orange, affidavit in the matter of war crimes, 12 June 1945.

As a decent Christian, I instantly came to an agreement with this decent Jew and allowed an exception, of which little practical use was made. You can see how a decent Christian can intercourse with a decent Jew.[87]

In his book *The Jews of the Channel Islands and the Rule of Law 1940–1945* David Fraser takes issue with the Bailiff's use of the term 'decent Jew' and sees this choice of terminology as proof for the latter's anti-Semitism.[88] What Fraser insinuates is that if the Bailiff used the term 'decent Jew' he must have also had ideas about the 'indecent Jew'.[89] I oppose this interpretation of the content of Pfeffer's report as tendentious, for three reasons. Firstly, the fact that the rendition of the meeting is not a direct quotation or a paraphrase of the conversation, but based on Pfeffer's memory. There is no guarantee that Pfeffer reported the meeting in an objective manner; context and words exchanged could have been entirely different. Secondly, Fraser omits giving any indication about the context of the Bailiff's utterance, namely that he was speaking to a German visitor and that – in line with 'restraint and influence' – he may have toned down his disapproval, adapting his verbal expression to suit his visitor, without necessarily sharing his opinion. If we reintegrate the omitted context and take account of posturing, a contrary interpretation is equally possible, namely that the Bailiff was telling a Nazi that living with Jews was possible. I have suggested that given the Bailiff's track record it is conceivable that the direction of the remarks was quite similar to that of the Danish foreign minister Scavenius, who is reported to have said to Göring in 1941 that there was 'no Jewish question in Denmark'.[90] Coutanche was not the only islander who seems to have adopted a posturing mode. Later Pfeffer, a sociologist, also asked a farmer whether he would rather be German or French. Predictably, the farmer answered 'German'. If one chose to one could interpret this as a sign of disloyalty on the part of the farmer, but one could also interpret it as a canny answer to an invalid question of an academic who should have known better. Asking a Jerseyman which of these two 'evils' he would prefer was never going to land an honest answer and reveals how little even educated Germans understood about islanders. The only thing one can deduct from this response is that the French were not popular and possibly that the farmer he interviewed was not going to

---

[87] Island Archives. FK 5–6. 'Bericht über Studienreise nach den britischen Kanalinseln vom 10. bis 25. September 1941', by Professor Karl Heinz Pfeffer (new translation in David Fraser, op.cit., 137). In a post-war translation of this report by the Home Office, the German original *anständig* had been translated with *respectable* (rather than *decent*).

[88] Fraser, David, *The Jews of the Channel Islands and the Rule of Law 1940–1945* – '*Quite contrary to the principles of British justice*', Brigthon/Portland, 2000.

[89] Fraser, op.cit., 137.

[90] Original: 'Es gibt keine Judenfrage in Dänemark', see Therkel Straede, 'Oktober 1943. Die dänischen Juden-Rettung vor der Vernichtung', <www.um.dk/publikationer/um/deutsch/oktober/oktober.doc>

land himself in prison for having 'insulted the honour of the German people' by giving the wrong answer. A proof of heart-and-soul collaboration this episode certainly was not.

The bottom line

Historians do not make good moral philosophers and until the recent arrival of political correctness it was considered inappropriate for a historian to profess any judgements at all and limit the job to accurate description and a modicum of interpretation. Robert Paxton did not give a direct answer to this issue in his classic study on Vichy France, but solved the problem of a final assessment in a roundabout way, by measuring the wartime performance of the authorities to the claim of post-war apologists that the regime had served as a 'shield' for the French. According to this myth Pétain avoided the 'Polandisation' of France, sacrificed the foreign Jews to save the French Jews and successfully defended the greater good. Paxton dismantled this myth piece by piece, determining, on balance, that the regime failed the French on all the tests. By hanging on to National Revolution and Nazi Germany – through thick and thin – they did exactly the opposite of what they had claimed: they worsened things for the French.[91] And just as Vichy, many other collaboration regimes in occupied Europe never even made good by the low standards of the 'greater number' principle, despite their promises and rhetoric. For them collaboration was a cynical political game in which the interests of the majority were of little consequence.

This is not something one could say about the Channel Islands administrations who were successful in their attempts to maintain public health and to provide an adequate supply of food and other items to the population. This may appear paradoxical, as so much has been written about the incompetence or inability of the authorities to deal with the black market and the fact that the food position was much worse than, for example, in England. However, such an Anglo-centric perspective overlooks the dire starting position in the matter of resources and transport which was one of the most unenviable in the whole of occupied Western Europe. Quoting the last hunger winter as the benchmark for the entire occupation is inappropriate, as by this time scarcity was induced by the military situation and had nothing to do with what the authorities did or did not do. Again, even in this situation the evidence weighs rather in their favour, as they did everything possible to realise the remarkable Red Cross salvage operation. The Channel Islands were also far from the only place where the

[91] See the last chapter in Robert O Paxton's *Vichy France. Old Guard and New Order*, New York, 2001 (reprint).

black market was raging. In France, a rich agricultural country, disruption and resource management was such that a very large number of French city dwellers were worse off than the average Channel Islander.[92] French black market prices for certain commodities, which saw anything from two- to ten-fold increases over the course of the Occupation, had nothing to envy the prices attained by their equivalent in the Channel Islands. Considering the circumstances – extreme scarcity, obstacles to importation and the draining of island resources by the Germans themselves – public management was good and the black market comparably tame. The milk herds were saved and children received their milk rations until the end of the Occupation. The view is confirmed in a 1945 UK treasury report which stated that the procurement from France, distribution and price fixing disclosed 'reserves of administration capacity' and that 'it was difficult not to remain impressed'.[93] The fact that the majority of the population survived in much better shape than the exposed position of the islands – on the edge of Europe – would suggest likely, was due to the authorities' tightrope walk. The second measure of the glory for getting these supplies across must go to the number of conniving Germans in high places who turned a blind eye or even supported island purchases on the French black market. Thus the survival of the civilian population was interlocked with the fact that this was the most heavily garrisoned outpost of German-occupied Europe. As one British observer stated in 1945, it was in the outback of the Nazi Empire, the Balkans and Greece, where the combination of scarcity, black market, indifference and German draining led to actual starvation and an uncharted reign of violence. In this sense the presence of a large German garrison was beneficial. The situation also influenced the financial position of the islands at the end of the war and explains how they could undercut and basically ignore the clearing procedure established between France and the Channel Islands in late 1942, for the duration of an entire year. Without this arrangement island debts to the banks would have been many times higher and the spectre of starvation may have hovered over the civilian population by as early as 1943.[94]

Old footage used in the landmark TV documentary 'The World at War' (1974) shows a rally of 50,000 Dutch Nazis listening to a speech by their leader

---

[92] Paul Sanders, *Histoire du marché noir 1940–1946*, 147–52.

[93] PRO WO 32/13750. Treasury document 'The Islands Budgets', 1945–46.

[94] PRO WO 32/13750. Report on the Financial and Economic Position of the States of Guernsey, 10 Jun 1945. occupation payments in Guernsey took a remarkable leap in 1944:

Year	Sum (£)
1940	107,966
1941	171,722
1942	243,755
1943	182,608
1944	1,219,272

Anton Mussert, in the summer of 1940. When Mussert asked the crowd whether they felt at war with Germany, he received a docile 'No'; the same question with regard to England was answered in the affirmative several moments later. At the end of the speech, a German Junkers flew over the crowd in salute, a mere six weeks after similarly low-flying Heinkels had bombed Rotterdam back into the stone age.[95] The all-too Anglo-centric approach to Channel Islands collaboration fails to realise the delirious heights to which collaboration did rise in other parts of Europe. The Channel Islands by comparison were a haven of sanity. Naturally, the Germans were interested in winning over islanders. Former Jersey Bailiff Sir Peter Crill was approached on one occasion, when he had to learn from a German that it was young people such as himself who should go to Germany to earn their place in the New Europe.[96] John Leale, the president of the Guernsey Controlling Committee, confirmed that the Germans were not indifferent when it came to what islanders thought about them. They became livid at the suggestion that they were callous about the fate of islanders and never forgot to remind them of the help provided in procuring supplies from France.[97] They were concerned about leaving the 'right' impression. Thus their attitude could have ripened into something 'warmer' had Channel Islanders wished it. The Germans were 'ready'; it was the Channel Islanders who 'held back'.[98] Had islanders responded to seduction, they could have secured themselves a very cushy corner in Hitler's Europe. In the end, the only warriors the Germans got for their 'New Order' were a tiny number of British renegades of mainland or Irish origin stranded in the Channel Islands when the Germans arrived. A singularly unimpressive harvest of ideological collaborators which showed islanders' remarkable *Resistenz* to Nazi sweet-talk.

On balance, we come up with a very mixed picture which, actually, is only straightforward if one argues from a partisan position of condemnation or island infatuation. Using Peter Davies' menu of 'collaborations' one can conclude that there is no evidence of heart-and-soul collaboration, wait-and-see collaboration or conditional collaboration, the last because the Channel Islands administrations were in no position to pose any conditions. The dominating influence was a definite 'submission on the grounds of superior force', interspersed with elements of 'shield philosophy' and 'tactical collaboration'. What is perhaps more sobering than collaboration itself is that so few influential islanders seem to have realised that it is not correct occupations with half-correct occupiers that

---

[95] 'The World at War: occupation', TV documentary narrated by Sir Laurence Olivier, 1974.

[96] Author's interview with Sir Peter Crill, 15 October 2004.

[97] PRO HO 144 22179. John Leale to Sir Francis Newsam (HO), Memorandum 'On Germans', 15 Jun 1945.

[98] PRO HO 45/22424. Report of the President of the Controlling Committee of the States of Guernsey on the activities of the Committee during the five years of German occupation, 23 May 1945.

captivate the imagination of future generations and stick in the collective memory, but examples of – if not sacrifice – then at least courage and imagination. In this respect the Channel Islands are no different from Ancient Greece, the Balkans, Afghanistan or Europe after the Second World War: it is the heroic deeds that are best loved and remembered by posterity. Although the authorities did the 'right thing', there was probably an even 'righter' thing – to resist, by whatever limited means available and, if necessary, behind the backs of those Germans with whom they had built relationships of trust but who were incapable of seeing through the criminal nature of the system they were serving. No measure of correction could ever compete with this. Still, one should not lose perspective of the wider scheme of things, in the light of which what the Channel Islands' elite did or did not do was relatively trifling. Comparison fades when we look at the enormity of European collaboration in the Holocaust. Although the Channel Islands authorities certainly did not cover themselves with glory when it came to fighting anti-Semitic legislation, there can be no comparison to the way in which thousands across Europe responded to calls to visit murder, rape and pillage upon their Jewish neighbours.

III

Resistance, Repression and Persecution

THAT THERE WAS 'no resistance' in the occupied Channel Islands has been the enduring cornerstone of critical interpretations, for several decades. The commonest stratagem in this respect consists in looking at the incidence of sabotage and partisan warfare in Europe and then in comparing this to the absence of any such thing in the Channel Islands. The inevitable conclusion drawn – amidst much Philistine finger pointing – is that when the British were faced with the Nazis they did not fight on the beaches, and the reader is then invited to reflect anew on British exceptionalism.[1]

Quite beside the point that the 'no resistance' paradigm is inaccurate, it displays ignorance of both the impact of geography, leadership and the operational realities of war on individual or group behaviour. One would have thought that its flimsiness would suffice to dismiss it as irrelevant. The trouble, however, is the frequency with which it is encountered and the verve in which it is upheld, in defiance of rational argument. This points to a more fundamental problem, linked to the uncritical, simplistic heroisation of the past, still today standard practice in Britain.

The rhetoric towards the Channel Islands hasn't always been so bad. One report based on 227 extracts from letters from the islands, drafted by the Information and Records Branch, was sent to the Cabinet Office in February 1945. The report spoke of 'courage and steadfastness not only in verbal expression but also in deeds' and referred more specifically to 'the tenacity in combating growing want and shortages' and the 'resistance to German attempts to prevent the reception and spreading of news from Britain'.[2] That escapee information was not always limited to incriminating islanders of collaboration is documented through a list of 'reliable personalities' in Jersey which is among the MI19 debriefings. They mention a solicitor at Bois & Bois, Le Gresley, who had

---

[1] See Bunting, op. cit., 191–2.
[2] PRO PREM 3/87. Information and Records Branch, Report on Channel Islands, 15 Feb 1945.

'helped many islanders to escape the Germans'. Mr W J Bertram, whose property on the road from Gorey to Le Hurel was the starting point for many escapes, was described as willing 'to gladly risk his life'. The same was said of Centenier Garden, the policeman in the parish of St Saviour who was involved in the Page case. Other names that appear are Fred Cooper, Major Manley, the acting head of the ARP, advocate Richardson and Alfred Sarre, the Guernsey representative in Jersey. States or government members mentioned for their 'good work' were food controller Cresley, and his assistant, Mourant, Captain Le Sueur, the assistant to Major Le Masurier and Jurat Dorey, the President of the Department of Finance who was described as the 'mainspring' between all departments. The odd one out on this list of resisters was Miss White, Lady Knott's secretary who was left in charge at Samares Manor. Miss White had formed close relations with Freiherr von Aufsess[3] and had the Manor taken into the personal custody of von Schmettow, which made many Jersey people consider her a quisling. The document stated that these allegations were false, without going into any further detail wherein the falsehood consisted.[4] No doubt opinions on some of the other men, especially those working in food control or essential commodities would have been similarly split. More than anything the list demonstrates how contested the issue of resistance really is.

Resistance in Europe did not spring out of a vacuum, but was actively built up by the Allies. One of the necessary conditions for such a build-up was a political or military objective. In the Channel Islands such objectives did not exist, as the islands were not an operational zone, nor were they ever seriously intended to become an operational zone. Home Office official Charles Markbreiter made the point clear enough in a correspondence with Brigadier French in April 1944, saying that '(i)n the Channel Islands [...] there has never been any question of active or passive resistance to the enemy as a policy designed to help us'.[5] This should not come as a surprise. On the Continent, German retaliation to acts of resistance inspired by Britain – by shooting or deporting 100 people – was unlikely to ever alter British determination. In such cases public opinion in Britain could be soothed by blaming any escalation on Nazi blood thirst. The matter was entirely different if the victims were Channel Islanders. In such an event public opinion could have very easily tied the government's hands. They could have no interest in being blackmailed over the fate of British citizens, for having stirred up resistance that was of no direct use to the war effort. Fundamentally, the best British interest was for things to remain as calm as possible in the islands. In this sense the course pursued by the island administrations could be described as an

---

[3] Von Aufsess's visits are mentioned in his *Occupation diary*, op.cit., passim
[4] PRO HO 144/22237. MI19. Report no 2510(S), 'Jersey Reliable Personalities. Further interrogation of three Jersey escapees', 27 Nov 1944.
[5] PRO WO 32/13750. Markbreiter to French, 4 Apr 1944.

exact mirror image of what was in the interest of British war strategy, namely to
maintain a benign form of Occupation in the Channel Islands, encourage
commanders to cultivate the islanders and avoid all confrontation with the
Germans that could lead to an escalation of violence. The situation was not
entirely unlike some of the hostage-taking situations that were to be become a
common feature of life in the second half of the 20th century.

The British decision to avoid stirring up resistance in the Channel Islands is
closely connected to the complex according to which Britain had 'forgotten' the
islands. This is another of the Occupation myths, still going strong after sixty
years. Some of the dilemmas of stirring up resistance already occurred in the
1941 V sign campaign. The idea had been conceived in the Belgian service of
the BBC – 'V' stood for 'Victoire' in French and 'Vrijheid' in Flemish – and
broadcast from January 1941. Quickly spreading across Western Europe, the
campaign was to 'encourage gentle disruptive activities in Europe'.[6] It did this in
rather innovative ways, not only encouraging people to daub V-signs across the
Continent, but also recommending how to engage in 'practical sabotage', by
'going slow' or by hiding metal coins and objects. The V-sign campaign also
worked with music and acoustics. The first chords of Beethoven's Fifth provided
the opening theme of the programmes and the 'V-sign' was associated with 'V
sound' – distinctive acoustic forms such as the clapping of hands or the rhythmic
sound of hammering. This 'intellectual invasion of the Continent by British
radio' became known through the galvanising voice of Douglas Ritchie alias
'Colonel Britton' who announced the 20 July 1941 as the day for the mobilisa-
tion of the V army. Politico-military intentions never underlay the V-sign
campaign, as it was never designed to have had operational impact; this is not to
say that the acts of passive or petty resistance it provoked were disregarded; they
were the little step to further more substantial resistance – when the right time
had come. The active forces should be made ready for future action. Although
Britton did advise 'unremitting caution', the problem of reprisals and precipitate
action soon became apparent. The campaign also lost momentum when the
Germans started to turn it around replacing 'V for Victory' with 'Viktoria'. The
ease with which the Germans turned the campaign and the success of their own
counterpropaganda showed that the campaign could potentially backfire.
Eventually 'Britton' continued to broadcast until May 1942, when his activities
were brought to an end on order of the Political Warfare Executive, until further
notice. The opinion had prevailed that encouraging resistance was so dangerous
that it should be left to the time when the end of the war was in sight.[7]

[6] Asa Briggs, *The War of Words* (The history of broadcasting in the United Kingdom, vol 3.),
Oxford, 1995, 338.
[7] ibid, 333–350; Edward Tangye Lean, *Voices in the darkness. The story of the European Radio War*,
London, 1943, 189–93.

Criticism of the decision to take off the airwaves any direct messages to the Channel Islands was voiced throughout the next years, but grew in particular force during the siege period. The majority of Channel Islands escapees who had arrived in England during the autumn had fuelled the allegation that islanders felt abandoned, deploring the fact that no special islands programs were being broadcast and depicting the enthusiasm every showering with leaflets in previous years had produced. The reaction, especially the feelings of isolation and abandonment, is comprehensible. But islanders were being left alone by Britain for their own best interest. In December 1944 the allegations that the BBC was doing nothing multiplied, with one article in *The Times*, a question by T J Brooks MP in parliament and a resolution from a Channel Islands Society in Britain. The BBC responded to these new allegations by informing Brendan Bracken, the Minister of Information, that in 1940 the BBC was told by the government that directing programs to the Channel Islands was 'undesirable' because 'such broadcasts might lead to reprisals against the inhabitants'. The policy had only been slightly adjusted in July 1944 when the BBC was informed that it could provide occasional items about the islands, but not *to* them.[8] Although in the light of the new circumstances Bracken was favourable to a further change in policy, the proposal was discarded, after consultation with the Home Office, 'in order not to provoke more stringent measures against listening on the part of the Germans'.[9]

The whole business of comparing the Channel Islands to partisan zones in occupied Europe also testifies to some authors' ignorance of what sabotage and partisan war entailed for the civilian population who ended up between the lines. Clearly this was not a scenario the British government could have wished for in an area of no importance to the speedy termination of the war. 'Setting Europe ablaze' was a catchy slogan, but the reality could not be reduced to 'hit-and-run' operations. The price paid by those civilians who had nowhere to run was often too high. The Special Operations Executive (SOE) support given to the 1942 assassination of Reinhard Heydrich in Prague, is illustrative of this point. Apart from executing the 'Hangman of Prague' this achieved very little in practical terms, and was chiefly designed to increase the leverage of the Czech government-in-exile under Edvard Benes in London. The human price was such that even today it suffices to drop the word 'Lidice' to be perfectly understood. The damage done to the strategic value of the Czech resistance itself was more than the Gestapo could have managed to do themselves. When the British came back in 1943 to ask the leaders of the Czech resistance to sabotage Skoda – at that time

    [8] PRO WO 32/11154. W J Haley (BBC) to Brendan Bracken, 7 Dec 1944.
    [9] PRO WO 32/11154. Ministry of Information (A S Hodge) to Home Office (J A R Pimlott), 14 Dec 1944; PRO PREM 3/87. Ministry of Information (A S Hodge) to Colville, 10 Downing St, 26 Feb 1945.

one of the most important arms manufacturers – the Czechs declined, pointing to the terrible bloodletting they had undergone only a year earlier.[10] The Channel Islands had the good fortune to not be embroiled in this kind of maelstrom. In France, as well, the targets were set higher, from an earlier stage, on embedding all sabotage and resistance support in the long-term strategy of an Allied landing. If sacrifices had to be made, they should be worth the price. No doubt, this relatively poised stance also owed something to the political and military intelligence of the Free French under de Gaulle in London who were less callous than the Benes government. SOE in France encouraged specific acts of sabotage and subversion, but sought to restrain resistance groups from indulging in activities 'which would lead to their premature destruction', such as the painting of V-signs. The policy was to persuade resistance groups to organise a common front and build up a force whose operations could be connected at a later stage directly with those of the Allies.[11] Indicative of the activities encouraged at this time were the networks running escaped or shot-down Allied personnel across the Pyrenees into the Iberian peninsula and from there back to Britain. This was an extremely wise decision, for the Germans had clearly shown in the hostage crisis of 1941 what they were capable of. The shooting of a pre-determined number of French citizens for every German assassinated by Communist Resistance groups, had made resistance unpopular. With some justification the ordinary French considered this assassination campaign – masterminded by Moscow and designed to stir up tumult – pointless. Had this campaign continued, this would have been a very unfavourable environment in which to groom French resistance.

The impact of geography and demography is another factor that cannot be discounted when dealing with the topic of island resistance. Captain Denning of MI5, on other occasions very critical of the conduct of islanders, admitted that 'the islanders enjoy none of the advantages of space or comparative freedom of action which have nourished the resistance movement on the mainland. It is difficult to be obstructive with impunity within parochial limits.'[12] Comparing a small island to larger countries is always a non-starter; for one thing the psychological make-up is not identical. Small size and congestion lead to a number of behavioural phenomena, such as crowding, which one does not find to the same extent in a larger country. The Germans never were in actual full physical control of France. It was impossible to comb the whole of the country. The only way of instilling fear was the threat of reprisals, spot-checks or pinpoint raids,

[10] See relevant chapter in Rab Bennett, *Under the shadow of the swastika : the moral dilemmas of resistance and collaboration in Hitler's Europe*, Basingstoke, 1999.

[11] J Ehrman, *Grand Strategy*, vol. V, August 1943–September 1944, 1956, 77 pp., cited in Asa Briggs, *The War of Words* (The history of broadcasting in the United Kingdom, vol 3.), Oxford, 1995, 401.

[12] IWM JRD.04. 'Channel Islands. Report on German Morale and factors likely to hasten or postpone capitulation', by Capt Dening 10 I(b), Sept 1944.

and for many partisans this was not deterrence enough. However, conducting thorough searches and turning upside-down small islands of this size was always possible, especially with the colossal German manpower reserves available. The odds were perhaps stacked too high to encourage a spirit of sacrifice. People do not act like lemmings and the futility of resistance under these conditions was often too obvious. But this wasn't all. The ratio of islanders to Germans and foreign workers is mentioned in almost every book on the Occupation and does not need to be regurgitated here, except perhaps that, proportionately, there were more Germans per square mile in these islands than in Germany. Congestion plus the frequency of denunciations were discouraging to an extent that, indeed, it could dissuade the most hardy from taking any action at all. Things were not made any easier through an island culture of proverbially stifling conformity. The islands were (and remain) extremely law-abiding places, this is one of the reasons why so many people elect to live here. It was no coincidence that Major Lanz, the first German Kommandant of Guernsey, noted in his report that, in its fifty years, there had never been any need for the Sark prison.[13] During the Occupation this conformity had been further enhanced by the authorities' decision to avoid anything susceptible to provoke the occupier. Much potential opposition was effectively stifled from the beginning, as a matter of policy.

If one said that the islands were at the very margin of what was humanly possible in terms of resisting an occupier, one would not have to forgive oneself for very much. With this in mind it is all the more striking that the most important argument against the 'no resistance' paradigm is its inaccuracy. It has been a perhaps too automatic reflex on the part of islanders to brush aside criticism with the fatalistic reference that nothing could be done. Nevertheless, considering the substantial impediments to any form of resistance, a large number of people were active in resistance. There was a definite potential and much of it was realised. Joe Mière, the former curator of the War Tunnels in Jersey, has counted around 4,000 sentences passed during the Occupation for breaking German law in the Channel Islands, a figure representing a sizeable part of the population. His figures of Channel Islands prisoners sent to the continental prisons and camps for 'offences against the occupying authorities' currently stand at 570; at least twenty-two Jersey residents and nine Guernsey residents did not return.[14]

---

[13] IWM JRD.04. 'Report by Major Lanz, 216 ID, the first German Commandant'
[14] JAS L/C/24/A/5. Joe Mière Collection. For offences against the occupying authorities 2,600 sentences were passed in Jersey and 1,400 in Guernsey; 'List of Channel Islanders deported to concentration camps and prisons', </www.occupationmemorial.com>, accessed March 2005. These figures bear no relation to the Channel Islanders internees in Germany who were a separate category.

The islands were predestined to foster covert forms of resistance. Naturally there were few opportunities for useful sabotage. One Jersey dairy farmer who claimed to have 'sabotaged' milk provisions – on instructions from Colonel Briton – and who had hoped to 'hurt' the Germans found himself in the Royal Court.[15] Considering that milk was the very linchpin of public health, the authorities were quite right in setting an example here. Passive resistance was a better option. One Guernsey resident stated that he ignored most German orders and refused to fill in forms and abide by preliminaries needed for the requisitioning of motor cars, tyres, refrigerators and other items which, instead he stored in secret caches. The Germans were not as thorough as their reputation suggested, and the author saw some success in refusing to give anything of value. He admitted, however, that this was easier for people living in isolated houses in the country than for those in more public locations.[16] Evasion and psychological resistance, in all its forms, were the name of the game. Consequently, the most typical offences tried by German courts during the Occupation were possession of a wireless set, spreading BBC news, countering German propaganda, 'dishonouring' the Reich or the German armed forces, sheltering escaped slave-labourers or German deserters, stealing German goods (or receiving these), blackmarketeering, sabotage, 'going slow', escape and weapons possession.[17]

Sheltering

The most significant, but also the most dangerous of these activities was giving shelter to escaped forced or slave workers. If a list of fourteen escaped prisoners in Jersey, in all probability established in 1944, is anything to go by, the great majority of the fugitives were Russian OT workers.[18] Louise Willmot has offered some interesting insights into the make-up of this sizeable population of helpers. The main motive was compassion, often coupled with a political or social element such as willingness to defy the Nazis, anti-Fascism or social marginalisation. On the other hand, many helpers were the exact opposite of marginals or non-conformists: 'doers' who were actively involved in community life.[19] This

---

[15] See correspondence re. Mr Sarre in PRO HO 144/22176.

[16] IWM JRD.04. Unknown author, 'Sabotage and Betrayal (Guernsey)', n.d.

[17] Taken from a list partly compiled by Michael Ginns, see JAS C/C/L. Occupation and Liberation Committee Files, letter of Michael Ginns to Jean Baird, 6 Nov 1996.

[18] JAS B/A/W50/165. List of escaped prisoners, Aug 1944. Another correspondence, of the same month, talks of thirteen Soviet nationals who had evaded recapture in Jersey and were living among the civilian population, see B/A/W50/165. Notice of the Festungskommandant Colonel Heine, 15 Aug 1944.

[19] Louise Willmot, 'The goodness of strangers: Help to escaped Russian slave labourers in occupied Jersey, 1942–1945', *Contemporary European History*, 11, 2 (2002), 211–27.

virtual resistance organisation grew organically and it was its inherent element of improvisation and heterodox nature which precluded detection and made it effective.[20]

Many of the escapees transited via the home of Stella Perkins in Hill Street. Stella's mother and aunt were Russian-born and it was known among islanders that the fugitives could find someone who spoke their language. Stella remembered the occupation years as a very difficult time, but also a time of much animated chitter-chatter with these strangers, many of whom were both interesting and refined. One tall Eastern Slav had a most peculiar idea of what it was to look like an Englishman. He took an old mouldy bowler hat from a scarecrow and dressed in clothes with short sleeves. Dr McKinstry was then alerted and went out in his ambulance to bring him in. [21]

Jersey clerk Bob Le Sueur was one of the relays for escapees in the island. He stated that eight or nine Eastern European escapees went through his hands from 1942. Bob was the ideal man for this task because of his mobility as an insurance agent and his talent for foreign languages. Security and discretion were of paramount importance: one of the precautions was to never leave an escapee longer than two months with any one shelterer. Town locations were considered safer than the countryside, which was perhaps against instinct. What he dreaded most was the fringe of town, as these suburban locations made it very difficult to hide things from the neighbours. Information was only passed on when absolutely necessary. The less people knew the better and Bob was never aware of more than three or four people up or down the life-line at one time.[22] The risks certainly were there, as is shown by the case of Jerseywoman Louisa Gould who took in a young Russian, Feodor Buryi (Bill) in autumn 1942.[23] Gould owned a shop at La Fontaine Millais, St Ouen, and having lost one son in the war, treated Bill as surrogate son. Gould was not a distrustful person and she had perhaps a too high opinion of her co-parishioners. Bill's presence in her house soon was an open secret. On occasions he was seen serving customers in the shop or doing little errands. In May 1944 the inevitable happened, Louisa Gould received a tip-off from a sympathetic islander who had gotten wind of a letter of denunciation that was on its way to the Feldkommandantur. Bill was immediately ferried to another location by Bob Le Sueur and the house was purged of any trace of his presence, but when the Feldgendarms raided the next day they still found enough evidence, including a

---

[20] Unfortunately, its lack of centralised organisation and absence of hierarchy also provided the basis for the belittlement of this important and significant effort after the war.

[21] IWM Misc. 2826 189/2 (Tape 4446 o/L). Interview with Stella Perkins

[22] Author's interview with Bob Le Sueur, 21 July 2004.

[23] See also Michael Frowd (et al.), 'A Russian in hiding – Feodor ("Bill") Burriy', *The Channel Islands Occupation Review*, 1999 (27), 59–70.

radio, to arrest her. The trial took place in late June 1944 and involved a number of other people who had received radio news: her brother Harold Le Druillenec, her sister Ivy Forster and two of Gould's closest friends, Dora Hacquoil and Berthe Pitolet. After the trial Gould, Le Druillenec and Pitolet were transported to the Continent (Ivy Forster evaded deportation by having been taken into hospital). The procedure until spring 1944 had been that condemned Channel Islanders sent to the Continent still served their terms in penitentiaries under the authority of the Reich Ministry of Justice first. By summer 1944, however, under the pounding of the Allied guns, German administration of justice in Western Europe had disintegrated and things were no longer done by the book. Therefore these prisoners were fed straight into the concentration camp prison: while Pitolet escaped during a bombing raid in France, Gould was sent to Ravensbrück and her brother to Neuengamme. Le Druillenec just about survived the horrors of Belsen, where he had been sent to in spring 1945, but his sister was gassed in Ravensbrück, on 13 February 1945.[24]

Especially in the rural northern and western parts of Jersey a large number of families provided assistance to slave workers, if only by passing on food. Some went as far as inviting slave labourers to their houses.[25] Perkins knew of twenty-two people who were involved in providing assistance, but is certain that there were many more. Information which Bob Le Sueur was able to collect after the war led him to believe that the total number of people directly involved in the sheltering of escapees in Jersey must have been about 100.[26] Jersey farmer William Sarre sheltered three Russian prisoners, among them Peter Bogatenko, Grigori Koslov and a man whom he had only known as Vasili, over varying periods of time. Vasili came to his house on Boxing Day 1942, to beg for food. He could not stand, 'his legs being like bamboo sticks', and the family took him in, stripped him, gave him a bath and put him to bed, before calling a doctor. They kept him for about five months until it became too dangerous to keep him. One week after he left the Sarres he was caught. As a result of Vasili's account of conditions, Sarre made it his 'business' to go out to the Five Mile Road in St Ouen's Bay.[27] A minority of farmers did not play along: Stella Perkins stated one case where a farmer tied up an escapee and called in the OT and another where an escapee was reportedly killed. However, she stressed that this should

[24] Paul Sanders, *The Ultimate Sacrifice*, op. cit., 65–80.

[25] Nan Le Ruez, a Methodist lay preacher in Jersey records multiple references to the feeding and sheltering of slave labourers in her diary, see *Nan Le Ruez Occupation Diary*, Bradford on Avon, 1994, passim.

[26] Author's interview with Bob Le Sueur, 21 July 2004; see also Louise Willmot, 'The goodness of strangers: Help to escaped Russian slave labourers in occupied Jersey, 1942–1945', *Contemporary European History*, 11, 2 (2002), 227

[27] PRO WO 311/11. Statement of William Sarre, Jersey, taken by C Kent, St Helier, 2 Jul 1945.

not be the basis upon which the 'kind, but fearful' majority of Jersey people should be judged.[28] Whether escapees were reported or given shelter relied to some extent on the first impression they gave to Channel Islanders. And it is true that in this respect not all forced workers were an example of rectitude. Whether the first impression slave labourers foraging for food left was the disappearance of someone's hens or rabbits or whether they approached the population with a modicum of civilised behaviour could make all the difference in the world. One December night in 1943 two Russians helped themselves to bicycles from the garage of a St Clement resident and then went on a food foraging 'tour' of the district, which involved several break-ins. The following day they were arrested by local police, brought into town and then handed over to the OT.[29] Could their fate have been different if they had asked nicely?

In Guernsey the scope for salvage activities was more restrained than in Jersey, which doesn't mean that they weren't taking place: Lambert, the French consul in St Peter Port sheltered one escapee in 1942, for thirteen months. Mr Troubil, a shoemaker, sheltered another OT worker for about two years. After this lapse of time the man came out into the open but was denounced and taken back to the OT.[30]

The most politicised and hierarchically structured resistance group in Jersey was formed around Norman Le Brocq and Les Huelin. Its members were mostly left-wing sympathisers who started off with regular meetings discussing the possibility of post-war reform, later pooling their energy into political expression through the formation of the Jersey Democratic Movement and the Jersey Communist Party. Needless to say that they were not equally popular with all islanders; some went to the point of scape-goating the group's criticism of the island authorities as an attempt to undermine their authority, thus supposedly benefiting the German occupier. As the Occupation dragged on, the group focused on ways of meaningful resistance, closing ranks with a number of Spanish workers with similar political leanings. When the Germans sent delousing parties – again consisting mainly of Spaniards – to the OT camps during the 1943 typhoid outbreak, they seized on the opportunity to get in touch with Eastern European workers. These men then smuggled leaflets written by Le Brocq's group, but also food and clothing into the camps. In late 1944 Le Brocq closed ranks with a German soldier, an industrial chemist by the name of Paul Mühlbach who approached them in order to circulate leaflets among the garrison. Mühlbach, the son of a trade union official who had died at the hands of the Nazis, had an authentic anti-Fascist pedigree and Le Brocq helped him desert,

---

[28] IWM Misc. 2826 189/2 (Tape 4446 o/L). Interview with Stella Perkins, n.d.

[29] JAS B/A/W50.124. The Constable of St Clement, S G Crill to C W Duret Aubin, Attorney General, 6 Dec 1943.

[30] PRO WO 311/12. 'Secret Report on OT – Guernsey', 1945.

with a view to fermenting a mutiny of the garrison, on May Day 1945. How far these efforts ripened and whether the mutiny would have succeeded is difficult to ascertain. In any case this eventuality was precluded by the changed situation following Hitler's death on 30 April.[31] Perhaps more than actual results, the efforts of Le Brocq's highly politicised group had a stirring up effect, providing people with an alternative consciousness to the complacency and inaction of certain members of the island elite. As a relay for channelling dissent and know-how between different atomised groups and individuals, Le Brocq was in a vital position. Working towards changing the atmosphere of the place did bear results.

That there was a potential to exploit, even among the ranks of the German armed forces, becomes clear through the case of Kurt Hälker. This navy telegrapher came to Jersey in autumn 1941, for six months. Early in 1942 a particularly devastating RAF pinpoint raid by low-flying British bombers occurred in the harbour area of Guernsey, sinking one freighter and blocking the entry for a considerable period of time. The navy was convinced that a raid of such accuracy was only possible because it was directed through the transmission of detailed information, probably via a radio link, from the islands to England. As was going to become increasingly common throughout 1942, they set a military intelligence (Abwehr) officer with the rank of Korvettenkapitän on the tracks of the elusive resistance network they considered responsible. Hälker says that when this man arrived for his short intelligence-gathering mission he was the highest navy rank in the islands, thus demonstrating the high priority attached to the case. Based at the Hafenkommandantur, on the premises of the Royal Yacht Club, the officer would spend most of his time at his desk, but would occasionally go out in plain clothes. Hälker and his colleagues were warned not to salute him, should they bump into him in the streets of St Peter Port. What his intelligence gathering consisted of was soon to become crystal clear, for one day Hälker saw him bring back a civilian, covered in blood, for interrogation. Hälker's aversion to the regime – already in gestation since summer 1941, when he had witnessed the daily executions of hostages in France – was reinforced during his time in Guernsey. When he returned to the mainland, he worked in Cherbourg and Paris and, by 1943, formed a cell with two other navy colleagues, passing on sensitive Navy HQ information to the French Resistance. Shortly before the Liberation of Paris he deserted together with a few others, joining the 'Nationalkommittee Freies Deutschland (West)'[32] and ending the war in the ranks of the US army.[33]

[31] IWM Misc. 2826 189/2 (Tape 18 4394 O/L). Interview with Norman Le Brocq, n.d.; Norman Le Brocq, 'Clandestine activities', *The Channel Islands Occupation Review*, 1999 (27), 39–58.

[32] 'Nationalkommittee Freies Deutschland' was an anti-Fascist organisation founded by German prisoners of war in Soviet captivity. Its members represented a cross-section of the German prisoner population, but Communist influence was, naturally, important.

[33] Author's interview with Kurt Hälker, Berlin, 30 Dec 2004. Kurt Hälker settled in East Germany after the war.

From early autumn 1944 islanders would find themselves in the shoes of the
Russian fugitives, as they were making their way across the gulf of St Malo to
the newly liberated Cotentin peninsular. The escapes had been few and far
between in the preceding years, mainly from Guernsey, in 1940 and then again
in 1943. The perhaps most spectacular escape was that of Jerseyman Denis
Vibert, before the war a merchant navy trainee. Vibert escaped in the
Ragamuffin, his 8ft boat, in October 1941, and this was his second attempt after a
failed attempt, ten months earlier. All escapees and would-be escapees took
great risks, as was demonstrated in the cases of three youngsters, Peter Hassall,
Maurice Gould and Dennis Audrain, who had tried to leave Jersey in May 1942.
While Audrain drowned in the attempt, his companions were imprisoned in
Germany where Gould perished.[34] The worst that could happen to their successors, two years later, was to be shot or locked up in the Jersey prison, but this
was not deterrence enough to dent their enthusiasm. The eventual number of
Channel Islands escapees would run at 225, of which 150 left from Jersey and 75
from Guernsey. Thanks to these large numbers of escapees, the British soon had
a steady stream of information on the islands, including material on the fortifications and German morale. The positive denouement of May 1945 could not be
foreseen when most of the escapes occurred, in 1944. Had it come to the crunch,
requiring the British to land troops in the islands, this information would have
saved hundreds if not thousands of lives.

Radio offences

If one had to choose a symbol of the Occupation, it would be hard to find a
better one than the radio. This was by far the most iconic image. Radios came
to embody the very idea of freedom of thought and sparked the most idiosyn-
cratic form of resistance in the Channel Islands, after they had been confiscated
in June 1942. Defiance came in two forms: the receiving of news and the
spreading of news in the form of typed out newssheets. While the Germans were
certainly not soft on the first act, the second one was the one they took a particularly dim view of. The confiscation itself was an initiative of the combat troop
commanders in the islands, their military superiors on the mainland and the
security establishment. The Feldkommandantur opposed it, as they felt they
had enough work on their hands already and did not want to rock the boat with
islanders who might stop cooperating if such a drastic measure was taken. On
the surface the measure was justified by security concerns, namely the idea that

---

[34] For a lists of escapees see Richard Mayne, 'People who escaped from Jersey during the
Occupation', in: *Channel Islands Occupation Review 1975*, 22–4; Roy Thomas, *Lest we forget. Escapes and
attempted escapes from Jersey during the German Occupation 1940–1945*, Jersey, 1992, 2; 128–129.

island resistance may receive instructions through radio messages from the UK and that details of troop deployment, fortification work and other sensitive information could reach the UK via wireless receivers which had been converted into transmitters. This interpretation was very much at the basis of the repeated confiscations of wirelesses after the V-sign scares of summer 1941. The second rationale – more important than the first – was that troop morale was being undermined by the availability of enemy news, the reception of which was punishable by death in Germany. This paradoxical situation was untenable, considering that this was the only place in occupied Europe where the local population was allowed to listen to enemy broadcasts; invariably, this information also spread among German soldiers who often came to appreciate the Allied news bulletin more than their own.[35] Guernsey GFP (Secret Field Police) man Einart stated that local youths who met German soldiers were spreading BBC news and that this led to 'growing unrest among troops'. When this situation capable of undermining German morale got to the ears of the OB West in Paris, the latter demanded confiscation.[36] This took place in June 1942 and was a heavy blow to the civilian population. Nevertheless the German decision to ban radios was based on concerns about the value of the troops as a disciplined force rather than a desire to punish the civilian population. Confiscating the sets was only half the problem, as – and this is a good guess – only half of the radio sets had been handed in. In no time radio listening parties were organised where groups of islanders would congregate to listen to the news. The Germans never tackled the problem of radio offences. They launched occasional campaigns against radio listeners (one is documented for November 1944), they gave wide publicity to the trials of prominent islanders caught with a radio to deter others, but islanders countered the threat by switching to the near undetectable crystal sets. After D-Day these became a standard feature, as the radio signals from liberated France could be picked with no problem.

As with the wireless ban, the apprehension of wireless offenders was also, first and foremost, an issue of maintaining German morale. Two escapees who went over to England in August 1943 said that most Germans understood by then that they could not win the war. One of the duo admitted that he had sat in many a German mess where he had been able to witness the morbid atmosphere following the announcement of air raids on German cities. Many men were recalled home after raids, among them one seaman who lost his entire family in Hamburg, and they returned with harrowing news which spread around the island in no time.[37] The truth was only reluctantly admitted in the German

[35] Paul Sanders, *The Ultimate Sacrifice*, op. cit., 104–21.

[36] IWM JRD.09. Document signed W Einart re 'Confiscation of Wireless Sets', 20 May 1945.

[37] PRO HO 144/22834. Report MI19/1742, 'Channel Islands Guernsey, interrogation of two Channel Islands escapees', 1943.

media (or not at all) and, paradoxical as it may seem, many Germans sought
contact with the local population to get the 'real' picture.[38] One of the informants
found German soldiers asking him for the news on his way to work in the
morning and, on the whole, felt that there was less danger from these Germans
than from many islanders. One German with whom he listened to the news was
interested in improving his English, another listened to the BBC news in
German.[39] The Germans were never in one mind about the hounding of radio
listeners and in certain quarters this category of people was viewed with
sympathy. This became evident in April 1945 when sentences of radio listeners
were suspended and they were released from the public prison.[40] If there was a
category of wireless offenders the Germans took a dimmer view of, this would
have been the people deliberately spreading news, an offence viewed akin to
sabotage. One illegal press service was the Guernsey Active Secret Press, (GASP),
which was being edited by the elderly L E Bertrand. Although Bertrand was a
World War One invalid whose health was frail, his doctor had been unable to
talk him out of producing newssheets. When the radios were confiscated
Bertrand handed in one set, but retained a small one-valve radio which was
easier to transport and hide. Betrand had twelve agents who would meet at Mr
Moullin's bicycle shop, a place where suspicion was drowned out by the contin-
uous bustle of people whose bikes needed attention. These agents then spread the
newssheets among reliable and trustworthy civilians.[41] One agent also recruited a
number of foreign agents through whom the news reached labourers. Quite apart
from their morale-boosting value, the sheets also had a practical value for
fishermen, as these would find a pretext to stay in harbour whenever Supreme
Command HQ issued instructions to stay clear of certain zones. One of the most
sought after items, the BBC Editors 'Survey of the Week' broadcast on Sundays
at 3 pm, even reached the Bailiff, through the wife of one of Bertrand's agents,
who was a States employee.[42] This fact may have been at the origin of the tip-off

[38]   See JAS Reverend Ord diaries, op. cit., passim.
[39]   PRO HO 144 22834. Report MI19/1742, 'Channel Islands Guernsey, interrogation of two
Channel Islands escapees', 1943.
[40]   JAS B/A/W81/11. Correspondence re release of prisoners from the public prison (Jersey),
April 1945.
[41]   The agents were: Deputy Inspector Banneville (police); his doctor, W B Fox; Charles Taylor,
who also made his crystal set; Sr Clayton and Sr. Marquand for the Emergency Hospital; William
Nant, George Wingate, Claude Trachy, Mr H S Snell, for St Peter Port; Fred Wellington for St
Stephen's District; Mr H R Bichard for Vale; Mr E Pill for St Martin's; Mr E Bisson for St Peter
Port; Mr W Blatchford for St Peter Port; Mr J Le Garff and Mr A Bonathan for Vale and St
Sampson's; Mr Frank Le Vallée for St John's; Mr P W Warley for the Post Office; Mr A L J
Bertrand for the Foreign Workers and PoWs; Mr A V Dorey for St Sampson's. Betrand also
thanked the Fruit Export Co Ltd, T Robin & Co Ltd and the GUB for their loyalty.
[42]   After Liberation Carey voiced his deep appreciation of the risk they had run and that he
looked forward 'most eagerly' to the Editors Weekly Survey, see L E Bertrand, *A Record of the Work*

they received from a local police detective. The latter informed Bertrand that the bicycle shop was being talked about too much as the place to get the 'real news' and that he should 'go easy'. This policeman continued to tip him off when the Germans were planning a raid in a particular district. An interesting point is that German raids often followed broadcasts which were particularly popular with islanders: Churchill's speeches, the Editors' reports and anything which bore a connection to the Channel Islands. Among the many delicate problems was how to obtain replacement batteries. Bertrand was not a complacent observer of the Guernsey scene and did not deny the disturbing fate which had caught up with underground newsagents such as GUNS. At times the issue of whom one could trust seemed like an almost insuperable obstacle. He finally found a man to whom he offered his cigarette ration but whose behaviour in accepting his cigarettes each week he did not find 'quite British'. Bertrand admitted that his group had been lucky in having avoided detection. Although much of this was probably due to the fact that he had a police contact, another part of his luck would have been precisely the fact that he was operating his wireless in a garden shed which was right under the Germans' noses: they had an anti-aircraft battery HQ only 50 ft away. This also provided an additional blessing in disguise: at some point Bertrand was unhappy about the performance of his radio, a fault due to an aerial, mixed with other wires in a small greenhouse so as to evade detection, which was both too low and too short. He had often looked with envy at the German telephone wires passing over his garden and leading to the anti-aircraft battery HQ, until one night nature came to his assistance by blowing one of these wires right across his garden. Early next morning he sabotaged 80 feet of this wire and left the remainder in a heap on the ground. However, there were a number of close calls, without these his account would somehow lack credence. As many Channel Islanders Bertrand had maps pinned to the walls showing the Allied positions, and this almost proved his undoing: one day the maps were spotted by a German who had come to collect fruits. When the man asked Bertrand whether he had radio, the latter denied and said this it was all made on the basis of the local news available in the German controlled papers. Although the German did not believe him, the thought of denouncing Bertrand did not occur to him. Later the same man brought his friends along to study the map. Bertrand and the Germans even went to the point of having arguments as to who was going to win the war, until, one day, the flags on the map had disappeared. Bertrand surmised that this had been done by one of his own people who had considered that this bit of fun was not worth the risk. Bertrand took considerable risks to keep the current of news flowing. Another close call with fate occurred at the time when electricity was getting scarce. The man responsible for charging

of the Guernsey Active Secret Press 1940–1945, published by the Guernsey Star & Gazette Company, December 1945.

his battery was already exceeding his supply and Bertrand committed an act of desperation: every night he borrowed a battery from a German car which he then returned to its proper place afterwards. Fortunately, a few weeks into this exceedingly dangerous daily chore instructions arrived through the BBC on how to make crystal sets. Later, when electricity was cut, Bertrand was caught siphoning off diesel oil, which he needed to provide light, from a German tank at the Electric Station. His ID card was confiscated by the man in charge, a Frenchman, and Bertrand was convinced that surely his time had come to pay a visit to the local gaol. But things took a different turn: on the next day he was handed back his ID card by the Frenchmen who had been pressurized, under various pretexts, by the second in charge, a Pole called 'Alex' who also happened to be one of Bertrand's radio news recipients.[43]

Another newssheet was the Guernsey Underground News Service (GUNS), animated by journalist Frank Falla, from 1942 to 1944. In opposition to Bertrand's seven lives, Falla's luck, and that of his helpers Charles Machon, Cyril Duquemin, Joseph Gillingham and Ernest Legg, ran out in February 1944 when they were denounced. Tried the following spring, they were sent to the prison of Preungesheim (Frankfurt/Main), in June 1944. When the group arrived, they found fifteen Channel Islanders already serving their sentences. By then Preungesheim had become one of the principal detention centres for Channel Islands offenders in Germany.[44] As a rule all residents of the Western occupied territories sentenced by German courts to longer prison terms were transferred to penitentiaries in Germany, usually after first serving time in the Channel Islands and in France, especially Villeneuve St Georges and Dijon.[45] While until 1942 people serving shorter sentences in France could be sent back to the Channel Islands, this practice became increasingly uncommon from later that year. The principal routes into the German prison system were, for men, the prisons in Saarbrücken and Wolfenbüttel (via Freiburg or Karlsruhe) and, for women, Cologne.[46] Because of overcrowding in Saarbrücken, Channel Islanders were sent to Preungesheim[47] from December 1943.[48] Preungesheim had four five-floor blocks, filled with 850 prisoners of all European nationalities.

[43] L E Bertrand, *A Record of the Work of the Guernsey Active Secret Press 1940–1945*, published by the Guernsey Star & Gazette Company, December 1945.

[44] BA-R 22. RMJ 1341. Army Notification Bulletins 1944, 10th edition, 18 May 1944.

[45] BA-R 22. RMJ 1342 (Microfilms). OKW Memo re. transfer of Belgians and French to German penitentiaries, 13 May 1942.

[46] BA-R 22. RMJ 1341. Army Notification Bulletins 1944, 10th edition, execution of sentences in area of military government in France, 18 May 1944.

[47] BA-R 22.RMJ 1341. Military government in France, Sec. Ib (Kommandostab)-Group 3, 1 Dec 1943, re Order concerning the execution of sentences, 21 Oct 1943.

[48] Sentences over two years were executed at Bochum prison, see BA-R. 22. RMJ 1341. Army Notification Bulletins 1944, 10th edition, 18 May 1944.

The blocks led onto a central building which Frank Falla described as 'a kind of platform and enclosed cabin in which worked the prison administrators, complete with Nazi uniform, Iron Cross, other medals, sword and all the trappings that were supposed to impress us.'[49] Prisoners frequently had to join work-parties clearing rubble or removing unexploded bombs from the devastated streets of Frankfurt. No air-raid shelters existed for prisoners and the frequent air bombardments on Frankfurt sent waves of terror through the prisoners who were confined to their crowded cells. One particularly heavy attack scored many direct hits in the immediate vicinity of Preungesheim prison on February 4, 1944.[50] Preungesheim also served as place of execution for both Germans and foreigner civilians tried by special Nazi courts and the 'People's Court'[51] , and in mid-1944 executions were taking place at a weekly rate of 30.[52]

Falla survived the war and returned to Guernsey to tell the tale. The overwhelming majority of prisoners from the Channel Islands were not so fortunate. A particularly harrowing fate awaited the Revered Clifford Cohu, formerly canon of Allahabad and acting rector of St Saviour's, Jersey. Cohu was the ringleader of a wireless circuit and he defied the occupier in a rather bizarre manner, by publicly declaiming the latest news while riding into town on his bicycle. Everywhere he went, including the General Hospital where he served as chaplain, he disseminated information which on one occasion earned him the reprimand of a nurse. It is difficult to comment on Cohu's motives, except that this was a particularly eccentric (and foolhardy) form of resistance, which could not last. There was no question that the Germans would tolerate such as slap in their face and in March 1943 they arrested Cohu together with eighteen other parishioners. The ensuing trial demonstrates the German occupiers' increasing nervousness to offenders against the wireless confiscation order and it provided a perfect opportunity to stage a show trial that would deter others. The Germans did make sure that the trial – which took place in April – received a lot of publicity and large crowds thronged Royal Square outside the States building where the trials was being held, to hear news of the verdict. As could be expected, Cohu received a tough 18-month jail sentence; however, his principal

---

[49] Francis Falla, The Silent War. The Inside Story of the Channel Islands under the Nazi Jackboot, Guernsey, 1994 (reprint), 114.

[50] Eyewitness account by Emil Schmidt, a political prisoner in Preungesheim, in: SPD Preungesheim, 8. Mai 1945, 8. Mai 1985. Preungesheim 40 Jahre danach – erinnern oder vergessen?, 6.

[51] Falla, op. cit., 122. This special jurisdiction under the Nazi judge Roland Freisler was responsible for high treason cases such as the trials against the members of the failed plot to assassinate Hitler on July 20, 1944.

[52] Falla, op. cit., 116; SPD Preungesheim, 8. Mai 1945 – 8. Mai 1985. Preungesheim 40 Jahre danach – erinnern oder vergessen?, 29.

helpers, parish cemetery worker Joe Tierney and farmer John Nicolle received even longer sentences. These men, together with the non-native British among the indicted, were transported off the island, Cohu in July 1943, first to Dijon, and then, in late December 1943, to Germany.[53] After the war Cohu's wife testified that her husband had remained in solitary confinement at the prison of Frankfurt-Preungesheim. Conditions in Preungesheim were severe, but up to the D-Day landings inmates could communicate with their relatives in Jersey once a month. The last time she heard from him was in July 1944. In his letters to his wife he frequently referred to the gruelling conditions in prison, particularly the cold and the hunger. On a weekly bread ration of four and a half pounds,[54] emaciation had already taken its toll: Cohu's weight had dropped from 10 st. 3lb. when he left the island to 7 stone in May 1944.[55] When Saarbrücken prison suffered heavy bomb damage and Preungesheim became overcrowded, the Channel Islands prisoners were transferred to Naumburg-on-Saale[56], in July 1944. Here conditions were even worse than in the previous prison and the majority of detainees wasted away. Cohu's sentence officially ended on 24 September 1944 and the sentence of his brother-in-arms Joseph Tierney on 25 March 1945. During their imprisonment in Frankfurt both men had laid the groundwork for an early release.[57] On 16 August 1944 Cohu had made one last appeal to the court of FK 515 in Jersey and he was discharged two weeks later on the grounds of a 'suspension of sentence'.[58] He expected to be sent to an internment camp, but with the Gestapo waiting outside the prison gates was sent to a 'work education camp' under SS authority, in Zöschen, 22 miles from Naumburg. He arrived there with a group of fifty prisoners, on September 13, 1944, at a time when the camp population had swollen to 500.[59] Conditions in 'work education camps' were primitive and reputedly worse than those in most concentration camps. Typically, thirty men were cramped into small round paper tents, with nothing but straw spread out on the bare soil. Cohu attracted attention and became a prime target for abuse, the minute he set foot in the

[53] Paul Sanders, *The Ultimate Sacrifice*, op. cit., 21–7.

[54] Falla, op. cit., 122.

[55] JAS B/A/L15. Bailiff's Liberation Files. Inquiries for relatives, letter of Mrs Cohu to Lt-Col. J W Taylor, British Military Authority, Military HQ, Jersey, 18 May 1945.

[56] Letter of Chief Prosecutor in Frankfurt to the Prosecutor at Frankfurt District Court re Order of the RMJ of 8 Oct. 1943 , 4 Jan. 1944, see Preungesheim prison records at State Archives Hesse, Wiesbaden (Reference: 409/4, file 2).

[57] On 11 October 1944, Tierney sent a plea for clemency to the court of FK 515, see State Archives Hesse, Wiesbaden. Files of Prosecutor's Office, Frankfurt District Court (Reference 461, Nr 18894/2).

[58] State Archives Hesse, Wiesbaden. Preungesheim prison records (Reference 409/4, Nr 2); files of Prosecutor's Office, Frankfurt District Court (Reference 461, Nr 18894/1).

[59] PRO FO 950/766. 'Index to names of British subjects in enemy concentration camps and statistical survey of camps', post-war.

camp. His position could not have been less enviable: being the only British prisoner was exposure enough; in addition, he was also a priest, which provoked the guards' perverse ingenuity. Feeble and thin, he was unable to lift a shovel, which earned him the direst of abuse ('You English swine, you want to bomb us, we will bloody show you, you cripple') and continual beatings. The camp SS were bent on bringing about one guard's ominous prognosis that he would not last longer than seven days, and their brutality prevailed on September 20, 1944. That day Cohu finally succumbed to the privations of an ordeal which had begun eighteen months earlier with his arrest in Jersey. When preparing his body, Przemysl Polacek – the Czech survivor who broke the story of Cohu's death – found a small bible tightly pressed against his breast.[60] Cohu's tragic disappearance was painfully felt in the island and it was not long after the war that a commemorative plaque was set up in his honour in St Saviour's church. The targeting of clergymen was certainly no coincidence. They were a group of persons particularly well-suited to be singled out for sowing deterrence. The family of the Methodist Reverend Mylne were 'framed', as they were receiving news; apparently an example was to be made of them. Although the radio found in their house was unworkable, Mylne, his wife and his daughter Vivienne were sent to prison for a year, principally for having refused to give away the names of the other 'circuit people'.[61]

Another extraordinary cleric was the Jesuit padre Charles Rey, a seismologist of international renown who worked at the Highlands observatory, in Jersey. Born in Senegal in 1897, Rey was the son of a French colonial official who had studied at the Jesuit seminary in Jersey from 1917 and who had returned there after some years in Madagascar as a missionary and scientific observer. During the Occupation Rey – one of the few brothers to have remained there – was the 'keeper' of the valuable 200,000 volume library at Maison Saint Louis. Part of Maison Saint Louis was taken over by the Germans as a training college. Naturally, as Rey was a Jesuit, the Germans had a thick dossier on him. But although he was burgled by German soldiers and had one brush with the GFP over his African crystal collection, they never seem to have been willing to take him on. Ironically, Rey, who was running the only meteorological station in the island, was allowed to retain his radio set after the June 1942 confiscation, as this was required to pick up the time signals sent by stations all over the world on special wave bands. Not that Rey would have used this to listen to the BBC, as he was rather expert in fabricating small crystal sets to specifications: some

[60] For an account of Cohu's seven days at Zöschen, see Przemysl Polacek's letter to the British Embassy in Prague, 25 Oct. 1945, in: JAS D/Z Law Officer's Department.

[61] JAS L/C/20/D/9. 'Under the Crooked Cross, Jersey 1940–1945. 4. German Justice', by the Reverend Mylne, post-war.

people wanted them built in the back of their watches or in matchboxes, others in their telephone.[62]

The interpretation of the duties of good Christians was extremely varied. While most clergy and Christian laymen in the islands kept a low profile, there were Channel Islanders who believed that this was a particularly good time to put their beliefs to the test. Some did this by engaging individual Germans in religious and political discussion and drawing them over to their own side. Others took their commitment further and became genuine witnesses in the faith.

In a similar league to Canon Cohu, was Marie Ozanne. A native Guernseywoman and a member of the Salvation Army, Ozanne had come to Guernsey in March 1940, for a holiday with her parents, and was bound to return at the end of the summer. Stranded in the islands by the Occupation, Ozanne had sent her first letter to Feldkommandantur official Dr Reffler, on 19 July 1941. The letter consisted in a plea filing a protest against the disbandment of the Salvation Army and the closure of their halls. A second letter followed four days later. In this she said that it had been a 'great mistake' to have allowed the Germans to go ahead with the closure and that she would reopen the hall at St Sampson. On 26 July Ozanne appeared in uniform at the Nebenstelle office. Inspector Sculpher of the Guernsey police was called and instructed to take into custody the uniform and all the other articles. This order was executed and Ozanne was declared not responsible for her actions. Over the months Ozanne was cautioned several times by the police for having attempted to preach in public, but her letter-writing did not recommence again before August 1942 when she complained about the treatment of the foreign workers. By this time the Germans seem to have finally decided to rid themselves of Ozanne's obstructions. On 31 August the FK ordered that she be medically examined as to her sanity, and either be sent to hospital or be court-martialled. A subsequent medical examination pronounced that she was 'sane and fully responsible', but diagnosed her as a 'religious maniac' whose intention was to get herself arrested so as to be a martyr. In a letter written to the Feldkommandant from prison, on 6 September, she explained her reasons, adding that she did not want to 'take back a single word'. She said that she could not stand by and that she had learnt to love everybody regardless of nationality, but revolted against hatred and oppression. True to the Christian precept of 'love thy enemy' she sent the Feldkommandant her regards and gave rise to the hope that after the war

---

[62] Journalist Mollie Leach ran a story in 1962 claiming that Rey's scientific resistance went further than crystal sets. Allegedly, with the help of an Alsatian radio specialist drafted into the German army, Rey managed to make a set which jammed German radio transmissions. Unfortunately this information is uncorroborated by any other source, see Mollie Leach to Rev. Père Rey S.J., 11 May 1962.

understanding between their nations would improve. Two weeks later, on news of the deportations, she wrote another letter stating the wish that she wanted to go to Germany to be helpful to the people who were being deported. Proceedings against Ozanne were suspended in October, on the grounds that she was 'preoccupied with religious fantasies' and that it was best to ignore her petitions in the future, and she was released, but died in February 1943, presumably as a result of maltreatment received during her imprisonment.[63]

The most creative resistance was that of French artists and stepsisters Lucille Schwob and Suzanne Malherbe.[64] Schwob was born in 1894, to a Jewish publishing family that owned the newspaper and press *La Phare de la Loire* in the city of Nantes. Her attachment to the Anglo-Saxon world started at an early age: in 1906 she was sent to England for schooling, to escape the anti-Semitic environment poisoning France at the time of the Dreyfuss affair, spending her summer holidays in Jersey together with Malherbe. After the First World War both worked in Paris, Schwob as a poet and photographer under the pseudonym 'Claude Cahun'; Malherbe as a graphic artist under the pseudonym 'Marcel Moore'. Although they are widely considered Surrealists because of their close ties with the movement around André Breton, they were perhaps even more important as symbolists. Transcending convention and exploring identity, including sexual and gender identities, was at the centre of Cahun's photographic auto-portraits, collages and photomontages. Having intermittently resided in Jersey since 1922, both left Paris for good and settled at La Roquaise, in St Brelade's Bay, Jersey, in 1937. Both sisters opposed Stalinism as ardently as Fascism, a commitment that went back to their involvement in the Trotskyite *Fédération internationale des artistes indépendants* in Paris. When they were faced with the choice of evacuation in June 1940 they deliberately decided to stay and stand their ground. This was in itself a position rather similar to Christians who believed that the Occupation was a time to put to the test their religious convictions.[65] From 1940 they engaged in small acts of resistance, in particular counterpropaganda aimed at the soldiers, not the islanders. As internationalists and anti-Fascists, they were not germanophobes and they made a particular

[63] IWM JRD.09. Force 135, I (b). Report 'Resistance: Marie Ozanne', 1945; Richard Heaume, 'Marie Ozanne', *The Channel Islands Occupation Review*, 1995 (23), 79–82.

[64] For the following section see Claude Cahun, 'Le muet dans la mêlée' and 'Confidences au miroir', in *Ecrits*, edited by François Leperlier, Paris, 2002; Kristine von Oehsen, 'Claude Cahun'-Published/Unpublished. The Textual Identities of Lucy Schwob 1914–1944', PhD thesis, University of East Anglia, 2003, passim; Jersey Archive, 'Claude Cahun', <http://jerseyheritagetrust.jeron.je/wwwopac.exe?DATABASE=supplier&LANGUAGE=0&DEBUG=0&BRIEF ADAPL=../web/infnam&DETAILADAPL=../web/infnam&%250=2208>, accessed November 2004.

[65] An example for this attitude is the Methodist environment of Nan Le Ruez in Jersey, see *Nan Le Ruez Occupation Diary*, Bradford on Avon, 1994.

point of dissociating Germans from Nazis. Their activity was based on the conviction that there was a potential to bring down to earth soldiers' delusions about the nature of a war in which they and their compatriots were being sacrificed by an abusive regime. The somewhat over-optimistic aim was to lay the base for mutiny or resistance within the army. The resistance work they produced over these years has few parallels. Their parish, St Brelade's, was an ideal base, as it housed the German military cemetery. They planted black crosses on the graves with the inscription 'For you the war has come to an end'[66] and placed a placard above the altar reading 'Jesus is great but Hitler is greater, for Jesus died for men whereas men died for Hitler'. Naturally they kept their radio in 1942, writing news bulletins, slogans, tracts and short dialogues between soldiers on thin cigarette paper. Thousands of these were deposited together with collages under the pen name 'The soldier without name'[67], in pockets, briefcases, parked staff cars and between the pages of magazines. Until 1942 they also sent mail through the post to houses occupied by officers. In 1943 the authorship was extended to 'The soldier without name and his comrades'[68] to give the illusion of a large network. This worked so well that for a long time after their arrest the GFP did not believe that the two women had acted alone, suspecting an wider organisation, possibly led by a German or Central European émigré. Malherbe's fluency in German – a fact they assiduously hid – was one of the reasons for the power of their work. This included a rewrite of Heinrich Heine's famous poem *Loreley*. Another text is titled 'Kraft durch Vezweifelung [*sic*]', a parody of the 'Kraft durch Freude' movement. The poem 'HITLER leads us' offers a good short example of their style:

HITLER führt uns	HITLER leads us
HITLER führt uns…	HITLER leads us…
GOEBBELS spricht für uns…	GOEBBELS speaks for us…
GOERING frisst für uns…	GOERING eats for us…
LEY trinkt für uns…	LEY drinks for us…
HIMMLER?…Himmler ermordet für uns…	HIMMLER?…Himmler murders for us…

Only known as 'the French ladies' to the local population, Schwob and Malherbe kept largely to themselves, attracting as little attention as possible. Schwob was concerned about being found out as a Jew through her Jewish sounding pen name and had therefore reverted back to her original name. Interviewed by the Feldgendarmerie in March 1944, ostensibly to give details

---

[66] 'Für Sie ist der Krieg zu Ende'
[67] 'Der Soldat ohne Namen'
[68] 'Der Soldat ohne Namen und seine Kameraden'

about her name and family background, she allayed suspicion by responding that she was an orphan from Alsace – where the name Schwob was common – who had resided in Jersey for 30 years. A house search produced no results. By July, however, the GFP traced the source of the paper they were using and identified them on a bus trip out of town. Finally, on 25 July 1944, they struck the final blow. The exchange of dialogue between the two women and the German policemen, related in a subsequent prison letter from Malherbe to Schwob, is not without its merits: four men, among them Karl, Erich and an unnamed third presented themselves at La Rocquaise to begin a search, effected in the 'most proper manner'. Not that Malherbe gives her tormentors the benefit of a flattering description: Erich was as a 'character with jug ears' and the 'face of a degenerate' , only saved from looking like a 'congenital idiot' because he actually had a neck. The unnamed third is simply described as a 'gangster américain'. As the search unfolds, Malherbe, cigarette in hand, is looking on, knowing only too well that it is a matter of time before the other two fumbling through Schwob's bedroom are bound to find the typewriter and the incriminating suitcase which, fatally, had not been taken to its hiding place that day. To cut the silence she quips: 'If you told me what you are looking for, we'd have finished sooner', to which Karl – with the look of someone just having had 'a nail driven up his backside' – responds: 'Thank you, I prefer to find it myself'. Three minutes later there is the inevitable 'Karl! Wir haben es alles!' from the other room. Now the inspector says in a severe tone: 'You know what we have found?' (pronouncing 'have' like 'haf'). This remark, later qualified as 'stupid', earns him the response: 'Of course I know it. I'm not an idiot'. After the typewriter and the wireless are discovered Malherbe tries her luck again, pre-empting Karl with: 'May I tell my sister to come up and change? I suppose you want us to go with you?' Karl, whose show she had stolen, responds, somewhat irritated: 'Yes, you will sleep in jail tonight'.[69]

Both women had made a suicide pact for the case of arrest. Overdosing on gardenal, they survived, however, and awoke one week after their arrest, in their prison cells. Paradoxically, this attempt to end their lives probably had the opposite effect, as during the intervening time they could not be court-martialled and transported off the island to a fate similar to that of Le Druillenec and Gould. In this respect they were extremely lucky, only having been discovered by the GFP in the last week of July 1944. By the time they regained consciousness and could be interrogated, the last boats had left for France and the islands were cut off. Unstinting in their attitude, the two women used their trial, which took place in November, to propagate their views. The first charge of listening to the radio carried a long jail sentence. The second charge, inciting troops to rebellion,

[69] JAS JHT/1995/00045/22. Malherbe to Schwob, 12 Nov 1944.

carried the death sentence, prompting Schwob to ask in court, with characteristic sang-froid, which sentence they were to serve first. This wasn't their first attempt to turn the tide and followed on top of rather embarrassing asides as to the quality of the defence counsel and the principles under which the court was operating. Although this revealed knowledge of recent radio news, Schwob could not resist the temptation to catch them off their guard, asking them the hypothetical question what they would do if at that very moment they were called upon to sit in judgement of German women in Aachen who had done the some thing they had done.[70] Their death sentence was finally commuted after an intervention of the Bailiff of Jersey who argued that no death sentence against women had been executed for time immemorial and that this was susceptible to upset the local population. The women may have also benefited from the established principle that no death sentences against islanders were ever executed in the islands during the Occupation. Whatever the reason, considering the humiliation they had visited upon the mighty occupying power, it was a miracle that they were spared.[71] After liberation in May 1945, they returned to their home in St Brelade. Although they tried to recover their belongings, the majority of their extraordinary art collection, including works by Max Ernst and other expressionists, was either destroyed or looted. Although there was no manifest maltreatment, Schwob never fully recovered from the deprivation of her nine months in prison and died, prematurely, in Jersey, in 1954.

Administrative resistance

Despite the official dogma of 'no resistance', there were a number of island officials who gave this dogma a different interpretation: for them 'no resistance' meant 'no armed resistance', but not acquiescence, which could still leave open a large spectrum of options; that is if one was prepared to jump the fence and use one's position. That genuine administrative resistance was possible, however, is demonstrated by the case of Dr Robert Noel McKinstry. Born in Northern Ireland in 1892, McKinstry had arrived in Jersey in 1929 and was appointed Medical Officer of Health in 1939. His wartime efforts and successes in preventive medicine have been documented in a previous chapter, but he was also

---

[70] Aachen was the first major German city to have been taken by the Anglo-Americans after a heavy battle, at the time of the trial.

[71] Judge Harmsen also indicated that a Swiss representative was present for the trial. He added that the plea for mercy was sent to Berlin where it was okayed and then returned to the island. The rescue of the two women is all the more astounding as by this stage of the war not only soldiers but also ordinary citizens in Germany were being routinely executed for sabotage (Wehrkraftzersetzung), for much less than what the two women had done. One cannot quite escape the impression that the court had 'caved in', see IWM Misc. 2826 189/2. Interview with Judge Harmsen, n.d.

engaged in other activities which took on a distinctly more political allure and reflected his centre-left and anti-Fascist views. McKinstry was one of the key persons in the rescue effort of Russian escapee slave labourers for whom he provided, not only medical help and assistance in finding shelter, but also with false IDs and ration cards. In 1944–45 this type of help was extended to Jersey people on the run.[72] One of the other high points of McKinstry's resistance career was his undoing of a German plan to evacuate the Jersey Mental Hospital in St Saviour, in spring 1942. That the Germans were intent on going ahead with this plan is documented through a letter written by Knackfuss to the division, in January 1942. This letter stated that 'for reasons of population policy' the removal of the 450 'mentally ill' in the islands was 'particularly desirable and already arranged'.[73] This was somewhat premature. Although the Mental Institution in Guernsey had to relocate in December 1941, as the building was taken over by the division as a military hospital, there is no indication that any of mentally ill were sent off the islands.[74] In Jersey resistance went even further, to denying the Germans the first step of relocating the patients. On 25 February 1942 McKinstry wrote to the President of the Department of Public Health informing them that Dr Blackwenn had requested, for the first time, a report on the possibility of evacuating the Mental Hospital. McKinstry was alarmed over this matter 'of very serious import' which he felt should be 'placed before the Superior Council' for comment.[75] The response was almost immediate: only three days later the Bailiff of Jersey, on behalf of the Council, wrote to the Feldkommandant urging him to consider 'the disastrous consequences which must inevitably follow the removal of so large a number of persons of unsound mind from the only place in the island suitable for their detention'. Coutanche must have sensed the direction of Dr Blackwenn's initiative, for he resisted, on principle, any suggestion of removal to an alternative location in the island. To the thought at the back of some people's heads, to remove them from island, he responded in uncharacteristically sharp manner that this was, 'a step which most assuredly would lead to the death of many of them and the suffering of most grievous discomfort by the remainder. In addition, the shock to the feelings of the relatives and to the inhabitants of the island generally would, it is feared, produce the most serious consequences.'[76] McKinstry did not make abhorrence

[72] Louise Willmot, 'Noel McKinstry', *The Channel Islands Occupation Review*, 2003 (31), 25–30.

[73] BA-MA. RH 26/319/8. KTB 319. I.D., Anl. 179. FK 515 to 319 I.D., betr. Abbeförderung der nicht eingeborenen Inselbevölkerung, Bez. Schreiben v. 15 Dezember 1941, 23 Jan 1942.

[74] BA-MA. RH 26/319/8. KTB 319. I.D., Anl. 155. Bericht des Divisionsarztes, 31 Dec 1941.

[75] B/A/W66/3. Letter of McKinstry to the President of Department of Public Health, 25 Feb 1942.

[76] B/A/W66/3. Bailiff's Chambers to FK, 28 Feb 42; see also commendation of Dr Le Brocq's management of the Jersey Mental Hospital by the Superintendent of St James Hospital, Portsmouth, 4 Sept 1945.

of illegality a convenient screen for cowardice. Such was his involvement that historian Louise Willmot wrote in a recent article for the Channel Islands Occupation Review that he 'was linked with every major form of organised resistance' and sustained 'channels of communication between disparate individuals and groups'.[77] Another good example of administrative resistance was Jersey deputy Edward Le Quesne who, it seems, had an axe to grind with the Attorney General, Duret Aubin. In his occupation diary he cites several cases where he tried to frustrate Duret Aubin's designs: in September 1943 he undercut a news embargo, on the instigation of the Attorney General, designed to prevent a 'sympathetic demonstration' at the funeral of American airmen found at Bonne Nuit bay; in January 1944 he entered a successful protest against the fact that the paid police in St Helier, which came under the Attorney General's authority, was assisting the Germans in finding the addresses of shorthand typists.[78] As has been demonstrated throughout, Bailiff Coutanche also made a better figure than many of the men working under him: he threw in whatever political weight he could muster on several occasions, petitioning the Germans to commute death sentences and furnishing escapees with letters to the British government that outlined the food situation. Neither was he heedless of the plight of the slave labourers. In his memoirs he details a talk with von Schmettow on this subject; and in spring 1945 he took the initiative to approach the Red Cross for permission to distribute additional food parcels to forced workers remaining in the island.

Repression

A number of German courts were operating in the Channel Islands. In Jersey the majority of civilian cases were dealt with by the court of the Feldkommandantur 515, whereas islanders in German employ were tried by air force, navy or army courts. Once more Guernsey residents in trouble with German authority seem to have gotten a rougher deal, as they were tried by the court of the 319th Infantry Division. Shorter terms of up to three months were executed in the islands, but longer sentences were served in continental prisons. The Germans also brought their own police forces and intelligence service to the islands. While the military intelligence people of the Abwehr only came over from France on a few missions, the Feldgendarmerie and the Geheime Feldpolizei (Secret Field Police - GFP) were permanent features. Although there was no Gestapo as such in the islands, the GFP included professional policemen

[77] Louise Willmot, 'Noel McKinstry', *The Channel Islands Occupation Review*, 2003 (31), 28–9.
[78] Le Quesne, Edward, *The occupation of Jersey day by day*, Jersey, 1999, entries of 24 Sept 1943 and 12 Jan 1944.

and, occasionally, Gestapo members in their ranks who had been drafted into the forces.[79] These German policemen were a far cry from an elite force. The Reverend Ord relates an excellent example of the 'one-track mind' in his diary: a house was being searched for black market food – because the orders were to search for food – and not for the wireless which was standing on the floor during the search; in the end nothing was found, the Germans conducting the search apologised and took their leave.[80] How far they would have gotten without the precise information included in denunciations is more than doubtful.

Stella Perkins' mother and aunt were Russian-born and both took an active role in the effort to help Russian escapees in Jersey. Had the German police wanted to solve this 'problem' once and for all, then this is where they would have had to start. As things went, however, neither of the women was seriously importuned. When their house was searched one day this was done in such a haphazard way that a Russian fugitive named 'Michael', who was present in one of the rooms at the time, sneaked past the German search party and escaped onto the street. Not only were the policemen singularly unsuccessful in their search, but they had also ignored standard procedure which was to post someone at the entrance. It was the combination of doing some things not exactly by the book and other things exactly by the book which doomed many of their ventures to failure.[81] Some of the contradictions with regard to their professionalism become clear when we study the history of this branch. GFP Group 131 was formed in Jena, in November 1939. The personnel were not volunteers, but men called up according to their linguistic abilities and experience abroad: businessmen, lawyers, schoolmasters, priests. They were trained in Cologne until May 1940 and took part in the Western Campaign, first taking up office in Amsterdam and Harlem, and then moving on to Antwerp and Ghent. In 1941 they were transferred to the GFP post in Dinard, of which Jersey and Guernsey were outposts. Early on there were two GFP groups in the Channel Islands: one group had military tasks, Group 131 surveyed the civilian population. Members of the latter circulated between Guernsey and Jersey and back to HQ on the mainland. The only criminal case investigated in 1940 was a rape in which customs officers were implicated. Otherwise there were only a few cases of carrier pigeons. In late 1941 a case against the former British Consul in St Malo, Ferrers, was opened. Ferrers, who resided in Jersey with his wife, was arrested because his wife had been wearing an RAF badge on her evening gown while dining at the Ommaroo Hotel. The then head of the GFP branch, Steinberger, was asked by another officer to persuade Ferrers that his wife

[79] Gessner, Klaus, 'Geheime Feldpolizei – Die Gestapo der Wehrmacht', in: Mallmann, Klaus-Michael/Paul, Gerhard (Ed.), *Die Gestapo – Mythos und Realität*, Darmstadt 1995, 492–507.
[80] JAS The diary of the Revered Douglas Ord, entry of 18 Jan 1943.
[81] IWM Misc. 2826 189/2 (Tape 4446 o/L). Interview with Stella Perkins, n.d.

should abstain. This was followed by an argument between the couple and Steinberger in the hall, at the end of which both were arrested and imprisoned in France.[82] The heyday of the GFP was probably the V-sign campaign of 1941 which was viewed with the utmost gravity, and pursued through vigorous investigations. The search for a scapegoat produced numerous denunciations and the GFP toured schools to issue warnings to the children. A further period of activity came in 1942 when they assisted in deportations. After D-Day the hunt for radios was somewhat intensified and again the denunciation letters were put to good effect. Other cases the GFP were involved in was the 1942 murder case of the German physician Goebel, in Sark. Suspicion had first fallen on islanders, but it was soon determined that a German soldier was the culprit. There were also a number of corruption cases: one official sent by the Goebbels ministry, Goettmann, was arrested for larceny and sentenced to three years, one OT leader received six years for selling Wehrmacht property on the black market. In February 1943 there was a case of seventeen Frenchmen who had attempted to evade the compulsory labour scheme by sailing to Ireland, and who were picked up off the Channel Islands coast.[83]

The 'face' of the GFP in Jersey was a man called Karl-Heinz Wölfle who spoke fluent English with a Canadian accent. Although a subaltern NCO, many islanders believed that he, and not Bode, was in charge. Wölfle admitted having contributed to the 'Gestapo myth' himself by introducing himself to people as 'Wolf, of the Gestapo', a rather effective sales pitch which is still going strong after sixty years. Wölfle was born in 1905, in Berlin, he grew up in Vienna and then left for Canada in 1923. Until 1935 he worked in London (Ontario) as a city clerk and then returned to Germany to take up a managing post in the firm of his father-in-law. When he was called up in 1939, his knowledge of English was identified as a key asset and he was sent to the postal censorship department in Frankfurt. Later he probably opted for a training course where he found himself with 300 former export managers, lawyers, priests, teachers and others who had lived abroad. Their pedigree was very similar to his: a good general education and foreign languages. After a short spell in Cologne Wölfle was sent to the Channel Islands in December 1940 or January 1941. At that time he was in charge of the GFP in both islands, but then went back to mainland Europe. He did not return until April 1943, and by then Bode was in charge. After the war Wölfle made various claims, some of them bordering on the ridiculous,

---

[82] It is indicative that a Colonel Vierbahn, of Army HQ in St Lô, who visited the islands with Colonel Schmundt, of the Führer Headquarters, in November 1941, criticised the handling of the Ferrers case on the grounds that Hitler 'wished to deal with the Channel Islands population with the utmost tact and leniency' and that the islands should be differentiated from Northern France, IWM JRD.09. Force 135, I (b), History of the GFP in the Channel Islands, 1945.

[83] IWM JRD.09. Force 135, I (b), 'History of the GFP in the Channel Islands', 1945.

grotesque, or both: he tried to sell the fact that he had grown up in 'democratic countries' and had been active in the Canadian Boy Scouts movement. His request to join the party in 1937 had allegedly been turned down because he was 'politically unreliable' due to his activities in Canada. Worse, of course, than Wölfle's stories was the naïveté (or plain madness) of those British officers who thought it was a good idea to task him with the re-education of German PoWs in a camp in England, while British intelligence sources were describing the man as a 'nasty piece of work'. What we also know for certain is that Wölfle had also been 'up to his ears' in the black market, partnering with a well-known Jersey butcher. He was also the drinking buddy of Mr Moyse, the fallen angel of the Jersey insurance business, and presumably a number of other islanders.[84]

In Guernsey the GFP resided at Mon Plaisir, St Jacques, a country house one-and-a-half miles from St Peter Port. They had relocated to this quiet location after an air raid on a radar installation in the vicinity of their former base, Les Terres, in June 1944. When the British investigators arrived in May 1945 they found Red Cross tins in the possession of one Inspector Jassner, an ex-CID from Elbing, East Prussia. Jassner was the only professional policeman and he left no doubt about his contempt for the other men in the unit whom he entrusted with no independent work and who were constantly scrutinised. Einert, the most active and successful of the team, had been a businessman before the war. He was a well-known hunter of illicit radios in the island, but stated that enquiries of this nature become fewer as the end drew near. The most interesting of these characters was certainly Spohr, the former missionary, who had arrived in the Channel Islands way back in 1941. When the British investigators searched the GFP hide-out they found Spohr's bedroom stocked with theological literature while notes for an exhaustive monograph on a text from Timothy littered the table. When questioned how he reconciled his religious calling with the duty of a secret policeman he declared that he had always preserved his conscience. He is reported to have reacted with genuine distress on being shown photos of Belsen. Spohr had lived in Southern China from 1929 to 1935, during which time he had joined the Nazi party in Hongkong. He stated that he had wanted to believe what Hitler was saying about the fundamental role of Christian religion in the new Germany, but became disillusioned when he returned. He was reprimanded twice for his politics, but this did not prevent him from being drafted into the GFP, much to his surprise. Spohr held on to the belief that God had subjected him to a particularly trying test and that he had to help in the Christian spirit wherever he could. While certainly no martyr to the cause, he was not enthusiastic about his task and received criticism for his meagre results

---

[84] PRO WO 208 4643. Wölfle, Niederschrift, 30 Apr 1946; PRO WO 311 11. Statement of Karl-Heinz Wölfle taken by Capt Kent, 6 Jul 1945; also Michael Ginns, 'Wolff of the Gestapo', *The Channel Islands Occupation Review*, 2003 (31), 112–125.

and openly professed anglophilia. The British were not too far off the mark when they described him as a man with 'a complex of deep religious convictions and the dumbest apathy towards a tyrannous political regime he professed to dislike'. This also seems to emerge from his incongruous lamentations about a Fräulein K., an ethnic German from Yugoslavia, whom he first suspected of having sold her soul to the British intelligence service and with whom he later seems to have had an affair burdening him with ever more guilt.[85] Overall, morale in the unit had slackened sometime in 1943 as the realisation grew that there was nothing of a major security or espionage interest in the confines of the island. The only high ranking officer to have ever visited the island was Dr Berger of the Einsatzstab Reichsleiter Rosenberg who came twice in 1941 to supervise the dissolution of the Masonic lodges. There were no repeats of the early scares of 1940 when one commando raid followed another. However, respect for the British Intelligence Service never faltered and was manifest in the 'pathetic and deluded eagerness to discover the ramifications of an omnipotent Secret Service in the most innocent circumstances'. Einert's bedside reading was Dennis Wheatley's *File on Bolitho Blane*, a clue-stuffed crime file complete with red herrings and the like. Towards the end of the Occupation an attitude of 'live and let live' prevailed which considered pointless all attempts to stem the black market or faltering morale.[86]

The German police force was not the elite force it was sometimes made out to be after the war. Besides the minute number of regular paid informers who were of public notoriety, a great deal of its efficiency was owed to voluntary informers from the population. Money rewards of up to £100 paid for the apprehension of 'offenders' certainly had a role to play. Some made denunciation part of their business practice: one Channel Islander, Raymond J., approached German officers hinting that he knew where people had hidden wirelesses. J.'s condition for surrendering names was for the Germans to shield his illegal cattle slaughtering, throwing in the additional promise of a share of the meat as an extra. In one reported case the information J. gave was accurate, in others he gave false information.[87] Equally as powerful as lucre, however, were private motives; the desire to hurt, gain power over or 'get rid of' an unwanted neighbour, rival, husband or wife.[88] Besides ancient or more recent grudges, often rather petty in nature ('If I had to hand in my radio, why should someone else be allowed to keep his'), there was something more systematic about denunciation. The sad

---

[85] IWM JRD.04. Written statement by Spohr (GFP), 1945.

[86] IWM JRD.09. Force 135, I (b), 'GFP in Guernsey', 20 May 1945.

[87] IWM JRD.09. Fc 135 I (b). Document signed W Einart, 20 May 1945. The link between illegal economic practices and denunciation has also been proven for other occupied countries, see Paul Sanders, *Histoire du marché noir 1940–1946*, Paris, 2001.

[88] See Gellately, Robert, *The Gestapo and German Society. Enforcing Racial Policy 1933–1945*, Oxford, 1990.

truth is that many people did not consider the changed atmosphere in which they were living. Some also underestimated the danger, disregarded simple security measures or engaged in loose talk. The Reverend Ord commented about a woman who – as late as January 1943 – still was more or less openly passing on news in a shop, with a clear description of the source. His wry comment was:

> We have evidently failed after two and a half years of living among spies and sneaks to acquire the technique of self-adjustment to such amenities.[89]

How many conversations like this fell on less forgiving ears? To Ord this was a matter of 'old habits die hard', the essential pre-war freedom of speech and culture of gossip characteristic to a small community could not be driven out of people. It took until 1944 for people to really adjust and change their ways.

But there is an even more insidious element to denunciation than 'loose talk'. The fatal change in atmosphere was precisely that once collective reprisals for the acts of individuals had been forced upon the community, once the 'greater good' doctrine was common knowledge, it was only a small step to a culture of fear, and denunciations. The disposition was magnified by the 1942 'Order for the Protection of the Occupying Authorities' which bound the local authorities to reporting all offences against Occupation law. This is certainly no invention in order to exculpate Channel Islanders. When the German authorities were searching for Bernard Turpin, a Channel Islander who escaped from the Jersey prison in August 1944, they criticised the attitude of the local authorities for their lax attitude and lack of energy in apprehending escapees. The message, addressed to the Bailiff by Heider, the successor of Knackfuss[90] could not have been clearer:

> In regard to the local notice dated 10th December 1942 (i.e. the order for the Protection of the Occupying Authorities), not only do individuals make themselves liable to penalties for concealing strangers, but parishes also may be liable to collective penalties, as I pointed out to the Constables in March of this year in the case of Basil Martin in St Martin.[91]

The reference to 'Basil Martin', a Russian OT labourer who had lived in the parish of St Martin before his recapture is highly interesting.[92] Not only does this case mirror the case of Feodor Buryi in St Ouen, but, more importantly, that the

---

[89] JAS Diaries of the Reverend Ord, 3 Jan 1943.

[90] Knackfuss was court-martialled and relieved of his post for 'defeatist remarks', in 1944.

[91] JAS B/A/W50/165. Platzkommandantur I to the Bailiff of Jersey, re search for Bernard Turpin, 15 Aug 1944.

[92] Basil (or probably Vasili) was absorbed into the community to the point that he played in the football team; 'Martin' was a pseudonym, see Leslie Sinel, *Occupation Diary*, op. cit., entries of 31 Jan and 6 Mar 1944.

local police were, indeed, dragging their feet. Although no collective measures were taken, threats were probably enough to make some law-abiding citizens buckle. Anyone could become a potential informer in such an environment, believing that this was in the ultimate interest of the community. Reality had all of a sudden become very complex. The only antidote in such an environment was discretion: neighbours could be expected to ignore or look the other way as a long as a stranger was not a permanent and visible feature of the scene. And it was good not to expect too much even from sympathetic Germans either, as this would have placed them in a impossible situation.[93] Indiscretion, on the other hand, evaporated the rules of privacy, involving the community as a whole. And this was dangerous. People in the neighbourhood were now potential accomplices to a punishable offence. This would have worked wonders on the anxious, the nervous and the fearful and there were multiple factors which would have contributed to such dispositions during the Occupation. Some may have decided that they had no obligations – as they had never been asked their opinion.

None of the discretely working escapee 'networks' was ever detected or compromised. Stella Perkins makes clear in her interviews that her family was not reckless and valued security. They realised very well that their situation was too exposed to shelter escapees and therefore limited themselves to becoming the 'placement bureau' which arranged hiding places. Many islanders knew of the existence of the two Russian ladies, to whom many of the escapees were despatched. The fact that they were never caught was not merely the result of an unprofessional German police force with particularly unbalanced priorities, but that when it came to the crunch many islanders were prepared to hold tight: the conspiracy of silence was stronger and more developed than the culture of denunciation. It also demonstrates the importance of basic security measures and the need to limit talk to the bare necessities and people one could trust. Again the distinct island environment ensured that people were bound to know more about each other than in larger continental countries, and stringency was *de rigueur*. In this sense the pre-war holiday island could very well become a variation on Sartre's *L'enfer*. Some of the resisters who were caught in the net, such as Canon Cohu or Louisa Gould, had either made no secret of their opposition or had been too liberal with trust and security. In an interview Bob Le Sueur stated that he had warned Harold Le Druillenec that it was dangerous how his sister was going about things – Bill was known throughout the parish of St Ouen and had never been moved. Le Druillenec, however, replied that the Germans were simply 'too thick' to ever find out about Bill.[94] This is not a case of blaming the victim for his misfortune, but rather an admonishment to never

[93] See the case of Dr Woelken mentioned in Michael Frowd (et al.), 'A Russian in hiding – Feodor ("Bill") Burriy', *The Channel Islands Occupation Review*, 1999 (27), 66–7.

[94] Author's interview with Bob Le Sueur, 7 Dec 2004.

underestimate one's enemies. In some cases, people were faulted by their judgement.

Persecution

In 2003 Jersey physiotherapist Albert Bedane was the first Channel Islander to be recognised by Yad Vashem as 'Righteous Among the Nations'.[95] Bedane's sheltering of Mary Richardson, a Dutch Jewess on the run from the Jersey police in 1943, points to the case of the two Jewish 'U-boats'[96] in Jersey. The other Jew who had submerged and was hidden by a local woman, Dorothea Weber, also in 1943, was Hedwig Bercu, a Romanian national.

For a very long time the exact story of the Jews in the Channel Islands was shrouded in oblivion, until the discovery of a number of important files including the diary of the Jersey Aliens Officer, Clifford Orange, in the 1990s.[97] One of the great omissions of practically all the historiographers of the Channel Islands Occupation, up until then the idea of what happened to this group was that they had been registered by the authorities but had all survived unscathed. How and why was of no further interest; and that there were foreign Jews among this population was virtually unknown. *Guardian* journalist Madeleine Bunting was the first to open the can of worms, muddling her way through the materials and stirring up an immediate controversy in the Channel Islands with an appendix on the Jews in her book *The Model Occupation*. Quality of research aside, more than anything else the instant outrage demonstrated how much knowledge of the subject had been repressed during the preceding five decades. This state of affairs continued for some time, in characteristic stalemate and interspersed with acerbic press coverage and the intercession of self-styled 'experts', in both the UK and the islands. Only after publication of further research by a Jersey resident, Frederick Cohen, were the waves calmed.[98] This was due principally to the quality and depth of Cohen's evidence, but also his offer of an exit strategy to the dispute through his unbiased and dispassionate matter-of-fact style.

As part of the overall administration of the military governor in occupied France, anti-Jewish measures in the Channel Islands followed the pattern of

[95] Bedane's resistance credentials already appeared in the British report based on escapee information mentioned in an earlier footnote, see PRO HO 22237. Report no 2510(S), 'Jersey Reliable Personalities. Further interrogation of three Jersey escapees', 27 Nov 1944.

[96] The term was much used in Berlin where several thousand Jews thus survived the war.

[97] Frederick Cohen, *The Jews in the Channel Islands during the Occupation 1940–1945*, Jersey, 2000 (2nd edition), 12–3.

[98] The sub-chapter is based on Frederick Cohen's *The Jews in the Channel Islands during the Occupation 1940–1945*, Jersey, 2000 (2nd edition); other materials or special references are indicated with footnotes.

France and were enacted in orders, most of which – with the significant exception of the eighth order in Jersey – were registered into the laws of the islands.[99] Caution is necessary, however, as anti-Jewish policy in France was being conducted from two ends: the German and the official French side. The situation in the Channel Islands mirrored German measures in France; but in notable exception to France, there was no Vichy government to legislate and institutionalise persecution through a Statut Juif, a Commissariat Général des Questions Juives or an Institut d'Etudes Juives, all of which exerted additional pressure on the French Jews. This was a political manoeuvre of the Vichy government to maintain leverage, a point worth bearing in mind when making comparisons.

The one dozen orders against the Jews covered a number of discriminatory measures. The first was approved in October 1940. Its principal requirement was that all islanders with more than two Jewish grandparents had to register as Jews. The second order soon followed in its tracks, in November 1940, and was mainly aimed at liquidating Jewish economic undertakings: registered Jews had to state and were dispossessed of their business interests; managers or administrators were called upon to declare the part of Jewish capital in local businesses. The third order in mid-1941 extended the definition of 'Jew' to people with two grandparents, under the condition that they belonged to the Jewish religious community or were married to a Jew; benefit of doubt was officially eliminated in undecided cases where someone belonged (or had belonged to the community). Most economic activities were now also being declared 'off limits' for registered Jews, showering unemployment and destitution upon this group of people. The next significant orders – in the main curtailing freedom of movement – followed in 1942. The order which stands out from amongst these is the eighth order, the requirement for Jews to wear the six-pointed yellow star inscribed 'Jew'. Bailiff Coutanche decided that this was 'a measure too far' and opposed its registration, thus adding Jersey to the ranks of those European countries – such as Denmark – which opposed, on principle, the introduction of this vital step in singling out the Jews for persecution and extermination. The reasons of the Bailiff are still not known with absolute certainty, but it is most probable that he realised that branding the Jews in this manner was an important threshold which went against his ethical and political instincts. That Coutanche was not an anti-Semite is documented by his defence of the Jews in an interview with Professor Karl Heinz Pfeffer, in September 1941.[100] In

---

[99] The origin of the orders clearly emerges in some of their stipulations, such as the decree that Jews who had fled from the occupied zone to the unoccupied zone (of France) during the German invasion were prohibited from returning there. This was irrelevant in the Channel Islands.

[100] The episode is detailed in the preceding chapter. Cohen also reminds us that this was the time of the radio confiscation when, after an anonymous letter signed 'the British Patriots' which

Guernsey, however, the eighth order passed unopposed, on 30 June 1942.[101] Here the only principled intervention seems to have occurred before, when Jurat Abraham Lainé, an important member of the Controlling Committee, refused to give his consent to the first order.[102]

If it were for mere numbers, the story of the Jewish civilian residents in the occupied Channel Islands would pale in comparison to the tragedy of the several thousand-strong population of slave workers – a population which incidentally also included Jews. What is more, of the eighteen[103] individuals who registered themselves as Jews in both Bailiwicks the majority survived the war. The continuing problem with the Jews in the Channel Islands lies rather more in the fact that while the island authorities could easily wash their hands in innocence over the slave workers – after all it was not they who had brought them to the islands – they could not deny some responsibility for these civilian residents.

The high proportional number of survivors – in the past cited as an exculpatory device – had nothing to do with efforts made by the authorities, but was due to the victims' British or Commonwealth nationality, or their marriage to British or Commonwealth nationals which made them potential exchange material. This is cast into relief by the fate of Jews with the 'wrong' passports, which was as grim as that of Jews on the Continent. The most exemplary case in this respect was that of three single women with German and Polish nationality – Therese Steiner, Auguste Spitz and Marianne Grünfeld – who were deported from Guernsey to France in April 1942 and then, three months later, to Auschwitz where they perished. All three had fled persecution in Central Europe in the late 1930s, but had been unable to evacuate to England in 1940 under the terms of the Aliens act.[104]

---

accused the Jersey authorities of collaboration with the Germans, pressure from the population was starting to build up. Considering the pressure Coutanche was under in summer 1945 to explain the measures against the Jews to the British, it is unlikely that his career would have survived had a Jersey Jew actually had to wear the yellow star, Cohen, op. cit., 41, footnote 51.

[101] Cohen, op. cit., 41. As far as the islands were concerned the order had no effect, as no Jew there ever had to wear the star. The matter was superseded when the Channel Islands Jews were sent to internment camps in 1943, as the SS seem to have passed over the matter, most probably on the grounds of nationality.

[102] The episode is referenced in Sherwill's unpublished memoirs, cited in Cohen, op. cit., 80; Lainé was acting Vice-president of the Controlling Committee and stood in for Leale at meetings, see Island Archives. Ken Lewis diary. Lainé's objection had no practical effect on the promulgation of the order.

[103] The total number of Jews in the islands was higher – anywhere between thirty and fifty. A significant number of Jews (e.g. Mary Richardson and Lucille Schwob) preferred not to register, actively hiding their Jewish origin; Richardson lied about her birthplace which she gave as British Guyana and stated her maiden name as Algernon (instead of Olvenich), Cohen, op. cit., 72–78.

[104] Cohen, op .cit., passim.

Another now defunct stratagem was the claim that no British or British-related Jew ever came to harm. If by 'no harm' was meant that they spent a peaceful life in their homes, this certainly is inaccurate. As one can imagine, many of the registered Jews were those who were either too elderly or too ill to evacuate. Neither were they the most affluent section of the island Jews. A number of these lives ended in suicides or early deaths. In addition, most of the island Jews, regardless of nationality, were deported to internment camps, in February 1943. This deportation of civilians followed a British commando raid on Sark, on 3 October 1942, which had come to the attention of Hitler and the German High Command. They then decided that not all 'unreliable elements' had been removed from the islands in the September deportation of the non-native British and ordered that further categories of islanders be readied for removal to internment. These 'undesirables' and 'useless eaters' included, apart from the remaining Jews, Freemasons, former officers and reserve officers, clergy, the 'politically suspect', persons with previous convictions, young men without 'useful employment', leading public figures and wealthy people susceptible to exert anti-German influence plus a number of Sark inhabitants. The island Jews were being deported with their families, mostly British nationals and only a few exceptions were granted on medical grounds.[105] For a Jew, regardless of nationality, it was wise to keep a low profile, even in an internment camp.[106] As is made clear by a number of cases, the path from internment to concentration camp – and vice versa – was a short one. Two Anglo-Italian non-Jewish internees, father and son Rossi, had this experience in 1944. Their tragedy was to have successfully argued their way out of Kreuzburg internment camp, by claiming to be Italians, following their arrival in early 1943, but to then have insisted on being sent back to Jersey instead of accepting a German offer to go to Italy – which to these non-native British men was a foreign country. When the tides of war turned in autumn 1943 they were picked up by the Gestapo and sent to Blechhammer, one of the Auschwitz satellite camps. While the father Rossi survived, his son, Marcel, died at Flossenbürg in 1945.[107] One of the Channel Islands Jews interned in Germany, John Finkelstein, had a similar fate. A former government official in the colonial administration of Egypt who had retired to the Channel Islands in the 1930s, Finkelstein was a Romanian

---

[105] Cohen, op. cit., 59–60. In one case a Jewish man from Jersey scheduled for internment in Germany did not take his prescribed medication in order to spare his family this ordeal.

[106] That she made an attempt to attract as little attention to herself as possible emerges from the diaries of Jerseywoman Esther Pauline Lloyd. In one entry she makes a clear reference to the camp gossiping which could be detrimental; Lloyd also was critical about Mrs Duquemin, one of the other Guernsey Jews who, she felt, was overexposing herself and the small group of Jews, cited in Cohen, op.cit., 65.

[107] Paul Sanders, *The Ultimate Sacrifice*, op. cit., 90–2; PRO HO 144/22833. Letter of W C Duncan, Liverpool to Miss Thornton, 23 Oct 1944.

national. This country's anti-Jewish policy was extremely ambiguous, even contradictory. Evocative of the position is Romanian responsibility for some of the worst pogroms of Jews of the entire war, in Bessarabia and Odessa in 1941; at the same time they did not concede to deportations of Jews from Romania. Finkelstein was taken by the Gestapo from Laufen internment camp, at about the same time in late 1943 when the Germans finally made good on their threats against Romanian Jews in Nazi-controlled Europe, whose repatriation to the homeland they had demanded repeatedly.[108] He spent the remainder of the war in various concentration camps, surviving Buchenwald and managing to make his way back to Jersey after the war. [109]

Sorcerer's apprentices

The view prevalent for many decades was that once the German imposed a measure, it was impossible for the occupied to countermand this in any way. This interpretation has been revised in recent years, under the weight of evidence showing that the authorities were not entirely powerless onlookers and, indeed, had some discretion in the implementation of measures. Firstly, one must ask why the authorities registered measures against the Jews at all. Wasn't the consternation over this measure in the civilian quarters, but also with the returning British power in 1945, caused by the fact that the expectation that

---

[108] The Romanian government declared to the German Foreign Office in August 1942 that they had nothing against the deportation of Romanian Jews from Germany (and by analogy from all other countries under German domination). Then however many consulates and the embassy in Berlin – probably on instructions of the Romanian Ministry of Foreign Affairs – intervened, claiming they had not been informed by their government. The Romanian consulates also made reference to the example of Switzerland and Italy, demanding that their nationals be treated the same way. The first secretary of their embassy in Berlin had already declared to the Germans a month earlier that Romanian reluctance was a matter of prestige, making a particular reference to the treatment of 'other foreign Jews'. What he was really saying was that Romania expected to be treated like Hungary and that as long as no similar thing was being asked of the Hungarian government with regard to their Jewish nationals resident abroad, they could not allow the deportation of Romanian nationals. Although the Romanian government told the Germans again and again that they could include Romanian Jews in the deportations, the uncertainty continued well into 1943. Romania appears on a list of ten countries, drafted by Eichmann on 5 July 1943, which were supposed to repatriate their own Jews from Germany and German-occupied Europe by 31 July 1943. Again, this was not the first time Romania had appeared on such a list. On 5 March 1943 Ernst Kaltenbrunner had already made a similar ruling with regard to Romanian Jews who could be treated according to the regulations in force in their countries of residence, i.e. they could be deported to the East, see H G Adler, *Der verwaltete Mensch. Studien zur Deportation der Juden aus Deutschland*, Tübingen 1974, 261–6; 272–3.

[109] Only for insult to be added to injury – this time by the Foreign Office – who kicked up a fuss over his pension because of his status as a technical 'enemy alien', see Cohen, op. cit., 62; 99.

measures against the Jews would be opposed on principle had not been met? Surely opposition would have come at a price, a price the authorities were unwilling to pay.

The authorities in both islands seem to have been somewhat surprised by the fact that not all Jews had evacuated in June 1940 and considered it unwise to antagonise the German occupier early on in the Occupation, when so much seemed to depend on German goodwill.[110] When the episode was being investigated by the British in summer 1945, Coutanche justified the measure with the reasoning that the number of people concerned by the measures was small, that moderation was shown in the execution and that undue harshness was avoided due to the intervention of the insular authorities.[111] Of these claims only the first seems to have been precise. It is hardly deniable that the tightening grip of discrimination did have a negative impact on the lives of the registered Jews, despite the Bailiff's amply documented interventions. But even the first argument of the 'small number' is not entirely convincing: if their number was small why not let them slip through the net? Why could the Channel Islands authorities not shrug off this measure and let the Germans implement it with their own administrative resources? Why did the Jersey Aliens Officer, Clifford Orange, and the Guernsey Inspector of Police, Sculpher, have to be the officials dealing with the direct implementation of these measures? There is no direct answer to this question. No official would have commended his exact motivations to paper; this is a false understanding of how bureaucracy works and a not altogether unusual situation for the historian. But evidence exists by implication. The Page case clearly reveals that the authorities were willing to engage in utilitarian calculations, in a sweeping manner that did not always demonstrate the required level of finesse. The story of the island Jews is of such great interest because it documents the classic case of one battle among a number of battles the authorities did not elect to fight.[112] As in the case of the Channel Islands 'offenders against the occupying authorities', this small number of people was not considered worth the trouble. In line with the principle of 'restraint and influence' the islands authorities held back, thinking that they were creating a debt with the occupier that could be invoked in situations where more important numbers were at stake.

The impact island endorsement of discrimination had is still underestimated: whether the local authorities of a country in occupied Europe lent support to the

---

[110] That the authorities grew bolder becomes clear through their refusal to submit further lists of islanders after September 1942 or the considerable initiative they displayed in 1944–45. It is indicative that from autumn 1942 the Germans dealt more directly with the Jewish question. Entries in the Jewish files of both Orange and Sculpher end in late 1942, see Cohen, op. cit., 48–9.

[111] PRO HO 45/22399. Memorandum, Alec Coutanche to Sir Donald Somervell, 3 July 1945.

[112] See also the comments of David Feldman, whose parents' business in Jersey was aryanised, *Sunday Telegraph*, 14 May 2000, cited in Cohen, op. cit., 99.

discrimination of the Jews made a difference. An administration opposing such measures was sending out a strong signal that it was equivocal about its justification. This was often the prelude to further action enabling Jews to avoid the sights of the persecutors and slip into illegality. An administration endorsing or even executing discrimination itself, emitted the opposite signal and encouraged people to comply. Registration of orders in the Royal Courts of Jersey and Guernsey gave them a legal imprimatur which a unilateral German measure would not have had and which would have been much easier to disobey. Jerseywoman Esther Pauline Lloyd, one of the registered Jews deported to internment, illustrates the impact in one entry to her diary, in May 1943: 'never shall I be honest again if I had not declared myself this wouldn't have happened – its dreadful [sic]'.[113] By bestowing legitimacy on these measures the authorities also gave a bad example to other islanders. Civilians now not only had to fear punishment from the Germans, but also had to reckon with their own authorities. Facing such pressure, it is no surprise that individual islanders did come forward with information on Jewish holdings in Channel Islands companies or enquired about members of their staff.[114] The population appears largely blameless in this matter, for the creation of an atmosphere conducive to 'reporting' seems to have had only limited impact.[115] A significant number of people with Jewish names who had not declared themselves – among them three Guernsey spinsters by the name of Cohen – were not denounced.[116] Other islanders threw up virtual screens by engaging in fictitious aryanisations of Jewish business interests which, after the war, were fully restored to their Jewish owners.

Unfortunately this is not all, for on top of granting discrimination a lease of life, certain members of the islands' administrations were also strangely proactive in their implementation of anti-Jewish measures. This applies in particular to the Jersey Aliens Officer Clifford Orange who applied over-inclusive criteria to the process of registration. Orange appears not only more rigorous than his

---

[113] Lloyd diaries, now in possession of Wiener Library, London, cited in: Cohen, op. cit., 47.

[114] See the case of the manager of the Ommaroo Hotel in Jersey who enquired about Simon Moss, one of his employees, Cohen, op. cit., 34.

[115] How powerful a tool denunciation was in implementing racial policy in Germany is shown in Robert Gellately's book *The Gestapo and German Society*, op.cit. In contrast Cohen uncovered a mere two denunciations in relation to Jewish residents (or residents believed to have been Jewish) in the occupied Channel Islands. One concerned Julia Brichta, a Hungarian national married to a local Guernseyman; the other one concerned a blackmarketeer in Jersey, Cohen, op. cit., 22; 83. The lower incidence of denunciation in the Channel Islands seems to allow the conclusion that rather than denunciation many of the unaccounted for successes of a German repressive apparatus which was substandard in many ways were due to the cooperation of the authorities. For the role of the civilian population see also Cohen's concluding comments on page 99 of his book.

[116] Cohen, op. cit., 72.

Guernsey counterpart, Sculpher[117], but even more thorough than the Germans themselves.[118] The best example of Orange's pernicious impact is the case of Hedwig Bercu who should have never been on the list of registered Jews in Jersey, but nevertheless was, thanks to the dedicated efforts of the Jersey Aliens Officer.[119] Technically, all the elements were there to exempt her: an illegitimate child, Bercu had never known her father, and her only connection to Judaism was the fact that her Gentile mother had married a Jew named Goldenberg. It is particularly damning for Orange that the OT transport sub-organisation NSKK accepted Bercu for work as an interpreter, obviously attaching no importance to the fact that she was a registered Jew and had an unmistakable 'J' stamped across her ID. This could have very well been because they realised on what flimsy grounds her registration was based. Bercu went into hiding to evade the prospect of a criminal case in November 1943, the outcome of which would have spelt disaster. Apparently, she had been passing on German petrol coupons, a serious offence. This was a dangerous position to be in, as demonstrated in the case of Julia Brichta, a Guernsey resident denounced as a Jew who was caught dabbling in the black market. The German stance on the black market certainly was contradictory, but, regardless, an accusation of this type in addition to a question-able racial status was enough for deportation; and this time not to an internment camp, but to a prison or a concentration camp.[120] Another good case to demonstrate Orange's pro-activity is the discussion surrounding the assets of Catherine Hill (née Jacobs), a 1940 evacuee. Mrs Hill's administrators – who did not know whether she was Jewish – submitted the case to Orange who decided that Jacobs must be a Jewish name, putting her holdings on the list of Jewish property in the island. In this case hiding or destroying some of the evidence would have cost him very little. Embarrassingly, it was the Germans who had to remind Orange that Jacobs was not necessarily a Jewish name and ordered further enquiries. Only after tenuous investigations of the Aliens Officer was it decided that, indeed, the Jacobs assets were Jewish.[121] Another case, that of Jerseywoman Esther Lloyd, proves that there was some German elasticity in the definition of Channel Islands Jews (which the islands authorities did not exploit).[122] Lloyd managed the extraordinary feat of talking her way out of

---

[117] With Orange's documented efforts to identify Jews and Jewish property there can be little doubt that had the three Cohen sisters lived in Jersey they would have surely attracted his attention.

[118] Orange eliminated benefit of doubt when determining Jewish origin even before the Germans demanded a more restrictive interpretation themselves, in their third order of 1941.

[119] Cohen, op. cit., 68.

[120] Brichta was deported to Ravensbrück, from where she was released in April 1945.

[121] Cohen, op. cit., 35.

[122] That there was some negotiation potential is also proven by the case of the Rossis who were offered the choice to go to Italy.

internment – with help from her husband who petitioned the Feldkommandantur in Jersey – and was finally sent back home, in 1944. This favour was usually only granted to internees reclassified 'essential workers', but in any case never to Jews. No information survives on how she went about this – probably by arguing that she was not Jewish – but it is unlikely to have ever occurred had the Germans been stringent.[123] The slackness of the Feldkommandantur in implementing anti-Jewish measures also emerges from the case of Annie Wranowksy, a Czech citizen registered as a Jew in Guernsey who was trying to prove her Aryan status in 1942. Had Dr Casper been as rigorous in his application of the principles as Orange, he would have included her on a list of Jews in a June 1942 correspondence submitted to the the Higher SS and Police Führer in Paris, the superior SS authority and direct representative of Himmler in France. The SS, charged with deporting the Jews of Europe to the East, were now enquiring about Jews in the islands and Casper seems to have decided that his authority granted him the right to let a liberal interpretation prevail.[124] In the same correspondence Casper also seemed to be dragging his feet over the introduction of the 'yellow star' order, asking the SS in Paris whether this order also applied to British Jews and whether they could supply him with the actual stars. A genuinely zealous Endlöser[125] (such as of the format of Alois Brunner in France) would have certainly found a way of fabricating these pointed stars and forcing them upon the local population. By late 1942 the stars had still not arrived and there is reason to believe that the German Foreign Office had decided – on the assumption that the Jewish Channel Islanders were British – that they need not wear the yellow star. Of course, Casper's downplaying of the Jewish dossier, evident in his remark that there was only a small number of Jews in the islands, also had a political aspect. From what we know there was general agreement that the Germans in the Channel Islands – mostly military – did not want the SS mucking around in their backyard. Only too often their radicalism in anti-Jewish policy had served as an inroad to increasing political leverage over the military whom they accused as being lukewarm in the question.

Was it anti-Semitism?

The biggest question is, of course, what motivated the islands authorities. Keeping in mind this disappointing record it is no wonder that a recent publication[126] by Professor David Fraser portrays the island administrations as

[123] Cohen, op. cit., 66.
[124] Cohen, op. cit., 42; 115.
[125] Executor of the Final Solution
[126] Fraser, David, *The Jews of the Channel Islands and the Rule of Law 1940–1945* – '*Quite contrary to the principles of British justice*', Brigthon, Portland, 2000.

unthinking and inhuman bureaucracies, dedicated to positivism and peopled by closet anti-Semites. This follows a pattern already set in Madeleine Bunting's *Model Occupation.*

Fraser must be credited with the highly significant discovery of the particular occupation group dynamics which saw some groups benefiting and others not benefiting from protection through the island administrations. He contrasts in particular the protection accorded to British forces personnel in 1940 and the prevention of measures against the Freemasons with the surrender of the Jews.

The Masonic temples in the islands had been ransacked by the Einsatzstab Reichsleiter Rosenberg (ERR) in January 1941. The ERR was a special squad operating under the authority of chief Nazi ideologue, later Minister for the occupied Eastern territories, Alfred Rosenberg. Among art experts it is best remembered as Göring's main rival in the looting of European art treasures, but it was also tasked with confiscating archives and other material from enemy organisations or individuals in order to further and document Germany's combat against her chief ideological foes, Jews and Freemasons. According to an ERR report of 1 February 1941 the coup in the Channel Islands was the most important Masonic booty they had ever made up until then. What intrigued the ERR in particular was the level of detail now available, which enabled them to identify Masonic lodges in the UK down to the last member; also the evidence of close connections between Masonry and Monarchy not only in Britain, but also in the Nordic countries.[127] In a letter to Hitler's secretary Martin Bormann, Rosenberg stated that the finds were confirmation of an alliance between 'Jewish world finance', 'British plutocrats' and other 'conspiracy centres'.[128] Rosenberg was particularly ecstatic about a Union Jack which he claimed carried a Jewish star of David and Masonic symbols.[129] In Jersey the ERR had taken great care to strip the entire furnishings and interiors, complete with library, banners and museum from the Jersey Masonic Temple, only burning items considered minor in a pit. The complete booty was paraded to Berlin in triumph where it was reassembled to replicate its original layout, thus constituting the centrepiece of an anti-Masonic propaganda exhibition destined to enlighten ordinary Germans on the insidious connections between Jews, Freemasons and the British Empire. This, however, is as far as the discrimination of the Freemasons went. When an order arrived from France, in late 1941, to liquidate Masonic property the islands authorities interposed themselves, using island legislation to transfer the assets to both States, thus providing protection for the duration of the Occupation. No individual Freemason suffered physical or material damage –

---

[127] IfZ MA 544/455–60. Aktenverm. Auswertung des Logenmaterials der Kanalinseln Jersey und Guernsey, ERR Paris, 1 Feb 1941.
[128] IfZ MA 544/385. Letter of Rosenberg to Bormann, 10 Feb 1941.
[129] IfZ MA 544/455–60. Note of Rosenberg sent to Bormann, 4 Feb 1941.

the way the Jews had – because he was a Freemason. Integral parts of island society, many Freemasons, such as Bailiff Carey of Guernsey, were members of the island elites. That a veil of protection had been drawn over them was cast into relief when an express order emanating from the German High Command which demanded the inclusion of 'all Jews and high-ranking Freemasons' in the ensuing February 1943 deportation of islanders to internment camps in Germany, was not executed with regard to the Freemasons.[130] Though one of the main targets of Nazi wrath, no anti-Masonic measures were ever passed into the law of the islands; and it wasn't for want of the Germans trying. The island Masons had escaped by the skin of their teeth.

David Fraser's conclusion from these facts is that only deeply engrained anti-Semitism could have accounted for the difference in treatment.[131] But, as has been made clear in two recent critiques, Fraser's one-pronged argument of island anti-Semitism is a very biased (and lame) interpretation of the available evidence, which overshoots the mark.[132] What is more, Fraser's reductionist agenda fails to explore other valuable avenues of enquiry, especially in the field of political science and social psychology.

Social research on insularity credits islands as being more democratic than larger countries, but also more nepotistic, with a higher incidence of insider dealing and influence peddling.[133] That an enemy occupation would increase rather than decrease this proclivity can be considered established. The Jews who stayed behind – frightened, of modest or no wealth, foreign, often advanced in age or ill – were the part of the pre-war community least suited to influence this environment. The distinction drawn between privileged, integrated Jews and underprivileged, often foreign Jews definitely transcends the cloaking of assets of established island Jews by their fellow islanders, and the return to their owners after the war. The importance of 'patronage' – and by implication a refutation of the argument of anti-Semitism as the main driver of island discrimination – also appears in the case of Marianne Blampied, the Jewish wife of Jersey artist Edmund Blampied. No doubt as appreciated by the occupiers as he already had been by islanders, after having designed the new Jersey pound notes and stamps, Blampied was an island celebrity. Unsurprisingly, neither Mrs Blampied nor her

---

[130] Fraser, op. cit., 214–22; Dennis Perrin, 'The Occupation and Jersey Freemasonry', leaflet produced by the *Provincial Grand Lodge of Jersey*, 9 May 1995.

[131] Fraser, op. cit., passim. The lengths to which Fraser goes in order to prove his point have been illustrated in his interpretation of an interview between Professor Pfeffer and the Bailiff of Jersey in September 1941, detailed in chapter two.

[132] For a more comprehensive critique of Fraser's thesis, see Donald Bloxham's review article 'The Jews of the Channel Islands and the Rule of Law 1940–1945 by David Fraser', *English Historical Review*, CXVII. 470, Feb. 2002, 226–7; also Sanders, *The Ultimate Sacrifice*, op. cit., 162–7.

[133] See for example Henry Srebnik, 'Small island nations and democratic values', in *World Development*, 2004 (32), 329–41.

husband found themselves on the 1943 deportation list, as they should have, had everything been 'done by the book'. That there were still a few strings to be pulled demonstrates the marked contrast of the Channel Islands to the rest of Europe where no such shilly-shallying was allowed. One may want to conclude from this that, rather than the result of racism, the fate of the island Jews was a function of their inability to leverage influence in a crisis situation.

Secondly, to portray Jews as the only 'out-group' – on which the thrust of Fraser's argument relies – is a step too far. Clifford Orange, the Aliens Officer, was busy tracking down many 'categories' of people, before, during and after the war. The case of Huyssen, as descibed in chapter II, is an example.[134] Other 'out-groups' were the Channel Islands civilians who fell foul of the new order by committing offences against the occupier. While they were not subject to racist measures, once caught many of them were sitting in the same boat as the Jews. How sourly their activities were regarded is demonstrated by the fact that practically no instances are known where they benefited from interventions on the part of the island authorities. The very existence of offenders was an embarrassment to the island authorities, whose bargaining depended on presenting islanders as calm and in no way disposed to opposition. Offences against the Germans invalidated this claim.

Thirdly, the argument of anticipatory zeal, in a situation that would have required a more distanced stance, applies in the main to Jersey. And the principal difference between the two islands was the differing personalities of the two officers charged with the anti-Jewish dossier, Inspector Sculpher and Aliens Officer Clifford Orange. While nothing special appears from the routine dealings of Sculpher, there was a troubling tendency in Orange, described as a 'stuffy stickler for principles', to overdo his job. It is perhaps not too surprising that the one individual who had the nerve to tell his staff that they must on no account assist Bolshie slave workers was also at the forefront of the implementation of anti-Jewish measures. Orange's action tallies with the experience of occupied Europe where many bureaucrats had their pre-war powers considerably extended and – instead of treading more carefully than before the war – responded with the opposite reflex of the sorcerer's apprentice. This often made them more dangerous than the Germans themselves, especially if, as Clifford Orange was, they were incompetent. One can draw no other conclusion from the fact that all of the registration forms – except that of Marianne Blampied – had been completed by Orange himself. As already noted several of the individuals registered as Jews had provided information to Orange which qualified them for exclusion from the registration order.[135] This level of

---

[134] For the entire Huyssen affair, see JAS Law Officer's Department. D/Z/H5/171.

[135] Bercu had no Jewish grandparents; Lloyd claimed to have had only one Jewish grandparent; another of the Jews registered in Jersey, Nathan Davidson, also had only one Jewish

incompetence was only possible because it found a feathered nest in the Channel Islands. Orange's position as Aliens Officer denotes the ambiguous feelings of an island community towards outsiders, especially non-British outsiders. Foreigners, especially those arriving as labour migrants, always were at the bottom of the social hierarchy in the islands and Orange's activity had all the hallmarks of a bureaucrat who had been given too much power over them, in addition to not even understanding the legislation he was implementing. Taking into account the considerable proportion of foreign or foreign-born among the island Jews, Orange acted 'in character', treating this group with the same mix of parsimoniousness and suspicion as any group of foreigners before the war.[136] It is not difficult to imagine the slightly coarser atmosphere that would have reigned in the Aliens Office. People who ventured there in order to clarify their status were betrayed; the mere fact that they had turned up at the office seems to have been taken as an implicit recognition of their Jewish status. Orange's disposition and understanding of his role was reinforced by a bureaucratic culture which had little regard for the wider scheme of things. Similarly pathetic attitudes existed at all levels of an administration where blind obedience reminiscent of a bygone age was rather more prevalent than civil service professionalism. This is why the few cases of administrative resistance and the diligent action of a Coutanche or McKinstry stick out so much.

It would be simplistic to make Orange alone responsible for this malaise. Orange's failure was also that of his superiors. This is also what the British investigators seem to have thought in 1945. Orange's activity partly informed the negative bias of the British against Jersey on the Jewish dossier.[137] This is somewhat paradoxical, as the Guernsey record – with three foreign Jews deported straight to Auschwitz – was worse. Having said this, with someone like Orange at the helm it is doubtful whether the fate of single Jews with a Central European nationality, had they existed in Jersey, would have been any different. Jersey simply made a lucky escape.

The fate of the Jews in the Channel Islands certainly brings the utilitarian 'greater number' calculations – of which both administrations made liberal use –

grandparent; only one of the Jews in Jersey professed the Judaic faith and it would have required very little effort to exempt the majority from having to register at all, see Cohen, op. cit., 84–5.

[136] Cohen mentions that Orange applied a similar degree of rigour to the registration of other categories of individuals, see Cohen, op. cit., 84. Xenophobia as a rationalisation for anti-Jewish action would tally with the experience in many countries, in particular France, where the first Jews to be targeted were the foreigners; the survival rate among Jews with French citizenship was significantly higher, see for example Serge Klarsfeld, *Le Calendrier de la persécution*, CDJC Paris, 1994.

[137] The other reason why more attention was drawn to the implementation of anti-Jewish legislation in Jersey was the more politicised nature of this island. Home Office files clearly indicate that more civilians from this island were prepared to come forward with information that was critical of the authorities.

to a head. Arguing from an Anglocentric perspective is not very helpful in this matter. One needs to integrate the actions of the islands authorities into the wider scheme of wartime Europe. The Channel Islands administrations certainly were not the only authorities to have operated on bargaining and trade-off principles. To the Germans it was quite obvious that keeping in place indigenous administrations, with their special expertise, was essential for the smooth running of the Occupation. In France the Germans succeeded in exploiting prewar political divisions and winning over those members of the conservative elite who had been dissatisfied with the Third Republic. The Germans clearly knew whom they wanted on the job and that there was absolutely no point in trying to run the country through reliance on the handful of French Nazi enthusiasts and rightist cranks. To this end they employed a rather astute carrot-and-stick policy, promising a lot, obtaining French concessions and giving practically nothing of any real substance in return. Vichy reacted to this situation with a policy of pre-empting German wishes, based on the utilitarian calculation that, ultimately, the sacrifices of today would lead to tomorrow's concessions. A small price, they thought, to pay for a better place in the 'New European Order'. Vichy delusion became suicidal after November 1942, when the Germans occupied the South of France, unmasking the mirage of Vichy sovereignty in its lack of substance. The logic of the regime now became based on the principle of power for power's sake. It would be flawed to view bargaining tactics as the mere domain of regimes such as Vichy which had already travelled a long way down the slippery slope of collaboration. Even for a nation as steadfastly self-assertive and fiercely passionate about its independence as Finland, this independence came at a price: recent research by Elina Suominen has revealed that the number of refugees, Soviet PoWs (among them many Jews) and, as it appears, even Finnish citizens with the 'wrong' political pedigree handed over to the Gestapo between 1941 and 1944 was much higher than previously admitted.[138] In the words of Max Jakobson, a senior diplomat and prominent member of the Helsinki Jewish community, the findings indicate that they were 'made pawns in a cruel diplomatic game'.[139] If even independent national governments with an otherwise untarnished record – the exemplary and principled protection accorded to Finnish Jews should be borne in mind – faltered, what more could be expected from the Channel Islands authorities? This is not

---

[138] Unto Hämäläinen, 'More than just eight deportations to Nazi Germany. New book reveals 3,000 foreigners handed over during World War II', *Helsingin Sanomat International Edition*, 4 Nov. 2003, <www.helsinki-hs.net/news.asp?id=20031104IE14>. The book in question is Elina Suominen's *Luovutetut – Suomen ihmisluovutukset Gestapolle* (*The Extradited – Finland's Deportations to the Gestapo*), published in 2003.

[139] Max Jakobson, 'Wartime refugees made pawns in cruel diplomatic game. Elina Sana book describes history of refugees extradited from Finland to Nazi Germany', *Helsingin Sanomat International Edition*, 4 Nov. 2003, <www.helsinki-hs.net/news.asp?id=20031104IE7>.

equivalent to condoning their action. The treatment of the island Jews was a chapter where neither the Guernsey nor the Jersey authorities covered themselves in glory. In retrospect nothing remains to commend the exposure of this small but symbolic group of people, instead of engaging on a path of obstruction from the beginning. In both islands a lack of imagination reigned in measuring the import of a policy of discrimination so unprecedented in the islands' history. The price for non-compliance would have been very small; chances are that the Germans wouldn't even have noticed. At the same time one must conclude that the sacrifice of this small group was based on utilitarian politics – as that of the 'offenders'. Collaboration in the Holocaust motivated by anti-Semitism this was not.

IV

The Culture of Survival

THAT 'MAKE DO AND MEND' is such an omnipresent theme in Occupation reminiscences is not an unwarranted spleen. While this was not a reign of terror, the pressure and anxiety islanders had to contend with on all fronts drove many to the very edge of their wits. The fixation on food was something they shared with most Europeans during this period; only they had to be even more resourceful than their continental counterparts. Survival also depended on the inner resources islanders could muster. And the Occupation certainly stretched their legendary ability to adapt to new situations to the limit. It is by looking at this theme that one approaches the very core of islanders' attachment to the Occupation as a collective experience and arguably the major episode in their modern history. Many believe that this was their 'finest hour', of a somewhat different and largely unknown sort.

Rationing and price control were the necessary evils accompanying restrictions. The simultaneity of their appearance led many to believe that the restrictions were actually caused by economic control measures, which is false. Rationing affected the population in all islands in a fairly similar way: the main foods such as bread, meat, fats and potatoes were rationed. Bread rationing began in August 1941, at four and a half pounds per week, until February 1945 when it was cut to one pound. In Guernsey the unprecedented situation arose where no bread was issued at all from 14 Feb to 7 March, owing to German requisitions in November 1944.[1] Pork and poultry disappeared entirely after 1942, as did many cats and dogs after 1944–45. The dairy herds, and milk production, were maintained almost to pre-war numbers. While children were treated on an equal basis everywhere, receiving a pint of full milk a day, Jersey adults were perhaps more fortunate in receiving full milk rather than skimmed milk, as in Guernsey.[2] As a

---

[1] JAS L/D/25/M4/10. Official report on Essential Supplies, Guernsey, post-occupation.

[2] A Leslie Banks, 'Effects of enemy occupation on the state of health and nutrition in the Channel Islands', Monthly Bulletin of the Ministry of Health and the Emergency Public Health Laboratory Service, 1945 (4), 184–195.

result of the shortage, vegetables – not rationed and available in relative abundance during the summer – were the only elastic food reserve, thus turning islanders into a nation of vegetarians. With the vast amounts they needed to cover energy requirements they were in fact eating double the quantity of vegetables and potatoes as in the UK. Fish and seafood, a potentially abundant and highly nutritious food source, did not live up to expectations: arrivals were very irregular, owing to a number of factors such as German restrictions, scarcity of petrol and the mining of many areas. On a number of occasions, such as after escape attempts, boats were not allowed to leave harbour at all. Also at least 20 per cent of the catch went straight to the Germans, the rest was sucked up by the black market. The only fish or seafood to have reached the parish of St Martin, in Jersey, were spider crabs which, according to the anonymous 'Watchman', were not appreciated by the occupying force.[3] In late 1943 a mere 25 boats were still fishing from Guernsey. Three or four boats at a time were escorted out of three harbours, St Peter Port, St Sampson and Portelet, by a German patrol boat. The patrol boat would then go back to harbour, take out another group and sail between the groups. Boats were not allowed to land anywhere on the coast, all single fishermen or fishermen with UK relations were banned and the fishing limit was reduced to three miles offshore.[4] Bar the ten to fifteen per cent of the population who, according to the Reverend Mylne in Jersey, felt none of the deprivation of the Occupation either because they were 'toadying' with the Germans or simply too affluent, the rest of the population had to revert to the almost universal practices of 'gleaning', 'limpetting' and 'wooding'.[5] Islanders became expert at producing substitutes: parsnip, barley and acorn provided the basis for ersatz coffee, carrots for tea or jam, potato flour was mixed into the island bake, salt being a rarity of the first order, people would use sea water for cooking. Fish was prepared in nettles which replaced herbs and currants were made from dried elderberries. Sugar beet was the most versatile of all as it could be turned into a Horlicks' food, tea, coffee or syrup, which mitigated the sugar shortage. One Guernsey escapee reported in 1943 that some experiments were the source of much laughter such as vegetable marrow milk pudding which the writer claimed was 'really quite enjoyable'.[6] Almost as serious a problem as the lack of food was the absence of cooking and heating facilities. Kitchen ranges could certainly not be used and much cooking was done on top of five-gallon oil drums,

---

[3] JAS L/D/25/M3/6. *A Jersey country parish during the time of occupation*, by Watchman (London, Society for Promoting Christian Knowledge, 1946).

[4] PRO HO 144/22834. MI19/2144. Report Channel Islands Guernsey, further interrogation of informants 2132, 2136 and 2141, 24 Apr 1944 (info as at 1 Dec 43).

[5] JAS L/C/20/0/7. 'Under the Crooked Cross. Jersey 1940–1945. 2. Domestic Life' by the Reverend Mylne.

[6] PRO HO 144/22834. 'Guernsey August 1943', memo written by J T D Hubert.

packed with sawdust with a hole in the middle for a tiny flame. These contraptions would take several hours to cook potatoes and then a kettle would replace the saucepan for tea. Only in the coldest weather did people bother to light a fire. The scarcity of fuels can perhaps be gauged from the fact that furnace coke in St Martin ran out as early as Christmas day 1941 and thereafter they had to continue in 'hideous cold' for three and a half winters. 'Watchman' made a particular point in stressing the courage of the island women, 'the real heroines of the time': 'We marvelled at the good appearance the children made – only a few of us knew at what cost to the woman who loved them.' Many were not only deceiving their children over the fact that they were sacrificing their own rations, but their husbands as well, prompting the writer to state that a 'Passion-tide week-day service [...] had a reality such as similar services have ever had.'[7]

One of the curious effects of the Occupation was that people would sleep more; this withdrawal into sleep was not only motivated by the intention to conserve warmth and energy, but it also provided a psychological escape. As 'Watchman', the pen name used by a parishioner of St Martin, Jersey, wrote: 'Some had to find refuge in bed and in their nightmares saw the Germans requisitioning their blankets.'[8] Although there were times when people went to bed without knowing what they would eat the next day, in the long term early exposure to scarcity and deprivation was an advantage, as it braced people for the worst and gave them a chance to adapt while there was still time. Over the months islanders learnt to make do with practically nothing. By the time they had to face their toughest challenge, in the second half of 1944, many survival strategies were already well-established practice.

The achievements of ingenuity were particularly impressive in medicine and the islands were extremely lucky to have had such a dedicated bunch of medical officers, doctors, nurses and pharmacists. Jersey, under the revered Dr McKinstry, saw a revival in alternative medicine, improvised on the basis of island resources. One of the many feats was the development a gonorrhoea vaccine on the basis of E.coli; the only things island doctors and pharmacists could not improvise, it seems, were insulin, certain other vaccines and anaesthetics.[9] Equally impressive exploits in improvising medical and pharmaceutical products are reported from Guernsey: when Boots the Chemist started to run out of stock, they launched their own line of Guernsey-manufactured drugs. By 1944 the product-manufacturing branch of the business employed a total of five full-time assistants. Besides the rather standard influenza and indigestion mixtures, and bronchial lozenges, they made a number of other

[7] JAS L/D/25/M3/6. op. cit.
[8] JAS L/D/25/M3/6. op. cit.
[9] Val Garnier, *Medical history of the Jersey hospitals and nursing homes during the Occupation 1940–1945*, London, 2002, 16–19.

supplies, concoctions and mixtures at the request of the island doctors and hospitals which were the subject of a letter of commendation by the island Health Services Officer after the war.[10] Thanks to these combined efforts the medical system came close to collapse only in late 1944. Similar wonders were also worked in toiletries. Boots turned out – among many other items – various creams, tonics, shampoos and powders, bath crystals, hand jelly from carrageen moss farmed at low spring tide and a range of perfumes with enticing names such as *Les Fleurs, Imperial Chypre* and *Gardenia*. Mr A Butterworth, the Boots manager, claimed that the perfume counter for Christmas 1942 was up to 'Bond Street level', earning the shop the reputation of being the one in Guernsey that preserved much of its pre-war appearance. In 1943 Butterworth developed another perfume, *Fleur de Tabac*, which became a hit with local men, for sweetening up the local tobacco.[11]

An assessment of the effect of living conditions on overall public health holds some surprises. One of the most immediate effects of 'green eating', combined with the high fibre content of the local bread, was looseness of bowels. The severity of the phenomenon usually abated after three months of adaptation, but 'bowel motions did not return to the pre-war habit of one motion daily'. Constipation disappeared. Also people who had suffered from the side effects of being overweight, especially chronic cardiac disease, showed remarkable improvement.[12] On a more general level there was a net regression of diseases of affluent societies related to alcohol, tobacco, fat and sugar. Both islands were remarkably free from influenza and common colds during the Occupation, but there was a rise in some infectious diseases such as TB, scarlet fever and whooping cough. A diphtheria epidemic brought to Jersey by the forced workers resulted in 277 civilian cases, resulting in 15 deaths, in 1942–43.[13] The most serious epidemic, however, was the outbreak of typhus in Guernsey, in 1942, with an acknowledged 30 German deaths. How many foreign workers died from this disease is not known, but, remarkably, the disease did not spread to the civilians. The few epidemics that occurred carried higher death rates than previous epidemics – owing to lack of vaccines and lowered resistance – but worse was prevented through inoculation campaigns. Another negative feature of the Occupation years was the rise in septic skin conditions and the slow

---

[10] PRO HO 144/22176. A N Symons, Medical Services Officer to the Managing Director, Boots Drug Co., Nottingham, 23 May 1945.

[11] PRO HO 144/22176. Report of Business during German Occupation to the end of September 1944 by A F Butterworth, 27; 30.

[12] A Leslie Banks, 'Effects of enemy occupation on the state of health and nutrition in the Channel Islands', *Monthly Bulletin of the Ministry of Health and the Emergency Public Health Laboratory Service*, 1945 (4), 188.

[13] Val Garnier, *Medical history of the Jersey hospitals and nursing homes during the Occupation 1940–1945*, London, 2002, iii; 14.

healing of wounds which was also attributed to the weakened resistance of patients.[14] However, by far the commonest manifestation of malnutrition was lack of energy and concentration, plus stamina loss. The situation for the island children on the whole was satisfactory, Guernsey being particularly lucky in this respect as four-fifths had been evacuated in 1940. The evidence for Jersey suggests that although their development suffered somewhat, especially in St Helier, within a few months of the end of the Occupation most children had recovered in weight, if not in height. Dental health, by contrast, was better than in England and better than before the war. This was based on a combination of factors such as wholemeal bread, full cream milk, more chewing of vegetable food and absence of sweets. When the Regional Dental Officer of the Ministry of Health visited in September 1945, she found that of the six-year-olds who had spent the Occupation in Jersey 50 per cent had retained all their teeth, compared with only 13 per cent amongst evacuees. Fewer than 13 per cent of school children had required dental treatment in 1943 and 1944.[15]

The increase in the crude death rate during the Occupation is always associated with insufficient diet, but this is only half of the story. Paradoxically, scarcity of food was not *the* 'killer factor' as it has been interpreted over the past 60 years, otherwise the effects would have been more easily spread over all age or social groups. But this was not the case; not all islanders were equally affected by the restrictions. This was also the tenor of a Home Office survey which pointed out that there was no general starvation and that the effects of the Occupation on the food situation were uneven: some people fell through the social net, others did not.[16] V V Cortvriend quoted a Guernsey medical practitioner in 1947 who said that the situation was 'fairly good' in terms of health, but people would break down 'if [they were] confronted with any considerable mental or physical strain'. According to this doctor three factors helped stave off such strain: the black market, the adaptability of the people and the way in which restrictions were imposed gradually. Overall the hardships were 'mental and spiritual more than physical', caused by separation from loved ones, uncertainty and anxiety.[17]

In terms of calories the rations were sufficient, or almost sufficient. Dr Noel McKinstry, the Jersey Health Officer, stated that energy consumption from July 1940 to July 1943 fluctuated between 2,100 and 2,500 calories per day.[18] Dietary

[14] A Leslie Banks, op. cit. 190.
[15] JAS D/Z/K/15/6. Survey of the Effects of the Occupation on the Health of the People of Jersey, by R N McKinstry, 1945.
[16] PRO HO 144/22833. Home Office. Internal memo 'Food situation in the Channel Islands', n.d.
[17] V V Cortvriend, *Isolated island. A history and personal reminiscences of the German occupation of the island of Guernsey, June 1940 – May 1945*, Guernsey, 1947, 124; 147.
[18] JAS D/Z/K/15/6. Survey of the Effects of the Occupation on the Health of the People of Jersey, by R N McKinstry, 1945.

surveys concluded that Jersey people got most of their nourishment from oatmeal, potatoes, bread and milk. Not counting black market purchases, a middle-class family of three could typically afford the additional benefit of flour and butter, thus receiving up to 2,640 calories per head, whereas a working-class family of eight living on state relief received a minimum of 1,677.[19] The rations fell in the closing months of 1944 and reached their lowest point – an average of 800 calories per day per head – in February 1945. Luckily, by this time the Red Cross parcels became available which gave everyone an extra daily 600 calories, in addition to still obtainable vegetables.[20] What becomes clear from these figures is that the issue was less one of lack or absence of food than one of getting a balanced diet. In fact, had it been possible to supplement more unsaturated fats and proteins, the overall diet would have been healthier than is the case today. What Channel Islanders suffered from was malnutrition or false nutrition, not starvation.

The death rate was typically on the rise during the winter months, when the combination of unbalanced diet with other factors such as lack of heating and clothing, plus depression created the worst effect. [21]

Guernsey – Death rate (per 1000)[22]

	1941–42	1942–43	1943–44	1944–45
December	17.1	25.5	21.4	31.8
January	41.1	20.5	28.7	45.0
February	37.0	18.3	33.9	31.1
March	32.0	29.7	33.9	24.6

According to these official figures from Guernsey the worst month on record was January 1945 – not altogether a surprise – while, arguably, the worst consecutive period was January to March 1942. Although somewhat unexpected, this concords with the diaries of The Reverend Douglas Ord which record a notable increase in deaths, in particular among the elderly, during winter 1941–42. Mr Butterworth, the manager of Boots in Guernsey, mentioned that during the winter of 1941 his staff grew particularly thin. During this time, he said, most people had to rely solely on rations, as no other food – not even swedes – was

---

[19] A Leslie Banks, 'Effects of enemy occupation on the state of health and nutrition in the Channel Islands', *Monthly Bulletin of the Ministry of Health and the Emergency Public Health Laboratory Service*, 1945 (4), 184–195.

[20] JAS D/Z/K/15/6. op. cit.

[21] In Guernsey things were not made easier by the fact that the diet, according to the Ministry of Health, was 'at a somewhat lower level than in Jersey and that a greater number of families suffered hardship than in Jersey', see A Leslie Banks, op. cit. 188.

[22] JAS L/D/25/M4/10. Official report on Essential Supplies, Guernsey, post-occupation.

obtainable.[23] The death rate was also affected by German requisitions of 1,027 tons of potatoes – mostly for export – after the 1941 harvest.[24] One of the associated psychological reasons for the high death rate in 1941–42 was the large number of evictions which sapped many elderly people's willpower. A Ministry of Health official visiting in the summer of 1945 confirmed the importance of the psychological element, saying that 'so long as stocks of food existed, there was a feeling of security and hope for the future, whereas when they were exhausted the whole prospect looked black'.[25] Intriguingly similar scenarios were also being played out in other countries. In France the winter of 1941–42 was the worst of the Occupation.[26] As in the islands French city dwellers had still been able to rely on pre-war stocks or what was available in the shops the previous winter; whereas this time around these sources of supply simply defaulted. Many had failed to use the summer to stock up sufficient supplies or adapt to the new conditions through improvisation – cultivating their own back garden or keeping rabbits. People didn't make the same costly mistake twice, and 1942–43 was a much better winter for most.

Food was one factor in the higher death rate; but almost as much depended on the ability to withstand psychological pressure and the power of adaptation. In this respect some groups were more favoured than others. Therefore the rise in the death rate affected mainly the middle aged or elderly, and some members of larger families on small incomes. Not surprisingly the elderly were also over-represented in that group of people with medical conditions, such as 'unusually sensitive gastro-intestinal canals' and who could not adapt to the new diet. [27] They often suffered from the perforation of pre-existing peptic ulcers or persistent diarrhoea, leading to chronic starvation. Another group who had a tougher time surviving were the English residents (not all of whom were wealthy), as they often did not have the same social networks in the countryside as native islanders.[28] V V Cortvriend also mentions 'land workers' (i.e. agricultural labourers) as one of the disadvantaged groups.[29] This seems decidedly odd, as agricultural labour was scarce. Also one would have thought that direct contact with the countryside was an advantage. This is not the first nor is it the

[23] PRO HO 144/22176. Report of Business during German Occupation to the end of September 1944 by A F Butterworth,

[24] JAS L/D/25/M4/10. Official report on Essential Supplies, Guernsey, post-occupation.

[25] A Leslie Banks, 'Effects of enemy occupation on the state of health and nutrition in the Channel Islands', *Monthly Bulletin of the Ministry of Health and the Emergency Public Health Laboratory Service*, 1945 (4), 190.

[26] Paul Sanders, *Histoire du marché noir 1940–1946*, Paris, 2001, 125–61.

[27] A Leslie Banks, op. cit., 188.

[28] IWM Misc. 2826 189/2 (Tape 23 4399 O/L). Interview with Leslie Sinel, n.d.

[29] V V Cortvriend, Isolated island. A history and personal reminiscences of the German occupation of the island of Guernsey, June 1940 – May 1945, Guernsey, 1947, 129.

last paradox of this period. The underprivileged status of agricultural workers and industrial workers living in rural districts certainly ties in with what is known about conditions in other occupied countries where these workers and labourers were often worse off than their urban counterparts. The reasons were two-fold: naturally this group was more dependent on the official rationing and distribution system than the agricultural producer or the retailer. Unfortunately the official system was more dysfunctional in the countryside than in the urban centres which were prioritised on the assumption that rural inhabitants had more direct opportunities to acquire non-rationed items or agricultural surplus. In addition social disturbances due to insufficient material conditions, a scenario all wartime administrations wanted to avoid, were also more likely within the more politicised urban milieu. The idea that rural inhabitants were better provided for disregarded the fact that the higher black market prices paid in the cities and towns acted as a powerful mechanism to drain. Often the lower classes in the countryside had to rely on the charity of individual farmers, a factor that was not always a foregone conclusion.[30]

That the analysis of food shortages as an associated factor in the higher death rate is correct, becomes clear when one adjusts the increase in the crude death rate for the change in population structure, notably the departure of younger members before the Occupation. The resultant difference from the pre-war average – at least in Jersey – is only slight.[31] The evidence for Guernsey points in the same direction: here the only population group to have suffered a significantly higher death rate than before the war were the over-65s.[32] The Channel Islands Occupation Birth Cohort Study, a retrospective longitudinal study examining the effects of the Occupation on the health of Channel Islanders born in the islands further confirms some of the above findings. It is surprising that although conditions in the islands during 1944–45 were rather similar to those of the Dutch 'Hunger Winter' of 1944–45, the Channel Islands experienced none of the short-term increase in mortality, decline in fertility, increased number of stillbirths and fall in average birth weight that took place in the Netherlands. Even on the issue of long-term effects, Channel Islanders born during this time seem to have escaped the increased prevalence of high blood pressure, diabetes and other subsequent effects which one finds in adults born during or after the Dutch 'Hunger Winter'. Dutch women born during this period were likely to deliver themselves smaller babies later in life.[33] Up to the present time the

---

[30] Paul Sanders, Histoire du marché noir 1940–1946, Paris, 2001.

[31] JAS D/Z/K/15/6. Survey of the Effects of the Occupation on the Health of the People of Jersey, by R N McKinstry, 1945.

[32] JAS L/D/25/M4/11. States of Guernsey medical report for 1944, 1945.

[33] George Ellison et al., 'How did the Occupation affect the health of Channel Islanders? A rationale for the Channel Islands Birth Cohort Study', *The Channel Islands Occupation Review*, 1998 (26), 39–43.

cohort study has found no evidence of even a modest increase in adult disease similar to what has been observed in the case of Holland.[34] What this indicates is that stinging into action the human power of adaptation was primordial for survival. In the Channel Islands, food started to run short from the onset; the deterioration and rise in mortality set in as early as 1941 and peaked in 1942, corresponding with an overall negative outlook that also led to one of the lowest birth rates on record.[35] Once they survived this Calvary, one could almost say that things started to look up once again. Holland, in comparison, was a land of plenty from the summer of 1940 to the summer of 1944, when the Dutch had expected to be liberated. Then, suddenly and unexpectedly, they were cut off from all essential supplies. Starvation was the inevitable result for a population that had not tested and experimented with other options over the preceding years as the islanders had. The Dutch had acquired none of the skill and experience needed to survive when they were hit by this calamity. The Channel Islands' case probably proves that over the long run 'less was more'. Despite their predicament as small, occupied islands with limited resources, in terms of overall living conditions, the Channel Islands were not only a better place to live in than Holland during the 'Hunger Winter', but – at least until 1944 – they were also a better place to live in than the larger French cities. The wonders of improvisation and adaptation already point to the importance of cohesion. That is where living in a small place with a homogenous population proved an advantage. Equally as important as early adaptation was better control and distribution of available resources by the authorities and social networks that took better care of the individual. Once more the Channel Islands' Occupation proves good for a surprise.

Fraternisation: necessary evil or evil necessity?

As for the entire occupation experience, it is not an easy task to put a definite tag on relations between islanders and occupiers, at least not as easy as many authors have pretended. Within a matter of weeks the islands had gone from being very special places exuding freedom and elevation at every turn of the corner – the favourite holiday and retirement spot in the British Isles – to vulgar army encampments. Worse was to come with the arrival of the 'Todts' and their army of slaves or half-slaves and thousands of additional troops. Islanders were

---

[34] 'The Channel Islands Birth Cohort Study' www.lsbu.ac.uk/health/research_exfunded.shtml, accessed 3 March 2005; telephone conversation with Michelle Irving, PhD candidate in the 'Channel Islands Birth Cohort Study', 4 Mar 2005.

[35] Val Garnier, *Medical history of the Jersey hospitals and nursing homes during the Occupation 1940–1945*, London, 2002, 36–7.

now to experience the full weight of the German security apparatus, hemmed in their existence of further restrictions and endless security checks. The beauty of the islands was defiled by brutal military architecture bearing all the hallmarks of a totalitarian and militaristic dictatorship. The wall of iron, steel and concrete being erected around the perimeter and across the islands was imprisoning people in their own homes. With a few exceptions access to the beaches became a thing of the past. One German soldier described the omnipresence of bunkers as 'a bad dream'. Each hill on the islands was equipped with a strong point and each bay, beach and meadow adorned with wooden posts against airborne troops.[36] A leisurely stroll in town also was a pastime of a bygone age. His weekly venture described in Mr Attenborough's Jersey diary in June 1943 has the touch of a major expeditionary foray, affording him several close calls with the occupier exercising his full armed might at his every step. Preparing to turn towards home he wrote that he was 'confronted with part of the invading army' running down the slopes with great gusto. Being in the line of fire he hastily made his exit towards the opposite side of the road, only to be confronted with soldiers lying flat out between the rockery, shrubs and bushes. As he advanced the muzzle of a gun faced him every two feet, making him wonder whether it was safer to advance or retreat, an NCO meanwhile bawling his instructions to the men, but obviously missing seeing the civilian.[37] No doubt, the suffocation of all civilian life in Guernsey was even worse. Children were particularly alienated in this pitiless environment. The granddaughter of entrepreneur-inventor Fletcher would hear the noise of tanks coming up behind her on her way to school and she would stand rooted to the spot until the noise had passed.[38] Most islanders understood and resented their degradation to the status of rightless inhabitants of their own native soil, stripped of all possibilities of redress; but they also had to survive; and survival depended on a modicum of accommodation, a conciliatory conduct, whatever the cost in pride.

Many Germans themselves realised all too well the emotional dilemma of islanders. Whenever the question is mentioned in interrogations or interviews there are always about as many Germans who feel that islanders were friendly as there are Germans who feel that, despite the 'correct' attitude, people left no doubt that they considered them the enemy. While one should factor in that people have (and keep) their secrets, there is no basis to discard the notion of a relationship characterised by a majority which kept their distance, in favour of the rather unsubstantiated idea that islanders as a group threw themselves into

---

[36] IWM Misc. 2826 189/2 (Tape 4489). Interview with Werner Grosslopp (sic). The spelling in this name is manifestly incorrect.

[37] IWM 02/17/1. Diary of Mr and Mrs G Attenborough, June 1943.

[38] IWM Diary of R E H Fletcher, 1940–42. Appendix: short anecdotal memoir by his granddaughter Mrs C Tarran, n.d.

the arms of the occupier.[39] In a relatively recent interview, one of the former judges at the court of Feldkommandantur 515, Harmsen, characterised the relationship as correct, 'without closer friendships'. He remembered the frequent short conversations with islanders in the street, polite small talk about the weather and other things.[40] This appreciation is not confined to civil servants such as Harmsen, but is also borne out by statements of the rank and file. Alfred Schmidt, a German civil engineer captured in St Malo and considered 100 per cent reliable by his British interrogators, stated that the relationship of islanders and Germans was characterised by respect, but as enemies nevertheless. Schmidt reconfirmed what many other Channel Islanders wrote or said, namely that they had little against the privates, but had a healthy dislike or even loathing for the officers. In the latter part of the Occupation the major part of the scorn seemed to have been shifted to the Russian battalions serving in the German Army.[41] A variation on the theme of 'selective appreciation' is offered by a 1945 report, by the Information and Records Branch (Cabinet Office), based on the analysis of letters from the Channel Islands. This read that '(t)hose who express appreciation of the correct behaviour of the German authorities rarely go further and evince pro-German sympathies – at the most, they differentiate between the afore-mentioned and the Gestapo and Nazi officers.'[42]

[39] Equally instructive is an analysis of intercepted letters from the Channel Islands being written to or received by German PoWs in the UK, in 1945:
PRO HO 144/22176. List of persons German PoWs are writing to/receiving letters from since being transported from the Channel Islands, document created in June 1945.

Analysis (number of letters)

Week ending:	12/07	19/07	03/10	10/10	24/10	07/11	14/11	21/11	28/11
Friends	24	8	12	30	9	5	7	5	3
Acquaintances ('greetings')	24	3	2	14	11	7	6	4	9
Sweetheart/fiancé/mistress	17	4	3	2	3		1	1	2
Wife/relative	1	2		3	2	1			1
Religious connection						1	1		
Official				1					
Unclear relationship	2	2	3						
Business						1			

Note: The letters figuring under '12 July' include interceptions of the preceding June. Otherwise the set of these letters is not complete; there is a gap between July and October, but the letters give some indication of the nature of relationships between Germans and islanders. The range of greetings in the 'acquaintances' category include 'friendly greetings', 'greetings' as well as indication of 'non-committal' or formal acquaintances. Many of the soldiers in the 'acquaintances' category had been billeted with islanders. A fair number of friendships and acquaintances were based on 'anti-Nazi sentiments' which the writers held in common with the recipients of the letters. One letter written on 19 July 1945 was that of a German PoW of Polish extraction; a second written on 10 October was in Polish.

[40] IWM Misc. 2826 189/2. Interview with Judge Harmsen, n.d.

[41] PRO WO 199/3303. Interrogation of Alfred Schmidt, captured in St Malo on 11 Aug 1944, 24 Aug 1944.

[42] PRO PREM 3/87. Report based on 227 extracts from letters from the CI dated Nov and Dec, 15 Feb 1945.

Another group that was disliked were the OTs (Organization Todt); and this not only because of their public bullying and beating of workers under their supervision, but also their brash treatment of the locals. In August 1942 complaints to the FK that German OT staff in various states of inebriation were gaining 'unauthorised access' and 'pestering' Jersey farmers to sell them produce reached such dimensions that the OT saw it necessary to remind them that such practices were 'verboten'; in the future culprits were to be 'severely punished'.[43] The idea of accommodation with the 'regular guys' and hearty dislike of the hierarchy also follows from a diary entry of Jerseywoman Mary Deslandes in September 1941:

> The army of Occupation seems to have settled down to a steady 8,000 now and we have grown quite accustomed to having them around. No one hates the poor wretches individually. They provoke no one and a better behaved, more inoffensive body of men it would be impossible to find. What one does hate, with a bitter, corrosive hatred is the system they represent and the conditions which their presence here imposes. They are very much the dominant autocrats in possession, and only by favour of their much vaunted magnanimity are the natives allowed to live on their own island, on sufferance, shorn of their rights and almost of their liberty.[44]

Mary Deslandes committed these thoughts to her diary before the advent of the crash-building programme, but a 'clash of systems' is already pre-configured in her writing. Only a few months later, multiple new pressures would bring out the real face of German rule. After the arrival of the Russian slaves and the deportation of the non-natives most people of sane mind realised that the concept of 'correct relations' was a mere façade. Herr Kassens, another former occupier, confirmed that the relationship with civilians deteriorated rapidly in 1942 because people resented handing in their radios. He also mentioned the Sark and St Nazaire raids which were closely studied by officers in the Channel Islands and resulted in yet more barbed wire, mines and other items of fortification.[45] If islanders could not always keep the required distance, this was most probably due to one factor: they depended on the Germans. This is nothing entirely new. The Home Office reflected on this point in a memo predating Liberation saying that the native population almost certainly benefited from the fact that there was so large a garrison and foreign labour. According to the British it was in places with a comparatively small German force in a large area that inhabitants were starved and maltreated.[46] The allusion clearly was that in

[43] JAS D/AU/V5/2. OT Abschnitt Jakob (Jersey), Rundschreiben, 6 Aug 1942.

[44] 'The Diary of Mary Winifred Deslandes June 1940 to May 1945', entry of 3 September 1941, in: *An Island Trilogy*, op. cit.

[45] IWM Misc. 2826 189/2. Interview with Herr Kassens, n.d.

[46] PRO HO 144/22833. Internal HO memo 'Food situation in the Channel Islands', n.d.

the Channel Islands the Germans had to contain extremes: they could not let the food situation deteriorate beyond a certain measure; neither could one afford to let disease get out of hand. A degree of interdependence, and a limited amount of leverage, stemmed from the fact that the Germans, after deliberation, had decided to leave the civilian population in place. Symbioses were created that were based on the unholy trinity of billeting, barter and food dependence. In Guernsey, in 1942, 10,800 Germans soldiers alone were billeted directly on the population or in the houses of evacuees, i.e. an average of one soldier for every two islanders.[47] This is without counting the substantial numbers of OTs and NSKK (their transport sub-organisation) members who lived with families and shared their food.[48] The food given to islanders by Germans, often better quality than what was available in the islands, was used for bartering of other goods[49] Statistically almost every Guernsey islander – and this includes the children – had his own very personal German marching up and down, and sometimes in and out of, his own four walls. Some Germans would bring their 'mates' along for binges – which is precisely what emerges from the diary of the Reverend Douglas Ord. Jersey diarist R E H Fletcher described the arrival of a German platoon in his own back garden in July 1941, to install an anti-aircraft gun. In the same month all houses of evacuees in his vicinity had already been occupied. Insight into their quartermaster's store, conveniently located in this now-military compound, gave him a glimpse of copious provisions stocked with food of all descriptions, tobacco, cigarettes and cigars, also French cheese and table wine, dates, sweets, freshly ground coffee, beans, meat joints, sugar, all luxuries for islanders. The men were generous and sold him some of this plenty at prices much lower than the local black-marketers. Fletcher also managed to supply friends and relations with left-overs of soup and stews from the German kitchen operating right under his bedroom window, this resulting in a constant to and fro, of up to 12 families with pots, at his house. Fletcher certainly had little good to say about the Germans in his diary and his most characteristic stance is derision or scorn. Despite his evident antipathy, he was fair enough to say, however, that the soldiers were 'well behaved', and more significantly, asked for no favours in return.[50] It is perhaps for this reason that he qualified the one

[47] JAS D/AU/VI/3. FK St Helier, Vermerk, 5 Mar 1942. In Jersey 6,503 German soldiers were billeted on the civilian population, mostly in properties of evacuees, giving a much lower ratio of 1:6.

[48] IWM JRD 09. Document signed W Einart (GFP Guernsey), Force 135, I (b), 20 May 1945.

[49] IWM Misc. 2826 189/2 (Tape 4425). Interview with Tom Mansell, Farmer, Guernsey, n.d.

[50] That the Germans were not always an example of good behaviour (or good manners) emerges later on when Fletcher admits that the soldiers were 'swarming about his property' and on one occasion removed a workbench for their own use 'without asking'. A relative trifle, however, compared to what was going on in the houses of evacuees, see IWM Diary of R E H Fletcher 1940–1942, n.d.

or two people who refused his offer to supply them with soup, as 'foolish' and their reaction to 'let it go to the pigs' as 'a strange way of showing their patriotism [...] one can only sympathise with them in their ignorance'. That many of Fletcher's circle could ill-afford such gestures becomes clear in the fact that many had already – we are still in 1941 – reached a stage of material deprivation where humans lose their pride and start picking up cigarette ends, or half-sucked lemons 'for use in a pudding'.[51] It is not entirely accurate to say that the Germans asked for nothing in return, or that islanders had little to offer in exchange. There was one highly prized item to which only islanders had access: news. Until the June 1942 wireless confiscation this was the sole place in occupied Europe where people were allowed to listen to the BBC and there is multiple reference in diaries to troops going into civilian houses to hear the news. Many Germans began to trust the English news rather than their own and found even bad news better than being taken advantage of. After June 1942 the practice died down, but it continued, albeit more discreetly, as punishment was severe.

How to 'manage' the relationship with the Germans is also the major theme in the diary of the Reverend Douglas Ord, arguably the most significant document to have emerged from the Channel Islands' Occupation. The Reverend Douglas Ord was a serving Methodist minister in Guernsey. He had fought during the First World War and spent some time as a prisoner of war in Germany. A well-read and scholarly man, he had studied in Leipzig before the war and was the only cleric in the island who spoke German. Ord understood the Germans, their intellectual brilliance, but also their culture of blind obedience, and their militarism, described by him as 'gallantry without chivalry'. As a point of reference for his own reflection Ord uses, intermittently, the German Occupation of Belgium in World War One and Ludendorff's memoirs, repeating his own mantra '*on peut militariser un civil, mais on ne peut pas civiliser un militaire*'.[52] He says the Occupation was an experience *sui generis* (unlike any other). From the onset Ord took the position that it was impossible to avoid Germans altogether; and we know that this is not an excuse – in particular in the case of Guernsey. Instead one should strive to dissociate the system from those individuals who may be trustworthy and who can be converted. To negotiate the difficulty of living with the enemy Ord developed his own 'golden rule': 'Watch every man circumspectly. Should he prove to be a decent fellow, treat him accordingly, otherwise be on your guard.' The approach was in the true Christian spirit: to distinguish between system and individual, not to give in to hatred, encourage those who come for counsel, be an example unto others. Ord was keen on belying the German propaganda of the British and hoped that

---

[51] ibid.
[52] 'One can "militarise" a civilian, but one cannot civilise a soldier'.

contact would undermine the received opinions of 'docile and gullible folk'. The very idea that there may have been a 'decent fellow' among the enemy was very British; this was not what the Germans were being told about their enemies, and it certainly did impress. Ord spent a considerable part of his time 'sounding out' the Germans he came across and limited himself to those he trusted to be genuinely opposed to Nazism. Sounding out the 'good' Germans was also a survival strategy, as it offered protection against the predator and hoodlum element within the German forces feasting on the civilians. He declared his Church neutral ground, German worshippers were neither encouraged nor excluded, and he formed a circle of loose friendship with a small number of Germans – mostly Churchmen or people connected to the Church – who came to rely on each other for material and spiritual sustenance. This was a middle course between the extremes of another Guernsey clergyman who – according to German documents – was pro-German and the strategy of avoidance advocated by the Rector of St Martin, in Jersey, who told his flock to pass the 'forces of evil [...] in the street as if they were not there, but if we were stopped and asked questions to answer them as politely and as shortly as (they) could.'[53] Ord was not a naive idealist or an opportunist and he does not give clerics automatic credence. He sticks to his golden rule throughout, describing the divisional chaplain for example, a Dr Ebersbach, who is introduced to him in October 1941, as a 'pompous stuffed shirt' who, as a minister of god, disappoints on all counts.[54]

When the wirelesses are confiscated Ord's house becomes a news exchange: his German relations bring news from Germany, he contributes news received from wirelesses operating in the island, they collate it with the controlled Guernsey press and thus get nearer to the real picture. Throughout the diary Ord relates that people in England would neither understand the coming and going in his house nor believe the things which were being said in the confines of his four walls. Ord's position is not without contradictions but he manages to reconcile them without betraying his principles. The strangest contradiction is that he rejoices in every step forward on the path to Allied victory – including the bombing of civilian targets in Germany – but is at the same time on speaking terms with men whose families are being showered with bombs. While empathising with their plight he does not waver in his opinion that all *this* was necessary. One of his German relationships is the result of a chance encounter in a book store in September 1941: Dr Gunkel, the son of the eminent Old Testament scholar Herman Gunkel during the inter-war years, with whose works Ord was familiar. We do not learn which duties Gunkel may have had to

---

[53] JAS L/D/25/M3/6. *A Jersey country parish during the time of occupation*, by Watchman, London, Society for Promoting Christian Knowledge, 1946.

[54] JAS Diary of the Reverend Douglas Ord, entry of 31 Oct 1941.

administer after his transfer from the island, and whether his conscience would have been shaken even further. What we do learn is his exasperation at the dismantling of the democratic legal system which had preceded Hitler but which, after years of thorough Nazification, no longer deserved the name 'law'. In Oct 1941, when one member of Ord's congregation, Basil Martel, is falsely denounced by a woman purchasing an expensive eiderdown on behalf of German soldiers and put on trial for anti-German speech, Gunkel, after an intervention by Ord, makes sure the trial is conducted fairly and the accused is immediately acquitted. Two months after Gunkel's departure in December 1941 Ord receives a call from Heinrich Bödeker, a minister serving in the navy, with an introduction from a German scholar – a mutual acquaintance. While considering him technically an enemy, Ord held that in the end they were fighting a common cause. Bödeker had supported Pastor Martin Niemöller, founder of the 'Confessing Church' and one of the few genuine resisters from within the ranks of the Protestant Church in Germany. After clashing with the Gestapo, Bödeker apparently sought refuge in the armed forces, the only place into which the long arm of the Gestapo did not extend. Bödeker's view of the inside of Nazi Germany and his depictions of the slow but steady inward decay were rather uplifting news to Ord's ears, as it exposed the rifts within the German camp. In March 1942 he told Ord that his entire battery were listening to the BBC, after sounding out the trustworthiness of each new arrival. Finally there is another one, Reinhold Zachmann, from Saxony, a friend of Bödeker's and of a similar disposition. These two men are Ord's principal points of contact during the Occupation. Both had fairly unorthodox views and were certainly no whingers as were so many other Germans once the bombs started to fall on their own cities. Zachmann's family – all regular BBC listeners – were sick of the Nazi lies and hoped for a British victory. His father held the opinion that the bombing campaign was something the Germans had brought upon themselves and now had to endure and denounced anti-Semitism as a reaction of the incompetent who could not adapt to modern economic conditions and needed someone to blame for their failure.

Ord's confrontation with these ordinary, but educated Germans strikes a number of highly interesting points: none of the Germans he meets have an inkling of how to resist and all rely on the Allies for delivery. Their political immaturity and naïveté drives home the point that Germany was incapable of self-deliverance. In a way Ord's German contacts deserve their fate: although they had been cowed into submission and dared not speak up out of fear, their inability to imagine any bolder action with practical implications is rather typical of German political culture of the day. What attracted educated Germans to people such as Douglas Ord was the free flow of ideas and the intoxication of outspokenness, fair judgment and honesty, qualities that were sorely lacking in

Germany. Ord had no illusions that the Occupation of Guernsey had any immediate impact on the outcome of the war, the culture of obedience always took the better of even the decent Germans, but he counted on the all-embracing power of ideas: the confrontation with truth and the spreading of doubt in the hearts of the enemy could not fail to produce results. While this is not measurable in military terms, out of the available options this, one must admit, was probably the best use of available resources. Ord's policy of selective friendship with Germans who were on the same wavelength was probably more useful in the long run than a stubborn avoidance of the 'Hun', which at least in Guernsey was out of the question anyway. One could advance that for Germans in the Channel Islands receptive enough for the gospel, democratic re-education commenced long before 1945, through their contact with a British population.

The British passion for their radios was the decisive factor in this battle of wits and ideas, confirming once more its iconic status. Ord described this as a 'lifeline':

> (E)ach item of news obtained at risk from proscribed wireless sets constituted a milestone on our journey and has a definite relation to the varying moods of depression or elation.

Radio news was a particularly important tool in breaking the power of rumours and countermanding their often damaging or demoralising effect. Many of these rumours originated with the German police or their paid informers anyway. As Ord indicates, Channel Islanders owed their relative sanity and stamina to the fact that they had continued to gain access to news. It wasn't the food that was keeping them going. Ord also confirms the backfiring effect of outright propaganda lies on the disposition of the troops, as these were able to compare German news with British news and often came to the conclusion that the latter was more balanced and as close to the truth as possible under the circumstances. Thus the iron bond of trust between *Volk* and leadership was broken on more than one occasion by the fact that Nazi propaganda was exposed for what it was. The grip of the spoken word was such that when it emerged, in October 1942, that many German soldiers who had radio sets in their billets, were permitting their civilian hosts to listen-in, countermeasures were taken to prevent soldiers from giving such facilities, either by padlocking or moving out the sets.[55]

Particularly heart-rending are Ord's depictions of the evictions of civilians from their houses. These gather particular speed in mid-1941 and continue through to 1942. Apparently sanctioned by divisional command, these 'requisitions' became a euphemism for outright plunder: soldiers penetrated civilian properties at their whim, carrying away family heirlooms, libraries, even

---

[55] JAS Diary of The Reverend Douglas Ord, entry of 9 Oct 1942.

chiming clocks. Some owners were turned out of their houses within minutes; others having been given more time were ordered to return furniture or other property already salvaged from the house which then disappeared or was broken up for firewood. On 10 October 1941 Ord wrote:

> Accounts of the treatment of evicted families pour in daily, and even hourly. A house is taken and in a few minutes German lorries appear with soldiers who are directed to load up the furniture under the very eyes of the rightful owners, who are given ten minutes to pack a suitcase and be gone.

These evictions were no less swift than elsewhere in Europe, with the significant difference, however, that Channel Islanders were spared severe physical maltreatment and death. The lame excuse given to such a flagrant violation of the solemn guarantee of life and property given in July 1940 was usually that the Allied occupation armies in Germany after the First World War had acted no differently. Ord himself was lucky enough never to have been turned out of his house, most likely because of his acquaintance with Judge Gunkel, but he has an unpleasant brush with a man who introduces himself as a historian from Jena university, invites himself into his house to inspect Ord's library and tries to coerce Ord into parting with a number of valuable books which the latter resists. Ord comments at great length on the disgrace of once proud houses being turned into wrecks soiled from top to bottom by troops who then simply move into the next, the scouring predators setting their eyes on choice properties to take over for their uses, the binge drinking, parties and sexual escapades of Germans billeted in his surroundings. But he proves his fairness by also mentioning the German youth billeted with neighbours, who is polite and considerate, leaves everything in perfect condition, supplies them with radio news and never fails to return from his leaves with extra food supplies.

Another Guernseyman to have studied the German occupiers was John Leale. According to Leale the German attitude made life easier to begin with, yet was deceptive. The first contacts in 1940 made many a Guernseyman over-optimistic, but this was to turn out a superficial first impression. Leale, who by all accounts had a more realistic appreciation of the German system than his predecessor, Sherwill, said that there was 'no way around the fact that the Germans were in occupation, despite the politeness'. Rather perceptively, he commented that the sabre-rattling and militarisation merely compensated for a profound inferiority complex, an opinion echoed in the work of many eminent sociologists such as Norbert Elias. Leale sees this complex at work in needless self-assertion which, to him, made individual German officers and officials either 'dangerous' or 'meddlesome'. Fear of losing face made them unwilling to learn; much interference and opposition was merely done for the sake of doing so.[56]

---

[56] A principle well-illustrated by *The von Aufsess occupation diary*, op.cit.

Leale found it 'extremely irritating' to be told by soldiers what was good for the island and cited the example of the Glasshouse Board as an instance of ignorant German interference. While at first it was amusing to see these amateurs (who had never seen a glasshouse) giving advice to Guernseymen who had spent a lifetime in the industry, some faces soon turned sour: the Germans were intent on turning the glasshouses into 'vegetable factories' that would produce all year round. All too often the occupied had to listen to platitudes such as that 'nothing was impossible' – this could have come straight out of the mouth of Hitler – which led to unnecessary argument and work. The other side of the inferiority complex, of course, was the respect of the Germans for British people. That this should have been the principal reason why the Channel Islands' Occupation was relatively mild is not convincing. However, that – as Leale maintained – the German attitude could have ripened into something warmer had Channel Islanders wished, seems a sound judgement. The Germans were ready; it was the Channel Islanders who held back. The Germans were certainly not indifferent about the impression they made and became agitated at the mere suggestion that they might be callous, constantly reminding islanders of their help in procuring supplies from France. Leale used this weakness to try to shame them into sticking to their promises, a tactic that did not always work; in which case the unexplainable was routinely attributed to 'higher authorities' or 'military necessity'. Leale saw through the German system and the rhetoric according to which they 'treated people according to that people's culture'; what this meant in practice was made clear daily in the fate of the foreign labourers.[57]

While there certainly was an affinity, the respect for the British was, as was the disrespect for other nations, founded on stereotypes and clichés, a large part of which were based on the reading of spy and murder mystery novels. Not that sorting out the relationship with the British would have been a preoccupation for the majority of the Germans; here the main worry was how to escape boredom, homesickness and other related afflictions. The ennui is certainly evident in the 1944–45 diary of Baron von Aufsess who apparently spent more time out of his office than in his office at College House Jersey; the inference being that, in fact, there was very little to administer at that time. The time he did spend at his desk he seems to have been trying to get involved in the intrigues and back-stabbing behind the scenes, always pretending to be a major player. His particular ire was directed towards another aristocrat, the right hand of the Befehlshaber, von Helldorf who, in comparison, was a real power broker. Von Aufsess's power, meanwhile, was limited to deploring and intervening in

[57] PRO HO 45/22424. Report of the President of the Controlling Committee of the States of Guernsey on the activities of the Committee during the five years of German Occupation, 23 May 1945; PRO HO 144/22179. Jurat Leale, Memorandum 'On Germans', sent to Sir Frank Newsam (HO), 15 June 1945.

the cutting down of old trees. Von Aufsess clearly had too much time on his hands to have been part of the inner political circle. He certainly did not belong to those Germans who were bored, devouring every genre of books and films that got into his hands and criss-crossing the island, often on horseback, cultivating relationships with compatriots and a select few islanders alike. The ordinary private, in comparison to someone of the status of von Aufsess, had much less freedom of action. The Germans who came over in the summer of 1941 still had enough time on their hands to go for a swim and lie on the beach in the afternoon, after morning drill practice. Germans could indeed mingle incognito among the local population engaged in similar pursuits.[58] These opportunities all but faded the following year when the drill 'became stricter', leaving soldiers less leisure time, access to beaches was restricted and the relationship with the locals was on the downward slope.[59] One unnamed German soldier who served at Mont Orgueil described his existence as a routine of guard duty, sleep, playing cards or chess, riding out and the odd visit to the Soldatenheim.[60] Understandably, military personnel thus employed had little contact with the population, except to barter food.[61] Some soldiers could develop 'island madness': in one documented case a corporal simply ran out of his bunker in Gorey, Jersey, one afternoon, loaded his machine gun and shot out to sea without reason, thus putting the entire east of the island on alarm.[62] In response to isolation and 'culture shock' the German authorities put on entertainment or let alcohol flow. They also tried to cultivate interest in island culture, by publishing a number of guide and illustrated books, a rather unprecedented and unwarlike move. One of these, rather touchingly, written by von Aufsess himself. In other cases the toll was even higher, resulting in suicide or suicide attempts, which the Germans in their eternal wisdom decided to condemn as sabotage. When these became more frequent, troop commanders were admonished to keep their eyes open for signs of suicidal tendencies and provide counsel.

Those Germans who had the opportunity were often desperate for the human touch. This is another thing that emerges rather clearly from the von Aufsess diary. Contrary to popular belief his contacts with islanders were few and far between, the Attorney General, Duret Aubin, with whom he has frequent official business being one of the few exceptions. Jerseyman Fred Woodall

[58] IWM Misc. 2826 189/2. Interviews with Hühnegarth and Kassens, n.d.

[59] IWM Misc. 2826 189/2 (Tape 4489). Interview with Werner Grosslopp [sic]. He made a particular mention of a deterioration of relations with the farming community. This may indicate that farmers were less willing than before to accede to the wishes of individual Germans in terms of additional food purchases.

[60] IWM Misc. 2826 189/2. Interview with unnamed German soldier, n.d.

[61] IWM Misc. 2826 189/2 (Tape 450). Interview with Herr Huhnegarth, n.d.

[62] IWM Misc. 2826 189/2 (Tape 4489). Interview with Werner Grosslopp, n.d.[

related in his war diary 'that most Germans (were) so lonely that they would do anything to be invited into someone's house to have a cup of tea or anything'.[63] Jersey youngster Don Filleul remembers one German passer-by who took to his piano playing, one Occupation summer day. This young sympathetic character was clearly disposed to striking up a closer friendship, but Don decided that this was not the right time or the right place for fraternisation while one's country was at war.[64] A similar fate befell former curator of the Underground Hospital, Joe Mière. In his Occupation reminiscences[65] he relates the pain of falling in love with an attractive German nurse who was killed in an air raid later into the war, and then having to end the budding relationship before it got more serious, for similar reasons. Islanders faced tough choices and not all were as consequential in drawing the line; many failed, for whatever reason, to comprehend the intrusion of politics and war into their private world.

If one had to categorise the Germans one would probably find as many compulsive 'complainers' who – almost as a matter of principle – were always bored by life in the islands, longed for home and drowned their sorrows in alcohol, as there were Germans who found the offer of cinemas, cafes, book store and theatre performances quite plentiful so that they were never bored.[66] A parallel exists between those Germans who found Channel Islands' women indifferent or hostile to any advances and the proactive roamers stating that Channel Islands' women were very approachable. Herr Grau, a former soldier, said that the women regarded the Germans as enemies, but that contacts were also determined by language problems. Germans who could communicate in English had better chances.[67] In spite of this and other evidence from Germans posted to the islands, the most enduring image on the issue of the approachability of British womankind is that created by the self-indulgence of a Baron von Aufsess and other male boasters. Why they are given automatic credence by many intelligent people often beggars belief. Other accounts, such as an infamous escapee report of 1944 that made headlines on its release from the Public Record Office in the 1990s, also leave an impression that Channel Islands' women who did not have a German lover were a minority. Unsurprisingly a lot of bad blood was created on the release of Madeleine Bunting's *The Model Occupation*. This book is adorned with photographs of women of unspecified nationality[68] together with their German admirers, carrying a catchy sarcastic caption reading 'Island women found the attractions

---

[63] IWM Woodall diary, entry of 21 Mar 1943.
[64] Interview with author, Nov 2004.
[65] Joe Mière, *Never to be forgotten*, Jersey, 2004.
[66] IWM Misc. 2826 189/2 (Tape 450). Interview with Herr Huhnegarth, n.d.
[67] IWM Misc. 2826 189/2. Interview with Herr Grau, n.d.
[68] See Bunting, op.cit., first set of photographs between pages 120–121.

of the Germans difficult to resist'. However, at least in the case of the group photograph there is evidence that it was shot elsewhere. Closer examination of the original photograph (Bunting's book only presents a blow-up) proves that the dresses and hairstyles of the women, the house and the surrounding vegetation are more suggestive of Northern France than the Channel Islands. In any case, to deduce from the fact that this photograph is in the collection of the Jersey Heritage Trust that it was actually shot in Jersey is a step too far. None of the photos warrant such a libellous caption and the outrage of the majority of island women who steered clear is understandable. It seems that when it comes to some of the trickier aspects of the Channel Islands' Occupation some writers and journalists would prefer their readers to suspend belief. That the sexual pursuits of a Baron von Aufsess or a Colonel von Helldorf were not given to the underdog who, at most times, had to stand guard duty, hovering between boredom, depression and eager anticipation of his next trip back home, should have been pertinently clear. As for the rest, it is probably safe to say that the ten to twenty per cent enterprising and hormone-driven predators, womanisers or charmers one can find in any male population, at all times, would have been responsible for the great majority of these love crimes.

Although many allegations were indeed exaggerated – and one has to factor in the impact of male fantasies on both sides – it would be equally foolish to deny the reality of horizontal collaboration. The figures certainly exist for the number of illegitimate children although it is debatable whether they suggest any extraordinary tendencies of sexual collaboration. The Germans themselves believed that they had been responsible for sixty to eighty illegitimate births in the Channel Islands and were undertaking steps to facilitate the emigration to Germany of the children together with the mothers at the time of the Normandy landings.[69] The British press, on the other hand, quoted a figure of 800 in 1945, which was too high. [70] In Jersey 176 births out of wedlock were registered between July 1940 and May 1945[71], but these figures are too low, as Jersey law recognises all children born to married women, even of another man, as legitimate. Although edging closer to the real figure of illegitimate births would have merely involved checking the names of the men stated as fathers against the list of men who had been out of the island during the Occupation, the Jersey

[69] BA-R NS 47/48. Lebensborn. Uneheliche Kinder deutscher Besatzungsangehöriger auf den Kanalinseln. FK 515 an den HSSPF im Bereich des Mbf Frankreich, Paris, 27 Apr. 1944.
[70] PRO HS 452. Sir Oscar Dowson, Home Office legal adviser to W E Beckett, Foreign Office re. children born out of wedlock during the Occupation, 20 June 1945; PRO HO 45/22399. Attorney General of Jersey to Howard (HO), 7 July 1945; see also the reaction to these allegations of the Medical Officer for Jersey, Dr McKinstry, in Louise Willmot, 'Noel McKinstry', *The Channel Islands Occupation Review*, 2003 (31), 29–30.
[71] A Le Gros, Superintendent Registrar, Jersey, 10 July 1945, relayed to the Home Office on 16 July, see PRO HO 45/22399. Attorney General of Jersey to Howard (HO).

authorities were certainly not interested in delving any further into the question.[72] In Guernsey, where the law was similar to English law, 259 illegitimate births occurred between July 1941 and June 1945 – with an estimated 140 of German fathers – with further births of this kind expected after June 1945.[73] By August 1945 the Security Service had been able to up the total figure to 320 illegitimate births in the Channel Islands, of which 'it was certain' that 180 were of German fathers. By what means this information was extracted is unknown, but determining German paternity beyond doubt must have been no mean achievement in the days of pre-DNA sampling![74] In the end, one should perhaps congratulate the Channel Islanders for not having taken these methods any further. The Channel Islanders also avoided the deplorable scenes of often indiscriminate violence played out against real – and imagined – horizontal collaborators on the Continent. Most islanders with their level-headed attitude realised that the rationale for such orgies of violence against women was to deflect attention away from subjects more meritorious of reproof, such as the people who had cashed in during the Occupation.[75]

The essence of conquest lies, to a certain extent, with the conqueror having his way with the females of the occupied territory. This feature of warfare was certainly feared by the Channel Islanders in the beginning and it worked in favour of the Germans that on this front they were better than their reputation. Like other more seasoned observers, the Reverend Douglas Ord believed that especially younger girls found the lure of the uniform irresistible. Other oft-repeated reasons for these relationships were that some women liked to 'show off', or were of low morality. In Guernsey a curious story was circulating at the beginning of the Occupation: a lady is walking up St Julian's Avenue with a friend, when they see a motor car being driven by a German sailor who is accompanied by a lady friend. The lady turns to her friend and says: 'Look at this – my maid and my car!'[76] Horizontal collaboration was also a revenge of the lower classes, a reaction to the class-riddled British system that appealed to the underdog.[77]

Reality was certainly even more complex than that. There were, of course,

[72] PRO HO 45/22399. Attorney General of Jersey to Howard (HO), 7 July 1945.
[73] PRO HO 45/22399. Home Office document 'Illegitimate children born in the Channel Islands during the Occupation', 30 June 1945.
[74] PRO KV 4/78. Consolidated report: 'The I(b) Reports on the Channel Islands', by Major J R Stopford, 8 Aug. 1945.
[75] JAS L/F/64/C/1–4. The opinion expressed in a newssheet of the minuscule Jersey Communist Party distributed on Liberation. The Communists were not alone, however, in their rejection of 'acts of hooliganism against foolish girls and women'.
[76] IWM P338. Diary of Miss Lainé, The German Occupation of Guernsey 1940–1945.
[77] Philippe Burrin writes that many of the horizontal collaborators were from 'modest backgrounds' and 'often worked for the occupying forces', Philippe Burrin, *Living with defeat: France under the German occupation*, London, 1996, 206, cited in Davies, op. cit., 106.

genuine love relationships. While this was certainly not the right time to fall in love with the enemy, it was human and in some cases inevitable. Who would want to sit in judgement? The Germans' taboo-lifting air of sexual liberty also challenged the consensus of prudishness, blowing a breeze of fresh air into stuffy old-fashioned Victorian society. This would have definitely endeared them to the hedonists intent on having a 'good time'. While it is certainly no excuse for sleeping with the enemy, there was a strange fascination or chemistry between some Channel Islands' women and Germans that seemed to precipitate such relationships. Some clearly found that the Germans were better love makers.[78] Here the role of perception is primordial. A similar phenomenon was spotted by behaviourists studying the relationships between GIs and British women during the American 'occupation' of Britain in 1943–44. Both groups, the British women and the Americans, claimed that the other side was particularly 'sexed' and that they found this attractive. The scientists then determined that every human group has its own ritual of love-making which proceeds according to a principle called 'the ten stages of love-making'. While all cultures have a limited number of steps, the order of steps can differ greatly. In British cultural coding kissing would come rather late, as a prelude to sex, whereas the Americans had this on their menu much earlier, but then threw in a few more steps before sex which were missing in the British code. What happened was that the inadvertent jumping of intermediary steps reinforced the impression that the other side was highly sexed and therefore precipitated rather than delayed the final stage of love-making. At what stage kissing came in German coding is unknown. Von Aufsess, the great expert, at one point 'compares' the 'swift' love-making of the Englishwoman to the profligate courtship required to bed a Frenchwoman.[79] Whether he was right to say such a thing is not the point; what counts is that such an idea would have occurred to him at all. It suggests that the 'ten stages of love-making' may have had relevance in the occupied Channel Islands as well.

What one should not forget is that in many other cases the often romanticised, supposedly voluntary act of 'sleeping with the enemy' was not a matter of choice, but of necessity; a halfway house between paid sex and a semi-permanent relationship mainly geared towards obtaining benefits of various kinds.[80] One Guernsey informant reported that food was the initial bait in many cases, suggesting that there was no other plausible explanation for why many married and respectable women would be living with Germans.[81] The real

[78] See the case of Guernsey girl Dolly Joanknecht in Bunting, op.cit.

[79] See relevant paragraph in *The von Aufsess occupation diary*, op.cit.

[80] There is no word in the English language to define such an arrangement. In Russian the term is '*sponsorstvo*' (literally: sponsoring).

[81] PRO HO 144/22237. Report from Guernsey, autumn 1944. The Report continued to mention a secret club which pledged to punish some of these women, known as the GUB (Guernsey Underground Barbers), in parody of the Glasshouse Utilisation Board.

nature of many relationships between Germans and island women is another point which was gravely misinterpreted by Madeleine Bunting: although she had the answer staring her in the face, she used the sexual boasting of an Oberleutnant (second lieutenant) Kugler to the effect that the Channel Islands were like a 'German port city' and that all young soldiers had 'girl friends' to demonstrate the high incidence of horizontal collaboration.[82] The allusion to 'port cities' should have been sufficient to gauge that 'girl friend' in this context was certainly synonymous not with horizontal collaboration, but with what in Germany is termed as 'horizontal trade'. This story repeated itself millions of times across wartime Europe, and into the post-war period. Estimates of illegal prostitution in occupied Paris suggest a figure as high as 100,000[83], which is not altogether surprising considering the material conditions of a majority of the population. It also explains the magical attraction the city continued to exert on the Germans and why so many would risk disciplinary measures for 'getting lost' there for a few days, during transfers to other, no doubt less well-provided places. In occupied Germany tens of thousands of other women sold themselves to the Allied forces for stockings or cigarettes[84], and the overriding motive still was to eat and survive. This is not a topic for sensationalist exploitation, it rather drives forward the consequences of war and occupation on women fending for themselves; yet another deserved nail in the coffin of an all-too romantic vision of war. The Germans recognised the problem of illegal prostitution and opened brothels destined to keep sex between natives and soldiers, and VD, down. One of these brothels was the Maison Victor Hugo in Jersey, run by French madams under German medical control, with as many as 36 French prostitutes.[85] One 1944 escapee said that the incidence of illegal prostitution in Jersey would have been higher had it not been for these 'professionals'. Another determining factor were the penalties introduced by the German hierarchy for sleeping around in the local population, in particular the fact that married Germans caught out with VD had certain allowances cut, thus bringing the problem to the attention of their wives. The same informant, a medical orderly at the General Hospital, revealed that there were 15 VD cases per week, and said that this was only an indication of the true scope of the problem as seeking treatment was akin to self-denunciation. The Guernsey figures for 1944 certainly go in the same direction: in the course of that year there was a total of 1,345 attendances at the clinic, with a 25–75 split between men and women.[86] Still, these figures give no indication as

---

[82] Bunting, op. cit., 56.

[83] Fabrice Virgili, *Shorn Women – Gender and punishment in Liberation France*, Oxford, 2002.

[84] Willi A Boelcke, *Der Schwarzmarkt 1945–1948. Vom Überleben nach dem Kriege*, Braunschweig, 1986.

[85] PRO WO 32/13750. MI19. Report Channel Island of Jersey, eighteen-year-old male nurse, arrived UK 13 Aug 1944, 18 Aug 1944.

[86] JAS L/D/25/M4/11. Medical Report for 1944, Guernsey, 1945.

to the source of contraction which might have been the many other foreigners or remaining Britishers in the island. As can be gauged from the number of male civilian attendances at the Guernsey VD clinic this part of the population was by no means inactive. German medical documents discovered by British security after Liberation were more satisfactory in this respect. They were to ascertain that a total of 110 Guernseywomen were treated for VD during the Occupation, contracted by reason of their association with Germans.[87]

Wherein lies the ultimate significance? Surely these were not unique events. In France the Germans were claiming to have fathered a total of 85,000 babies.[88] The uniqueness of horizontal collaboration in the Channel Islands only really lies in the fact that it pulverises the stereotypes and mythology of the Second World War. Otherwise it is a story of human flesh and blood. Often it is also forgotten that the overwhelming majority of these flirtations never went beyond the platonic stage and were motivated by curiosity or genuine interest. The mother who exclaimed that her daughter's relationship was for reasons of 'cultural exchange' may have had the right idea after all.

---

[87] PRO KV 4/78. Security Service. Force 135, I(b), The I(b) reports on the Channel Islands, 8 Aug 1945.

[88] BA-R NS 47/48. Lebensborn. Uneheliche Kinder deutscher Besatzungsangehöriger auf den Kanalinseln. Vermerk Einwandererzentralstelle, Paris, 15 Oct 1943.

In June 1940 everyone lent a hand to fill sandbags. Here a group of children do their duty by the front of the West Park Pavilion in St Helier's Lower Park.

June 1940. In Jersey, the queues of people registering for evacuation stretched from St Helier Town Hall all along the Parade.

June 1940. Despite the heat of the June sun, evacuees wore as many clothes as possible to be able to carry more in their suitcases.

July 1 1940. The Bailiff, Attorney General and the Governor's Secretary meet the invaders at Jersey's new airport.

Luftwaffe troops taking part in the Victory parade in St Helier, August 1940. The tall man without a rifle on the right of the column was Lt Richard Kern – the first German to land in the island.

Throughout the summer of 1940 islanders had to get used to thousands of foreign troops in their home. Life went on and many islanders tried to ignore the obvious.

St Helier, May 1941 – German uniforms became part of the landscape.

Women who had relationships with German soldiers were shunned as "Jerrybags" by fellow islanders.

A must for every German serviceman was to have his photograph taken alongside a British "bobby".

The SS *Diamant* in Granville, 1941. This ancient Norman port was one of the main staging posts on the way to the islands and the HQ of the Channel Islands Purchasing Commission.

The Pioneer company (engineers) of the 319 Division en route to Guernsey on board the SS *Diamant* in 1941.

A view of St Peter Port harbour from Tower Hill, taken by one of the Pioneer Company in 1941.

Amongst the many organisations proscribed by the Germans was the Freemasons. Masonic regalia was removed from Jersey to Berlin on the orders of Reichsleiter Alfred Rosenberg who featured it in an exhibition, *British Freemasonry*, in March 1941. The doors of the St Helier Temple were officially sealed by the Feldkommandantur to ensure it remained closed.

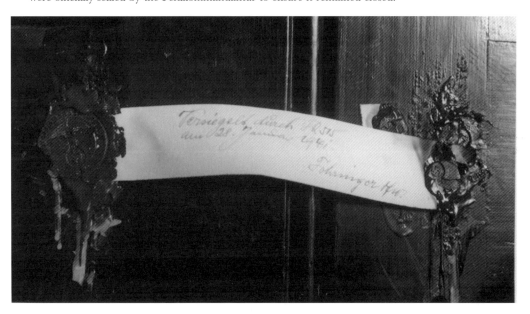

Starting in late 1941 islanders were fenced in and denied access to the sea. As the Occupation wore on, life in the islands became increasingly constrained by and subject to the harsh restrictions of life in a fortress.

This blockhouse by Gorey Pier which housed a 7.5cms anti-tank gun was camouflaged to look like a seaside bungalow.

(*Left*) Albin Ballauf (right), here in his billet in Alderney, was a member of the Pioneer company (engineers) of the 319 Division posted to the island at the height of the fortification programme in the summer of 1942.

(*Above*) SS Hauptstrumfuhrer Maximillian List, Commandant of the Sylt Concentration Camp in Alderney.

(*Below*) Prisoners from the Sylt camp in Alderney working under guard.

FOR SALE BY TENDER

THE

UNDERTAKING

Including the Stock-in-Trade of Gentlemen's Outfitters carried on by

A. KRICHEFSKI & SON,

HALKETT STREET,
JERSEY.

Tenders to be sent prior to 25th March, 1941, to—
LE MASURIER, GIFFARD & POCH,
Solicitors,
23 HILL STREET, JERSEY,
from whom all particulars may be obtained

FOR SALE BY TENDER

THE

UNDERTAKING

Including the Stock-in-Trade of Costumier and Milliner carried on by

MADAME PERETZ,

9 KING STREET,
JERSEY.

Tenders to be sent prior to 25th March, 1941, to—
LE MASURIER, GIFFARD & POCH,
Solicitors,
23 HILL STREET, JERSEY,
from whom all particulars may be obtained

FOR SALE BY TENDER

THE

UNDERTAKING

Including Stock-in-Trade and fittings of

Messrs. LOUIS ET CIE

(Mr. Louis Feldman)

trading in Ladies' Gowns, Millinery, etc., at

No. 5 NEW STREET,
JERSEY.

Tenders to be sent prior to the 25th March, 1941, to—
Advocates OGIER & LE CORNU
(Acting for the Administrator),
ROYAL COURT CHAMBERS, JERSEY,
from whom all particulars may be obtained

(*Left*) Notices in the Evening Post announcing the Aryanisation of Jersey's Jewish businesses.

(*Above*) One of Jersey's Jewish businesses, Madame Peretz in King Street, with the "Jewish Undertakings" sign displayed in the centre of the window, October 1940.

(*Below*) Two Guernsey women, Mrs Adele Masurier and Mrs Dorothy Michael, were deported to the continent for their part in sheltering the British soldiers, Nicolle and Symes.

BEKANNTMACHUNG.

Im Monat Juli wurden auf der Insel Guernsey 2 englische Offiziere zu Erkundungszwecken an Land gesetzt. Die beiden Offiziere hielten sich zeitweilig bei ihren Angehoerigen auf, ohne die deutsche Militaerbehoerde von ihrem Aufenthalt ordnungsgemaess in Kenntnis zu setzen.

Die Namen der betr. Angehoerigen sind:

Frau Adele Masurier, geb. Martel, wohnhaft West-Craft, Queen's Road, St. Peter-Port und

Frau Dorothy Madeleine Michael, geb. Moorhouse, Le Paradou, Forest.

Um in Zukunft jede Unterstuetzung seitens der Zivilbevoelkerung von weiteren britischen Spaehversuchen auf den besetzten Kanalinseln zu unterbinden, wurde vom zustaendigen Armeeoberkommando angeordnet, dass die beiden Frauen nach einem auf dem Festlande gelegenen, mindestens 15 km von der Kueste entfernten Platz gebracht werden und sich dort taeglich bei der Feldkommandantur zu melden haben.

Feldkommandantur 515.
Der Feldkommandant
gez. Schumacher.
Oberst.

NOTICE.

During July two British officers landed on the Island of Guernsey for the purpose of gathering military information. Temporarily, they put up with relatives without informing the German military authorities of their stay according to regulations.

The relatives are:

Mrs. Adele Masurier, née Martel, Westcraft, Queen's Road, St. Peter Port, and

Mrs. Dorothy Madeleine Michael, née Moorhouse, Le Paradou-Forest.

To prevent the civil population of the Channel Islands from supporting henceforth British Agents on occupied territory, the Commander in Chief of the Army ordered the two ladies to be removed to a place on the Continent, at least 9 miles distant from the coast, where they will have to present themselves daily before the local Feldkommandant.

Feldkommandantur 515.
Der Feldkommandant.
(Signed) Schumacher, Colonel.

Peter Hassall photographed just before his escape attempt in May 1942. He served three years as a *Nacht und Nebel* prisoner in Germany's prisons and concentration camps. He was the only one of three friends to survive the war.

Dennis Audrain was only 17 years old in May 1942 when he drowned while attempting to escape from Jersey with Maurice Gould and Peter Hassall.

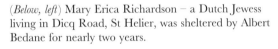

(*Below, left*) Mary Erica Richardson – a Dutch Jewess living in Dicq Road, St Helier, was sheltered by Albert Bedane for nearly two years.

(*Below, right*) Albert Bedane risked his life on several occasions to hide fugitives from the Germans. In 2000 he was posthumously recognised by the State of Israel as one of the 'Righteous Amongst the Nations'.

(*Top left*) Some Germans found the relative isolation of the islands hard to contend with; however, it was regarded as being better than serving on the Russian Front.

(*Bottom left*) German funeral at Fort George, Guernsey.

(*Right*) Swastikas daubed in tar on the homes of suspected German sympathisers remained part of St Helier's townscape for years. This image was taken in Dumaresq Street in 1947.

(*Below*) German Police in Guernsey, 1944.

The two Bailiffs, Coutanche and Carey, discussing the arrangements for the visit of the Red Cross ship *Vega* December 1944

Guernsey's Bailiff, Carey and Admiral Huffmeier meet with Red Cross officials on the arrival of the *Vega* in St Peter Port harbour in December 1944.

The Red Cross ship SS *Vega* in St Peter Port harbour.

JLiberation Day, 1945. In St Helier, a jubilant crowd hoists onto their shoulders one of the first Royal Navy sailors to land. Partly obscured by the sailor's elbow was Claude Cahun, the Surrealist photographer, recently released from the island prison where she had been held for anti-German activities.

Rapturous crowds watch British troops marching down New Street, May 1945.

The large numbers of German POWs were shipped out of the islands to camps in the U.K. and elsewhere within days of the Liberation. Here, a column of prisoners stretches from West Park to First Tower in St Aubin's Bay, Jersey.

Unlike these, most
forced workers in
Alderney were not
given the dignity of a
marked grave.

British war correspon-
dents demonstrate the
use of the re-usable
coffin found in
Alderney.

V

The Visitors

Islanders had many names for the occupier, none of which was particularly flattering. For some they were simply 'Jerry', for others 'the greenflies'. Alexander Coutanche is reputed to have referred to them, in his own distinguished and unmistakable style, as 'ces messieurs' which – as the linguists will recognise – carries an oh-so-slight whiff of disapproval. Those more advanced in age stuck to the by then old-fashioned 'the Hun', in particular those who, like Jerseywoman Dorothy de Gruchy. wanted to have nothing to do with them; whereas for the more French-inclined they were simply the Boches. Others tried to ridicule the situation with the deprecating humour so characteristic of the wartime generation, by referring to them as 'the Visitors'. And some did, indeed, treat them like another bunch of tourists who would return home when they had had their fill of sea, sun and fun. Clearly islanders never were in one mind about these new 'Visitors'. For some they remained humourless automatons, a disposition made clear by one joke circulating in Guernsey:

> A Guernseyman goes to a hairdressing saloon for a hair cut and a shave, and is asked to take a seat. Then a German naval officer comes in who is asked to do the same, but expecting to be attended to at once.
> *Assistant:* 'Excuse me, sir, but this gentleman was in first so I must attend to him first.'
> *German:* 'If Mr Anthony Eden came in would you ask him to wait?'
> *Assistant:* 'It would not be necessary. He is too much of a gentleman to want to take anybody else's turn.'
> Assistant fined 20 RM.[1]

Others were quite surprised to discover that the Germans could have a sense of humour all of their own. Islander John Blampied reported that when the Germans found some thousand copies of 'The Siegfried Line' 'they thought [...] it was a great laugh', buying up the lot and sending it back to Germany.[2]

---

[1] IWM P338. German Occupation of Guernsey 1940–1945, diary of Miss A Le M Laine
[2] IWM Misc. 2826 189/2 (Tapes 4394 O/L and 4396 O/L). Interview with John Blampied, n.d.

Some of the Germans brought a hitherto unknown culture and worldliness to the Channel Islands. Jersey girl Stella Perkins had enough reason to dislike all the German marching and singing, but enjoyed being taken to hear a string quartet by her music teacher, some time in 1944–45. While three of the players were locals, the lead musician was a white-haired German who looked and played 'like an angel' – starvation had reduced many soldiers either to old men or young children.[3]

Of men and morale

Who were the men under the Wehrmacht uniforms? What was behind the grey monolithic mass as they often appeared to islanders?

The first occupation troops in the island were the men of the 216th Infantry Division (ID). This unit was set up shortly before the outbreak of war, in August 1939, and originated in Lower Saxony. The 216th was a division of the third wave which consisted of reservists and home guard members, many of whom had seen active service in the First World War. In December 1941 the 216th was moved to the Eastern Front, to Smolensk. It vanished out of existence two years later, after fierce fighting around the city of Orel. The 319th ID had arrived in strength in the Channel Islands in June 1941. The chain of command extended from the division to the LXXXIV Corps stationed in St Lô, the 7th Army, and finally the Oberbefehlshaber West. This 319th belonged to the 13th recruitment wave and was set up as late as November 1940, in Thuringia. The 319th was one of nine new divisions formed with the task of garrisoning occupied France and the Channel Islands. One third of the troops were taken from divisions of the second, seventh and eighth waves. The rest were fresh recruits of the age groups of 1905 through 1919. Their equipment included much French war booty and they were seconded by coastal artillery, a machine gun battalion, two mobile units and one Panzer unit. The 319th was the only division which remained permanently stationed in the occupied West. The other eight garrison divisions were sent East in 1942 where they saw action at the battle of Kursk in July 1943. Only one regiment of the 319th seems to have been withdrawn to the Crimea, in October 1943, and was replaced by 3,000 troops of the 'Russian Army of Liberation' and 1,500 Italian auxiliaries. The German troops were also filled up with Polish and Czech draftees and a Georgian battalion was to follow in April 1944. Russian speaking German officers also visited the eight Russian labour camps to persuade them to join the Wehrmacht, which, according to informants, none accepted.[4]

---

[3] IWM Misc. 2826 189/2 (Tape 4446 o/L). Interview with Stella Perkins, n.d.

[4] Georg Tessin, *Verbände und Truppen der deutschen Wehrmacht und Waffen-SS im Zweiten Weltkrieg 1939–1945*, Biblio Verlag, Osnabrück 1974; Michael Ginns, 'The 319 Infantry Division in the

The troops and operational command were not the only German military entities in the islands. The other hierarchy was the civil affairs unit, the Feldkommandantur (FK) 515. Although staffed by men in uniform and despite its name, its principal tasks were non-military. Broadly, the FK assumed the rights of the sovereign; it was responsible for the civilian population as well as for the maintenance of law and order. The FK 515 was formed in May 1940, trained in Luxemburg and arrived in Jersey in August 1940, with a personnel consisting of officials, city employees, government workers and a few army officers. Of the 150–160 men in the unit when it was formed only a small number were sent to the Channel Islands. Although the personnel changed from time to time and men could be transferred to other jobs in occupied Europe, about 30 per cent of the original personnel remained in the islands in 1944.[5] An important accessory to FK duties was its responsibility for providing troops with supplies. Therefore, not surprisingly, food production and agriculture were at the top of the FK's overall agenda. On a more unpleasant note, the FK also supervised the German police force, had jurisdiction over islanders who flouted German regulations and implemented anti-Semitic measures, wireless confiscations and deportations. Manpower shortages made the Germans adopt the principle of 'indirect administration' in occupied Europe, and the Channel Islands were no exception. This 'control administration' (Aufsichtsverwaltung) was loosely modelled on the example of colonial administrations, with a stress on the supervision of all domains of state and society, and direct interference in key strategic areas only. The actual number of FK staffers was tiny; their main tasks consisted in establishing directives, passing them on to the local authorities and double-checking whether these had been duly executed. On a large number of issues the island authorities were co-opted, a mandate bringing FK officials in close working contact with islands officials. The majority of FK officials were recruited directly from the civil service, receiving military ranks commensurate with their civilian status and wearing uniform. This was resented by the professional soldiers who certainly did not regard these *Zivilisten* as equals deserving automatic rank without first earning it. The aversion would have been compounded by the organisational culture of a civil affairs unit, which cultivated the art of compromise and political tact, not something hardened Prussian soldiers were known for. Neither would FK officials have endeared themselves by letting it be known that army officers were over-reacting or by their attempts to water down measures. Politically, the FK bureaucrats belonged to the conser-

Channel Islands', *The Channel Islands Occupation Review*, 1991 (19), 40–68; PRO HO 144/22237. Report Channel Islands Jersey, Interrogation of 4 Russian OT labourers (info as at 13 Dec 1943), 4 Jul 1944.

[5] PRO WO 199/3303. Information obtained from KVI Taborsky, PLK, captured near St Malo 13 Aug 1944, 22 Aug 1944.

vative right, which meant that although critical, they would have approved important sections of the Nazi agenda, especially the revision of the Versailles treaty, German hegemony in Europe, anti-liberalism and anti-communism. Although they may have abhorred some of the cruder manifestations of Nazi prejudice, they did not shed a tear when Jews and other minorities were being packed off to unknown destinations.

At least in theory the FK should have had substantial say in the running of the islands, mirroring military authority. Dr Casper – chief administrator from 1941 and 1943 and a *Landrat* (county councillor) before the war – certainly believed that the military administration had more freedom of authority in the Channel Islands than in France. He based this on the idea that the FK 515 had less interference from civilian agencies than its counterparts in France.[6] What he overlooked was that, with such a strong garrison, combat troops and OT (Organization Todt) exerted more than the usual influence. Thus the final word in many areas, even on measures concerning the civilian population, lay not with the Feldkommandant but with the commanders of the combat troops. Perhaps the most illustrative example of their influence was the suggestion of deporting the entire population, an idea that surfaced in the beginning of the fortification of the Channel Islands in 1941 and again in late 1944. In the opinion of the combat troops the presence of civilians was anathema to the smooth running of a fortress. The FK, on the other hand, insisted that the presence of civilians in the islands was beneficial, as it reduced the scale of German imports from France. While radical plans of total evacuation never materialised, the basic idea of removing groups of people was implemented on several occasions. The availability of food and labour, political and racial 'reliability', and the demands of fortification served as the rationale underpinning most decisions on whom to deport, and the FK was called upon to strike the balance between 'essential workers', e.g. those active in food production, and 'undesirables', 'unreliables' or 'superfluous eaters' who served no purpose in the German sense. The internal power struggle for authority in the Channel Islands was also visible in the radio confiscation of 1942 and in a number of other areas. It climaxed in April 1943 when divisional command demanded the complete dissolution of the Feldkommandantur and transfer of its duties to the 319th ID. However, these steps were thwarted in unison by the competent superior authorities in France, the Oberbefehlshaber (OB) West,[7] and the Military Governor in France,[8] who insisted on the usefulness of the FK 515 as a buffer between military and civilians. It was equally conceded that the Channel Islands' Occupation was sensitive in

---

[6] AN AJ 40/547. FK 515. 'Verwaltungsüberblick über die Kanalinseln', Wilhem Casper, June 1943.

[7] German Military High Command in Western Europe

[8] The term in German is *Militärbefehlshaber in Frankreich*.

terms of foreign policy and propaganda, and that relations between military and locals should continue to be managed through an appropriate hybrid agency.

The Channel Islanders were not used to dealing with such a Byzantine bureaucracy. Had they known what was going on in the German camp – the crude politicking and backstabbing, continually shifting alliances and imbalance of power – they may have been surprised. But it is doubtful whether they ever knew what was going on – with the notable exception of the last months of the Occupation when the contours of a 'power struggle' between army and navy could no longer be hidden. Alexander Coutanche's memoirs confirm the impression that the islands' authorities were left out of the bigger picture. The combat troop commanders always remained in the shadows and the dealings with civilians were relegated to the FK underlings. Questioned after the war on whether he could give a description of General Müller, Coutanche said that he was unable to, as he had never seen Müller. His only other contact apart from the Feldkommandantur people was von Schmettow. His successor Hüffmeyer, however, Coutanche only saw twice: when the latter arrived as von Schmettow's 'guardian angel' in late 1944 and when the visitors' visit drew to an end, in May 1945. The Occupation experience coincided with a considerable disempowerment on the part of the authorities whose access route to the real decision makers was a roundabout one and who were often being used as political pawns.

The quality and morale of the conglomeration of fortress troops is a different question. Their mind-set would seem to answer this question in the negative. All ideology provides a simplification of the world. Its reduction of complexity simplifies life, but there is a threshold where the undoubted benefits ideology bestows for selecting and processing information turns into a harmful distortion of reality. The Nazi mind-set embraced a form of political paranoia that would fit this description rather well. Its vigour remained intact in the context of offensive war, but being forced back onto the defensive was like a negative recall of everything that had gone wrong in German history. The fortification of the Atlantic Wall was the expression of paranoia cast into concrete and steel. It bred a fortress mentality that numbed the flexibility and tactical skill German commanders had displayed in their early military campaigns. Their participation in delusions such as the alleged British priority to re-conquer the islands or the chimera of enemy agent infiltration seems to prove how far removed from reality they became. As a fighting force the 319th was as good as any other division, but fortress life lulled its alertness in comforting monotony. Channel Islanders soon spotted this weakness. Jerseyman Alf Vibert stated that it was as though they had a drill for every eventuality, but were caught out when something unexpected or 'impossible' happened.[9] Not that tedium did not exist

---

[9] Interview with Alf Vibert, Jersey, 21 November 2004.

in other armed forces, but the subservient spirit reigning in the German armed forces seemed to sap independent initiative. Examples for this disposition abound. In the autumn of 1944 escapes were taking place at a rather regular pace from the south-eastern part of Jersey, notably Pontac beach, which 'rather stupidly ' was left un-mined and un-patrolled.[10] During all this time troops were only alert when they received an order to be alert. One party stated that they had made 'a lot of noise' and were even spotted by two Germans, but were allowed to leave undisturbed.[11] By November the Germans had finally woken up and increased patrols on this part of the coast, but they still did not know the exact locations from which people were escaping. One of the obstacles to singling out Pontac was that they remained convinced that it was impossible to get a boat over the 14 foot seawalls on to the beach. When a party had left they did not believe that it could have reached the mainland and said that it was 'at the bottom of the sea'. One party of escapees put this down to their diminished ability to believe in any 'individual initiative or ingenuity'. The party reported that it was safer to make all preparations in broad daylight, as the Germans didn't believe in such a possibility; in consequence they didn't 'see it happening'.[12] Most Germans, most of the time, simply didn't care. Posted in this isolated outpost of the Third Reich, the inevitable onslaught of fortress mentality sapped their 'creativity'. Contact with the local population, who gave no reason for offence, did not enhance their fervour either. Two Guernsey escapees who arrived at Dartmouth in a fishing boat in mid-August 1943 said that the Germans understood that they could not win the war. One of them had sat in many a German mess and seen the morbid atmosphere on the announcement of air raids on German cities. The depression which had followed the fall of Tunis and the bombing of Hamburg had even outweighed the reaction to Stalingrad and was compounded when many were called back home after raids. The effects of bombing were no longer hidden and the news had spread around the island in no time.[13] Six Jersey escapees interviewed in October 1944 stated that the food shortages were getting the Germans down; mashed potatoes and mashed tomatoes were now the fare of some officers' messes in St Helier. The Germans were reading leaflets and diaries on the sly. One informant had observed a

[10] PRO HO 144/22237. German measures to prevent escapes from Jersey. MI19 report to Mr McIvor at Southern Command, 4 Nov 1944; MI19, Report Jersey More notes on Germans and Islanders, interrogation of 5 men and 1 woman from Jersey who left the island on 8 and 9 Oct 44, 14 Oct 1944.

[11] PRO HO 144/22237. German measures to prevent escapes from Jersey. MI19 report to Mr McIvor at Southern Command, 4 Nov 1944.

[12] PRO HO 144/22237. Report no 2510A. Jersey German Activities. Interrogation of three Jersey escapees, 27 Nov 1944.

[13] PRO HO 144/22834. MI19/1742. Report Channel Islands Guernsey, interrogation of fisherman and driver, 1943.

German sit down on a tree stump, hold his head down in his hands, then after a while quickly spread a leaflet put under his face while remaining in this position.[14] Two men who left Guernsey on 3 November 1944 said that German morale had fallen considerably since D-Day. The soldiers intimated that they would not fight. A sign of the time was the rioting of 48 men billeted in the Victoria Hotel in St Peter Port over food. The only thing that seemed to cheer them up was the arrival of the mail plane.[15]

It would be a mistake to conclude from all this that morale was weak. Despite an Allied approach to negotiate surrender in September 1944, the German garrison continued on for another eight months through a disastrous winter of deprivation.[16] That there were paradoxes in the German stance was made clear by a civil engineer captured in St Malo and considered 100 per cent reliable by his Allied interrogators. This man stated that listening to the BBC was the rule rather than the exception and that he was always aware of the London viewpoint. At the same time he maintained that it was no use inducing von Schmettow to surrender. The majority of the officers were 'hardened veterans of the Russian campaigns and would not think of giving in'. Leaflets were of little avail; they only told what Islanders and Germans already knew.[17] The redistribution of troops in 1943 when many of the crack troops were replaced by very old and very young men, plus foreigners, did not undermine morale.[18] One British report of September 1944 considered the 2,700 Georgians an 'uncertain factor', but had little faith in any rumblings on the part of the Czechs, Poles and Russians who would 'do as they are told as long as normalcy prevails'. Revolt was only to be expected, if German supervision was weakened or removed, otherwise stout resistance was to be expected 'as a matter of well rehearsed routine'.[19] Any wavering was compensated for by the high morale in the Luftwaffe which consisted of young officers and former Hitlerjugend members who remained enthusiastic about the regime and were described by various sources as the cleanest and smartest German soldiers.[20] Further 'cement' was provided by fear of punishment and the fact that the officers were there to make sure that nobody

[14] PRO HO 144/22237. MI19. Report Jersey More notes on Germans and Islanders, interrogation of 5 men and 1 woman from Jersey who left the island on 8 and 9 Oct 44, 14 Oct 1944.

[15] PRO HO 144/22237. Report Guernsey Defences and German Morale, further information given by two Guernseymen who left Guernsey on 3 Nov 1944, 19 Nov 1944.

[16] For the failed attempt to get von Schmettow to surrender, see Cruickshank, op. cit., 251 pp.

[17] PRO WO 199/3303. Interrogation of Alfred Schmidt on 11 Aug 1944, 24 Aug 1944.

[18] PRO HO 144/22237. Report Channel Islands Jersey, interrogation of 4 Russian OT labourers (info as at 13 Dec 1943), 4 Jul 1944.

[19] IWM JRD.04. Channel Islands Report on German Morale and Factors likely to hasten or postpone capitulation by Capt Dening 10 I(b), Sept 1944.

[20] IWM Misc. 2826 189/2. Interview with Killmann (Luftwaffe), n.d.; PRO HO 144/22237. Report Jersey German Activities, interrogation of three Jersey escapees, 2510A, 27 Nov 1944.

stepped out of line. Von Schmettow, by this time Befehlshaber of the Channel Islands, was the archetype of such an officer. Born in 1891, von Schmettow was a Silesian cavalry officer who served in the First World War and then later in the '100,000 Army' of the Weimar Republic. According to a British intelligence report his military career was undistinguished, even 'singularly inactive' for a German General Officer, but this could have been caused by his loss of one lung during the Great War and the fact that he was a long-time TB patient. Before being sent to the Channel Islands he had served as the military commandant of Breslau (Silesia), in April 1938. Von Schmettow arrived in the Channel Islands as early as September 1940, seconded, until his departure in 1945, by his ADC, Lieutenant Colonel Hans von Helldorf. During this initial period of his command the garrison comprised a few battalions and anti-aircraft detachments. In spring 1941 Major General Erich Müller arrived with an additional division and replaced von Schmettow as the head of military command in the Channel Islands. [21] Müller – who outranked von Schmettow – became the key actor in the histrionics of German power-play and it was only after Müller's departure that the Count took over as commander of the reinforced division. Von Schmettow had a reputation for paying attention to meticulous detail and he certainly knew how to motivate his men and was well liked. At least once a month he completed a tour of inspection over his command, down to the last machine gun nest. His visits to the strong-points were routinely accompanied by extra rations sent from the nearest Soldatenheim. It was also said that he enjoyed the 'reluctant esteem' of the civilian population. Von Schmettow was brought up in Prussian tradition and although no fanatic and 'apparently inexperienced in its more practical and brutal application', there was no indication that his loyalty would waver.[22] At least a British report of September 1944 saw no sign of imminent disintegration or collapse. The mix of fanatics for whom final victory was historical fact and professionals, such as von Schmettow, was a powerful one, and gave little reason to be optimistic. It was feared that any frustration of an attempted landing would be a considerable blow, 'inflicting damage far outweighing the value of the operation if successful'. It surmised that von Schmettow:

> Must be watching the present debacle in France with pain and anger and would no doubt welcome reviving German military prestige by a local success [...] He knows that surrender is inevitable, but wants this to be neither ignominious nor premature. Many of his officers are Eastern Front veterans and will support this stance.[23]

[21] PRO WO 309/192. Statement of Oberstleutnant Hans von Helldorf on Channel Islands, 27 Dec. 1945.

[22] IWM JRD.04. Channel Islands Report on German Morale and Factors likely to hasten or postpone capitulation by Capt Dening 10 I(b), Sept 44; PRO WO 199/3303. Second interrogation report of Alfred Schmidt, 1944.

[23] IWM JRD.04. ibid.

The Channel Islands were not the only German outpost deep inside 'enemy territory'. Similar 'fortresses' existed in Kurland, Finland, Norway, across France and in the Balkans. They owed their existence to the German doctrine to continue fighting the war as far as possible from Reich borders. This move was founded on the idea of delaying and dissipating the enemy force and to be effective at this they had to prove as much of a nuisance as possible.[24] In the spring of 1945 the time had come to act. A February 1945 report from Guernsey confirmed the high state of alert and stated that all officers and probably one-third of the garrison would rather die than surrender. The Ardennes offensive had raised morale and since January 1945, 400 especially picked troops were undergoing commando training for raids on Continental targets.[25] Considering that several hundred German soldiers were suffering from the effects of starvation – many were already being hospitalised – this was indeed an astonishing new development. Whether the men undergoing commando training were more motivated by the extra rations they were receiving or whether it was Nazi fervour that carried them is unclear. The idea had been conceived well before Admiral Hüffmeyer took up overall command, by the 'good Kommandant' von Schmettow. The first of these raids was the raid on Granville harbour, in March 1945. Less well known than the Granville raid is the 'Malzan' demolition party, named after first lieutenant Malzan, the trainer and leader of the first group. Two more groups were sent over from Alderney and the raiding party left Guernsey on the night of the 3rd and 4th April, first for a stop-over in Sark and then, the following night, on to France. Their mission was to disrupt rail traffic near Cherbourg, by blowing up a bridge near Le Pont. Marching during the night and resting during the day, they became disoriented. Finally, at 2 am on 7 April, they were spotted by allied forces who opened fire. One of the lieutenants, Heinrich Grosskurth, shot himself in the temple rather than face capture, which resulted in total blindness.[26]

High, high society

Among the Germans the Channel Islands had a reputation as 'Europe's air raid shelter'; the less talked about reputation was that it also acted as a preferred 'hang-out' for the German aristocracy in uniform. Prince Waldeck, Prince Oettingen, von Schmettow, von Helldorf, von Aufsess are only some of the most commonly heard names, but there were many others. To which factors this very

[24] IWM JRD.04. ibid.
[25] PRO HO 144/22237. MI19. Report Guernsey Situation of German defence, further interrogation of informants 2555A, 1 Feb 1945.
[26] PRO WO 199/3303. Interrogation of PoW officers re. 'Malzan' demolition party, 1945.

high concentration of aristocrats owed its posting to the islands is not known, but connections, no doubt, played a role. That the German nobles would have felt a particular affinity with a place where pre-modern feudal rule was still partially intact is an inescapable conclusion. The German aristocrats brought with them their consensus, their abhorrence of the Nazi parvenu, and their peculiar snobbishness and arrogance. One typical case is von Aufsess whose petty excursions into the world of art and literature conveyed in the pages of his occupation diary are rather blasé. Von Aufsess also enjoys moralising about others. Whether he has any right is a different matter: it is certainly not below him to have helped himself to books from the looted library of French artists Schwob and Malherbe.[27] Von Aufsess himself provides an excellent illustration of an aristocrat who believed that inherited position still equalled influence, and that this followed him wherever he went. The Channel Islands – where many of the attributes of the by-gone aristocratic age were still alive – were the perfect place to massage his ego. His diaries do tell us about the politicking going on in the islands in the end phase of German rule – and to a certain extent he is involved in this. What is strange, however, is that von Aufsess never gets to the bottom of the matter, which reveals his status as a superseded busybody rather than someone of any genuine importance. Considering the seriousness of the situation during the 1944–45 siege, von Aufsess has far too much time to spend on books, intellectual dribbling with like-minded compatriots and a select crowd of self-important islanders, and the pursuits of the country gentleman.

European nobility is a small world and many of the vons who came to the islands during the war already had some well-established connections there. The Dame of Sark, who had visited Germany in the 1930s, wrote that Prince Oettingen – stationed at the Guernsey Nebenstelle – was a 'charming man' and that 'they had many friends in common'.[28] The Dame of Sark was not the only island seigneur to whom the vons paid their respects. They also bonded with Mrs Riley, the Dame de Rozel in Jersey, and the Countesses Radziwill and Blücher in Guernsey. In her autobiography the Dame of Sark stated that she could benefit from the exploitation of aristocratic leanings by extracting from her visitors the same degree of rigid formalism as they would have been expected to adhere to in Germany:

> The stiff German formality worked in my favour because it showed the Germans that I expected to be treated in my home with the rigid etiquette to which they were accustomed in their own country.[29]

[27] Max Freiherr von Aufsess, *The von Aufsess occupation diary*, Chichester, 1985, entry of 2 Dec 1944, 87.
[28] Sybil Hathaway, *Dame of Sark: an autobiography*, London, 1961, 131–5.
[29] ibid.

Although symbolic, such rituals were important as they showed who was boss; from what is known about living conditions in Sark, there is no indication that the Sarkese were any worse off for that.

The German aristocrats and their dedicated followers acceded to real fame in the post-war period when they were assigned the role of 'figures of light', required to breathe life into the paradigm of 'benign occupation' and 'correct relations'. The retrospective purpose was to show that the Channel Islands' authorities, in their course of non-confrontation, had been right all along and owed their benign occupation to these 'officer gentlemen'. Praise has been heaped on the first island Kommandant of Guernsey, Lanz and his deputy Dr Maas, a former medical student at Liverpool University. Major Bandelow, another Kommandant, is quoted as having been on excellent terms with Sherwill in Guernsey. Typically, he only thought he was 'boss', but obviously went a promise too far when he guaranteed safe conduct to British personnel in hiding in the autumn of 1940. Then there is the universally acclaimed von Schmettow. The uncritical gushing about personalities conveniently overlooks the fact that the 'benign occupation' was a matter of policy rather than personality. Nevertheless the myth of the 'good Kommandant', recently immortalized in a Granada TV mini-series,[30] has been irreversibly 'burnt' into popular imagination. The main problem with the 'good Kommandant' is that this static idea does not correspond to the continually shifting power bases, replacements, dismissals and transfers in the German camp. There was a lot more to the German organisation (or lack of organisation) than blind reliance on the title 'Kommandant' can suggest. As a result there is quite a menu to pick from: island Kommandant (of which island?), Feldkommandant or Befehlshaber?[31] Another issue is how good slave workers, Jews and 'radio offenders' would have found the 'good Kommandant'. On occasion the sheepish infatuation with the 'Kommandant' and German high society also extends to his helpers in the administration. Equally good as the 'good Kommandant' were the 'good administrators' such as Knackfuss who was good enough to remind islanders that he deplored the mistreatment of slave workers, but that this was the only language they understood. Rather intriguingly Major General Erich Müller, the Kommandeur of the 319th, never seems to be in the running for the title even though he was the most powerful man in the Channel Islands from 1941 to 1943. The reason seems to be that he was nowhere as 'highfalutin' as the other small and large Kommandants peopling the German services. Müller was a rather less agreeable personality for that matter, feared by his own troops as a pedantic slave driver. While he was calling the shots from Guernsey, von Schmettow, the

---

[30] 'Island At War' was screened in the UK in July–August 2004.
[31] To get a grasp on the complexity of the problem, see Cruickshank, op.cit., chapter six; Michael Ginns, 'The Kommandant', *Channel Islands Occupation Review*, 1981, 6–10.

prime contender for the 'best Kommandant' label, was practically 'in exile', reduced to the level of local island Kommandant in Jersey charged with 'keeping an eye' on fortifications and troops in that island.[32]

Another busy bee in the creation of legends was Dr Wilhelm Casper, von Aufsess's predecessor as chief civil administrator in the Channel Islands from 1941 to 1943. While von Aufsess's legend retains an element of charm and honesty, the legend of this opportunist, with its multiplication of lucky coincidences, half-truths and outright lies, is distasteful. Over the years this early spinmeister has had many voluntary and involuntary helpers, such as the Woods who wrote in their history *Islands in Danger* (1955) that he was one of the 'most praised' German officials.[33] During the war Casper managed the astonishing feat of landing himself in high-profile posts where things were relatively quiet, owing to considerable tactical skill combined with pulling the right strings. His superior during his time in the Channel Islands was Dr Werner Best – a high-ranking SS doctrinaire who had changed into the military camp after a feud with Heydrich – who later invited him to join the team he was setting up in Denmark where he was Reich plenipotentiary from the summer of 1943. Another acquaintance was the president of the International Committee of the Red Cross, Burckhardt, whom Casper claims to have known when the latter was High Commissioner for Danzig. After the war Casper settled in Bonn where his career at the Ministry of Defence flowed on without interruption and where he cultivated high-level relations with, among others, two presidents of the Federal Republic of Germany. Casper, seemingly, was always the right man in the right place at the right time: in one correspondence he says that an article he published during the war in a reputable German journal had an effect on Allied bombing of supply ships, as it was heard on both sides after its parallel publication, in the UK, by the Channel Islands Monthly Review, in August 1943. He also credits himself with a key role in the Red Cross relief effort to the Channel Islands in 1944–45 which he claims was the result of his contacts with Burckhardt. Casper also claims having advised both Bailiffs that under international law they had a right to claim supplies through the Red Cross. What Casper certainly does not make a fuss about is that his signature graces practically all pieces of anti-Jewish legislation in the islands. In another correspondence he has a convenient lapse of memory, saying that his office, the Feldkommandantur, had no connection with the island of Alderney after the 'SS took over'. It would be hard to find a more appropriate demonstration of 'alibi of a nation'. After his departure from the Channel Islands Casper's legend continued in Denmark where he claims to have been connected to one chief of

[32] PRO WO 309/192. Statement of Oberstleutnant Hans von Helldorf on Channel Islands, 27 Dec. 1945.
[33] Wood and Wood, op.cit., 95.

the Danish Underground whom he 'instructed' to let the Jews escape; a
variation on the ludicrous story that Casper conferred with Prince Oettingen to
let three Jewish women from Guernsey slip away to England in a boat, a chance
they did not take up as they decided to 'return home'. Casper's words speak for
themselves, making irrelevant the fact that he was not a Nazi. There is nothing
in Casper's activity to suggest that he was more than an ordinary and effective
administrator.[34]

Manufacturing perception

The Channel Islands elicited some academic interest and German observers
could be divided into two groups: one interested in the cultural and political
peculiarities of the Channel Islands while another assuming that autonomy was
humbug 'wherever England set foot'.[35] In the long run the view of the first
prevailed. Characteristic is an article published in the *Magdeburger Zeitung* in April
1939, under the title 'In the World's Smallest Feudal State'. The author
described Sark, with some sympathy, as a 'fortunate isle [...] remote and untrou-
bled [...] on the periphery of [...] European politics [...] and penetrated by the
essence of an Old Germanic and Nordic spirit' which had protected its inherited
traditions against 'the decadence of the rest of Europe' pervaded by plutoc-
racy.[36] Such interpretations were in line with the opinion voiced by chief
administrator Dr Casper who described the islands as a 'constitutional nature
reserve' which the Feldkommandantur had sought to preserve as much as
possible.[37] Not every German visitor was as flattering: a report of the German
propaganda unit in Jersey detailed in-breeding, sexual promiscuity and
alcoholism.[38] Others criticised the social divide, the influence of the churches
and the numbers of rich English idlers who still had time to play tennis and sip
cocktails, but refused to labour for the occupier.

The most 'highbrow' of these observers, a professor from Berlin, arrived for a
two-week sojourn in September 1941. Karl Heinz Pfeffer was not a nobody, but

---

[34] JAS M/19/A/1. Correspondence with Mr Musso (spanning several years); Wilhelm Casper,
In the eye of the hurricane. Remembrances from the Channel Islands 1941–1943, Jersey, 1991; letter to author,
27 Jul 1997.

[35] Sonderberichterstatter Dr Otto Reich von Rohrwig, 'Abstecher nach den Kanalinseln', *Die
Neue Ordnung*, 16 Aug 1942.

[36] 'Im kleinsten Feudalstaat der Welt', *Magdeburger Zeitung*, 3 Apr 1939.

[37] AN AJ 40/547. FK 515. 'Verwaltungsüberblick über die Kanalinseln', Wilhem Casper, June
1943.

[38] Island Archives. FK 5/11. Leutnant Seyferth, Aussenstelle Jersey der Propagandastaffel
Nordwest, 'Historische, staatsrechtliche und bevoelkerungspolitische Betrachtungen ueber die
britischen Kanal-Inseln unter besonderer Beruecksichtigung der Verhaeltnisse auf Jersey', n.d.

the very archetype of the new Nazi intellectual. The son of a high school professor, he was born in Frankfurt in 1906. Studying English, German, history and philosophy at several universities from 1925, he was a member of several rightist organisations from an early age. In 1928–29 he received a grant to study in Stanford, obtaining a doctorate in 1931 at Berlin, on 'England in pre-Civil War American literature' where he contrasted the achievements of the 'white race' in North America – and its continuing connections with Old England – with those of other races who had settled there. After his doctorate he went to London for a year, where he tried in vain to represent the social studies of the 'new Germany' in the through-and-through liberal environment of the London School of Economics. This stint was followed up by an academic visit to Australia on a Rockefeller scholarship, in 1932–33. During this time he formed close connections with the Nazi party through the German consul in Sydney. When he returned to Germany in late 1933 he taught sociology at Leipzig, joining the SA, and the Nazi party. One source stated that he was one of the few university personnel who wore SA uniform on duty. In 1940 he moved to the German Institute for Foreign Studies (DAWI) at the University of Berlin where he was offered a chair in British Studies, becoming a full professor in 1943, aged 36. Pfeffer, like most of the other Nazi academics he was surrounded by, was woefully young and their steep career path – which they owed to their close association with Nazism – bore an element of opportunism. At DAWI Pfeffer became the close associate of another Nazi professor, Franz Six, who was even younger than Pfeffer, born in 1909. How close the two men were is demonstrated by the fact that Pfeffer – who was less politically tainted, as he was not a member of the SS – found Six a hiding place when the latter was trying to evade Allied prosecution in 1946. DAWI, a Six brainchild designed to address the challenges arising from the conquest of Europe – especially ideological penetration and economic exploitation – was perhaps the principal Nazi research institute. It spun off a number of think tanks and had close contacts with the SS, the Reich Security Main Office, the Abwehr, the Foreign Ministry and German consortia such as IG Farben.

Six himself is definitely worth a detour, as he was one of Reinhard Heydrich's early recruits when the latter was setting up his new Security Service (SD) – a Nazi party offshoot – in 1934. In his capacity as chief of ideological education and indoctrination the young academic became the mentor of a number of other SD recruits, such as Adolf Eichmann and Herbert Hagen, all of whom would gain infamy through their having masterminded the Final Solution. After the SD was integrated with the State Security Police (consisting of Gestapo and Kripo) into the Reich Security Main Office, Six became the chief of Amt VII, specialising in 'enemy research'. In September 1940 Six, who was tipped to become SD chief in London, headed a working group planning the invasion of Britain. Had Six ever set foot on British soil, he would have masterminded the confiscation of archival material and the repression of political and ideological enemies. The working group, which must also have received substantial inputs from Pfeffer, was not only responsible for compiling a special blacklist of 2,700 people to be arrested in Britain, but also published an information booklet with descriptions of industrial installations, enemy organisations and state bureaucracy. Owing to the postponement of military operations against Britain, Six, who spent most of his time whizzing around Berlin, missed out on all the action again. Therefore, shortly afterwards Six's name was on a list of SS intellectuals who, in Heydrich's opinion, needed some real 'hands-on' experience. In June 1941 these men were sent East for service in the Einsatzgruppen where Six led the SD Vorauskommando Moskau (Moscow advance party). As hapless in reaching Moscow as he had been in reaching London the year before, Six had now become a mass murderer. After his return from the East Six left the RSHA and joined the Foreign Service, at which point Pfeffer – who had deputised during his absence – took over as DAWI dean. Publications such as the institute's Yearbook were standard reference works in Nazi Germany. In 1943 Pfeffer founded a think tank, the Europa Seminar, which had Six as well as Professor Albrecht Haushofer, the doyen of German Geopolitik, among its eight permanent members.

The 1941 study mission to the Channel Islands was one of many missions in official employ. By this time, Pfeffer had become Germany's foremost academic 'authority' on Britain and the Empire. In 1934 he had already been sent to the US and it is also thought that he used several pre-war visits to Britain – his wife was British – to gather information and establish contacts. During his visits he collected information on various aspects of political or cultural life, giving free flow to the dogma of race as the key to an accurate understanding of history. As one would have expected his main target was the Jews, which can also be gauged from the title of one of his wartime publications, loosely translatable as *The English war – Another Jewish war* (1942). [39] Fiercely anti-Semitic, he is reported to have said that Jews were not a Volk, but merely 'parasites'; his report provides evidence that he did not miss the opportunity to spread his poison during his short stay in the Channel Islands.[40] It is for other reasons, however, that Pfeffer's report[41] – despite its inherent bias – is one of the most revealing

[39] *Der englische Krieg – auch ein jüdischer Krieg* (1942), see Hachmeister, Lutz, *Der Gegnerforscher. Die Karriere des SS-Führers Franz Alfred Six*, Munich, 1998, 228–29.

[40] Kommittee zur Untersuchung der Verhältnisse an westdeutschen Universitäten (ed.), *Die wissenschaftliche und politische Karriere des Dr. phil. Habil. Karl Heinz Pfeffer, Professor für Soziologie der Entwicklungsländer an der Universität Münster. Eine Dokumentation*, Leipzig, 1963; Hachmeister, Lutz, *Der Gegnerforscher. Die Karriere des SS-Führers Franz Alfred Six*, Munich, 1998, 228–29; 277; passim.

[41] PRO HO 45/24756. 'Historical peculiarities of the Channel Islands', report of Prof Karl Heinz Pfeffer on research visit, 10–25 Sept 1941. The German original is preserved at the Guernsey Island Archive. FK 5/6.

documents of the Occupation. The principal aim of Pfeffer's visit was the exploration of options available to the occupying force in exploiting the situation in the islands. Analysing the structure of the population, Pfeffer admitted that the Germans had not adopted a 'uniform and consistent line [...] in regard to the inhabitants'. He indicated two possible avenues: total evacuation; or a strategy of 'divide and rule' based on sowing dissension between native Channel Islanders and British migrants. For a number of reasons – mainly economic, but also the desire to keep options open – he seems to have favoured the second. He saw this preference confirmed by the basic direction of German policy over the fifteen months preceding his visit (we are in late 1941). Taking as an example British colonial rule in Malta, where the Maltese language had been 'artificially groomed'[42] against the Italian language, Pfeffer recommended that the Germans appeal to the Norman heritage and treat the islands as 'Germanic micro-states' whose personal union with England was an accident of history that could be reversed. Intriguingly Pfeffer ended the section with an admonishment that the success of a policy designed to win over the natives depended on the leading German personalities in the islands who had to be able to 'combine tact and self-confidence with evident severity'. Although singularly unsuccessful on this count – Pfeffer admitted that Channel Islanders were unresponsive to seduction[43] – his report seems to have informed future orientations such as differential treatment between native Channel Islanders, mainlanders and foreigners. Under 'points of fracture' he referred to a 'few fascists on the islands', but said that genuine penetration depended on winning over poorer sections of the population with social changes.

The third major point in the report is the significance of the Occupation as a trial case for contact with a British population. According to Pfeffer the conditions between occupier and occupied were such that they constituted 'an important advance of German propaganda for the post-war period'. If after victory the Germans intended to draw part of the English people over to their side 'the prevailing conduct of the German occupation troops (could) be abundantly employed as propaganda'.

Other interesting details in Pfeffer's report are his reference to the opinion of German officers that the start of the war in Russia had seen 'a hardening' and a considerable 'cooling off' of 'private relations' with the civilian population. Pfeffer cited Dunkirk and Crete as the low points of islanders' morale and the

---

[42] 'Supported', the translation given in the English version does not echo the rather more colourful 'hochgezüchtet' in the German original, see preceding footnote.

[43] The relevant passage reads: 'Altogether the behaviour of the inhabitants who after all lived with England up to June 1940 shows that up to that time there had at least been no change from a personal or political standpoint in regard to the situation in the summer of 1939. During the year of occupation the islands inhabitants have continued to remain in that state.'

beginning of the war in the East as the beginning of 'high hopes'. The rest of the paragraph is quite flattering for the 'British or British-thinking inhabitants' who regarded 'the occupation as a temporary storm in which they almost commiserate with the individual German soldier on account of his unpleasant duty.' The Attorney General of Jersey was quoted as 'amiable', but 'quite impenetrable'. From the absence of a last word in the relevant paragraph one can only infer that Coutanche's small-talk about decent Jews and decent Christians was an equally disappointing affair for Pfeffer.[44] Other islanders 'dished up' the latest 'babblings of British wireless propaganda', telling Pfeffer about 'the tremendous losses in the East' which were weakening (the Germans) 'decisively'. Pfeffer was baffled that '(t)he permission to listen to the British wireless was exploited so that they placed loud-speakers at the open windows' and found islanders' appeals to the Hague rules in the face of German demands 'impudent'. Pfeffer must have had a premonition when he wrote that 'the whole population could at any moment get the scent of quite another wind owing to this running off the rails.'

[44] The episode is detailed in chapter two.

VI

The Practice of Modern Slave Labour

Alderney – Another planet

THE OCCUPATION of the Channel Islands was unlike the occupation of other northern nations, such as Holland, Norway or Denmark. There the role of the military was rather reduced and was graced with German civilian governors and a plethora of official and semi-official services, agencies and plenipotentiaries who followed in their wake. Here it was fully determined by the German military. But within the spectrum of military occupation there was variation. Thus the Jersey Occupation was the most civilian and the Alderney Occupation the most brutal and the most militarised, while the Guernsey Occupation took a median position. Alderney's destiny as a devil's island was principally owed to the absence of civilians, practically all of whom evacuated to England in June 1940. Little did they know that their abandoned homes would set the stage for murder. The desertion and desolation brought on by their exodus was an omen of things to come. As an experiment in racism and group dynamics the Occupation of Alderney was highly significant. This sealed environment was in a way the perfect laboratory for applied National-Socialism: in Alderney the German occupiers had a tendency to close ranks, forming a 'joint venture' based on a tight symbiosis of OT (Organization Todt), Wehrmacht and SS. The predisposition to racist excesses was compounded by the isolation of the place and the resulting decomposition of discipline.

The main sources for the history of the Alderney camps still are the accounts written by former MI19 officer Theodore Pantcheff. In June 1945 the War Office sent Pantcheff, one of their top interrogators, to the islands to investigate alleged atrocities against slave workers. It is understood that he also received this task on the basis of his knowledge of the island, which he had gained through numerous holiday visits to his uncle, Dr Ramsbotham, one of the three doctors practising in the island before the war. The results of his lengthy investigation were consolidated in a report, which was forwarded to the Soviet authorities for further prosecution. For reasons which defy rationality, the English original of the report itself has long been lost and today only the Russian translation exists at the Russian State Archive in Moscow.[1] However, the bulk of the evidence upon which the report was based survives intact at the National Archives in Kew. At first a major nuisance, the need to plough through the Alderney investigations is a blessing in disguise, as it allows one to address omissions and attempt a number of reinterpretations. Pantcheff also kept a sufficient amount of notes which laid the basis for a short treatise published in 1981, entitled *Alderney Fortress Island: The Germans in Alderney, 1940–1945*, which he wrote during his retirement in Alderney.

After the departure of the civilian population the island accommodated a small German garrison and work parties sent over from Guernsey to collect perishable foodstuffs, livestock and unharvested crops. Looting from the properties of evacuees was inevitable under these conditions and in the spring of 1941 some men of the Guernsey work parties were put on trial. It is doubtful, however, that they would have been the only or even the worst looters. After Hitler's invasion of the Soviet Union the Occupation of Alderney started to gather in momentum. On 24 July a reinforced company arrived whose commander, Captain Karl Hoffmann, took over as island commandant. By November 1941 numbers had risen to 2,500 and they would eventually peak at over 3,000. In December 1941 when command over Alderney was transferred from the 83rd infantry division to the 319th division which was already deployed in the other islands, Hoffmann lost his title as island commandant which was now held by a senior rank, but he remained the tactical specialist responsible for the planning and execution of fortification work and armour.[2] The fortifications which eventually would grace the island were three heavy coastal defence batteries manned by the navy, AA batteries, two anti-tank walls at Longy and at Platte Saline, the wiring, booby-trapping and polluting of the cliffs and beaches with 37,000 mines. Anti-airborne landing charges were later added to in Longy Common, all supported by earthworks, underground concrete emplacements, passages and storage tunnels.[3]

---

[1] GARF. Report on crimes committed in the Alderney camps from 1942 to 1945, by Captain Pantcheff, 23 June 1945, submitted by the representative of the Council of Ministers of the Soviet Union in charge of Repatriation to the Commission on the Investigation and Detection of Fascist Crimes, 23 April 1947.

[2] Hoffmann's successors were: Lt Col Rohde (Jan 1942), Colonel Zuske (Feb 1942 – Nov 1943), Lt Col Schwalm (Nov 1943 – May 1945). The latter was described as 'a mealy-mouthed bastard who always had his hair cut [...] in the Concentration Camp "Sylt", but who knew nothing of what went on (or so he said)'. The residence of the island commandant was in Connaught Square, later to become the Connaught Hotel, s. JAS L/D/25/A/4. Appendix to Col B E Arnold, *The Alderney Story*, information provided by Theodore Pantcheff, n.d.

[3] JAS L/D25/A/4. Appendix to Col B E Arnold, *The Alderney Story*, information provided by Theodore Pantcheff, n.d.

A short time later, at the beginning of 1942, work got under way on the camps. The workers employed on this task were French volunteers and they accomplished their task by mid-1942.[4] At about this time another contingent of workers arrived whose pedigree as 'volunteers' was less than sure: first 300 Spaniards who had sought refuge in France after the collapse of the Republic in 1939 and who had been kept in internment camps. In 1939–40 some of them had volunteered for service in the French Army which grouped them together as foreign labour auxiliaries. When the Germans started to comb France for labour in 1941 they were among the first foreigners to be rounded up or – if they happened to come from the unoccupied zone – sold down the line by the Vichy government. The Germans gave them a choice between work or repatriation to Franco's Spain, which, for obvious reasons, most declined.[5] The first batch of 1,000 Eastern workers followed closely in their tracks in July 1942, followed by two more batches of 900 each in August. They were predominantly Soviet citizens – mainly ethnic Ukrainians and Russians – with a smaller number of Poles.[6] Only a minority of these 'Ostarbeiters' were genuine volunteers, the remainder were press-ganged by various means such as coercion of the village elders to hand in a required number or swoops which combed young men, women and children off the streets, out of cinemas or cafés and marched them to the waiting trains. At some point the OT also shipped in Soviet PoWs branded with the letters 'SU' across their backs. Seventy-six of these men arrived in May

[4] Pantcheff, T.X.H., *Alderney Fortress Island – The Germans in Alderney*, 1940–1945, Chichester, 1981, 4.

[5] ibid. 11. According to Pantcheff many Spaniards brought over in the first half of 1942 were shipped out again by end of year, op. cit., 8. Many appear to have regretted their decision to eschew repatriation for there is evidence that some had call-up papers for the Spanish army forwarded to them by the Spanish consulate in Paris, s. JAS D/A/U/V/52. OT Rundbrief, Abschnitt Jakob (Jersey), 6 Aug 1942.

[6] It has become an established procedure to refer to slave workers as Russians. Less frequently, Russians is also used as an amalgam of all categories of forced and slave workers, even though there were many more nationalities. The indiscriminate use of the term brings up the fundamental problem of terminology. The fact is that even the people of Slavic extraction most commonly referred to as Russians were a rather more mixed bag. In addition to a large number of ethnic Russians there were Ukrainians (or people of Ukrainian extraction, cognisable through the suffixes in their name endings) and a number of Poles and Belorussians who had lived on the wrong side of the 1941 German-Soviet border. There is also evidence of the occasional Caucasian or Central Asian. In short, a cross-section of the peoples of the Soviet Union. The first reason why these people were referred to as Russians was anti-Communism. Referring to them as 'Soviet citizens' was distasteful as it implied recognition of the regime; the other, more important influence was the unquestioning reception of Muscovite ideology – the unification, if necessary by force, and Russification of all Eastern Slavs under the 'Third Rome' – in the West. The Germans in their wisdom used 'Russia' as an umbrella term in the same way as they would refer to 'England' when actually meaning 'Britain'.

1943, having been transferred from a PoW camp near Vienna.[7] At its peak the total prisoner population, including Sylt, would have been around 4,000. While the number of SS prisoners oscillated between 800 and 1,000, the OT workforce in September 1943 comprised 700 Russians, 400 European volunteers, 100 French women, 700 German workers and 300 French Jews. [8]

The four camps were each named after a German North Sea island: Helgoland, Nordeney, Borkum and Sylt. Borkum was probably the very first of these camps. It housed between 500 and 1,000 specialist workers, highly paid volunteers from Germany, Holland and other countries, who were not subjected to the treatment which was customary in the other three camps. Of these Nordeney, with a maximum holding capacity of 1,500, was probably the worst. The population here was first Spanish, then Soviet, until August 1943. They were then replaced by a mixed bag of different nationalities, among them a large group of North Africans who had been rounded up in the South of France. The largest group, however, were 600 French Jewish men who had been spared deportation to the extermination camps because they lived in so-called 'mixed marriages' or because they were 'half-Jews'. These were rather a distinct group in so far as they belonged to the most assimilated part of the Jewish bourgeoisie. As one would imagine they made up a disproportionately large group of people with a higher or university education, among them many doctors or barristers forced out of their profession by the anti-Semitic legislation of Vichy. There was also a former MP, an acclaimed pianist, a high ranking officer of the French Army and a state councillor, all classed as non-specialist workers and clubbed into the most demeaning jobs. Wearing civilian clothes they were branded with a yellow star and had white stripes painted down the outside of their trouser legs. The third OT camp, Helgoland, was similar in size to Nordeney. The situation here was that the majority of the population was Soviet, and remained that way until the disbandment of the camp in early 1944. Overall, the most feverish period of activity surely were the 18 months from the spring of 1942 to the autumn of 1943. Practically all remaining Russians were sent to Cherbourg in October 1943. Helgoland was then dismantled and Borkum and Sylt were operating with a considerably reduced prisoner population, leaving the Jewish and French element at Nordeney much in evidence. To replace the departed Russians an additional 250 French Jews and 150 civilian prisoners arrived at Nordeney[9], and, from May 1944, a contingent of Norman

---

[7] PRO WO 311/12. Notes of statement made by Ursula Camp personnel, 1945.

[8] Pantcheff, T.X.H., *Alderney Fortress Island – The Germans in Alderney*, 1940–1945, Chichester, 1981, 9.

[9] Pantcheff, T.X.H., *Alderney Fortress Island – The Germans in Alderney*, 1940–1945, Chichester, 1981, 9; PRO WO 311/12. Statement of Sdf Wilhelm Richter statement taken by C Kent, Alderney, 1945; PRO WO 311 106. Aussage des Kgf Bauleiter Leo Ackermann, 2 Jun 1945.

resistance workers, among them two clerics, and internees from Vernet. According to a post-war report these two groups were particularly harshly treated and singled out for 'special duties'. The Jews were made to unpack and carry sacks of cement from the harbour, while the Resistance workers were sent to the quarry.[10] After June 1944 the only camp continuing in operation was Borkum.[11]

The German organisation is an important factor in understanding responsibilities. OT activity in the Channel Islands was subject to two command levels: army and OT. The army supervised and controlled OT construction activity through its Fortress Construction Command XV. Discipline and personnel superior authority was vested in the OT Oberbauleitung in St Malo (from February 1943 OT Oberbauleitung Cherbourg). For its purposes the OT divided the three islands into sectors codenamed 'Adolf' (Alderney), 'Gustav' (Guernsey) and 'Julius' (Jersey). The senior representative in each sector was the OT Construction Superintendent (Bauleiter). In Alderney this post was held by Büttmann who was relieved of his post in January 1943 and replaced by Bauleiters Goedhardt and his deputy Dr Panzer. Goedhardt left again in March and Panzer succeeded him as Bauleiter. Later, in August 1943, Leo Ackermann took over. The OT Bauleiter was responsible for the execution of all building in the island, co-ordinating his action with the Inselkommandant and the Fortress Engineers, the taskmasters. One step down in the chain of command was the Frontführer, the second-in-command and deputy of the Construction Superintendent. The other task of the Superintendent was to provide instructions to the OT Bauführers who each oversaw the different subcontractors carrying out work on specific sites. Each of these civilian firms was based in one of the camps from which it drew its workforce of about 200 each.[12] Four Lagerführers had authority for each of the four camps.[13] The main OT firms on the island were Deubau (Düsseldorf) and Kniffler (Saarbrücken), based in Helgoland, Sager & Woerner (Munich)[14] and Fuchs (Coblenz), based in Nordeney.[15] Other names appearing in the documents are Strabag, Westfälische Steinindustrie, shipping agents Karl G Blume, Colignon, a French

[10] AN F 9/5572. Amicale des Anciens déportés politiques de l'île anglo-normande d'Aurigny (M Azoulay) to Ministre des Victimes Civiles de la Guerre, rapport sur l'ile d'Aurigny, 3 Apr 1946.

[11] PRO WO 311/11. Haddock to Shapcott, 21 May 1945.

[12] PRO WO 311/12. Statements of Georg Preukschat and Bruno Zietlow, FestPioStb 2/11 Alderney, 1945.

[13] Pantcheff, T.X.H., *Alderney Fortress Island – The Germans in Alderney*, 1940–1945, Chichester, 1981, 7.

[14] Fritz Todt started his engineering career at this firm in 1922, see Pantcheff, *Alderney Fortress Island*, op. cit, 5.

[15] PRO WO 311/12. Additional note of Ackermann to his statement of 2 June 1945, 20 June 1945.

firm, and several Dutch sub-contractors of the German concern Wolfer & Goebel: Stork of Rotterdam and Bosland & DeWolf[16] with offices in Amsterdam and Paris.[17]

When the SS arrived in the spring of 1943, Sylt camp had been under the OT for half a year, since August 1942. During this time the population never exceeded 100 to 120 Soviet prisoners. The SS then extended prisoner capacity. The 1st SS Baubrigade was one of several flying squads deployed across Europe and consisted of 1,000 prisoners drawn from Sachsenhausen concentration camp. Before being sent to Alderney half of the brigade were stationed in Duisburg, half in Düsseldorf for the purpose of repairing air raid damage, from October 1942 to February 1943.[18] The prisoners represented a typical cross-section of the population of a German concentration camp: 200 Germans, political and criminal prisoners, conscientious objectors – among them Jehovah's Witnesses – and homosexuals. Besides practically all nations of Occupied Europe, the majority, however, were again Eastern Slavs, including 500 Soviet prisoners of war and partisans, many of them survivors of the mass starvation and killings of the autumn and winter of 1941.[19] The SS detachment of between 70 and 80, consisting mainly of Volksdeutsche – ethnic Germans from across Europe – was taken from Neuengamme where the prisoners were also registered, receiving numbers of the series 16,000 to 17,000.[20] The first commandant of the Baubrigade was Maximilian List, a Berlin architect decorated for services performed in Russia in 1941. List had a chalet built in the style of Hitler's Berghof outside the camp perimeter, with an underground passage linking it with the camp. List was seconded by Klebeck and Braun. The latter, according to Pantcheff, an 'uncured syphilitic', took over as commandant after the departure of List and Klebeck in December 1943.[21]

In the somewhat isolated and alien environment of Alderney the Germans drew ranks, resulting in a wide degree of collusion between German services, OT, military and SS. Many admired the training of the SS, their ability to break the willpower of state enemies or other undesirables and turn them into purveyors of 'useful services', as well as their ability to liquidate prisoners without a breakdown in discipline. This had always been the problem: turning

---

[16] Pantcheff, T.X.H., *Alderney Fortress Island – The Germans in Alderney*, 1940–1945, Chichester, 1981, 7.

[17] PRO. HO 144/22237. MI19. Report Channel Islands Alderney, information as at June 1943, 27 Jul 1944.

[18] Martin Weinmann (ed.), *Das nationalsozialistische Lagersystem*, Frankfurt, 1990, 365.

[19] Pantcheff, op. cit., 6; AN. F9/5572. Amicale des Anciens deportes politiques de l'ille anglo-normande d'Aurigny (M Azoulay) to Ministre des Victimes Civiles de la Guerre, 3 Apr 1946.

[20] *Das nationalsozialistische Lagersystem*, op. cit., 365.

[21] Pantcheff, op. cit. 27–29.

ordinary folk into killers who did not become demoralised by their task, but were still capable of executing orders and remaining effective as a force. Naturally, the SS scorned the OT for their incompetent handling of prisoners. Georgi Kondakov stated in his book that while OT slaves were filthy and covered in cement dust, the SS prisoners faced severe punishment if they were not immaculately clean. [22] The OT were also clueless when it came to turning the prisoners against themselves, a technique of domination the SS mastered so perfectly through the system of privileges accorded to camp elders and kapos, many of them criminals or antisocial elements. In time the OT tried to copy these SS techniques. In a French investigation conducted in 1944, one of the prisoners, Dr Bloch, pointed out that the OT tried to drive a wedge between the prisoners, by specifically selecting friends or relatives to institute disciplinary beatings and who were themselves abused, if the beatings were not hard enough.[23] However, if Georgi Kondakov is to be believed the Russian OT slaves stuck together more than the SS prisoners did and these ties of solidarity between prisoners were a crucial step in surviving.[24] Nor were all military men the incredulous and powerless onlookers they portrayed themselves to be after the war. List, the commander of Sylt, regularly farmed out workers and other expertise to Captain Parsenow, the harbour comman-dant. Relations were more strained under his successor, Captain Massmann, but not necessarily because of the mistreatment of workers.[25] Further implicated were German civilians: while the Lagerführers were responsible for what happened inside the camps, it was the civilian firms who handled the men at their work.

The relationship between SS and OT only changed after the arrival of Leo Ackermann as the new OT Superintendent in the late summer of 1943. Ackermann felt that he should be in overall charge of the fortification and wanted to deploy the SS Baubrigade in the way he saw best, but this move was resisted by List, fiercely defensive of encroachments on SS independence. The trigger for open conflict was the fact that some OT prisoners who had been sent to Sylt for punishment without, however, being returned. This internal OT-SS arrangement had been hatched by his predecessor Dr Panzer, with the authorisation of his OT boss on the French mainland, Cardinal. Because it was impractical for the OT to

---

[22] *The island of dread in the Channel. The story of Georgi Ivanovitch Kondakov*, edited by Brian Bonnard, Stroud, 1991, 49–50, 74.

[23] JAS L/C24/B/1. Tribunal militaire permanent de Paris Caserne de Reuilly. Acte d'accusation dans l'affaire Heinrich EVERS et Adam ADLER, inculpés de coups et blessures volontaires et de vol, 20 Sept 1949 (Copy of CDJC document CDLXXXIX-45)

[24] See *Island of dread in the Channel*, op. cit.

[25] PRO WO 311/12. Statement Oberleutnant zur See Hey betr. Alderney, Einsatz von Fremdarbeitern und Insassen des KL Sylt sowie deren Gesundheitszustand und ihre Behandlung, 1945.

send foreign 'repeat offenders' to one of their punishment camps in the other islands or France, a scheme was arranged by which they were sent to Sylt for three weeks and then returned. This was put into practice and between May and late Aug 1943 a total of 60 OT workers thus entered Sylt; none of them, however, was released after the lapse of three weeks. Although the OT accepted this at first, Ackermann regarded it as a challenge to OT authority and confronted List. The reply he received was that they had since been enrolled in the camp register and that he had to await a reply from Neuengamme before he could accede to Ackermann's request of a release to the OT. Ackermann was more of a political animal than his predecessors and seemed determined to put a stop to SS encroachment on his own labour force. He therefore reported the architects of this grand scheme, Dr Panzer and Frontf Konnertz, to Cardinal.[26] Certainly no stickler for humanitarian principles, Ackermann seems to have disagreed about the amount of brutality that was necessary to get work out of the prisoners – an interesting departure from the OT's own abominable start in 1942. When he reprimanded a Deubau employee for beating up a Jewish prisoner and followed up with a written order to all firms prohibiting the beatings of foreign workers, the opponents of the new regime retaliated. Ackermann was denounced by Deubau and other 'old regime' OT men as 'being soft on Jews', a serious charge. The hierarchy, however, decided to ignore this denunciation. Eventually, Ackermann almost won over the SS, for in December 1943 the OT prisoners sent to Sylt for 'punishment' were finally returned, albeit in reduced numbers. Also the SS Baubrigade was withdrawn on his insistence to Cherbourg, on 20 December 1943.[27] Then, however, the military intervened, complaining that targets would not be met if the SS were withdrawn and insisting on their return. Thus within three weeks of their initial departure the SS Baubrigade returned.[28] The SS had also negotiated a new arrangement whereby they no longer came under OT authority, but were subordinated directly to the 319 ID and the Fortress Engineers.[29] The final withdrawal of the 1st SS Baubrigade took place suddenly, on 25 June 1944. The SS had clear orders from Himmler to prevent the capture of live prisoners in the case of an Allied attack, and it seems established that the repeated transferrals of Nordeney forced workers to the notorious 'tunnel', camouflaged as air raid exercises, during the spring of 1944, were a rehearsal in anticipation of this contingency.[30] In the absence of documentary evidence it is

---

[26] PRO WO 311/106. Protocol interrogation Bauleiter Leo Ackermann, 8 Jun 1945.

[27] PRO WO 311/106. Aussage des Kgf Bauleiter Leo Ackermann, 2 Jun 1945.

[28] According to Michael Ginns, General Marks, the commander of the 84th Army Corps wrote the letter of complaint to the 7th Army, interview with Michael Ginns, 20 Oct 2004.

[29] Pantcheff, T.X.H., *Alderney Fortress Island – The Germans in Alderney*, 1940–1945, Chichester, 1981, 32.

[30] Himmler told List in August 1943 to train his men for the case of Allied attack. Prisoners 'inciting revolt' had to be shot, if it continued all should be shot, see RFSS Himmler to List, 19

impossible to say whether the SS were on the brink of liquidating their prisoners and were only prevented from doing so by the military. The fact is that they returned to St Malo via a twisted route involving stopovers in both Guernsey and Jersey which took almost a week. When they finally arrived at St Malo, around 1 July, they were sent on to Tours, for bomb clearance work, where they arrived in mid-July. One week later they were loaded onto a train with Allied PoWs which first went across central France to Dijon and from thence northwards to Kortemark (Belgium) where they arrived on 29 July to work on a V1 launch platform. When the Allied advance drew near they were loaded onto trains again. It was clear that the prisoners were now being transported back to Germany; they knew that they would not get into such close range of the advancing Allied troops again and therefore took their chances. Several break-outs occurred after the prisoners left Alderney, the first in the early morning of 6 July. On 25 July and again on 26 July a number of prisoners in one truck strangled two guards and managed to escape. In retaliation those prisoners still in the truck were mowed down. The SS retaliated by mowing down prisoners in the freight trucks from which escapes had taken place. Eighteen of them were buried in Toul (France) the following day. The last of these escapes occurred at the encampment near Kortemark itself, on 1 September, the day before their departure to Germany. Four prisoners were gunned down in the attempt, but as post-war testimony confirms, 39 prisoners managed to escape and shelter with civilians.[31] The 570 SS prisoners who remained behind were sent to Sollstedt (Germany), where they arrived on 10 September, via another twisted route. While remaining stationary at this location, they were shifted from one camp register to another: Buchenwald in September; Dora in October and Sachsenhausen in December. In April 1945 the survivors were sent on a march through Bohemia and Austria until they were liberated near Steyr on 5 May 1945.[32]

The number of deaths in Sylt is almost as inscrutable a topic as the number of total deaths in Alderney. The Neuengamme camp records suggest that fewer than 100 SS prisoners died in Alderney, but this figure is certainly too

Aug 1943, facsimile in *Channel Islands Occupation Review*, no. 34 (2004), 20; the 'exercises' in the tunnel were confirmed by former Jewish prisoners who testified at the trial of Adler and Evers before a French military tribunal see JAS L/C24/B/1. TMP de Paris. Caserne de Reuilly. Acte d'accusation dans l'affaire Heinrich EVERS et Adam ADLER, inculpés de coups et blessures volontaires et de vol, 20 Sept 1949 (Copy of CDJC document CDLXXXIX-45)

[31] Staatsanwaltschaft, Landgericht Hamburg. Verfahren gegen Klebeck, Hartwig und Rometsch. Vermerk, 24 Nov 1969; Bericht über die 1. SS-Baubrigade, 10 Mar 1950; IV 404 AR-Z 57/67. Verfügung; Erlebnisbericht Erich Frost, Watch Tower Bible and Tract Society, German branch (copy from ITS Arolsen), n.d.

[32] PRO KV 4/78. Report from Sgt Bennett to I(b) HQ Force 135 re. Alderney, 23 May 1945; PRO. WO 311 12. Statement by Kapitän Krönke, 15 Jun 1945; *Das nationalsozialistische Lagersystem*, op. cit., 365; 493; 601.

low.[33] Otto Spehr, a former Sylt prisoner, cited a figure of 87 prisoners killed in the spring and summer of 1943 alone.[34] In a later interview he gave a total figure of 350 deaths[35], a figure which comes in close range of other figures. One Jehovah's Witness at Sylt stated after the war that the camp sustained a decrease in its population of 400 within a short time. Of these early deaths 220 were buried in the island and 150 prisoners, mostly sick with TB, were returned to Neuengamme as early as June 1943, in all appearance to be liquidated.[36] Wehrmacht and OT had insisted on this transport indicating that they were unwilling to support with food prisoners who did not work. After escapes had occurred during this June transfer, prompting a disciplinary enquiry against List and Klebeck in September 1943, sick SS prisoners were liquidated in Alderney. At least 30 were shot in the autumn of 1943 and this was not the only shooting of its kind, before the Wehrmacht intervened.[37] What seems significant again is the fact that most of the deaths occurred in the early period of the camp's existence. It is quite possible that the negative reinforcement of transport limitations having an impact on the despatching of prisoners to and from Alderney, the sudden decrease in prisoner numbers and, finally, the inability to get work done on time may have led to an improvement of conditions. It is indeed surprising to read the testimony of SS prisoners stating that camp discipline in Sylt was less harsh than in concentration camps in Germany, but for those who survived the first six months – and the war – this may well have been the overriding impression.[38]

---

[33] See Pantcheff, *Alderney Fortress Island*, op. cit., 86.

[34] Brian Bonnard, *Alderney at War*, op. cit., 68.

[35] Madeleine Bunting, The Model Occupation, op. cit., 292.

[36] Staatsanwaltschaft, Landgericht Hamburg. Erlebnisbericht Erich Frost, Watch Tower Bible and Tract Society, German branch (copy from ITS Arolsen), n.d. Klebeck spoke of 200 sick prisoners sent back to Neuengamme in June 1943, see Wannseevilla Berlin. Testimonies of the Holocaust. Disziplinarakte des SS-Hauptsturmführers Max List. Vernehmungsniederschrift, 23 Sept 1943.

[37] Staatsanwaltschaft, Landgericht Hamburg. LKA/NW – Dez.15. Zeugenvernehmung Otto Spehr, 22 Dec 1964.

[38] Staatsanwaltschaft, Landgericht Hamburg. Erlebnisbericht Erich Frost, Watch Tower Bible and Tract Society, German branch (copy from ITS Arolsen), n.d.; s. also opinion of Staatsanwaltschaft, Landgericht Hamburg. IV 404 AR-Z 57/67. Verfügung; Alexei Pyanov, a Russian labourer at OT Sylt, witnessed the arrival of the 'striped' of whom he said that they 'were fed better, they got half a loaf of bread for each man a day, but the discipline there was severe', see *Island of dread in the Channel*, op. cit., 75.

British civilians

The first British civilians sent to Alderney arrived from Guernsey, in the summer of 1940, to salvage food, goods, machinery and livestock. Other agricultural working and house clearing parties followed from the spring of 1941. This came about as a result of the legal argument that for all purposes of the Occupation, Alderney came under the jurisdiction of Guernsey and that, in accordance with the Hague Convention, they were responsible for running all non-military services in the island. A spurious argument, no doubt, for the island no longer had any civilian population in the proper sense and was nothing more than a German fortress. There is evidence that both Guernsey and Jersey argued that they could not be held accountable for the running costs of the island. The two main islands did attempt to disengage themselves from having to disgorge labour and finance for the Occupation of Alderney, by petitioning the FK. In the end the Germans decreed otherwise. One argument advanced by Guernsey was that Alderney was a separate entity within the Channel Islands, both from a historical and jurisdictional point of view. A request to separate Alderney from the military administration of the Channel Islands and attach it to the French department of La Manche was lodged by the FK in 1941, but rejected by a higher authority.[39] Jersey continued its resistance toward providing funds for the billeting of German troops in Alderney over the next few months, but was told in February 1942 that the payments had to be split on a 63-37 basis between Jersey and Guernsey. The Bailiff of Jersey was clearly reluctant and needed more reminders of his obligations before finally coughing up on 29 May 1942.[40] There is some reason to believe that, at least in the case of Guernsey, the evident paradox of arguing that Alderney was an entirely separate jurisdiction while continuing to foot the bill for German billeting costs was the result of a calculated intention to utilise the resources of Alderney for their own needs. When this was no longer feasible, they backed out. Until October 1942 a specialist appointed by the States of Guernsey oversaw harvesting in Alderney, the proceeds of which benefited the Guernsey civilian population (or so it was said). After that the OT took over cultivation, with three different overseers being replaced as heads of the now OT farm in a matter of three months. Only with the arrival of a new agricultural expert named Rebling, in February 1943, did the situation improve somewhat. Still the harvests were very small compared to German standards. The OT were assisted by a number of foreigners, but in the majority were 25 Channel Islands' workers who remained behind. Finally, in March 1944, the FK intervened, as no progress was being made and appointed

---

[39] D/AU/VI/5. Chef MVB A, KommandoStb, St Germain an FK 515, 5 Aug 1941.
[40] D/AU/VI/5. FK 515 an Bailiff von Jersey betr. Quartierleistungen Alderney, 26 Feb 1942.

an agricultural officer, the already mentioned Sonderführer Richter, who took over the farm from the OT. In the spring of 1944, multiple factors were blamed for the disappointing results: the area of cultivation was overgrown with weed, the drought in the spring of 1944, lack of machinery, threshing machines, tools, labour, feeds. The only light on the horizon was the successful rearing of a flock of 90 sheep which was in good shape.[41] It is perhaps indicative that OT management was not mentioned as one of these factors inhibiting agricultural efforts. Clearly whatever schemes the Germans mounted to improve yields they could never match the know-how of the skilled labour which had evacuated in 1940. And back out they did, eventually, for in April 1943 the civilian labourers were taken over directly by the Germans as the States' representative was being recalled. Most of the Channel Islands' civilian employees in the island (over 100 at peak) worked mainly as carpenters, glaziers, waitresses, cooks, farm hands and other menial workers. In practice, however, the distinction between Guernsey and German work was not always as clear as one might have wished. Some of the specialist workers, such as Albert Pike whose last job was the management of the electricity generating plant, alternated between German and States-paid work.[42]

A handful of Alderney people who initially left the island, also returned. One of the men was farmer Frank Oselton who, having obtained permission to look after his herd, came back in November 1940. He was accompanied by a labourer by the name of Ernest Clark. A condition put upon them was that they should confine themselves to the vicinity of the farm and they seem to have wiled away their time bartering milk and butter for bread, fairly undisturbed until June 1944. Only then did the Germans compel them to supply milk.[43] The oft-mentioned Pope family were not strictly speaking islanders, but were stranded there at the outbreak of war which had interrupted their sea voyage to New Zealand. Far fetched as this may seem, the fact remains that he was also allowed to return to Alderney with his family and subsequently served as a pilot between the mainland and the islands. Again it was never established conclusively whether he did so under compulsion or of his own free will. Oselton and Clark certainly had no easy relationship with Pope whom they accused of being an ideological collaborator to the point of extending the Hitler salute and toasting German victories. Very little is known about how the other Britishers adapted to this strange planet. Scotsman Thomas Creron stated that he was

[41] JAS B/A/W/9146. PLK I, Aussenstelle Alderney, Agricultural report Sdf Richter, 18 Mar 45; PRO WO 311/12. Nebenstelle Guernsey to FK 515, report on work trip to Alderney 26 – 28 March 1944, 30 Apr 1944.
[42] PRO KV 4/78. Sgt Bennett to Capt Dening, report on Alderney, June 1945; Pantcheff, *Alderney Fortress Island*, op cit., 42.
[43] PRO WO 311/12. Statements of Frank Oselton and Ernest Clark, 24 May 1945.

never ill-treated by the Germans and that he would have hit back, if they had hit him. Others were not so lucky. On one occasion an OT threatened to shoot a man by the name of Le Cocq for striking an OT who was maltreating a Russian. According to Creron, Le Cocq received 14 days in the OT prison.[44]

In the long run the Germans also used Alderney as a 'penal colony' to which undesirables from the other islands were sent. One of these was Gordon Prigent, a young Jerseyman requisitioned for civilian labour, who was sent to the island in November 1943 – together with fellow islander Walter Gallichan – as the result of difficulties at his workplace. Prigent first worked on the OT farm before being transferred to a 'potato peeling' squad of other Britishers and Irish at the Soldatenheim, where he scrubbed the floors. When they were caught listening to the news by two German nurses and refused to return to the OT farm, they were taken to camp Nordeney where Gallichan was severely beaten with a spade because the holes for planting cabbages were not correctly spaced. Prigent eventually returned to Jersey with a prisoner transport in the summer of 1944, waiting to be transported to the Continent when the communication lines were interrupted. Astoundingly he was then released and allowed to sign up as a volunteer policeman.[45] Another Englishman who had probably never imagined in his worst nightmares that he would find himself in such a god-forsaken place was Ernest Kibble. This Liverpool engineer had come to Guernsey in 1938 and had missed the boat to England in 1940. He was denounced for having a radio set and sent to Alderney to serve part of his sentence.[46]

One of the memories that stands out in the testimony of the Britishers is of the Normandy days, when the German garrison became extremely jittery, expecting the imminent arrival of an invasion. On orders of the Inselkommandant all civilians were gathered together: the women in a bunker in High Street, the men in a park opposite the bakery. They were guarded and instructed not to leave these premises. At this time troops had orders to shoot to kill civilians who absented themselves from these designated areas. The same applied to civilians engaging in such suspicious activities as bending down to pick up objects or roaming around outside curfew.[47] One of these nervous Nazis was Richter, the agricultural officer in charge of the OT farm. He ordered his British civilian workers to sleep out in the open. When one of them went back to his billet he started abusing the entire work gang, firing shots from his pistol and shouting

---

[44] PRO WO 311/11. Statement of Thomas Creron to Capt Kent, Alderney, 17 May 1945.

[45] JAS L/D25/L/52. Gordon Prigent, CIOS talk, 13 Oct 1982; IWM. Misc. 2826 189/2 (Tape 4390). Interview with Gordon Prigent, n.d.

[46] PRO WO 311/12. Statement Ernest Kibble, n.d.

[47] PRO WO 311/12. Statement Sdf Wilhelm Richter, taken by Sgt M Eversfield, Kempton Park Camp, 3 Sept 1945. Richter was a former District Farmer Leader in Germany, a position usually only given to reliable Nazis, as it involved the supervision and control of all farmers.

'you have not won the war yet, we'll still kick you out of France!' Richter also prevented Germans from listening to the radio saying that the BBC news was all nonsense.[48]

The Germans in Alderney

The ordinary German soldier considered a posting to Alderney as a punishment, both in the metaphorical and actual sense. Hans Riedel first came to Alderney in November 1942, to work in radio engineering. He left in March 1943, and went to one of the other islands, but was sent there again in November 1944, as a punishment for having made crystal sets for civilians.[49] Life in Alderney lacked the amenities and distractions of the other islands. Alderney was also more isolated than the other islands, its principal neighbour being Cherbourg. Materially as well, Alderney was less well off: food allocations were almost the only source of provision and there were no opportunities for purchasing fresh agricultural or horticultural produce as in the other islands. Gerhard Nebel, a German soldier who published his wartime experiences in a book after the war, was also sent to Alderney as a punishment in 1942. If Nebel is to be believed not only material conditions, but also moral conditions were worse than average, with Prussian officers using the special circumstances to drive chicanery and humiliation to ever greater heights. Nebel referred to his company commander as a Nazi full of 'pedantic pettiness' founded on stupidity and fear of superiors. Nebel described his existence in Alderney as 'hopeless', of 'insupportable misery'.[50] To make matters worse, in 1942 a mysterious epidemic struck, an infection causing diarrhoea and with very unpleasant side effects. It has been said that it was caused by a parasite linked to problems with the water supply. The population of Alderney during the Occupation was considerably higher than in normal times, more clean water was needed and more sewage was being produced.[51] Similar in size to Sark, Alderney also lacked the soothing presence of contact with normal civilian life. The Germans themselves were reminded with every step that this was a harsh little outpost of the Third Reich where military discipline alone accentuated the rhythm of life. A British escapee confirmed that German morale was worse in Alderney than in the other islands

---

[48] PRO WO 311/12. Statement of Obergefreiter Kraus, 6 Jul 1945.

[49] PRO WO 311/12. Statement of Hans Riedel, taken by C Kent, Alderney, 4 Jun 1945. Pantcheff also voiced the opinion that Alderney was dreaded by the Germans themselves, see JAS L/D/25/A/4. Appendix to Col B E Arnold, *The Alderney Story*, information provided by Theodore Pantcheff, n.d.

[50] Gerhard Nebel, Bei den nördlichen Hesperiden, Wuppertal, 1948, 81, cited in Cruickshank, op. cit., 175.

[51] Pantcheff, *Alderney Fortress Island*, op. cit., 62.

and that many did not know how to cope with claustrophobia.[52] The Germans tried to counter the negative effects of 'island madness' by putting on entertainment. In 1944 the German *Guernsey Zeitung* also published a brochure, similar in character to von Aufsess's *Impressions* and the short guide to the Channel Islands by Sonderführer Auerbach, to 'facilitate acclimatisation' and sensitise the 'visitors' to the unique topography, fauna and flora of the place.[53] Needless to say, the most shaping feature of occupied Alderney, the foreign workers, were not considered part of the fauna.

The three principal categories of workers in the occupied Channel Islands were voluntary, forced or slaves. The volunteers often were skilled or specialised workers who received high wages. A large proportion of them came from Germany, but there were also many other nationalities. Some of the French who joined as volunteers did so to avoid being sent to Germany under the compulsory labour service scheme of their government. Had some of them known that they would be sent to Alderney, they may have reconsidered their decision.[54] The forced workers comprised the Republican Spanish exiles, but also other 'undesirables' the Vichy government could dispense with such as North Africans.[55] A curious case apart, more forced than voluntary, were the Germans of the former 999 Brigade, a special unit created on Hitler's orders in February 1942. Fourteen of these workers were captured in the island on Liberation. Veterans of the trade unions, KPD, SPD and various other political parties, these German anti-Nazis were treated almost as prisoners. The purpose of the 999 Brigade had been to put a stop to the waste of precious Aryan cannon-fodder and accommodate fallen angels who previously had forfeited their civil rights and could not be incorporated in the army through the regular channels. Two of these men were interviewed by the British. Clemens Kriesbach from Essen had been involved in clashes with the Nazis since 1932 and locked away in a concentration camp when the Nazis took power in January 1933. In June of that year he escaped and crossed the border into Holland where he worked for a Communist underground movement. This sent him back to Germany where he was again picked up by the Gestapo and imprisoned for five years. Jacob Pfarr was another former KPD member, jailed for a first time in 1933, released and then again put into a concentration camp on 1 September 1939. After enrolment in the 999 Brigade both men were sent to Greece in 1943, but returned in the autumn and were then sent to the Channel Islands. The reason for this curious

[52] PRO HO 144 2223. MI19. Report by two informants, 19 Apr 1944.
[53] *Die Insel Alderney. Aufsaetze und Bilder*, Zusammenstellung von Hauptmann Dr Bessenrodt, deutsche Guernsey Zeitung, 1943.
[54] Michael Ginns, *The Organisation Todt and the Fortress Engineers in the Channel Islands* (Channel Islands Occupation Society, Archive Book No. 8), Jersey, 1994, 57.
[55] ibid.

occurrence is given in an appendix to an order of 8 January 1944 stating that the men's rehabilitation with the 999 Brigade had been cut short by 'incidents' and that they were unworthy of military service. However, they were to be afforded another chance to prove themselves, in the OT. At first given a swastika armband and treated as free workers, this new experiment soon went awry as they had been prone to 'abuse their position', resulting in the OT withdrawing their free workers status.[56]

Eliminatory prejudice

The brutalities prisoners suffered in the Alderney camps have been the mainstay of many descriptions over the last 60 years: beatings of varying degrees of severity and with diverse implements were a daily routine, at times degenerating into random shootings or other forms of cold-blooded killing. As their SS counterparts the OT guards were up for 'games', performed with alternating sadistic ingenuity. Gordon Prigent described one such 'game', the ultimate aim of which was to get prisoners to 'work harder'. First a guard would put a lump of sugar in a row of carrots, in sight of the worker. Predictably when the prisoner reached the spot, the guard moved it another 100 yards further, and so on, until, by the end of the day, the worker might be lucky enough to get one lump of sugar. Popular variations involved the use of Alsatians who were trained to tackle anyone who ran. Hubert Riegner, in charge of the OT farm, thus 'amused' himself with the 60 Sylt prisoners who were sent there to work, by letting loose his dogs on the prisoners. If they managed to disentangle themselves from the grip of the canines and get up from the ground Riegner would beat them down again so that the dogs could have another go. Quite frequently prisoners were dragged around until they were unconscious. [57] Abuse was not limited to the camps or worksites. Abuse was in the air, poisoning the atmosphere across the island. Scenes evocative of the western frontier in its worst days of lawlessness were acted out. Life was cheap in Alderney and stories of desperado culture were, indeed, legion. One night in 1943 a Russian worker who had had the audacity to gorge himself on the spot with food scavenged in a German billet was surprised by the occupants, two Feldgendarms, on their return from the mess. The outcome was predictable: he was killed in the ensuing fight. Other scenes were in the genre of Francis Ford Coppola's *Apocalypse Now*: in one reported case a very gung-ho German simply shot out of a window killing a worker prowling around

[56] PRO KV 4/78. Sgt Bennett to Capt Dening, report on Alderney, June 1945; PRO WO 311/11. Statement of Jacob Pfarr taken by Capt Kent, 18 May 1945.

[57] IWM Misc. 2826 189/2 (Tape 4390). Interview with Gordon Prigent; PRO WO 311/11. Statement of Wilfred Henry Dupont to Capt Kent, Alderney, 17 May 1945.

the Jenning farm one night in 1943. No questions asked. He later stated to the investigating Feldgendarm that he had shot out of 'fear'.[58] Other incidents had an even more sinister touch to them, such as the manhunt and public liquidation of Ebert, a former head Kapo at Sylt (SS). Ebert had attempted to get onto one of the ships plying the Alderney route. When his disappearance was noticed, an islandwide search was instigated and it was not long before he was found hiding in the church, between Victoria Street and New Street. Pursued by the SS and their helpers across the cemetery, he was hit by one or more bullets before reaching the street. At this moment a German Army captain arrived on the scene in his car. Ebert, already bleeding from several wounds, ran towards this man imploring him to protect him. The officer would have none of this, he simply shook off the prisoner and proceeded to his quarters in the Court House. When the SS caught up with him he was beaten and finished off with a shot in the back of the neck. After this an argument ensued between the SS, as some had wanted him alive for interrogation.[59] More important than 'hare hunts' was eliminatory prejudice which was definitely *en vogue* with some Germans. Werner Trautvetter, a naval rating who arrived in Alderney in September 1942, stated that his commanding officer, one First Lieutenant Hay, gave them orders that they should not give anything to the Russians because they were their enemies, adding for good measure 'that they should be exterminated'. Trautvetter's room-mate and comrade-in-arms, Paehlicke, a man he described as 'impossible to talk to […] as he could only talk about National Socialism', also delighted in hitting Russians.[60] Another German who had not yet been sent to the Eastern Front was reported to have boasted that finally he had killed his 'first Russian'.[61] As in the occupied Eastern territories, where army personnel followed mass shootings of Jews or hangings of partisans with an enthusiasm comparable to the Roman relish for gladiator games or the medieval zest for gruesome public executions, the Channel Islands saw their share of thrill-seeking and inhuman curiosity. Jerseyman John Pinel, a pre-war cabbie, became an OT driver in January 1942. He was profoundly shocked by the attitude of two German officers for whom a mortal accident witnessed while driving past a worksite was the cause of much amusement. Other Germans took photographs of skeletal Russians removed from the wards.[62] All these individuals found themselves well within the parameters of the Nazi canon.

---

[58] PRO WO 311/12. Statement Stabsfeldwebel Kurt Busse, Feldgendarm, taken at Kempton Park Camp, 11 Jul 1945.

[59] PRO WO 311/12. Statement of Uffz Rudolf Kupfer, driver in Alderney, 25 June 1945.

[60] PRO WO 311/11. Statement of Werner Trautvetter to Capt Kent, Alderney, 20 May 1945.

[61] PRO WO 311/12. Statement Balika Alexander, Alderney, 18 May 1945.

[62] PRO WO 311/11. Statement of John Pinel taken by C Kent, St Helier, 10 Jul 1945.

The Origins of Violence

The problem of arriving at a correct appreciation of the origins of violence is due to the fact that the worst killer in Alderney was not the beating to death or shooting of prisoners on the spot but rather more the systemic violence consisting of a combination of back-breaking work, deficient diet, primitive accommodation and sanitary conditions – even by the standards of an ordinary German camp, absence of adequate clothing, protection and medical care all of which gave rise to physical exhaustion, sickness and disease. The best demonstration of the systemic violence were the 'meals' prisoners received: ersatz coffee for breakfast, 'soup' for lunch and again 'soup' for supper, plus a loaf of bread for five men. 'Soup' was a mere euphemism for 'water' with bits of tomato, cabbage, carrot or minced potato floating in it. Other food was practically never distributed and it is obvious that a man doing hard labour on such food would be liable to physical exhaustion and eventual collapse.[63] This diet stood in bleak contrast to official 'paper' rations as determined by the island quartermaster of the 319th ID. Naturally, there were differentiations in the rations: Germans received the best meals, civilians from other European countries (including the Channel Islanders) came second, while political prisoners, Jews and Soviets found themselves at the bottom of the pyramid. But even set on a scale below Germans, the rations for foreigners should have still added up to 700 grams of meat per week and 600 grams of bread per day.[64] The difference between what they were entitled to and what they found on their plates was attributable to misappropriation at all intermediary stages of distribution, starting as far afield as France, and further tampering once the food arrived in Alderney. There the biggest fraudsters were the above-mentioned office of the army quartermaster and the two men responsible for the OT Central Supply Store, Helling and Standop. Both offices represented the black market in the island.[65] Corruption was by no means restricted to the OT in Alderney, nor to the OT alone. At Sylt the prisoners also did not receive their due in rations; the spoils of corruption, however, did not remain the exclusive domain of a few men, but were evenly spread out among the SS staff. Thus the 'savings' from prisoners' rations were put on sale at the canteen, profits were pooled into a

[63] PRO WO 311 12. Statement made by Ivan Amelin from Orel, 10 Jun 1945; JAS L/D/25/A/4. Appendix to Col B E Arnold, *The Alderney Story*, information provided by Theodore Pantcheff, n.d.

[64] Pantcheff, *Alderney Fortress Island*, op. cit., 15.

[65] These were the only two places of additional supply in the island. No food was available from the canteen located at the corner of Victoria St and High St near Lloyds Bank which only sold a few irrelevances at prohibitive prices, see PRO HO 144/22237. Report Channel Islands Alderney MI19, Further report by informants 2122, 2136, 19 Apr 1944 (info as at 8 Apr 43).

fund and at regular intervals SS men were paid dividends of 100 RM.[66] The SS quickly adapted themselves to the business environment running on pilfered resources. One of the other ventures they established at Sylt, in October 1943, was a schnapps distillery.[67] At OT Guernsey the overall principal was no different. Jaime Verdaguer, a Spanish worker at Camp Ursula, incriminated 14 people whom he knew had stolen worker rations. OT cook Bronislaw Gruschke, also stole Red Cross parcels and traded food on the black market, the medical officers, a French OT delegate, the men of the OT protection service (Schutzkommando) who co-operated with the Feldgendarmerie. Many OTs also fleeced workers of food, cigarettes or soap obtained in the island when they returned to the camp. OT-Truppführer Hermann Poehlke, the senior overseer of the camp and one of the worst pilferers, told workers that they had no right to procure extra food as they had their rations.[68]

The high incidence of systemic violence is reflected in the post-war statements taken from victims, bystanders and perpetrators. In comparison evidence of death by beating, shooting or other direct means was rare – although, naturally, such dramatic incidents were what stuck most in people's memories. Yet all statements taken together leave no doubt that the island was strewn with prisoners clearly on their last legs. This became such a common and permanent feature that it wasn't even considered special anymore. What most witnesses also confirmed was that the worst period was indeed the six months after the influx of the Eastern Europeans, until the spring of 1943. Deaths through ill-treatment and overwork did still occur after this period, but the highest exertion toll seem to have been localised with specifically designated categories – the Jews, half Jews and resistance workers who replaced the Eastern Europeans in late 1943. Generally, however, the regime eased.

The origins of this structural violence are less clear. Two hypotheses can be advanced. Starvation and overwork were the result of a combination of corruption and eliminatory prejudice at grassroots level; although endemic wherever the OT went, this combination took a particularly nasty turn in Alderney. This would imply that the potential for feeding, clothing and provision of minimal care existed, but was not realised. The second hypothesis is that prisoner deaths were a premeditated act of 'slow' murder, based on the fact that food was a scarce resource and that prejudice did not allow 'Untermenschen' to be fed on an equal footing with the German master race. A fixed mortality rate was agreed which factored in food supply, possible replenishment of labour and work schedules. All this made up the 'production process'. The most striking

---

[66] Pantcheff, *Alderney Fortress Island*, op.cit., 33.
[67] PRO WO 311/12. Protocol Statement Oberbootsmannsmaat Franz Docter, Hako Alderney, 7 Jul 1945.
[68] PRO WO 311/11. Statement of Jaime Verdaguer, 17 June 1945.

evidence in support of this second theory is that there was no shortage of food during the worst period of OT labourer suffering in 1942–43 and that many Germans themselves could not understand why these workers were being worked to death.[69] It is possible that an explicit order existed whereby certain workers were to be given lower rations. After all, while resources in the Channel Islands may have been adequate, on the level of fortress Europe there was a definite shortfall of food. How otherwise is the demented frenzy of denying prisoners even a single extra potato explainable? There is also no question that the Germans were aware of the death rates. Kurt Busse served as a Feldgendarm in Alderney after he arrived on 7 February 1942. A professional soldier who had joined the 'Army of 100,000' after the First World War, he developed something of a relationship with another middle-aged professional soldier, the Russian doctor overseeing the OT sick bay at Norderney. Busse testified that the doctor kept a record of deaths in triplicate, one of which was sent monthly to the OT Frontführung in Alderney and another to the Oberbauleitung in St Malo.[70] The situation in Alderney certainly does seem to bear some connection to the contradictions between a Utopian calling to reconfigure the racial landscape of Europe – meaning the disappearance of certain categories of humans – and the need for labour. It also appears valid to suggest that the 'mess' criticised by the OT commission in 1943 – the lack of registry, the state of the graves – was not a criticism of the overall conditions, but of the lack of observation of orders within the parameters set by superior authority. The duality of death and work existed in all the camps. The SS were the great camp experts in Nazi Gerrmany. Most of their camps consisted not of one, but of several establishments, with varying conditions, at times trying to negotiate a balance between the reduction of human beings and exploitation.

Tempting as a theory of premeditated starvation is, however, it is inconceivable that the OT was capable of the level of sophistication displayed by the SS who knew much better how to calibrate such a system and make it responsive to the varying demands for extermination or labour. An even more powerful argument is the uncomfortable truth that despite the harsher discipline and treatment in the SS camp, this camp sustained proportionately fewer deaths than the OT camps.[71] In addition, there was a considerable difference between the logic of death and violence in the SS and the OT. Violence in the SS camps was a practised ritual, the ultimate aim of which was to maintain camp discipline or –

---

[69] PRO WO 311/12. Statements by Johann Burbach and Josef Kratzer taken by Capt Kent, Alderney, 28 May 1945. Kratzer said that at one point they had so many vegetables, in particular carrots, that these were going bad.

[70] PRO WO 311/12. Statement of Kurt Busse, taken by Capt Kent, 22 May 1945.

[71] JAS L/D25/A/4. Appendix to Col B E Arnold, *The Alderney Story*, information provided by Theodore Pantcheff, n.d.

to use a better term – strike terror in the hearts of the prisoners. Death was not the result of chaos, corruption, starvation, exposure or disease (which is not to say that the food or medical conditions in the SS camp were good). The organisational experience the SS had gathered in running concentration camps since 1933 had made them expert in determining the minimum margins necessary to just about keep people on their feet. The SS had developed their own system of 'managed' violence, a well-greased machine which could be turned to all needs and intentions. The SS style of inhumanity was cold-blooded, calculated and rational, within the bounded rationality of Nazism. Himmler himself had stressed time and again that he did not want sadists, perverts and rapists among his elite, simply men who carried out orders. The fact of the matter is that the SS believed that murder without an emotional response on the part of the perpetrators was possible and desirable. Extermination by work, especially of racial inferiors, was executed as one disposes of rubbish. None of this applied to the OT, a civilian agency which, in a matter of months, had gone from supervising voluntary German workers to directing an army of work slaves. The OT violence strikes one as crude and without purpose. The beatings, starvation and torture in the OT camps did not reinforce discipline – neither that of the prisoners nor that of the OTs themselves – and it created a slave population that could not meet targets. Nor was the OT a force which could develop an organisational culture of discipline and blind obedience comparable to the SS who were an elite of a very particular kind. One OT circular detailing cases of disciplinary action taken against German OTs in August 1942 gives an impression of a fairly 'rough crowd': out of the ten men on this one list, seven had already spent time at the OT Education Institution in Pontivy, France. Most offences were connected to drunkenness, insubordination, disobedience, unruliness, lack of discipline, racketeering and only in two case the more honourable charge of having listened to the English radio. Other documents also mention lack of cleanliness and bartering of OT property against liquor. Another OT officer borrowed money from other OTs whom he was supposed to transfer through Paris and then disappeared for three days. The most picturesque in this collection of rogues, however, was one Julius Ordner. This man was arrested stark naked and stone drunk in the streets of Dinard. The explanation he gave was that he had bathed in the sea, but had failed to find his clothes upon return to the shore.[72]

---

[72] JAS D/A/U/V/52. OT ESG West Rundschreiben, 29 Aug 1942.

Mismanagement and corruption

The evidence seems to weigh rather in support of an explanation of corruption coupled with eliminatory prejudice. Breakdown of discipline is always a temptation in isolated positions such as fortress Alderney. Whatever may have been written elsewhere about the exemplary demeanour of the German troops in the Channel Islands, in Alderney an almost imperceptible, yet genuine disintegration of morale took place which found an outlet in corruption, alcohol excess, sexual debauchery and cruelty towards foreign workers. It is inconceivable that the goings-on were not known to the higher authorities outside the islands, as the signs of breakdown in discipline were splashed across the wall.

The system's inability to reform from within and the deep entrenchment of corruption is illustrated in the case of Johann Hoffmann, Commandant of camp Helgoland from January 1943. When Hoffmann arrived at the camp he found many signs of neglect. His deputy was drunk in his office, the camp was not properly fenced in and workers were leaving as they pleased. No reliable information existed as to the figure of the camp population, as no papers had been kept, and Hoffmann had to establish numbers himself, at the time about 900 mainly Russian and Ukrainian workers. Hoffmann seems to have had the intention of 'tidying up' the situation; he claimed having paid the workers – including the Russians – their due salaries, while also conceding that many of the firms never paid them out. Hoffmann did not get very far in changing the system. When he lodged a complaint about insufficient food and accommodation with his superiors in Alderney, Frontführer Linke and Bauleiter Büttmann, he was reprimanded with the comment that he did not know how to make ends meet. Sometime later the procedure was reversed and he was attacked for allowing an increase in the cases of illness because he was too lenient.[73]

Finally, the Germans only got a move on when the rot began to threaten construction targets, and then exemplary punishment was meted out. Major Karl Hoffmann, the tactical specialist in overall charge of fortification, confirmed after the war that at first all building went according to schedule, small bottlenecks existed – through disturbances in shipping – but nothing serious. Then in mid-1942 performance started to decrease continually. Hoffmann began individual controls and spot-checks and found that not all workers were at their sites. As a result an order was passed forbidding German soldiers to give food to workers who were absenting themselves. When a subsequent query with the division in Guernsey found that they did not have the

---

[73] Pantcheff, T X H, *Alderney Fortress Island – The Germans in Alderney*, 1940–1945, Chichester, 1981, 17; PRO WO 311/12. Statement of OT Frontf. Johann Hoffmann, Kempton Park, 1 Aug 1945.

same problem of keeping workers at their sites, the phenomenon was linked to the German organisation in Alderney. For all his failings – Hoffman lauded Sylt as 'the best labour camp he had seen during the entire war' – he could not have been popular with the OT, for he noticed far too many other things as well. Hoffmann criticised – perhaps inspired by what he had seen at the SS – that the OT did not get its priorities right and did not know how to create the basics of ordered camp life. Not enough clothes and shoe repair shops existed, but meanwhile resources were wasted on luxury standard accommodation for higher OT officers. In October 1942 Hoffmann also established that food in Alderney was not sufficient and attempted to remedy the situation by getting the divisional quartermaster to negotiate an increase in potato rations with the OT; only to be told by General Müller to keep his nose out of OT business.[74]

Nevertheless, an inquiry did, eventually, take place in early 1943. Feldgendarm Kurt Busse stated that in 1943 he was ordered by divisional command in Guernsey to conduct an inquiry, visiting Nordeney and Helgoland camps with the island Wehrmacht surgeon and conducting unannounced spot-checks which involved weighing and tasting the food. As could have been guessed, they found 'deficiencies'.[75] According to OT Frontführer Johann Hoffmann a medical commission sent all the way from Berlin removed records and ordered that crosses be erected on the graves.[76] It is very likely that the inquiry reached the conclusion that the human reservoir was no longer as abundant in late 1942 as it had been the year before and that, therefore, the OT could not afford to work to death labour on such a scale. From the Nazi point of view working certain categories of prisoners to death was acceptable as long as schedules were met. This was evident from the fact that no charge was brought as to the responsibility for the numerous deaths. The regular exchanges of exhausted prisoners also demonstrate that the system revolved around an officially condoned prisoner life expectancy. Prisoners were viewed as a mere production factor and as long as the supply was plentiful, a heavy-handed approach presented no particular problem. The really serious charge in this case was malfeasance, cheating the system by starving workers to death in order to realise black market profits.

[74] PRO WO 311/12. Statement by Major Karl Hoffmann, taken by T X H Pantcheff, Kempton Park Camp, 2 Sept 1945. Hoffmann was sent to Jersey in November 1943 when Müller left, and he was probably not too far off the mark with his speculation that this transfer was instigated by the OT.

[75] PRO WO 311/12. Statement of Kurt Busse, taken by Capt Kent, 22 May 1945.

[76] PRO WO 311/12. Statement of OT Frontf. Johann Hoffmann, Kempton Park, 1 Aug 1945; PRO WO 311/11. Haddock to Shapcott, 21 May 1945. The other source confirming that an enquiry did take place was Major Hoffmann. There need be no discrepancy in his statement that this was conducted by the divisional quartermaster and the divisional doctor, as they may have preceded the OT commission from Berlin, see PRO WO 311/12. Statement of Major Karl Hoffmann, taken by T X H Pantcheff, Kempton Park Camp, 2 Sept 1945.

As a result action was taken against a number of people. At the top both Frontführer Linke and Construction Superintendent Büttmann left the island in the spring of 1943, for trial or court martial in France. The same fate befell Tietz, according to Pantcheff, the worst of the Alderney OT bullies. Tietz was the first commander of OT Sylt and then, until January 1943, commander of Nordeney. He was court-martialled by the Germans in April 1943 and sentenced to one year and six months – for black marketeering and illegal bartering of food and cigarettes against watches and other valuables obtained from Dutch workers.[77] Helling and Standop were accused – not of workers' deaths – but of embezzlement, as it was found that they had over-indented actual ration strength by 600 heads. Both were sent away in the summer of 1943, Standop to stand trial in Berlin, Helling, after court-martial by the divisional court, to one of the notorious Emsland penal camps where he died in August 1943. The two quartermasters – and this should be no surprise – got off very lightly. The first, Krüger, was only reprimanded with a degradation whereas the other, Frank, committed suicide in April 1945.[78] What did raise eyebrows, however, was the military's indulgence in corruption of the flesh, the routine keeping, by officers, of mistresses and 'comfort women' recruited from the female employees or workers in the island. Emulating the OT establishment in Victoria Street – to which, if Theodore Pantcheff is to be believed, must go the 'laurel wreath' – Major Hoffmann even opened his own brothel in a quiet corner of the island.[79] For the rest of German manhood, prospects in Alderney were bleaker than in other postings such as Jersey and Guernsey, where the number of imported prostitutes was higher in comparison. An even greater danger than mere corruption of morals was the spread of VD. In the two larger islands control of sexual activity was enforced through regular medical inspections, whereas the situation in Alderney was out of control. A repatriation of 40 infected women in late 1942 did not remedy the situation.[80] In the summer of 1943 Lieutenant Colonel Schwalm was sent over from Jersey to replace the Inselkommandant, Zuske who, it was said, had set a bad example. Before Schwalm left for his new post he was briefed by von Schmettow who told him that his posting was necessary because of emerging friction between the Wehrmacht Fortress-Pioneers and the OT. He also revealed that the division had initiated the change in command within the OT – this may have been the reason for the fallout – and ordered him to report misappropriations of food. On his arrival Schwalm ordered the

[77] PRO WO 311/12. Statement of OT Frontf. Johann Hoffmann, Kempton Park, 1 Aug 1945; Pantcheff, *Alderney Fortress Island*, op. cit., 14.

[78] Pantcheff, *Alderney Fortress Island*, op. cit., 15.

[79] JAS L/D25/A/4. Appendix to Col B E Arnold, *The Alderney Story*, Information provided by Theodore Pantcheff, n.d.; Pantcheff, T X H, *Alderney Fortress Island – The Germans in Alderney, 1940–1945*, Chichester, 1981, 58–9.

[80] Pantcheff, *Alderney Fortress Island*, op. cit., 58–59.

return of all remaining mistresses, an order which some managed to dodge. It is indicative of military cronyism that Zuske was one of the few men involved in corruption who was not tried, but posted back to a cushy office job in Leipzig, his home town.

Workers' rations now improved from the previous starvation level to something slightly better. Jan Szulc, a postal clerk from Rowno (pre-war Eastern Poland), stated that bread rations as well as the soup got better in mid-1943. Prisoners now also received tomatoes. Potatoes and sugar, however, were not distributed before 1944 and there was no milk ration.[81] His compatriot Ted Misiewiec said that workers had more freedom in 1943 than the preceding year. They were allowed to visit other camps and there were even football matches between forced workers and Dutch or German volunteers. That this liberalisation had nothing to do with humanitarianism is perhaps best demonstrated through Schwalm's glib statements that he was on good terms with List. When he visited the SS camp he found things in 'particular good order' and had his hair cut by two Jehovah's Witnesses because 'work was done here cleanly and carefully'. Schwalm appeared to have been equally easy to please when, during a visit to a building site, he noticed a man cowering in a corner and was told that this was merely a 'slacker'.[82] One can understand why Pantcheff, who interrogated Schwalm, described the man as 'a mealy-mouthed bastard […] who knew nothing of what went on (or so he said)'.[83] Relatively speaking, the margins of survival increased in 1943. Most prisoners were now working on the borders of their physical ability rather than entirely in the red burn-out zone. Still, in some work parties the death toll from exhaustion remained as high throughout 1943 as it had been before.

The OT failure to meet production targets, combined with allegations of corruption in the OT and the military, were also the most likely influence on the despatch of the 1st SS Construction Brigade in the spring of 1943. The rationale behind this SS incursion into a predominantly military area has never been conclusively explained, but the situation presented precisely the sort of political scandal Himmler would have relished and, besides, an excellent peg to push through his own agenda. That the SS were informed about the situation is confirmed by the post-war statement of the ubiquitous Karl-Heinz Wölfle, of 'Gestapo' fame. While on duty in St Malo during the winter of 1942–43 he was approached by De Wolf, one of the co-owners of the Dutch firm Bosland & De Wolf. De Wolf complained that his workers were not getting enough to eat and

---

[81] PRO WO 311/12. Jan Szulc from Rowno, postal clerk Statement of 28 Jul 1945, Kempton Park Camp.

[82] PRO WO 311/12. Report of Oberstltn d R Schwalm re Alderney, 20 July 1945.

[83] JAS. L/D25/A/4. Appendix to Col B E Arnold, *The Alderney Story*, Information provided by Theodore Pantcheff, n.d.

that the people responsible for the rations were selling them on the black market, intimating that something should be done about this. Wölfle also took statements from Bosland and others who came to St Malo on leave, thereby confirming De Wolf's allegations, and then submitted a report to the SS Verbindungsstelle.[84]

Survival

Survival was conditioned by resourcefulness and the ability to figure out how the system worked. The first rule was to avoid, if possible, worksites with a particularly bad reputation. Russian survivor Georgi Kondakov explained in his account of Alderney, that chances of survival also depended on the character of the person in charge. As a rule those working at the harbour, in the unloading of the supply ships were in the best position to steal food or other items and spread these over the island. The worst work sites in Alderney were Westbatterie, the quarries and the anti-tank wall at Longis Bay which the Russians called 'inevitable death'.[85] Despite the frequent beatings of prisoners who dared to line up, gaining admittance to the sick bay was also the winning formula. Jan Szulc, a Pole who came to Alderney in the summer of 1942 and spent two years at Nordeney, was admitted to the sick bay after six weeks on the work site and when he left after two weeks he was sent to the camp kitchen. A second Polish prisoner, Antoni Budny, was lucky enough to have been transferred from Nordeney to Borkum, where he worked in the tailor's workshop. At Borkum even the small number of foreign workers escaped ill treatment and were better fed than in the other camps. The clue to his transfer is probably that, initially, Budny was brought to Alderney with a group of 50 Polish craftsmen, some of whom at least were transferred to better duties after a few weeks.[86] Another stratagem was to 'make a show of working hard', without breaks, which better suited the German foremen.[87] Escape certainly was not an option. According to Madeleine Bunting the only forced worker to have escaped from Alderney was Ted Misiewiec, a young Pole who had been sent to Sylt as a punishment in 1943.[88] After he escaped he hid in various places for some time, among them camp Helgoland itself, before enlisting the help of some Belgian prisoners who were on their way to Cherbourg. That conditions remained chaotic is testified by

---

[84] PRO WO 311/11. Statement of Karl-Heinz Wölfle, taken by Capt Kent 6 Jul 1945.
[85] *The island of dread in the Channel*, op. cit., 49–50.
[86] PRO WO 311/12. Statements Jan Szulc and Antoni Budny, Kempton Park Camp, 28 Jul 1945.
[87] *The island of dread*, op. cit., 33.
[88] Madeleine Bunting, *The Model Occupation*, op. cit., 179.

the fact that Misiewiec had no trouble taking the place of a prisoner who had died. On arrival in France he attached himself to a party of Russian workers logging timber, from which he absconded again after a few weeks' work, finally making it to Paris where he hid until Liberation.[89]

In the early period of the OT presence not even a genuine fence perimeter existed. It was logical for the OT to assume that in this isolated small island there was nowhere to escape to and nobody to whom the prisoners could turn. Nevertheless some workers had taken their chances. In one case two fugitives took refuge in a cave beneath the cliffs. Inevitably, one day, while they were out picking mussels, they were surprised by a sentry and shot.[90] Smoking was a more lethal habit than it is otherwise, as some, unable to quit, exchanged their food for cigarettes. Other slave workers were more clever as they realised that their only chance lay with those members of the garrison itself who did not agree with the way prisoners were being treated. Instead of relying on the civilian population, as in Guernsey or Jersey, workers had to find helpers among the Germans. That this was not impossible is confirmed by the post-war testimony of OT employee Maria Brock who said that even among the OTs in Jersey there were two types: those who liked and those who disliked ill-treating Russians.[91] To conceive of the Alderney camps as sealed environments is false, there was a considerable degree of fluidity. Despite orders prohibiting communication all 'populations' on planet Alderney mingled steadily. Civilian workers and soldiers even came into contact with the Sylt prisoners who were being farmed out across the island. As in Jersey, the German chiefs tried to put a stop to the helpers by issuing prohibitions on providing extra food to workers, the most common argument being that they were well catered for and only abused people's kindness. One such notice, published on 15 August 1942, demanded that all 'vagabonding and begging foreign workers' be arrested and handed over to the Feldgendarmerie. The order did not provide the expected results, for two months later Inselkommandant Zuske had to remind the troops of the preceding interdiction, criticising that some Wehrmacht units had 'misappropriated' labourers who were now working for them in exchange for food.[92] Other workers tried to survive by bartering firewood against food which, theoretically, was also outlawed.[93] When the warnings went unheeded, the authorities meted out punishment: Johann Burbach, an army mechanic, received three days' confinement for selling some bread to an Eastern European who worked with him at the electricity plant. Pity,

[89] IWM Misc. 2826 189/2 (Tape 3376). Interview with Ted Misiewiec, n.d.

[90] PRO WO 311/12. Herrmann Kuhn, Feldgendarmerietrupp 319, taken by T X H Pantcheff, Kempton Park Camp, 2 Sept 1945.

[91] PRO WO 311/12. Statement of Maria Brock, Jersey, 27 June 1945.

[92] PRO WO 311/12. Inselkommandantur Alderney, Ia, betr Abstellung russischer Arbeitskraefte zu Einheiten der Wehrmacht, 9 Oct 1942.

[93] PRO WO 311/11. Statement of Lorenz Gmeinder to Capt Kent, Alderney, 20 May 1945.

which he gave as the reason for his action, was not acknowledged as a valid motive.[94] Naturally, this demonstrates that prisoners were more exposed in Alderney than in the other islands, for Germans who stepped out of line were easier to discipline than the civilian population, especially if orders were reinforced by the self-policing environment created by group dynamics. Still many more may have helped, if the system had not been so largely in favour of the bullies.

Even more shocking than this realisation is the fact that for the Russian slave labourers, at least, conditions in the OT camps were not as unheard of as one might have imagined. Georgi Kondakov reminds us that deprivation and starvation practised as a political and economic weapon on its own population by a totalitarian regime already existed in 1930s Russia. Especially during the period of forced collectivisation, millions were evicted from their land, sent to camps or liquidated. Famine followed in the wake of the destruction of the traditional farming culture which wiped out more millions, among them many from Kondakov's home *oblast* of Orel. One of his brothers-in-arms believed that this experience steeled many of their compatriots as they already had acquired many relevant skills at home. 'Except for the killing work', Kondakov wrote, 'life on Alderney differed very little for me from life in Russia'.[95]

Deaths

The number of deaths in Alderney has remained a contested topic. It must be admitted that the evidential base is rather patchy and unsatisfactory, especially as prisoners were shifted back and forth all the time. Neither the register of deaths in the island nor post-war exhumations or searches proved conclusive. Pantcheff bases his figures on the results of a 1963 exhumation and the number of recorded deaths between February 1942 and June 1944: 389 (329 buried in the Russian cemetery and 60 in the churchyard), out of a workforce of forced and slave labourers which at most times was 3,000. Pantcheff determined that the worst months were November-December 1942, during which a minimum of 116 died (average age 26) of which 114 were Ukrainians, Russians and Poles. Men who had arrived in perfect health a few weeks before were reduced to skeletons. No single German death took place during these two months and even during the siege period of 1944–45 the German death toll was only 21.[96] While Pantcheff's

[94] PRO WO 311/12. Statement Johann Burbach, army mechanic, taken at Kempton Park Camp, 10 Jul 1945.

[95] *The island of dread in the Channel*. op.cit., 7.

[96] The aggregate death toll of the German garrison during the occupation of Alderney was 61, see Pantcheff, *Alderney Fortress Island*, op. cit., 71–4; JAS L/D25/A/4. Appendix to Col B E Arnold, *The Alderney Story*, information provided by Theodore Pantcheff, n.d.

prisoner death figures are indicative of a trend, the numbers do not agree with what is known about camp conditions and prisoner deaths. The best clue comes from Major Karl Hoffmann who gave a figure of 250–300 OT workers who died during his period of activity in Alderney from June 1941 to November 1943.[97] If we take into account that the Germans would have had a tendency to play down the exact number of worker deaths, that Hoffmann's figure does not include the SS deaths, and that no doubt more deaths occurred after his departure, we're probably edging closer to at least 700. Other sources seem to point in this way as well: van Amelin from Orel (Russia) stated that six weeks after his arrival with the Eastern Europeans in August 1942 the death rate at Nordeney was two to three per day.[98] The Amicale d'Aurigny, the association of French survivors of Alderney, provided a figure of 687 for the number of Russian deaths alone, while Ted Misiewiec estimated 800 deaths.[99] Other witnesses maintained that casualties until about mid-1943 could reach anything up to ten per day which would agree with the average 'prisoner working life' of six months cited across the board.[100]

The reason for the difference in the numbers relating to burials and deaths has remained the great mystery. This has given weight to the argument that some bodies were dumped in pits or thrown into the sea. Several survivors have confirmed such occurrences: Georgi Kondakov writes in his book[101] that at a point which he dates in December 1942, the workers were told that henceforth they were to receive the privilege of being buried in a coffin, another example of sick Nazi humour as it is well known that the coffin in question was a reusable one with a bottom that could be opened mechanically. If they were now to receive this 'privilege', where had the bodies of previous dead gone? The theory that bodies may have been disposed of in alternative ways open to the imagination of the OT has, over the years, been denied by those wishing to preserve intact the idea of a 'correct occupation' and who believe that such atrocities will reflect negatively on the civilian population, which is inaccurate. Their chief counter-argument is that no bodies were washed up on the shores of the islands or found during the post-war searches and exhumations. What such criticism

---

[97] Wannseevilla Berlin. Testimonies of the Holocaust. Evidence of Major Hoffmann and other persons as to persons in authority in Alderney. JAG analysis of statement of Karl Hoffmann, n.d.

[98] PRO. WO 311/12. Statement made by Ivan Amelin from Orel, 10 Jun 1945.

[99] JAS L/C24/B/123, 'Historique sur Aurigny – Ile anglo-normande d'Alderney', Amicale des Anciens Déportés Politiques de l'Ile anglo-normande d'Aurigny, n.d. (copy from CDJC (Paris) – DXLIII-7). They did not, however, give any indication of how they had arrived at this figure. Ted Misiewiec, a Polish prisoner, estimated the number of deaths at 800, see IWM Misc. 2826 189/2 (Tape 3376)

[100] This figure was advanced by Jan Szulc from Rowno, see PRO. WO 311/12. Statement of 28 Jul 1945.

[101] *Island of dread in the Channel*, op. cit., 53; see also testimony of Kyril Nevrov, Ivan Sholomitsky and John Dalmau in Bunting, *The Model Occupation*, op. cit., 289.

does not take into account is the considerable time lag of two and a half years between the period when the overwhelming majority of these slave labour casualties would have occurred and bodies dumped in the sea (late 1942) and the period when any inquiry worthy of the name was undertaken (May-June 1945). This would have given the Nazis sufficient time to erase any evidence of the real extent of their 'death by work'.[102] As to the issue of no bodies having been washed up elsewhere one should perhaps remark that this subject requires more detailed forensic research, especially into the issue of tidal current and range, which is extremely powerful in the bay of St Malo, before it can be settled. Also some of these bodies may have been washed up elsewhere without this having necessarily come to the knowledge of the civilian population. While it seems obvious that at least some bodies were disposed of in this or other 'extraordinary' ways it is not suggested that this was practised on a grand scale, but it *is* rather plausible as an accessory practice of disposal for the period of brutalisation until mid-1943; but perhaps less so for the ensuing period when the Germans were 'cleaning up' their act. Another key in solving the discrepancy lies in the exchanges of exhausted prisoners and the resulting fluctuations in the prisoner population. Pantcheff himself would not commit to any precise figure of how many died after leaving the island, but estimated that it must have been 'some hundreds'. [103] What he does say, however, is that 700 to 800 Russians were shipped out to Cherbourg in January 1943, at the peak of the most murderous two months:[104] at least 180 aboard the *Franka*[105] and, later the same month, a further 300 aboard the ill-fated *Xaver Dorsch*. These prisoners were confined below deck for three days, at the end of which the boat was wrecked at Braye Harbour in a storm, with considerable loss of life. [106] According to Josef Kaiser, a German Navy man who arrived in Alderney in January 1943, these two transports were made up of men who could no longer work and were being exchanged for others. Kaiser also stated that batches of prisoners used to stay a few months, seven at the most, and were then taken away, worn out.[107] This

---

[102] That the SS at least practised the systematic exhumation and obliteration of bodily evidence is demonstrated by the activities of several units, among them the Sonderkommando Blobel which commenced 'work' in 1942 in Ukraine, see 'Documents of the Holocaust, Part III, Evidence by Blobel on the burning of bodies and obliterating the traces of bodies of Jews killed by the Einsatzgruppen' <www1.yadvashem.org/about_holocaust/documents/part3/doc212.html>

[103] JAS L/D25/A/4. Appendix to Col B E Arnold, *The Alderney Story*, information provided by Theodore Pantcheff, n.d.

[104] Pantcheff, *Alderney Fortress Island*, op. cit., 8.

[105] The figure of 180 is advanced by Theodore Pantcheff in his book *Alderney Fortress Island – The Germans in Alderney, 1940–1945*, Chichester, 1981, 18–9. A German witness to the transport, Hans Schenk, gave a higher figure of 300 when interrogated in 1945, s. PRO. WO 311/12. Statement taken by Captain Kent, 21 May 1945.

[106] Pantcheff, *Alderney Fortress Island*, op. cit., 18–19.

[107] PRO WO 311/12. Statement of Josef Kaiser taken by Kent, 11 Jul 1945.

would suggest that such prisoner transports were more routine than has been realised up until now. Pantcheff himself confirmed one more such transport of prisoners ferried out on the *Dorothea Weber*, in October 1943. [108] Two convoys made up of a total of 200 exhausted Nordeney prisoners were evacuated in January and March 1944, and according to a post-war report of the French association of former Alderney prisoners, 12 of these prisoners succumbed – either en route or at their destination.[109] Finally, the sinking of the *Minotaure* on 3 July 1944 is though to have cost the lives of 250 people.

One must conclude that it is impossible to say exactly how many forced and slave labourers died in Alderney. What is clear is that the number of 389 deaths given by Pantcheff[110] is a strict minimum and that a large number of sick and exhausted prisoners died en route to or on their arrival on the Continent, of privations suffered in Alderney. The better-documented figure of about 300–350 deaths in the SS camp – one third of the camp population – together with the fact that conditions of survival in the OT camps were *not* better than in the SS camp, makes it reasonable to assume that at least 30 per cent of all forced and slave labourers who set foot in Alderney perished. Taking this axiom as a basic level of comparison the estimate is a minimum of 750, perhaps even 1,000. That this is not unrealistic is borne out by the official information provided by the Amicale d'Aurigny cited at the beginning of this section. If one includes those who perished en route one surely must arrive at a figure well in excess of the estimate of 1,250 advanced by Madeleine Bunting.[111]

The inability to put a final definite figure on the death toll of the Alderney camps is no doubt unsatisfactory; and it provides a good terrain for the genre of speculation as exemplified by Tom Freeman-Keel's sensationalist account *From Auschwitz to Alderney*. But even without a final figure, the evidence of wartime atrocities is incontestable. When evacuee Marion Bates returned to the island in 1945 she noted that there were no more birds left. For her it was especially eerie to experience Alderney without the sound of seagulls.[112] Alderney had lost her soul. The thought of the breakdown in civilisation that led to a holiday idyll being turned into hell on earth is both thoroughly depressing and thought-provoking.

---

[108] Pantcheff, *Alderney Fortress Island*, op. cit., 18–19.

[109] AN F/9/5572. Amicale des Anciens déportés politiques de l'île anglo-normande d'Aurigny (M Azoulay) to Ministre des Victimes Civiles de la Guerre, rapport sur l'île d'Aurigny, 3 Apr 1946.

[110] Brian Bonnard has recently raised this number to 437, see Brian Bonnard, in Cohen, op. cit., 148.

[111] Madeleine Bunting, *The Model Occupation. The Channel Islands under German rule, 1940–1945*, London, 1996, 291.

[112] IWM Misc. 2826 189/2. Interview with Marion Bates, n.d.

[113] IWM P338. Diary of R E H Fletcher, 1940–1942.

Foreign and slave workers in Jersey and Guernsey

It is one common misconception that the practice of slave labour was limited to Alderney. Forced and slave labourers also reached the shores of Jersey and Guernsey and their arrival engendered profound shock in the civilian population, many of whom commended their thoughts to paper. In an entry for 31 January 1942 Jersey diarist R E H Fletcher noted that Spanish, Italian and Belgians had arrived:

> who look the picture of poverty and misery, poorly clad and fed. In all my experience of 35 years work in various English seaports I have never set eyes on a rougher collection of human beings.[113]

In September 1942 Guernsey teacher Miss A Lainé reported similar scenes of foreign labourers begging and eating apple cores from streets or potatoes out of dogs' dishes.[114] Still worse was to come. The peak number of foreign workers, including German and other voluntary workers, forced and slave labourers, in the islands, in late 1942 was 16,000.[115] The workforce in Guernsey comprised about half of this total workforce: 1,600 German and 6,700 foreign OT workers on 1 May 1943. The camps in Guernsey were given, rather prosaically, female names: Ute, Erika I, Lotte, Else, Hannelore, Rosemarie, Annemarie, Ursula and OT prison 'Paradis'.[116] Out of these, firms working across the island were supplied with labour: Rose, Kronibus, Oelting, Klaus Ackermann, Mueller & Co., Schneider, Siemens und Schuckert, Raabel-Werke, Hoffritz, Westdeutsche Steinindustrie (Saarbrücken), Wilhelm Goetzky (Bremen), AEG Paris, Deutsche Asphalt und Tiefbau AG (Hamburg).[117] In Jersey the camps were named after German war heroes: Richthofen, Udet, Brinkforth, Mölders, Prien and Immelmann. OT punishment camp was at Elizabeth Castle. Another camp was at Fort Regent. As in Guernsey OT partner firms carried out the projects with the labour supplied from the camps: Oltsch & Co were laying a narrow gauge railway; Karl Ploetner was engaged on the anti-tank wall on the west coast; Hans Grimich was building ammunition tunnels; Heilmann & Littmann (Berlin and Düsseldorf) working out of Brinkforth on the Five Mile Road erected ferroconcrete bunkers; Olbricht was building ammunition tunnels and an anti-tank wall behind Grouville Bay; Westdeutsche Steinindustrie operated a stone

---

[114] IWM P338. Diary of Miss A Le M. Lainé.

[115] Cruickshank, op. cit. 59; 193–94. Of the 11,000 foreign workers in the islands on May 14, 1942, 3,000 were German and 8,000 foreigners, s. BA-MA. RW/49 97. Abwehr Command France (F/IIIc), Channel Islands – Commitment of labour resources, protective security measures 1942–1944. Zollgrenzschutz, Leiter der Befehlsstelle, RV189/42 g, 14 May 1942.

[116] PRO WO 311/12. Secret Report on OT – Guernsey, 1945.

[117] ibid.

crushing plant at Gorey. Most of the defences in the west and at Grouville were built by Russian labour, whereas in St Brelade the labour was mainly Spanish, North African and French. No Russians worked in the harbour of St Helier.[118] As in Alderney, worker numbers started to decrease with the closure of camps and the despatch of the population to fortification work in France, in the autumn and winter of 1943, bringing the Spanish and Russian worker presence in the islands almost to an end.[119] By July 1944 worker numbers fell to several hundred, in the majority North African PoWs, French and Spanish.[120]

One particular feature which Jersey had in common with Alderney were the Russians: the arrival of the first Russians in the summer of 1942 is one of the enduring memories of many a Jerseyman. Jersey bus driver Frank Luce remembered the arrival of the Russians among them women and children, in the late summer of 1942. Passing a pitiful column of these prisoners at the top of St Brelade's Hill, he noticed some of his passengers standing at the doors, where they gaped and wept in disbelief. He admitted that it had a worse effect on him than anything he had experienced as a soldier in the Great War.[121] The presence of mere children among these prisoners is confirmed by many other sources. Many described the Russians as boys not older than fourteen. While some islanders reacted in shock and disbelief, others were simply disgusted. A Jersey diarist wrote on 19 August 1942 that the long column she saw was

> in rags, bare bleeding feet. Some men in women's clothes – a terrible, heartbreaking spectacle as they were driven along the road from the harbour [...] by the Huns with revolvers, fixed bayonets and rubber truncheons which they used on the falling, worn out prisoners. The awfulness (is) a good lesson for the many vile St Aubin people who are so friendly with their country's enemies.[122]

For the more pessimistic the treatment of the Russian labourers had a powerful signalling effect of things to come for the islanders, especially if they 'misbehaved'.[123] Not surprisingly, when the non-natives were deported only a

---

[118] PRO HO 144/22237. Report Channel Islands Jersey, interrogation of four Russian OT labourers (info as at 13 Dec 1943), 4 Jul 1944; PRO WO 311/12. Statement of Maria Brock, Jersey, 27 June 1945.

[119] PRO WO 311/12. Statement of Alfred Leake, 11 Jul 1945.

[120] There were 371 workers in Guernsey in July 1944, see PRO WO 311/12. Secret Report on OT – Guernsey, 1945. The situation was similar in Jersey: most of the French were from Normandy and the Paris region; the 115 North African PoWs had arrived in 1943, see JAS L/D25/A/21. List of French citizens in Jersey, post-Liberation

[121] PRO WO 311/11. Statement of Frank Luce, Jersey taken by Capt Kent, St Helier, 12 Jul 1945.

[122] Diary of Mrs De Gruchy, Jersey (photocopies in author's possession). Characteristically for the many swings through which islanders went, De Gruchy, in May 1943, referred to them as the 'awful Russians' who 'are still thieving'. A somewhat understandable reaction to the strain of having seen sixty-five of her beehives destroyed by thieves.

[123] IWM Misc. 2826 189/2 (Tape 4480). Interview with Joe Miere, n.d.

few weeks later, many believed they were going to a similar fate as the Russians who had arrived in the summer. At the same time, it would also have been a good reason for increased concern over the fate of those people sent off the islands for anti-German offences and who did not return.

An insider view of the OT organisation in Jersey was given by Maria Brock in 1945. The wife of a Belgian working in Jersey she arrived in the island in June 1942 and was an interpreter at the OT personnel office (Gefolgschaftsstelle). When she started, there were about 1,500 Spanish, 1,500 French (including the North Africans) and about 600 workers from the Lowlands. Between August and December 1942 about 3,000 Russians arrived. Brock confirms that there was plenty of food in the island – especially potatoes, but also bread, butter, meat and other items. As in Alderney, certain categories of workers, such as the Russians, received the rations they were entitled to 'on paper' only. Officially employed by the firm Kehl & Co, many relevant records passed through her hands and Brock was able to ascertain that the stocks were delivered by the Wehrmacht to the OT Central Supply Store at Beaumont from where they should have been sent to the OT camps, every Tuesday. The OT Bauleiter in Jersey was Freiherr Rupert von Grienbacher, a Tyrolean aristocrat whom Brock described as 'very nervous'. Von Grienbacher was informed of all the aspects of OT in Jersey by Frontführer Helmuth Schuster, his second-in-command. Schuster's office was right opposite Brock's and as the overseer of all OT camps he had made it his 'hobby' to drive around the island to pick up workers roaming for food whom he then 'disciplined' in his office. Brock added that the office did receive complaints about the beatings of workers, sometimes from Germans themselves. As in Alderney, particular firms and particular men employed by these firms had a particularly brutal record. Her own superior OT-Truppführer Dökel once cautioned a Heilmann & Littmann foreman in charge of a column of 200–300 men from Udet about his treatment of workers. However, such dispositions were not encouraged by von Grienbacher who, sometime in 1942, explicitly authorised foremen to beat Russian workers in order to get more work out of them.[124] Brock's testimony is corroborated by other sources. Differences were made with regard to the supply of OT meal tickets. At the OT in Jersey meal tickets were blue for Germans, and brown for the Dutch, Czechs, Flemish, Poles and British. At the bottom of the pile were the white meal tickets given to Spaniards, French (in majority North African PoWs) and Russians.[125] Although the Republican Spaniards and North Africans were bullied and mistreated, they were not quite as disenfranchised and without rights as the Russians. Being PoWs, the North Africans, although despised,

---

[124] PRO WO 311/12. Statement of Maria Brock, Jersey, 27 June 1945.
[125] JAS D/AU/V/52. OT Einheit 40157 S, Frontführung-Gefolgschaftsstelle (Schuster-Jersey) an alle Dienststellen, Lagerunterkuenfte u Firmen, 16 Sept 1942 (handschriftl 2 Oct 1942).

received Red Cross parcels. Even more crucial was the fact that the Western Europeans, Spanish and Algerians were given days off, on which some of these workers used to go into town to procure food or other items.[126] Another significant difference between practice in Jersey and in Alderney was that the OT forced workers actually did receive the payment they were entitled to, again with the exception of the Russians.[127] The combination of no pay, lowest food rations, interdiction to move about the island and inability to receive any other resources that could be bartered for food made the Russians the most vulnerable group of workers. The only way they could get extra food was through scavenging and begging in the countryside, on their way to their work or during work hours, or by slipping out of the camps at night in order to scour farms, fields and dwellings for something edible. The result was a surge in burglaries which incensed public opinion, not necessarily about the behaviour of the labourers, but about what was driving them to such despair in the first place. First the Germans tried the propaganda route of causing animosity between islanders and labourers. When some islanders turned on Russians, the Germans exploited the piquancy of islanders turning against 'Britain's allies' in a press campaign designed to stir animosity towards the slave labourers. However, not everyone allowed themselves to be convinced and some islanders continued to give unstinting support. Most islanders understood the worth of Nazi propaganda – if they hadn't already – when they came face-to-face with atrocities. After having witnessed, on 19 February 1943, a Russian worker in the pillory at St Ouen, Jersey, with two tree branches tied tightly around his neck and attached to two trees, Senator Edward Le Quesne wrote in his diary:

> Some of us had imagined that the tales we heard of similar atrocities in Russia were simply for propaganda purposes […] Even those who have sympathised with Jerry can hardly do so after witnessing this or similar scenes.[128]

That same month the break-ins and robberies were reaching endemic proportions with more than 170 incidents across the island. The situation was particularly bad in the west of the island where 137 properties in St Peter, St Ouen, St Brelade and St Lawrence had been targeted. Embarrassingly, toward the end of the month, an attempt to break into the Bailiff's residence in St Aubin took place which was only averted at the last minute. It seemed that the Germans who were still pretending that this was the work of 'gangs of civilians' had to address the problem and von Schmettow himself ordered the island authorities

---

[126] PRO WO 311/11. Statement of Emile Boydens, Jersey taken by C Kent, St Helier, 12 Jul 1945. Boydens went to Belgium every 6 months.

[127] The confiscation procedure is described in Pantcheff, *Alderney Fortress Island*, op. cit.

[128] Edward Le Quesne, *The Occupation of Jersey day by day*, Jersey, 1999, entry of 20 Feb 1943, 182.

to mount an investigation. This established rather conclusively that these break-ins had occurred, in their majority, in the vicinity of OT camps.

In Guernsey and Jersey the slave labourers were not out of sight and islanders of all ages witnessed brutalities close up. Children came to see people being dragged behind lorries; in fact, such scenes were described as quite common-place. Drivers working for the OT and other services would find dead bodies strewn about, some with bullet wounds, others badly bruised. Many were little more than skeletons. Frank Killer, the teenage son of a local vicar, himself on the run from the Germans in 1945, described the labourers as 'starved, weak (with) boils and similar things'. In a post-war deposition he recounted how once, when passing a bunker on the Five Mile Road, he saw an OT man hitting a prisoner on the head with the 'flat of the spade'. Frank often passed along this stretch of beach where he would catch crabs, and 'cases of hitting the Russians occurred so frequently on the Five Mile Road that no other cases particularly stand out in my memory'. On another occasion he saw three Russians who had been hanged for stealing bread. How dangerous it was for Jersey families to shelter escapees is demonstrated by another of Frank's remarks, detailing the case of one young Russian who, after his recapture, was taken to the edge of a cliff. There he was threatened and told to reveal the name of the people who had helped him.[129] The 'non-execution' of the death penalty in the Channel Islands was starkly relative and, the way the Germans interpreted it, certainly no token of a model occupation. Another islander, Arthur James Scriven, secretary to the *Evening Post* (Jersey), was assigned to guard duties on the railway construc-tion at St Clement in April 1943. He described the slave labourers as 'clad in anything from sacks to rags, with nothing on (their) feet'. He witnessed, a few yards away, a demented attack by an OT guard on a boy aged perhaps eighteen. The boy first received a violent fist-blow in the face; this threw off the hat he was wearing; the guard then made him pick it up and put it on again. Another violent blow followed, knocking off the hat again. The guard made the prisoner pick up the hat three times and the same procedure was repeated each time. After the third blow the rules of the 'game' were slightly altered: when the prisoner refused to pick up the hat, the guard picked it up himself, put it on the prisoner's head and carried on with the procedure. Scriven saw this happen about 12 times before turning away in disgust.[130]

Evidence that a shift occurred in 1943 is also available for Jersey and Guernsey. A Jersey OT driver interviewed in 1945 was not the only witness to confirm that in early 1943 two OT doctors came to the island and carried out inspections. They visited the hospital and the camps, tasted the food and

---

[129] PRO WO 311/11. Statement, Frank Killer, 26 June 1945.
[130] PRO WO 311/11. Statement, Arthur James Scriven, 29 June 1945.

afterwards there were improvements, even in the conditions of the Russians.[131] One of the reasons may have been the typhoid epidemic in Guernsey, in January 1943. This had necessitated the quarantine of all OT camps for at least two months, during which time performance targets were not met.[132] Whether the epidemic also reached Jersey is not known, but Norman Le Brocq stated later that the German authorities in Jersey were alarmed about typhoid. He could recall this clearly because it was at about this time that his group was able to smuggle leaflets directly into the OT camps through the delousing parties which were being sent there.[133] John Le Quesne, the official undertaker appointed by the States of Jersey, stated that of the 73 Russians he buried in the Strangers' Cemetery at St Brelade, 70 died between 21 August 1942 and 24 April 1943, after which conditions improved. Bodies were usually brought to their private chapel and Le Quesne himself had an opportunity to see many of them before burial. He said that he had never seen such emaciated bodies and that some of them bore evidence of assaults, with dried blood still on them. Other foreigners usually had a short religious ceremony, but none was forthcoming for the Russians.[134] This also changed in mid-1943.

Earlier in this chapter it was established that the situation in Alderney was particularly vicious because there was no civilian population. The dangers of fraternisation to a frictionless occupation were well recognised by the Germans themselves. In 1943 they had intended to send as many as 2,000 French Jews and half-Jews to the Channel Islands, but this was rejected out of hand and the great majority was sent to Alderney only. Feldkommandant Knackfuss himself stated at a June 1943 conference with General von Unruh, Hitler's taskmaster for combing the Western European theatre of its last reserves of canon-fodder for the Eastern Front, that he feared fraternisation with local Channel Islanders, on the basis of their common language.[135] This is quite an instructive point, as it shows that the Germans knew that the balance could tip and sought to avoid anything that could increase ties of solidarity between the population and the OT workers.

The absence of a civilian population implied that no farming was being done. Not only did this eclipse the chance of finding anything edible on forays into the

---

[131] PRO WO 311/11. Statement of Arthur Samson, Jersey taken by Capt Kent, St Helier, 10 Jul 1945.

[132] IWM EDS. Bericht über den Baufortschritt auf den Kanalinseln im ständigen Ausbau (Stand vom 1.3.1943).

[133] The delousing parties consisted of Spanish medics with whom Le Brocq had good relations, see IWM Misc. 2826 189/2 (Tape 18 4394 O/L). Interview with Norman Le Brocq. n.d.

[134] PRO WO 311/11. Statement of John Le Quesne, Jersey taken by C Kent, St Helier, 13 Jul 1945.

[135] IWM Guernsey Nebenstelle files. FK 515, Besprechung mit General von Unruh in Rennes, 29 Jun 1943.

fields and glasshouses, but it also meant that all food and supplies were imported, thus entrenching corruption and reinforcing the pull of the German-dominated black market.

The absence of a civilian population also meant that there was nobody to offer food, support or even shelter. Naturally, not all Jersey and Guernsey people viewed the plight of the OT workers with sympathy, but still there was a sufficient number who were willing to help. Although scarce, food was not as tightly regimented in the larger islands as it was in Alderney.[136] In addition people in the countryside had their secret caches which some were willing to share. That this form of assistance was, indeed, occurring on a rather substantial scale is demonstrated by the fact that the Germans published notices in the press saying that it was a serious offence to give food to begging workers, in particular Russians. Notices such as these were published in the *Evening Post* (Jersey) on 11 and 13 November 1942, warning the population not to give in to fear or pity, as these workers were getting sufficient food.[137] The absence of a civilian population also meant that there was nobody around to protest or ask awkward questions which might shame those Germans with some humanity left in their bones into exerting whatever limited influence they had over the situation. Mr Harrison, the editor of the *Evening Post* in Jersey, reported that when he spoke to Baron von Aufsess at the time an order was issued obliging people to report escaped Russians, he told him that he did not think many people would comply because the prisoners were so manifestly ill-treated and beaten. Von Aufsess responded with indignant denial, but cheered up again when Harrison told him that the population was not blaming the German troops for this, but the OT. A short time later, however, his demeanour dropped again when Harrison said that 'whatever good the German propaganda machine was doing towards converting the islanders [...] it was being undone by the horror and disgust the people felt at the brutality meted out to the Russians.'[138] The Bailiff of Jersey, Alexander Coutanche, did what he did best during the occupation, he went all the way to the top and enlightened General von Schmettow on the appalling treatment of the labourers. Although von Schmettow merely voiced his regret, Coutanche thought it was significant that the latter was at least prepared to listen to him.[139] One cannot rule out that such negative reinforcement had an impact on the 1943 shift in German attitude and treatment.

---

[136] After the Germans had cleaned up their act, black market initiative shifted to the Moroccan PoWs in the island. Their monthly Red Cross parcels contained 200 cigarettes, a highly prized item which they could barter with the Germans who received a mere three cigarettes per day in spring 1943, see PRO HO 144/22237. MI19. Report Channel Islands Alderney, further report by informants 2122, 2136 (info as at 8 Apr 1943), 19 Apr 1944.

[137] WO 311/12. Statement of A Harrison, editor EP, 29 June 1945.

[138] WO 311/12. Further statement of A Harrison, editor EP, 29 June 1945.

[139] *The Memoirs of Lord Coutanche*, recorded and compiled by H R S Pocock, Chichester, 1975, 34.

Another thing one could not find in Alderney were groups of islanders or individuals who interposed themselves directly. One such incident had occurred at Brown's Café in Jersey, shortly after the arrival of the first Russians. Mary Brown and her daughter Constance ran this establishment, situated on the edge of St Brelade's Bay. From this vantage point the work on the sea wall which commenced in the spring of 1942, and which was to extend right across the bay, was easy to make out. The workers in those early days were predominantly Dutch and Spaniards, many of whom managed to slip away from work and have a cup of coffee. In August 1942 the Russians arrived on the site and it was immediately noticed how different this population was. For one thing they never managed to absent themselves from work and come to the café. Constance also reported that on several occasions in August or September 1942 she saw Russians being beaten and then collapsing. One day during that early period some of the patrons were taking their tea outside. They must have watched the activities unfolding for some time and it could not have been a pretty sight. Their fuse seems to have blown when they saw a Russian being beaten up before their very eyes and they started to boo and shout obscenities at the abuser. The man in question then came up, obviously trying to create an incident. Again the Germans involved did not take a light view of the occurrence which they could have simply ignored, for the following day Feldkommandant Knackfuss himself, together with other Germans, proceeded to 'Brown's' to say that the OT wanted the café closed down. During the ensuing discussion he said that he deplored the fact that the Russians had to be beaten, but that they had to be 'disciplined'. In the end the café stayed open, but it was now prohibited for customers to go down to the level where the wall was being built.[140]

Incidents where civilians interposed themselves are also known for subsequent periods. John Wickings, a young van driver for Jersey Dairy Ltd, made it a habit to throw them his packed lunch whenever he passed work parties in St Brelade or St Aubin. One day in October 1943, while delivering milk at the La Pulente Hotel, he chanced upon a slave labourer being knocked about by the OT Lagerführer (head of camp). Wickings went to a bungalow at the back of the hotel, from where he saw a young labourer being made to run around the outside of a cider press, while the OT man stood by and hit him as he passed. When the latter discerned Wickings, he shouted at him and Wickings immediately turned away to go, but was beckoned back. Hesitating at first, Wickings finally decided to turn back. When he approached the OT man the latter said something in German, which he followed up by hitting him under the chin. At

---

[140] PRO WO 311/11. Statements of Mary and Constance Brown, St Brelades Bay, Jersey taken by Capt Kent, St Helier, 2 Jul 1945.

this point Wickings, as he later deposed, 'lost his temper, hit him back and tried to get away to his milk van'. The OT man was, however, back on his feet, catching him by his moneybag and grabbing him by the throat. Other OT labourers were called to hold Wickings, who was taken to the bungalow where he was detained for five hours, from 1 pm to 6 pm. Although the ensuing phone call for the Feldgendarms diverted his attention for a moment, the OT man then recommenced his sadistic routine with his prisoner. Every time the prisoner slowed he was hit, until he was finally stopped and made to run around the other way. Once he fell down and the OT poured water over him, made him get up and continue. When the Feldgendarms finally arrived to interrogate Wickings, at six o'clock in the evening, he was 'roughed up' and taken to Bagatelle Road, and from there to the prison, where he stayed for one week. His trial took place the following week and he received a two-month sentence. [141]

While one might say that coercion reinforced compliance and instilled fear, it also made people angry and determined to defy the Germans in other more covert ways. Such other ways in which the continuation of civil and civilian life could have an impact on the chance of survival of foreign workers are often not immediately obvious. Until December 1942 the OT in Jersey referred their sick to the OT sick bay at Rosemount. After that they were taken to the Ladies College Hospital or to the German ward at the General Hospital. Nurse Violet Maggs stated that conditions on this ward, in particular food and medical care, were as good for foreigners as they were for Germans, as the majority of staff there were locals.[142]

[141] PRO WO 311/11. Statement, John Wickings, 29 June 1945.
[142] PRO WO 311/12. Statement of Violet Maggs, General Hospital Jersey, 1945.

VII

Epilogue: The Disposal of Occupation

FOR FIVE ARDUOUS years islanders whose understanding of 'loyalty to the Crown' also meant holding on to their pre-war beliefs of justice and fairness, had been prey to the nefarious activities of denouncers, profiteers and anyone callous enough to take advantage of the situation. How many times had they thought that this had to be the last Christmas under Occupation, and that Liberation would surely come the following year. As the Occupation stretched on forever, a large number of islanders found the strength to carry on with the thought that justice would come. The situation *was* being monitored on the other side of the Channel and the earliest reliable information on how the islanders were faring came to light when Denis Vibert was debriefed after his spectacular escape from Jersey in October 1941. In his interviews with the Security Service he acknowledged 'that Crown Officers were directed to remain at their posts', that they were 'doing their best to safeguard the interests of the Islanders' and 'that their difficult position had not been clearly understood by some of the evacuated Channel Islanders'. But Vibert also criticised a number of States officials who he said were 'co-operating [...] to an unnecessary extent' or even 'going out of their way to co-operate'.[1] Vibert's information set the pattern for all subsequent escapee debriefings. Thanks to the rising numbers of escapees, from late 1943 the mere trickle grew into a torrent of information. Unfortunately the exhaustion of occupation had blinded the power of discrimination of Vibert's heirs, many of whom could no longer muster the judicial mix of criticism and fairness which had characterised the latter's appreciation. The

---

[1] In this category Vibert included Attorney General Duret Aubin, Petrol Controller Clift, President of the Essential Commodities Department Major Le Masurier, President of the Department of Transport Messervey and Jurat Norman. How accurate Vibert's 'information' was is unverifiable: neither are Vibert's security service debriefings available nor is it known whether the men were ever investigated, see PRO KV/4/78. Security Service, 'The Administration of the Channel Islands under the German Occupation', 30 Jun 1945.

least equitable (and most damaging) of these escapee debriefings[2] occurred in October 1944 when the British received the visit of a number of Jersey youngsters, clearly fed up with sitting around and waiting for deliverance, who had set up an escape network. With them they had brought a large amount of information, partly evidence, partly hearsay, which allowed the British to draw up an extensive list of 'collaborators'. Alas, the fact that someone had had the guts to risk escape should not have lead to a suspension of critical faculties; nor do heroes necessarily make 100 per cent reliable witnesses. That these young men had a grudge would be an understatement; and much of this was based on the material deprivation of the Occupation. To all intents the report mentions the black market as the cornerstone of the Occupation, claiming that popular ill-feeling was due to the complacency of island officials and their botched food system. This was a justified grievance, but the problem was that they did not limit themselves to this in their criticism. Their vendetta soon turned against each and everything, in particular figures of authority. Famously, the report stated that '7 out of 10' island women had practised horizontal collaboration, producing '800–900 German babies'. Having besmirched the reputation of the island womenfolk, the report certainly did not stop short of the island officials; the most unfair criticism was probably that levelled at Edward Le Quesne who it was said was 'acting on behalf of his own political future' by 'appeasing the workmen with higher wages and less work simply to get votes in the future'. When he was caught with a wireless in autumn 1944 he was condemned to seven months' gaol, but left after two weeks. The escapee thus questioned (who did not have full knowledge of the facts) judged this as a 'typical instance of the way deputies, jurats and their friends can and do wangle things with the Germans'.[3] Small wonder that on its release into the public domain in 1996, the report was greedily wolfed down by the press, always hungry for 'sensations', who feasted on every word. The juvenile lashing out at the presumed cowardice of their parents should have raised alarm bells with everyone who set his eyes on these yellowed pages, but such is the passion that their passage into the canon of 'truths' was virtually unchallenged.

---

[2] PRO WO 208/3741. MI19/2438. Report Channel Islands Jersey, 2 Oct 1944.

[3] Le Quesne had appealed to von Aufsess, not for remission of his sentence, but for permission to leave the prison on Wednesdays and Saturdays to attend to his duties at the department of Labour. His sentence was then remitted, which von Aufsess qualified as a German blunder in his diaries (*The von Aufsess occupation diary*, op. cit.). Four weeks after his first correspondence Le Quesne approached von Aufsess again with the suggestion that the remission be extended to the other people under sentence for wireless offences. This request was granted as the prison was overflowing anyway. We know that some Germans – and von Aufsess was among these – looked upon wireless offenders with some sympathy as they did not deem their acts as reprehensible as other offences, see JAS B/A/W91/41. Correspondence between deputy Le Quesne and Freiherr von Aufsess, 26 Sept to 6 Nov 1944.

Fifty years earlier the effect was even more devastating, as this type of report was the very foundation of suspicion on the British side and the source for much of the enthusiasm in favour of the prosecution of collaborationist crimes and misdemeanours. The three categories which came in for attention were war crimes – this included offences in violation of the Hague rules such as the 1942–43 deportations – atrocities committed against slave labourers in the islands and alleged collaboration, both of civilians and the island authorities. Those islanders, however, who had hoped for swift justice were in for a rude shock. On 14 May, a mere five days after the end of the Occupation, the Home Secretary, Herbert Morrison, visited the islands for a short two-day trip. For the island authorities – short of Churchill himself sharing in the Liberation – this was a hugely reassuring affair and a clear signal that the British government was willing to accept their version of things. Many members of the general public, however, found that this easy-handed absolution left something to be desired, raising more questions than it solved. On his return Morrison wrote a memorandum to his Cabinet colleagues stating that the Channel Islands author-ities had discharged their duties in 'exemplary fashion' and that there were practically 'no cases of collaboration involving active disloyalty' on the part of any islanders. There is a mere hint of criticism – it is clearly localised – in his reference to a 'few cases' of horizontal collaboration or of people working in German employ. The 'most serious problem' in Morrison's view were the Eire citizens in the islands who – he had been told – had exploited their position as neutrals to obtain favours.[4] Considering the ecstatic mood of the days preceding his visit – where it would have been difficult to make much definite sense – as well as the fact that the Home Secretary had had a mere two days to acquaint himself with the situation, these were surprisingly far-going assertions. The only practical measure for which Morrison seems to have seen an immediate need was a campaign to put islanders in touch with the realities of post-war Britain and satisfy their information hunger. Morrison had noted that islanders, fed on a mixture of gossip and second- or third-hand BBC news since mid-1942, were suffering from an acute information 'under-load'.[5] The idea certainly was that lack of knowledge was the principal reason for many misjudgements and that the rumour mill was kindling polemics which might wreak havoc in this sensitive situation. Overall Morrison offered very little for the more sober-minded who were already casting their thoughts to the end of the party and the long-awaited day of reckoning. That the Home Office would take such a view was hardly surprising. As Sir Frank Newsam of the Home Office would later explain to Lord Justice du Parq, British policy would start off by recognising the status quo

---

[4] PRO PREM/3/87. Home Office memorandum about the Home Secretary's visit to the Channel Islands, 14–15 May 1945, 24 May 1945.
[5] PRO HO/144/22176. Letter of Herbert Morrison, June 1945.

ante and leave any move for change to the islanders themselves.[6] The Home Office maintained that – under the circumstances – the island authorities had acquitted themselves well. This was not an expression of complacency, but reflected the Home Office role as the established go-between between HM Government and the islands. Their role in the disposal of the detritus of war was to be limited to that of facilitator. This lack of ambition was an obvious reflection of the constitutional status of the Channel Islands within the realm and the Home Office had no intention to use the occasion in order to enlarge UK prerogatives. Their perspective was long-term. Newsam had made this position clear in a note written to Brigadier Snow on 28 September 1944, stating that constitutional changes could only be engineered, if representations from islanders reached HM in Council as a petition, in accordance with the usual procedures.[7] Morrison's scheme of non-interference, which he relayed to the Commons on his return, was spread by Home Office grandees such as Sir Alexander Maxwell. In a letter to the Treasury Solicitor, the body charged with war crimes investigations, he stated that the delegation had gained the 'general impression' that the Germans had 'behaved in a correct manner' and that there were no grounds for any such investigations.[8] Although two cases concerning the September 1942 deportations were already under investigation, the Treasury Solicitor conceded Maxwell's point. He merely added that having regard to the public notice given to war crimes, they should wait until they had communicated directly with Channel Islands administrations and asked them specific questions with regard to possible breaches of the Hague Convention. In this case they would at least get an answer which would enable them to say that they had done all that they reasonably could in the matter.[9] It is accurate that the British war crimes investigators in the summer of 1945 had more serious cases to deal with than the Channel Islands deportations. There were concentration or forced labour camps to be dealt with in the British zone of occupation in Germany, or – closer to the Channel Islands – investigations into the Alderney atrocities. The general impression throughout is that the British government very early on set their minds on doing nothing about collaboration and that the rhetoric of future investigations was a screen whose principal purpose was to stem public discontent.

The greatest legacy of the Home Office view of the Channel Islands Occupation formed during those weeks of hectic activity was that it would firmly

---

[6] PRO HO/45/22399. Note of meeting between Sir Frank Newsam and Lord Justice du Parcq, 9 June 1945.

[7] PRO WO/32/11154. Sir Frank Newsam (HO) to Brigadier Snow (WO), 28 Sept 1944.

[8] PRO HO/144/22833. Sir Alexander Maxwell (HO) to Sir Thomas Barnes (TS), 17 May 1945.

[9] PRO HO/144/22833. Sir Thomas Barnes (TS) to Sir Alexander Maxwell (HO), 18 May 1945.

imprint future interpretations. Morrison's version, outlined in his memorandum to the War Cabinet and a speech in the Commons[10], represents the classic narrative of the Channel Islands Occupation, which held currency in many quarters well into the 1990s. The bottom line of this official version of history was that all or most Channel Islanders had behaved as real Britishers, with an attitude and in a manner that was poised, exemplary, steadfastly consistent and scrupulously fair. Curiously, in this version the entire situation was devoid of the humiliation, desperation or compromise of principle occurring across the rest of Europe. The exceptions to the rule were the feat of the foreign community and the 'few informers'. Decidedly sexist and racist undertones emerge in Morrison's unwarranted focus on the Irish and on women who consorted with the Germans. Otherwise a quiet heroism and dignity pervaded life and the 'stiff upper lip' was de rigueur. Even Occupation government was done 'by the book': the Bailiffs dispensed their duties 'according to their own judgement' and the relationship with the Germans was correct, unspectacularly correct, as the islands had had the good fortune to have been run by a group of aristocratic gentlemen officers and not some red-hot Nazis. The *grand absent* in this narrative were the forced and slave labourers who were such an integral part of the history of the Occupation and, of course, all those who didn't fit the bill: the nonconformists, resisters or outsiders. It was a view of history that left no place for the complexities and contradictions of enemy occupation. Dissonances were smoothed over or suppressed and the Channel Islands, now safely determined as a special case in occupied Europe, were encouraged to lock into British wartime history rather than dwell on the 'dark years'. Collaboration was dismissed by pointing to the fact that 'no collaboration involving disloyalty' had occurred. The entire occupation experience – essentially interpreted as a waste of time and a period of stagnation – was relegated to the cabinet of island curiosities. The entire stance betrayed a sense of embarrassment over the 'abandonment' of the Channel Islands and an urgency to mend the bridges by adopting a conciliatory position.

Attacking or even questioning any of these building blocks has been next to impossible, as over the years traditionalists have feared that even minute changes would lead to a collapse of the entire structure. In their view order has been deemed preferable to chaos. Unfortunately it is impossible to get to the real story without a measure of deconstruction; and this need not always be to the sole disadvantage of the islands.[11]

---

[10] PRO PREM/3/87. War Cabinet. Home Office memorandum about the Home Secretary's visit to the Channel Islands on 14–15 May 1945, 24 May 1945.

[11] Morrison is also seen by many as the source of one of the most tenacious myths, namely that of a post-war UK government whitewash. This contention is based on the universally peddled and seldomly challenged idea that during his 1945 visit he was supposed to have uttered: 'If anything

The public mood shifted within days of Morrison's departure, from insouciance and relief to anger and sterner demands for justice. The Chief Civil Affairs Officer of Force 135, Colonel Power, was already receiving substantial numbers of denunciations – some anonymous ('old habits die hard') – since he set foot in the islands. While the people of Guernsey seem to have given vent to their feelings mainly in this way, the public temper brewing up in the sister island was more political in its criticism of the establishment. In a memo to the Home Office Power explained that although there had been just as much or as little 'collaboration' in Guernsey as in Jersey, the complaints were more serious for Coutanche who was 'a dominating personality' than for Carey who was 'more of a figurehead'. In addition, John Leale had calmed the waves with his 'masterly apologies', a States address outlining the policy of the Controlling Council, as early as 23 May, whereas Coutanche had not taken any such step. When the Jersey Crown Officers met Colonel Power at the end of May, they did not feel that they could point out cases of behaviour among the population warranting criminal prosecution, unless retrospective legislation was introduced. Good lawyers as they were, they had read the Treason and Treachery Act more closely than most others interested in the issue. They were, however, genuinely concerned over the precedent which might be set by not censuring people who had been unduly friendly. The core legal problem in bringing justice to the Channel Islands lay in the fact that the defence regulations punishing the offence of giving aid to the enemy, did not cover the occupied Channel Islands as they had been revoked for technical reasons in 1941. Therefore the only basis upon which trials could be placed was the Treason and Treachery Act, which – at least in theory – carried the death penalty.[12] The other options were retrospective legislation – an alien concept – social ostracism or taxation. Coutanche suggested instituting an enquiry which would direct public discontent and examine possible prosecution, and it was agreed that Jersey should prepare evidence in two or three rather serious cases of paid informers for submission to the Home Office.[13] It would soon become clear, however, that

he (Coutanche) has done requires whitewashing, I will take care of it for him'. The quotation itself is from Alan and Mary Wood's book *Islands in Danger* where Morrison is said to have added this snippet, 'jokingly', during a speech in which he lauded Coutanche's 'sterling work, courage and integrity'. As is the case in most Occupation books, no source is provided for this aside, and one can but base oneself on guesses. Rather tragicomically there is some indication that the source may have been Coutanche himself, for a few phrases up, in the same paragraph, we learn that 'Morrison stayed with Coutanche, and that they talked most of the night'. Who other than Coutanche – whom the Woods interviewed for their project – could have provided this very detailed piece of information? The butler perhaps? Coutanche probably also provided the information on Morrison's intentional or unintentional slip of the tongue. This is decidedly a shaky base to build an argument of 'government whitewash', see Wood and Wood, op. cit., 292.

[12] IWM Misc. 2826 189/2 (Tape 4526). Interview with J Howard, Home Office, n.d.
[13] PRO HO 45 22399. Brief for Home Secretary re collaborationists in the islands, 4 June 1945.

two or three scapegoats would not be enough to calm the raging soul of the people. The signals of unrest in Jersey were immediately picked up by the Force commander, Brigadier Snow, who suggested to the War Office in the beginning of June that the Force remain for several months, instead of the scheduled ninety days. Besides technical reasons linked to the rehabilitation of the island, he cited that the present discontent was likely to increase further after the return of the Channel Islands evacuees from the UK.[14] Therefore the present Force should stay at least until all returnees had come home. The troop reduction from three to two battalions and the arrival of the two Lieutenant-Governors, a step which would see the end of unified command in all islands, should not take place before the end of September.[15] In those early days it was hard to predict which way things would turn out, but there was certainly enough military gear and ammunition which had passed from German to civilian hands to stir up a small civil war in Jersey. The suggestion was, however, refuted out of hand by Brigadier French, Snow's superior at the War Office. French insisted that the return of the Lieutenant-Governors and the reinstatement of the civil authorities was 'politically desirable', adding that 'bickering' had always existed in the islands, but that the idea of disorder was quite unthinkable.[16]

The intelligence service would have certainly welcomed the extension of the military mandate. Their wartime gathering of information did not tally with the Home Office line and led them to believe that many islanders – including many of their leading men – were collaborators. Present on the staff of Force 135 with a small team under Captain Dening, MI5, they were briefed to target security suspects, but the actual import of their investigations went way beyond these narrow terms. They were faced, however, with the serious disadvantage of inflated ambitions that were not matched by sufficient manpower. This appears in particularly stark contrast when comparing their small team to the CAU Public Safety Branch investigating collaboration and war crimes in the islands, which consisted of a full ten CID officers seconded to duty from the UK.[17] The intelligence people's ultimate goals also seemed obscure, other than that they seemed intent on purging and had no qualms about starting with the island elites first. For this purpose they had arrived with 340 white cards of 'alleged sympathisers' about whom they had been collecting information since late 1943.[18] As to their political orientations they certainly had little or no time for the Home Office line of status quo ante.

[14] PRO WO/32/11711. Brigadier French – Comments, 9 Jun 1945.

[15] PRO WO/32/11711. Note from Southern Command to the Under Secretary of State at the WO, 4 Jun 1945.

[16] PRO WO/32/11711. Brigadier French – Comments, 9 Jun 1945.

[17] IWM Misc. 2826 189/2 (Tape 4526). Interview with J Howard, Home Office, n.d.

[18] PRO KV 4/78. Security Service. Force 135, I(b), The I(b) reports on the Channel Islands, 8 Aug 1945.

Meanwhile the Home Office was getting stuck with a task it had never really wanted: the hunt for collaborators. The first meeting bringing together the Home Office, the Director of Public Prosecutions, Sir Theobald Mathews and the Attorney Generals of Jersey and Guernsey, on 13 June, focused on classification. They found horizontal collaborators, fraternisers, profiteers, informers, voluntary contractors and workers as well as 'certain persons who had sought to undermine the States administrations', a very unspecific category which, incidentally, comprised the Jersey Democratic Movement.[19] At this early point already it was determined that the first three classes could only be dealt with through ostracism and taxation; the 'paid propagandists' were the only ones who might fall within the jurisdiction of the Treason and Treachery Act. The other categories were more of a dilemma: they were clearly identified as a problem, but they fell outside the provisions of the Act.[20] This was confirmed a week after the meeting in London, when Jersey submitted a number of these cases to Mathews. The latter clearly felt that – though highly reprehensible – they did not amount to high treason or treachery. The Jersey authorities were also advised that retrospective criminal legislation required sanction of the King-in-Council and that this was unlikely to be forthcoming.[21] Meanwhile a petition by a group calling themselves the 'Jersey Loyalists'[22] was submitted to the States, demanding precisely what the Director of Public Prosecutions had just discarded: legislation for the constitution of a tribunal or court of enquiry charged with the investigation of all offences of collaboration in the island. This included not only categories such as informers, blackmarketeers, but also women who had consorted with Germans, workers in German employ, people who had entertained Germans and those who had assisted or collaborated 'in any way with the enemy'.

In addition the petition called for a veritable witch-hunt by demanding that, for the protection of members of the British forces,

> adequate means and measure be taken to create distinctions between female members of the population who have been loyal to British interests and those who have consorted with the enemy.[23]

[19] After the war the JDM was attacked for its wartime pamphlets which it was said had 'undermined' the local administration and therefore were well received by the Germans.

[20] PRO HO/144/22176. Meeting at Home Office to discuss treatment of 'collaborators', 13 June 1945.

[21] PRO HO/45/22399. Draft note on investigations in Jersey into allegations of collaboration, n.d. (after 21 June 1945).

[22] The most active members of the Jersey Loyalists included many veterans of the First World War: Major Manley, the late chief warden, acted as president; Captain Poole, chief clerk at Southern Railway, as secretary. Others included Mr Troy, news editor at the *Jersey Evening Post*, Mr Le Brun, Centenier in the parish of St Helier, Mr Michel, a grower, Mr Coutanche, Centenier in the parish of St Ouen and Mr Tregear, one of the largest wholesalers, see JAS Lieutenant Governor's files, 50/4 H. Note 'Jersey Loyalist Delegation', Sept 1945.

[23] 'The Jersey Loyalist Petition', *Evening Post*, 22 June 1945.

Under these terms almost everyone could have been targeted for some offence, real or imagined, and enquiry would have involved the invasion of the innermost privacy of many hundreds of people. Deplorable as the situation was, the lack of measure of the proposal was all the island needed to be set ablaze with anger and fury. The petition also went counter to one of the measures the authorities were probably already contemplating – the eviction of certain islanders – by suggesting that the guilty may seek to leave Jersey and that such attempts to escape their shame should be prevented. Presumably on these grounds it was greeted with a lukewarm reception in the States who however, supported the Attorney General's motion to institute a special committee to study the proposals.[24] The Bailiff, however, reiterated his interest in an inquiry or public statement on the conduct of the authorities in a correspondence with the Home Office in July.[25] Snow was also not toeing the Home Office line and allowing the investigation of twenty cases of alleged collaboration in Jersey.[26] In Guernsey the issue did not even make it to the States, the procedure for dealing with collaborators was merely made public through a notice in the press.[27]

The complaints from the public reaching the Home Office by the end of June were no longer of a general nature urging action against collaborators, but turned their wrath directly against the Channel Islands administrations. Again, the Jersey officials – in particular Coutanche – got more of a rap than their counterparts in Guernsey where things were comparatively quiet. The gist of these representations was that the authorities had not been 'bold enough' or did not 'adequately protect the interests of the islanders in resisting the German demands for local supplies'. There were also allegations that they had assisted the Germans in their deportations and, in Guernsey, encouraged islanders to denounce their fellow subjects for infringements of German laws. The Home Office had some doubts as to the veracity of these claims, but was not so unwise as to simply brush them aside: they discreetly asked the Director of Public

---

[24] The members of this committee included States members and 'independents': the Constable of St Clements Sydney Crill, deputies Philip Richardson (St Helier), Philip le Feuvre (St Mary's) and Wilfred Bertram (Grouville), George Billot, George de la Perrelle Hacquoil, Alexander Picot. There was some indication that the committee might at least investigate officials' alleged misconduct which could then receive disciplinary sanction, but in view of the continuing legal uncertainty the Committee only produced an interim report, JAS Lieutenant Governor's files, 50/4 H. Petition of the Jersey Loyalists to the States of Jersey, 20 June 1945; States Greffe notes on Special Committee submitted to the Lieutenant Governor, 21 Jun, 21 Jul, 4 Aug 1945; PRO HO/144/22176. Attorney General Duret Aubin and Jurat Dorey in States debate. Inquiry re conduct of certain people, 21 June 1945. For reference to interim report, see Lieutenant Governor's files, 50/4 H. Letter Bailiff of Jersey to Lieutenant Governor, 15 Sept 1945.

[25] PRO HO/45/25844. Home Office note, 18 July 1945.

[26] PRO CAB/121/367. Force 135 to War Office, 22 June 1945.

[27] PRO WO/106/3007. Force 135, Channel Islands Progress Report no. 2, week ending 27 Jun 1945.

Prosecutions for assistance, on the understanding that the ongoing investigations conducted by Force 135 on their behalf would also throw light on the new allegations. As the Director of Public Prosecutions was preparing a visit to enquire into the conduct of certain islanders under the Treason and Treachery Act, he was asked to identify evidence which would be useful in deciding whether there were prima facie grounds for further inquiry into the conduct of the administrations.[28] That there were misgivings over the authorities is also evident from a briefing of the Director of Public Prosecutions with Major Stopford, MI5, on 30 June. Stopford mentioned a conversation with Sir Edward Bridges on the subject of the award of decorations to the Bailiffs, a step initiated by the Home Office. Both had agreed that the award would have to be deferred and that meanwhile it would be their task to goad the Home Office into taking some action against collaboration. The Director of Public Prosecutions, when brought to the subject, also agreed that the idea of honours had been 'rashly conceived'.[29] He would be even more scathing after his visit to the islands: briefed by Dening, he agreed that the £25 reward episode as well as Carey's other derailments were offensive, but said that it was not worth more than 'four days in the market square'. Dening and Mathews found themselves wishing for a pillory in St Peter Port, with a population 'plentifully furnished with their own, preferably unmarketable, vegetable produce.' There were also misgivings about John Leale, but it was conceded that it was unlikely that his defence of having always wanted to act in the public interest could ever be overthrown. The criticism, however, did not dent his powers of judgement and Mathews stuck to his previous line that it was impossible to push charges as far as treachery. He also advised Dening against imposing an enquiry on both States as this would be faced with a wall of silence when it came to obtaining information. The impulse for reform had to come from within, and that reform was inevitable had been recognised in both islands.[30] Mathews made his position clear in a report to the Home Office on 9 July 1945, ruling out that there was any prima facie evidence for legal action against Channel Islanders and coming down firmly on the side of the advocates of financial sanctions and social ostracism.[31] The findings of the Director of Public Prosecutions almost coincided with the first of two reports issued by Major Stopford on 30 June 1945. Titled 'The Administration of the Channel Islands under the German Occupation', this was a consolidation of information received since 1941 from people who had escaped from the islands

    [28] PRO HO/144/22833. Frank Newsam (HO) to Thomas Barnes (TS), 25 June 1945.
    [29] PRO KV/4/78. Note on meeting with the Director of Public Prosecutions, Major Stopford, 30 June 1945.
    [30] PRO KV/4/78. Captain Dening to Major Stopford, 3 July 1945.
    [31] PRO HO/45/22399. Director of Public Prosecutions to Home Office, report on the conduct of the islanders and the administration, 9 Jul 1945.

during the Occupation. While it commended four Jersey politicians, Coutanche, Dr McKinstry and Jurats Dorey and Le Feuvre, it added, for the first time, names of Guernsey politicians to the list of usual suspects already mentioned by Vibert as far back as 1941.[32] All of these were thought to have exceeded the mandate given to them by the British Government in 1940, i.e. the good measure of cooperation required to maintain the administration of the islands during the Occupation.

Coutanche countered allegations levelled against his administration by disgruntled islanders in a 25-page note, on 3 July 1945. The original complaints, which were brought to Coutanche's attention on 18 June, have not survived, but they bore much of the lack of focus discernible in the petition of the 'Jersey Loyalists'. The criticism had centered in the main on cases of 'false collaboration', such as the reasons for the creation of the Superior Council, the deportations, the potato plan, billeting and looting, the 1940 evacuation, labour requisitions, the black market, the disappearance of Red Cross parcels. Some of the accusations, such as the criticism of the milk distribution, the quality of the bread and breakfast meal or the difference of prices in Jersey and in the UK, were downright unfair.[33] The critics had clearly been fishing around for reasons to corner the administration, but had ended up with a deluge of trivia or *faits de guerre* for which, ultimately, fate alone bore the responsibility.

Bailiff Carey had received copy of similar complaints referring to his three notorious press notices of 1941. He explained that two of these letters – the warnings after the cable sabotage and the appearance of the first V-signs – emanated directly from the Germans and had simply been rubber-stamped by himself. He admitted, however, that the £25 reward letter was of his own making and that he did this after a 'stormy interview' with the Feldkommandant, on the understanding that the Germans may take hostages – of which they had a list of 80.[34] What is even more disturbing is Carey's explanation that 'the majority of the population realised that [...] they were really German orders.' This statement stands in stark contrast to the constant

[32] PRO KV/4/78. Security Service, 'The Administration of the Channel Islands under the German Occupation' by Major Stopford, 30 June 1945. The names included the harbour master of St Peter Port J Penstone Franklin, Labour controller Johns, John Leale, States Supervisor H Marquand, the Reverend Romeril and Wiliam Vaudin of the Guernsey Press Office.

[33] PRO HO/45/22399. Note of the Bailiff of Jersey to the Home Office, re memorandum and re petition to HM, 3 July 1945. The allegations against Coutanche in many ways echoed a memorandum incriminating the Bailiff of Jersey sent to the Home Office at around the same time by F C Maugham, and which was very unfavourably commented upon, see PRO HO/144/22176. Memo re. Conduct of the Bailiff and Jersey officials, June 1945.

[34] PRO HO/45/25844. Reply of the Bailiff of Guernsey to allegations of collaboration received for further comment from the Home Office on 18 June, 25 June 1945. I would like to comment here that this is the only time that any such thing is mentioned in the sources and could have been an ex post facto embellishment of an uncourageous stance.

hammering of the population, reminding them that they were not to undertake anything naughty against the Germans. It is therefore extremely doubtful that the people of Guernsey understood the 'message'. What potential resisters would remember was not Carey's alleged *double jeu*, but John Leale's line which branded them 'worst enemy of the islands'.[35]

The dice were finally cast in August. On the 9th Colonel Power commented on the progress of the investigations of treason and treachery as 'slow', adding for good measure that 'evidence which has any value is extremely difficult to obtain [...] the sooner we end the atmosphere of suspense and admit there is not evidence the better.' He did, however, repeat that the situation was 'edgy'. The danger of disorder after the withdrawal of the Force was 'lessening but not negligible'. Power's report was an admission that the little enthusiasm in favour of enquiries which may have existed was petering out, a fact also demonstrated in the mere 2,000 signatures collected for a Guernsey petition to HM asking for a suspension of the Guernsey government and the institution of an official investigation. [36] During the summer the UK press had been full of 'imputations' against the Channel Islands authorities and the Home Office now felt that it was time for another speech in the Commons to set the matter straight. The situation was acute enough for Sir Alexander Maxwell to suggest that the outgoing Home Secretary make the speech, but in the end it was delivered by the new Home Secretary, Chuter Ede, on 17 August.[37] Before facing the House the Home Secretary had met Brigadier Snow who confirmed that there were very few substantial accusations of collaboration and that despite the deployment of professional policemen – among them the deputy chief constable of Sheffield – no 'dirty work' had come to light.[38] Those who had hoped for some real news were to be disappointed, as the speech was little more than a recast of Morrison's speech, three months earlier. The speech could, however, build on the perhaps most important of all the official meetings which had taken place in London, four days before, on 13 August 1945. Besides the Home Secretary himself, both Bailiffs, Jurat Leale and the Attorney General of Jersey were in attendance. The meeting, at which the Home Secretary advanced that 'mistakes had been made' and that there was a definite need for reform, was the final

---

[35] The attentive reader will have noted that the business of signing letters which really emanated from the Germans was a trap which Coutanche had consciously resisted; to the point that the Germans – demanding such a signed letter in order to facilitate their radio confiscation in June 1942 – published an unsigned letter in the *Evening Post*, the ultimate purpose of which was to cast doubt on the Bailiff in the eyes of his own population.

[36] PRO WO/32/11711. Further report of progress of work of 20 CA Unit, 18 June to 8 Aug 1945, by Colonel Power, 9 Aug 1945.

[37] PRO HO/45/25844. Alexander Maxwell to Herbert Morrison, 1 Aug 1945.

[38] PRO HO/45/25844. Conference between the Secretary of State and Brigadier Snow, 14 Aug 1945.

opportunity for self-criticism, which the authorities did not waste. A supplementary to this meeting lists the responses to the main misgivings towards the Guernsey and Jersey authorities and their responses: Carey had to defend his reference to Allied forces as 'enemy forces' in one order, his invitation to people to attend a German entertainment and the £25 reward for information leading to the arrest of the painters of V-signs, all in 1941. In the case of the order it was explained that it had never occurred to Carey to examine the text before publication. The invitation was described as 'extremely silly', with no further information given, leaving the impression that the Bailiff rubber-stamped everything submitted to him 'unless they were of a kind against which he ought to protest'. As to the reward the same reasons were given as in his correspondence with the Home Office on 25 June 1945. The three foreign Jewish women sent from Guernsey to their deaths in March 1942 do not even appear here. They had been entirely forgotten. This was different in Jersey. The registration of the Jews was the only topic Coutanche felt needed an explanation and he repeated all the known arguments of 'small number' and 'least possible harm'.[39]

The battle was now drawing to an end: on the day of the Home Secretary's speech MI5 issued a new report titled 'The Channel Islands under German Occupation' summarising their position. Based on previous communications, in particular the first MI5 report of 30 June 1945 and a consolidation of the I(b) reports, the most significant new development was the eleven cases where the evidence accumulated seemed to 'warrant consideration by the Director of Public Prosecutions with a view to possible prosecution' and the 180 cases where it had not been possible to collect satisfactory evidence, but which, according to Stopford, deserved some form of punishment. The latter category included profiteers, informers, women who had consorted with Germans, but also members of the island elites.[40] The far-reaching allegations of this report obviously aimed at a last minute extension of the MI5 mandate in the Channel Islands in order to continue investigations beyond the end of the military period, but the attempt backfired. The report, sent by Major Stopford to the Home Office was immediately transferred to Brigadier Snow for comment. Snow was irked, not least because MI5 had picked up his earlier assertion of June 1945 that he feared disturbances when the force was withdrawn. Snow had abandoned this position since, aligning himself more closely to the official view as expressed by French at the War Office. He was not too pleased to be reminded of it in this

---

[39] PRO HO/45/25844. Supplementary to the meeting of Bailiffs Coutanche and Carey, Jurat Leale and the Attorney General of Jersey with the Home Secretary and other officials, 13 August 1945.

[40] PRO KV/4/78. Security Service. The I(b) reports on the Channel Islands, by Major Stopford, 8 Aug 1945; PRO HO/45/22399. 'The Channel Islands under German Occupation', 17 Aug 1945.

manner and his criticism of the report was scathing.[41] It would be unfair, however, to portray Brigadier Snow as someone who had made up his mind in advance and who was unimpressed by new evidence. Dening himself more or less confirmed this in a letter he submitted to Major Stopford, on 26 August, where he stated that Snow had clearly changed his views at one juncture. It indicates that Snow was sympathetic to Dening's efforts, but expected results.[42]

Snow's criticism of the August MI5 report was that the evidence weighing in favour of the island authorities was just as valid as that against them. He commented that 'mountains' had been made out of 'molehills' and that everything had been shown 'in the worst possible light, imputing the worst motives to people on every occasion'. All in all, the report was a 'rehash of tittle-tattle prevalent in the islands but which nobody is prepared to come forward and substantiate'. Snow had a point: the information submitted by MI5 did not have the density one would expect to see in information that was to stand the test of a court or public enquiry. If available documentation is to be believed, MI5 had no major source in the islands which would have allowed them to give their wide ranging claims more credibility. As a result the report was a mere collage of various minor sources, none of which was in a position to provide information of the required import. More importantly, Snow noticed a serious lack of progression between the June and August reports and slated the information as 'out of date by 2 months'.[43] This admission could have very well been an expression of frustration on his part over what was now a manifest intelligence failure. Stopford and his men had been given a fair chance to enlarge their body of existing evidence during three months – from May to August 1945. When Snow realised that no conclusive information would emerge, he had no other choice than to come down firmly on the side of the Home Office view and pulled the plug. Dening concluded the affair in his 26 August letter to Stopford with the words that the Home Office were under the spell of a 'policy of appeasement' with opinions founded on 'the social impressions of high ranking officers', but that Snow was also at loggerheads with lower ranks – and in particular his I(b) staff – as regarded the evidence of collaboration. Bake [one of the CID officers seconded to Public Safety, Force 135] and Dening himself were considered 'unduly pessimistic'. Defiantly, Dening said that he stuck to the report: 'the Administration [sic] of the Islands during the occupation remains pusillanimous – particularly so in Guernsey'.[44] Stopford made one last attempt to get the ball

---

[41] PRO HO/45/22399. Brigadier Snow (Force 135) to Frank Newsam (HO), 24 Aug 1945.

[42] IWM JRD/09. Dening to Stopford, 26 Aug 1945.

[43] PRO HO/45/22399. Brigadier Snow (Force 135) to Frank Newsam (HO), 24 Aug 1945.

[44] IWM JRD/09. Dening to Stopford, 26 Aug 1945. Having gotten the wind of the 17 August report submitted by MI5 to the Home Office, Snow had called Dening to task 'for the expression of views' with which he did not agree. According to Dening, Snow had said, somewhat condescendingly, that he regretted such a junior rank should have been 'saddled with such a responsibility'.

rolling by submitting a list of names to the Director of Public Prosecutions in September 1945. The Director of Public Prosecutions, once more, responded that he was only interested in prosecuting the cases of islanders who had gone to Germany to broadcast, as these fell under the Defence Regulations.[45] Also in September a deputation of the Jersey Loyalists approached the Lieutenant Governor, Sir Arthur Grasset, to express their dissatisfaction over the way their petition had been received by the States and the lack of action with regard to collaborators. Although the Director of Public Prosecutions had been reluctant since June, the Lieutenant Governor still maintained that steps against informers were under consideration. It emerged during the meeting that the deputation were particularly upset about the Italian restaurateurs who were still in the island and some other people they deemed 'collaborators' who were 'back in business' or had been able to take up government employment.[46] When the Lieutenant Governor informed the Bailiff about the visit of the deputation, the latter wrote that the public did not realise that the legal situation precluded prosecutions.[47] By all means this was a hardly veiled allusion that someone should finally stand up and tell them, and that it wasn't going to be himself. As the Lieutenant Governor was not prepared to step in, the pretence was maintained that the enquiry was continuing. Although plans for the deportation of foreigners and certain categories of British citizens were being devised to act as a placebo, the Lieutenant Governor of Jersey obviously still believed that the Director of Public Prosecutions could be persuaded otherwise. As late as November 1945 he was still informing him that there were no signs of abatement of anger against collaborators in Jersey, and that the feeling was actually increasing. To contain this the Lieutenant Governor intimated that there were at least thirteen persons who he was quite prepared to evict, if this became necessary.[48] This may or may not have been a hint that the culprits should be tried under UK law. Although the Home Office continued to insist that there could be no trials without retrospective legislation, they submitted the Lieutenant Governor's letter to the Director

[45] The names on this list included some prominent islanders such as the Reverend Waterbury of Catel (Guernsey) and the Dame of Sark, other names included Mallet, Dyball, Cort, Pickthall, Cheesebrough, Hughes, Pope, Maud and Lily Vibert, see PRO KV/4/78. Security Service. Note of cases of allegations of collaboration to be submitted to the Director of Public Prosecutions, 4 Sept 1945.

[46] JAS Lieutenant Governor's files, 50/4 H. Letter of the Lieutenant Governor to the Bailiff of Jersey, 11 Sept 1945.

[47] JAS Lieutenant Governor's files, 50/4 H. Letter of the Bailiff of Jersey to the Lieutenant Governor, 15 Sept 1945.

[48] The names are in the public domain: Alexandrienne Baudains, John Dyball, Mr & Mrs Beckingham, Dorothy de Gruchy, John Quenault, Lilian Galer, Nicholas Tancred, Carmel Giard, Florence Jehen, John Hughes, George Romeril, Ralph Webber, Muriel Hunt, see PRO HO/45/22399. The Lieutenant Governor of Jersey to the Director of Public Prosecutions, 2 Nov 1945.

of Public Prosecutions. But the latter remained unenthusiastic: although he wavered a little, saying that there could be a possibility of trying them under English Common Law – for 'misdemeanour or affecting a public mischief' – he was against its use in criminal proceedings. Explaining once more the general position, the Director of Public Prosecutions said that it had never been legislated or considered what conduct was to be regarded as criminal during enemy occupation, and that this particular field was open as far as English law was concerned. Rather half-heartedly he agreed to a meeting with the Jersey Attorney General, to examine what could be done about public mischief trials under Jersey law. The meeting between Duret Aubin and the Director of Public Prosecutions, before Christmas 1945, was a foregone conclusion. The Attorney General had already indicated that the criminal jurisdiction of Jersey did not extend to such cases and had to be tried in England, whereas the Home Office was unenthusiastic and had made it clear to the Lieutenant Governor that any such trial in UK would have repercussions 'as there may have been other British subjects guilty of similar behaviour'.[49] The overall situation had also changed dramatically since the elections to the States Assembly in December, the results of which had taken much wind out of the movement in favour of collaboration trials. The force behind much of the discontent in Jersey, the Jersey Democratic Movement, had suffered a resounding defeat in the election, passing only one of its twelve list candidates. During the meeting with the Attorney General the Director said that the evidence in the twelve collaboration cases under investigation was insufficient and that they could not be tried in the English courts under the common law. He doubted the jurisdiction of English courts and thought the juries in England would be such as to lessen the chance of a conviction. Duret Aubin agreed, stating that if persons were tried in England and acquitted, this would probably be 'worse than the present situation'. On the other hand it was deemed equally impossible to get a proper trial in the Royal Court as public feeling in the Island was running 'so high'. Only the cases of two Eire citizens who had gone to Germany from Jersey should go ahead as planned.[50] In the New Year the Director of Public Prosecutions paid one last pro forma visit to Jersey for a public statement which was to finalise the position. With this the last window of opportunity for collaboration trials closed. Alternative options also remained unexplored: a petition of the Jersey Loyalists to the States, advocating the novel idea of a tribunal ruling on 'scandalous behaviour' on the basis of the Hague Convention was equally discarded with the arguments of retroactivity and lack of codified penalties. The special committee detailed to studying the

[49] PRO HO/45/22399. Frank Newsam (HO) to the Lieutenant Governor of Jersey, 26 Nov 1945.

[50] PRO HO/45/22399. File note re meeting between the Director of Public Prosecutions and the Attorney General of Jersey before Christmas 1945, 31 Dec 1945.

petition came to the conclusion that protracted investigations were not in the interest of the islanders. Instead it was suggested that legislation available to deport aliens and others should be used and that States employees be sanctioned with disciplinary action.[51] In mid-January the Home Office informed Coutanche – who still wanted to prosecute – that the legal opinion given by the Director of Public Prosecutions made it impossible to recommend, to the Privy Council, approval of retrospective legislation to deal with 'reprehensible conduct not amounting to treason or treachery.' Owing to the absence of legal machinery persons concerned could not be brought to trial, neither in Jersey nor in England. The Home Office ended with the wish that the 'unprecedented situation' would be 'appreciated'.[52]

None of these manoeuvres concerned Guernsey anymore where, by the look of things, it had never gotten to this stage. What fervour there was in favour of a purge died almost immediately after Liberation. Two petitions were filed with the States, in July and in August, the latter asking for an enquiry into the administration of the island during the Occupation, but neither mustered enough support to be submitted to the King-in-Council. The reasons for the lack of interest in collaboration trials were a lesser degree of political organisation than in Jersey; and a state of exhaustion which made the public rhetoric encouraging islanders to look forward, and not back, an extremely attractive proposition.[53] Over the months the absence of 'public feeling' would provide a welcome excuse for inaction. Finally, no candidates carrying enquiries or trials against collaborators on their political agenda made it past the posts in the January 1946 States elections.

The issue of official collaboration was raised one last time in October 1945, when the names of Carey and Coutanche were submitted to the Prime Minister for the list of honours. Attlee was puzzled by the discrepancy between this recommendation and the August MI5 report which he had seen.[54] Chuter Ede then unrolled the whole story of the investigations into the Channel Islands authorities. He stated that both Morrison and himself had gone to great lengths to ascertain whether officials had been guilty of any criminal offence or willing-

---

[51] PRO HO/45/22399. Rapport du Comité Spécial nommé avec mission d'étudier une Pétition du Comité Central d'Organisation des "Jersey Loyalists", 1945.

[52] PRO HO/45/22399. The Lieutenant Governor to the Bailiff of Jersey, 12 Jan 1946.

[53] Not everyone in Guernsey went along with this. One of the rebels was a States deputy named Cross, well known for his anti-establishment views. Cross had already protested against the formation of the Controlling Committee in June 1940. After Liberation he was suspended from the States for making disparaging remarks at a public meeting and in November 1945 he was put in his place by the Lieutenant Governor who refuted his claim in the *Guernsey Press* that the Home Office had an intention of sending a commission of enquiry to Guernsey, see *Guernsey Press*, 22 Jun 1940; 21 Sept 1945; 14 Nov 1945.

[54] PRO HO/45/22399. The Prime Minister to the Home Secretary, 31 Oct 1945.

ness to collaborate with the Germans 'in any sinister sense'. At the request of the Home Office the Director of Public Prosecutions had paid a special visit to the islands to ascertain that the authorities had 'behaved well, animated by the sole desire to act as a buffer'. The Force commander had said likewise that criticism was 'largely due to ignorance and misunderstanding'. Finally, the two Lieutenant Governors had been questioned personally by the Home Secretary about the conduct of the government and administration, confirming that both Bailiffs deserved commendation.[55] The letter to the Prime Minister demonstrates that by autumn all dissonances had been glossed over: Chuter Ede's depiction of the activities of the Director of Public Prosecutions definitely does not concord with the latter's comments before and during his visit to the Channel Islands in July 1945, in particular his agreement over the fact that the idea of honours had been rashly conceived. And the opinion of the Lieutenant Governors, at least in August when they were quizzed by the Home Secretary, would have counted for very little, as they had only just arrived at their new posts.

In the end the only cases with a Channel Islands connection ever to be tried under the Treason or Treachery Act were British renegades and conscientious objectors, often of Irish extraction, who had come to the islands for agricultural work under the auspices of the Peace Pledge Union, in 1939–40. During the Occupation some of these men followed up calls to work in Germany. These cases were peripheral, and they say nothing about Channel Islanders as a population; most of the accused did not even spend any significant amount of time in the islands. One of the men, Charles Gilbert, a Sandhurst dropout, was tried at the Old Bailey, in September 1946. Having arrived in the Channel Islands in spring 1940, Gilbert was already on his way to Berlin as early as late 1940, where he was to apply his talents to broadcasting news items and talks with the NBBS (New British Broadcasting Station). He stayed there, interrupted by a short spell in prison for a brawl with an SS guard in 1943, until the end of the war. Naturally, in this milieu his frequentations included the inevitable but less fortunate Joyces. Gilbert could have met with a worse fate than the nine-month prison sentence he received at the end of the trial; the jury had, in fact, interpreted his acquaintance with the inside of a German prison and his documented clashes with his German boss, many of them under the influence of alcohol, as a plausible sign of his disenchantment with the Nazis.[56] The most significant element of this and other cases is that they belie the argument that a death sentence was the inevitable outcome of treason and treachery trials, the principal argument with which any indictment of lesser collaborators had been

[55] PRO HO/45/22399. The Home Secretary to the Prime Minister, 2 Nov 1945.
[56] PRO KV/2/442. Gilbert Treason Trial at the Old Bailey, 1946. For others cases of this type see Mark Hull, 'Accidental tourists: Germany, the Channel Islands and espionage, 1940–45', Channel Islands Occupation Review, 29 (2001), 20–8.

refuted all along. These cases demonstrate that treason and treachery trials could result in relatively mild sentences. In terms of 'assisting the enemy' the difference between an informer in the Channel Islands and a broadcaster in Berlin was unclear, even though government lawyers would have probably found some reason to claim that there was one.

The failure to launch more comprehensive trials or a proper public enquiry had many sources: the Channel Islands authorities were not enthusiastic about treason or treachery trials and wanted a soft option which did not exist; the British wanted a return to normality as soon as possible and rejected any retrospective legislation. However, the most important impediment to collaboration trials was the intelligence failure mentioned above. It is common knowledge today that most battles are fought on the back of intelligence. This was little different in 1945. The point brings us back to the allegations of an establishment cover-up – in itself a very idle attempt to understand what exactly happened in summer 1945. Unfortunately the weight of intelligence was never strong or coherent enough to create the impetus required to help along the unprecedented action that trials of islanders would have been. Soon after the Liberation Colonel Power noted that the letters he was receiving 'contained very little in substance' and 'nothing on which official action could be undertaken.'[57] They may have contained more had the British CID used the methods of enforcement of their predecessors, the GFP, but this was the price to pay for the return of British justice. Testimonials containing imprecise, conflicting or misleading information were frequent. The difficulty of obtaining salient information is clearly confirmed by MI5 themselves. A letter written by an unnamed agent to Stopford, on 8 July 1945, provides conclusive proof: the agent in question had arrived in Guernsey in June. He stated that he had been stationed in the island in 1939–40 and had tried to revive some old contacts. In the end he had found that there was 'nothing definite' and that everyone was accusing everyone else of collaboration. As a result no man felt that he could inform for fear of being informed on himself. He came to the conclusion that nobody was unbiased and that the interdependence, intermarrying and 'smallness' of the island made it impossible to obtain any reliable information. In the view of this agent the 'much vaunted correctness of the Germans' was a 'security hatch' against attempts to criticise their own actions. The agent was clearly a professional in his field, but in the end there was little else he could suggest than that they try the Advocate General of Guernsey and the Attorney General of Jersey – in their capacity as heads of the island police forces – in order to obtain reliable information.[58] That no such working relationship with the Channel Islands authorities was sought was another considerable mistake of appreciation, as they were the only ones capable of providing the insider information required to build more elaborate cases

---

[57] PRO HO/45/22399. Brief for Home Sec re collaborationists in the islands, 4 June 1945.
[58] PRO KV/4/78. Unnamed agent to Stopford, Guernsey, 8 July 1945.

targeting specific individuals. In most European countries similar compromises were struck. Without a rehabilitation of the elites not even a minimum of *épuration* was possible. This was a more realistic – if Machiavellian – position than insisting on the thorough cleansing of society. The intelligence service had made the unforgivable mistake of taking the Channel Islands authorities for some colonial administration which could be forced into any particular direction.

Perhaps the most intriguing question of all is how the Home Office and the Intelligence Service could diverge so much in their appreciation of the situation. The simplest explanation, of course, is to assume a whitewash or cover-up. Unfortunately, most conspiracy theories are the handiwork of people who never really bother to look at the hard evidence. In all fairness, neither of the two groups was entirely wrong. This was not a dispassionate debate, but a process that addressed some painful and rather far-reaching issues. The very thought processes of officials at the Home Office and in the intelligence community – with the War Office people stuck in between – were structured by diametrically different outlooks and agendas which had a powerful impact on their percep-tions. The rift between Home Office and Intelligence embodied two visions of post-war Britain. The Home Office officials appear rather faint-hearted and old-fashioned in their tendency to subject almost anything to the preservation of the status quo – Morrison's visit to the Channel Islands is the very epitome of this. The intelligence people, on the other hand, stood for the bolder, more reformist faction favouring modernisation, including an overall constitutional shake-up. They made a serious miscalculation in disregarding the weight of tradition and failed to realise that the end of the war also heralded the wresting back of power placed in trust with the military by the civilians. Continuing to lobby for drastic measures that to many seemed informed by the demands of war – not peace – Intelligence went against a newly emerging consensus. Selective memory was operative on all sides, thus leading to the emergence of a number of 'blind spots'. This in itself is nothing sinister; it merely displays the tricks played by the minds of ambitious and determined people.

The other obstacle, preventing the British from making any real sense of the situation, was that they lacked a conceptual framework for dealing with collabo-ration that could have informed the legal and political process. The result, with everyone throwing around his own version, was utter confusion. One universally peddled idea in British government circles was that because 'a public servant [...] faithfully performed his normal duties and functions' this would have automati-cally benefited the civilian population as it would have avoided a German take-over of the administration and 'contributed towards the maintenance of some semblance of legitimate Government [*sic*]'[59]. We have seen in the Page case how

---

[59] PRO FO 371/40417. Draft memorandum concerning policy on collaborators, 26 Jul 1944.

insidious a principle this was and how it could work against civilians. Quite beside the point that the Germans never were interested in direct rule, it exonerated island officials from almost any responsibility. They could always point to force majeure. The natural conclusion from this was that '(any) public servant who has so acted and has confined himself to the duties of his post will not thereby be open to the charge of disloyal or improper behaviour, even though his activities have been of indirect benefit to the Germans also.'[60] Bravo. Whether this was simply a misinterpretation based on assumptions people had at the time about German intentions or a conscious post-war defence strategy is impossible to tell. Only one serious attempt was made – in the Force 135 counterintelligence plan – at providing a working definition of collaboration and defining what constituted acceptable and unacceptable behaviour. The plan conceded that collaboration to a limited extent was inevitable, in view of the civic responsibilities of the Bailiffs and the States officials. It continued:

> A broad view will therefore have to be taken as to what constitutes collaboration. Each case will be judged on its merits with due allowance for difficult circumstances. A useful yardstick will be on individual financial gain or evidence of gratuitous and not enforced assistance to the Germans.[61]

But these recommendations were never adopted into general policy. Most people in positions of responsibility seemed rather content on muddling their way through these blurred frontiers. To make matters worse the British confronted the entire question with a feeling of paramount distaste: many thought it below themselves to have to contemplate anything as unpalatable as the possibility of collaboration of Britishers. This distaste was again the result of unrealistic, but understandable premises, namely the British wartime paradigm. At its heart this identified collaboration as a continental and not a British phenomenon. At the same time the British interpretation never got around the contradiction that, yes, the islanders had to find a 'way of living' with the Germans. The basic human reflex was to leave the contradiction unresolved, without regard for the consequences. General Hind illustrated this attitude in a pre-Liberation report: while he betrayed some hesitation as to whether the working arrangement with the Germans was of a collaborationist nature or simply in the interests of the islanders, he mentioned – in the same breath and with some irritation – that the occupied Channel Islands were the only place in Europe without a resistance movement; as though this was the proof of a good pedigree. Then he swung back again to concede that this was not due to disloyalty or faintheartedness, citing all the common reasons used for explaining the absence of a movement, but failed to address the perhaps more important question whether a resistance

[60] Ibid.
[61] IWM JRD/07. Channel Islands Counterintelligence Plan, 1944.

movement would have been of any military use. This failure is so striking, as at
the of beginning of his report, he had sought to explain the 1940 evacuation and
the abandoned plans of a proposed liberation of the islands in 1944–45 in terms
of the strategic irrelevancy of the Channel Islands. What General Hind really
thought in the end is impossible to tell, for he concluded with the more enlightened statement that some 'responsibility for fraternisation must be borne by the
authority which ordered the evacuation of able-bodied men, but not of their
womenfolk who may since have fallen victim to temptation.'[62] This is not the
only British report full of blatant contradictions and swinging, like a pendulum,
from one extreme to another.

Finally there were also practical reasons which did not bode well for a grand
reckoning. Theodore Pantcheff, a good connoisseur of the islands, stated many
years later that cleansing from collaboration had to be done with great care in
order not to fracture the island societies beyond repair. He gave the random
example of a French woman who had had her hair shaved in Marseille, but
then moved to Lille to get on with her life. Moving from St Helier to St John, or
from St Peter Port to St Sampson with a collaborator's reputation would never
do the trick. Pantcheff added that it was terrible to contemplate perpetuating
some of the issues which could, at times, split through the middle of families.
Although at the time he had regretted the absence of a genuine payoff, he later
changed his mind and thought that the interests of the islands had been met.
One does not have to share Pantcheff's prescription of amnesia as a cure. What
worth was ostracism, forced emigration and taxation, if the facts were not
known? What if they hit the wrong targets? Nevertheless these were to become
the fundamental methods of 'disposal'. Already in May 1945, Mike Frowd, a
conscientious objector in Jersey, wrote in a letter to the editor of the *Evening Post*
that the 'witch-hunt' was turning against 'conchies', Italians and Irish – in
default of other targets.[63] In Guernsey another foreigner, Dutchman Gerrit
Timmer, was branded as the chief profiteer in the islands. Discussions toward
the deportation of the Irish and Italians started as early as November 1945.
Some Italians had created bad blood by scoring on the black market or
obtaining licences and supplies to run cafés which were frequented by
Germans.[64] The aversion against the Irish was based on the case of the eighty
Irishmen who were said to have volunteered for work in Germany and the 467
Irish (out of a total of about 1,000) who had registered as neutral nationals in
Jersey, in July 1942.[65] Finally, about forty Jersey collaborators, among them Mrs

---

[62] PRO HO/45/22399. Report by General Hind, pre-Liberation, 1945.
[63] PRO HO 144 22176. Letter of Mike Frowd, 1945.
[64] PRO FO/371/60551. Home Office letter to Foreign Office, 5 Apr 1946.
[65] PRO DO/35/1228. Political and Constitutional Relations. Deportation of six Irishmen from
the Channel Islands, 1946.

Baudains and her son, both regular GFP informers, and Mr Romeril, a notorious black market farmer, were deported to England on 23 March 1946.[66] They were followed by seven Irishmen, on 30 March 1946.

The Channel Islands elites did not remain entirely untouched by this upheaval, as is often claimed. One of the notable exceptions to the rule was Yvonne Riley, the Dame de Rozel, in Jersey. Mrs Riley was not the only member of the elite who had fraternised with the Germans (she was a confidante of von Aufsess); what tipped the scale was her Austrian heritage as well as the unpleasant personality changes that occurred when she was under the influence of alcohol.[67] She also angered other estate owners by having Rozel Manor placed under special protection by the Germans and was thus one of the few to have been preserved from the cutting down of trees imposed on the others. Already during the visit of their Majesties to Jersey in June she had been prevented from dispensing the traditional duties falling to the fief-holder of Rozel, namely to act as the Sovereign's butler in the island and attend to him on his arrival and departure. It was also felt in 1945 that she could no longer be summoned to the Assise d'Heritage for the purpose of performing her feudal obligations. Mrs Riley petitioned the King for permission to surrender her title and fief to her son Major Robin, of the Coldstream Guards, who had returned from active service. After some initial complications the request was finally granted in 1947.[68]

While the pros and cons of the abandoned post-war enquiry or trials for the scarring of the war wounds can be debated, there is one very serious impact which is irreversible: subsequent historiography suffered from the absence of official action. In most European countries enquiries or war crimes trials were held at some point. Although their main aim was to punish, they were also designed to inform, re-educate or to provide a catharsis after a particularly traumatic collective experience. Cleansing by judiciary means was also the first reflex of many countries of the former Eastern bloc after acceding to Western-style democracy in the early 1990s. Other examples where the judiciary became the institutional stage for dealing with the past are the International Tribunals for Rwanda and for ex-Yugoslavia, but one could also mention the South African Peace and Reconciliation Commission. What is sometimes overlooked is that such official proceedings also provided the critical mass of documentary evidence for historians. Without the documentation established for the purpose of trials many scholars would have written fundamentally different and – for that matter – poorer pieces of work. Nowhere is the impact clearer than in the study

---

[66] Information obtained at Jersey War Tunnels.

[67] JAS D/Z/H5/100. Law Officers department. Correspondence re. Yvonne Riley (née Lemprière), 1940–43.

[68] PRO PC/8/1541. Privy Council Office. Petition of Yvonne Riley to HM, 1945–1947.

of the Holocaust: already the trials conducted under mostly Allied auspices between 1945 and 1949 provided glimpses on which the first scholarly attempts, by Hilberg and Reitlinger, were based. The 1950s were a comparatively quiet decade, but in the 1960s a massive wave of trials began. The most reverberating was the trial of Adolf Eichmann in Israel, in 1961, which brought back the demons of the past, but also provided an opportunity to lay them to rest. The 1963 Auschwitz trial in Frankfurt had a similar effect in the land of the perpetrators. The impact in particular on the post-war generation critical of their fathers was profound. Hundreds of further trials were to follow until the last German trials in the 1990s. In other countries such as France, things did not start to hot up until the 1980s, but when the trials came they generated a seismic shift in attitudes. None of this would have come to fruition without the work of lawyers, among them Serge Klarsfeld.

All this is 'terra incognita' in the Channel Islands which are doubly disadvantaged: not only did the Germans manage to destroy the bulk of their files; but even the few enquiries conducted into Channel Islanders accused of collaboration offences in 1945, files which clearly existed at some point, were either intentionally destroyed or are now rotting away in some unidentified location. Over the decades the gap was filled by a deluge of oral history and personal memoirs, the most unreliable source, especially when so much time has elapsed. The unhealthy over-reliance on oral sources has created what is essentially unreliable oral history. The absence of official action in the Channel Islands is at the basis of the chequered views that persist until today and which make the historiography of this Occupation a considerably more trying affair than that of many others.

VIII

Conclusion

IN JULY 2004 columnist A A Gill created a small furore in the Channel Islands with a newspaper piece titled 'Islands struggle to keep us occupied'. What was perhaps more interesting than the usual volley of disparaging media remarks, was his hint that the makers of the TV mini-series 'Island at War' – using as a backdrop the Channel Islands' Occupation – were totally off the mark in their appreciation of British consumer taste. The man in the street was either indifferent or critical, particularly as this episode had never loomed large in British collective war memory. As locations conjuring the right sort of spirit Malta and Singapore had a lot more to offer.[1] Gill certainly had a point; which reduces to half a point if one digs a bit deeper. Perhaps Gill should have added that what he really meant was (positive) collective memory. Malta and Singapore are certainly more interesting for the aficionados of primeval, raw TV heroism à la Ray Meare or Jeremy Clarkson; but sometimes the more important things in life are the things that are not often, or never talked about; perhaps even the things one can't see. If one takes into account repression – the 'stuff' the 'man in the street' would rather not remember so much – you are spot-on with the Channel Islands. Quite apart from the point that it is inequitable to compare the Channel Islands with Malta or Singapore, frontline positions of global strategic importance which were defended, the Channel Islands offer a unique and heterogeneous psychological context. The paradox is: while the Channel Islands' Occupation is part of the British war experience, it has not been fully integrated as such in Britain's war history, except as an embarrassing footnote, hidden away somewhere out of sight. As Louise Willmot writes in an article on resistance in Jersey, much of the Channel Islands' Occupation remains to be discovered, like the city of Troy.

Much of this goes back to the 'family reunion' of summer 1945, which was pervaded by troubled feelings on both sides and prevented certain issues from

---

[1] AA Gill, 'Islands struggle to keep us occupied', *The Times*, 18 July 2004.

being addressed. The British certainly did not want to run the risk of being accused of having placed the Channel Islands in the predicament of occupation by their 'abandonment' in the summer of 1940, an argument that could have been used as a defence against too much criticism of the Channel Islanders. One of the sources of mistrust between mainlanders and islanders – the islands' antiquated pre-war form of government and 'deficits' in democracy – was quickly dealt with through post-war reform; the other important source – the essentially differing war paradigms[2] – ran much deeper, however. Still, with no place other to fit their war memory than the straightjacket of UK war memory – the Churchillian paradigm – islanders locked into the celebration of sublime heroism and unwavering steadfastness. The Occupation was stripped down to the dogma of 'political correctness' of the post-war period: 'our chaps' in the Channel Islands did a fantastic job in fighting their corner and defending the population. The Germans there didn't really behave too badly because they respected the British and, besides, were 'officer gentleman', quite similar to the British themselves; evacuees and escapees participated directly in the 'British war', their brethren indirectly, by keeping on smiling, eluding the 'Gestapo' bloodhounds and following the Allied news. Whether the Occupation fitted this bill was an entirely different question: in the list of illustrious episodes stretching from the Battle of Britain, the sinking of the Bismarck, Malta, North Africa, the exploits of Bomber Command, the Battle of the Atlantic, the Normandy landings all the way to the liberation of Belsen, the Channel Islands' Occupation was the odd one out. The story of the Occupation provides a dissonance on the self-image the British have adhered to as a nation over the past 60 years: there was panic in 1940 and the ethical choices were not always straightforward. Even worse, the Channel Islanders contradict the most potent image of the Churchillian paradigm, namely that the British were not a nation of victims, but victors. Suffice to say that islanders' experience had one element in common with the appalling experience of the PoWs in the Thai jungle – there was nowhere to run to. Many islanders who decided to stay in 1940 said later that, had they known this occupation would last five long years, they would have made sure to have caught the boat to England, never mind the Blitz. Islanders also diverged (and diverge) fundamentally from mainlanders in their assessment of Germans – individually and as a nation. There were, of course, islanders who continued and would continue to refer to them as 'the Hun'; the majority, however, had learnt more than they had perhaps wished for and knew how to tell apart the good, the bad and the ugly. While one had to watch one's words

[2] A paradigm corresponds to the framing of a particular problem or issue, it defines the way in which its parameters are determined, how the problem is approached. A paradigm community is the group of people which frames and deals with a given problem in a similar way. This binds the group together, but it also increases the tendency to develop blind spots.

and be discreet, one survived better by identifying people whom one could trust, even if they were on the other side of the divide. The British attitude towards the Germans, in contrast, was a great deal more aloof. For the adherents of Vansittartism they were ugly, degenerate brutes; others, such as the Foreign Office people working on post-war policy were more conciliatory, but dealt with Germans on a level of abstraction incomparable with the vivid richness of Channel Islanders' real life experience.

Dissenters trying to reconcile the rather facile official occupation memory with reality were in as bad a position as in other European countries which had gone down the chain of occupation-collaboration-resistance-liberation and endured several dramatic paradigm shifts in the matter of a few years. But while internal debates continued to rage in most European countries – one only has to look at 1960s France, Germany or Italy – the islands were in a rather peculiar situation, brought on by the cultural spell of the bigger brother nation. Because of the interlocking of Channel Islands and British war memory, any revision of the Channel Islands' Occupation has had to pass via a reappraisal of war memory in Britain, a victor nation where war memory is inevitably tied up with identity.[3] While the rhythm of popular culture churned products such as *Colditz*, *The Dambusters* and *The Great Escape*, there was very little understanding for alternative readings of the Channel Islands' Occupation – much of which was anathema. Certain aspects of those five years were blanked out in the public discourse; these were the 'dark years', best forgotten (or repressed), together with the people involved in those forgotten episodes. What emerged was a sanitized occupation memory focusing on fortifications, a superficially apolitical domain where it was valid to ask questions and be curious. The Occupation, taunted in tourist brochures, became part of island folklore. The collective trauma of the Occupation was only magnified by the absence of proper enquiries. The rummaging in the underbelly of public opinion, best avoided, was only allowed to emerge when there was no other way out, e.g. when compensation procedures had to be publicised in the 1960s or when war memorials were being planned.

The contested character of the Occupation – still a historiographical minefield – is at the origin of the continuing multiplicity of views. This, in turn, has had an important impact on interpretation. Islanders certainly were not in

---

[3] How powerful a mechanism this remains is confirmed by Oxford historian Adrian Gregory. In an interview he stated that despite the schizophrenic state British war memory reached by the 1970s, when the celebratory tradition of the fathers clashed with the counter-culture (and in particular anti-war culture) of the sons, the obsession with the war continued. The satirists of the day had a keen sense for this. Thus, the target of ridicule in the famous 'Faulty Towers' sketch are not the Germans (who barely say a word throughout), but Basil (i.e. the British) who is obsessed. Today, war culture is not about the war; it is about the fear of losing identity, see 'War, culture and memory', documentary by Clive Emsley, The Open University, 2003.

one mind after the Occupation and very different appreciations could hinge on rather anodyne things, such as where one was born, which internment camp one was sent to, whether one had been caught spreading radio news or what sort of German one met. While a minority of returnees – those who had been in prisons and concentration camps – were marked in their flesh, others had nothing more serious to regret than feeling that the five years of occupation had been a terrible waste of time. Again others would value the experience for the rest of their lives, and not always in a negative sense. Jersey teenager Stella Perkins said that without the Occupation she wouldn't have been the same kind of person. What Stella continued to cherish was that people had relied on their resourcefulness and imagination to keep alive; a 'great feeling of camaraderie' had existed and she found the thought comforting that 'one knew who one could trust'. Stella's 'mixed feelings' on Liberation Day were quite similar to people's reactions to the end of Communism four decades later: relief over the end of a dictatorship, regret that the sharing and solidarity which had existed between people would give way to greed and selfishness.[4] Not everyone would have agreed with Stella, though. Jerseyman Fred Woodall wrote in his diary that '(t)his occupation has made me lose more faith in humanity than anything else in my life'[5], but the point remains that multiplicity of view is the core associate feature of the event. Difficulty of coming to terms with multiplicity is also discernible in the most widely read account of the Channel Islands' Occupation in the UK, Madeleine Bunting's *Model Occupation (1995)*. Bunting certainly tried – and failed – to come up with a balanced view of the Occupation, and this failure was due to the 'yes-no' tendency inherent to her approach. Citing as many examples of resistance as of non-resistance, of collaboration as of lack of collaboration, in the end she comes down squarely in favour of the prevailing mainstream consensus of 'no resistance-collaboration'[6]; despite the fact that the presented evidence, with its dangerously complacent over-reliance on oral history and escapee reports, is not strong enough to pursue this path with such vehemence. Already at the time, John Keegan – a lonely dissonant voice among the cream of UK historians and commentators who fell over themselves in gushing praise of the book – criticised that the publisher, Harper Collins, had been 'trying to boost sales by suggesting that it contained evidence more damning than it really was'.[7] In the end, Bunting's book was more 'story' than

---

[4] IWM Misc. 2826 189/2 (Tape 4446 o/L). Interview with Stella Perkins, n.d.

[5] IWM Woodall diary, entry of 15 Dec 1942.

[6] The gist of the mainstream consensus on the Channel Islands Occupation can be gauged through the title of Hugh Trevor-Roper's review of Bunting's book: 'A little bit of Nazi Britain', *Sunday Telegraph*, 29 Jan 1995.

[7] John Keegan, 'Appeal of sleeping with the enemy – John Keegan finds a new history too fair to live up to its own hype', *Daily Telegraph*, 21 Jan 1995.

'history', pointing to a continuing insecurity over the real face of the Channel Islands' Occupation and indicative of what happens to history that does not seek its necessary distance from the UK media circus. It was all very instructive targeting a perhaps too complacent British self-perception at the time – much of which is built on Britain's role in World War Two – but Bunting's attempt (and that of her credulous commentators) overshot the mark.

In the past year the islands celebrated 1204, the year marking the inception of the islands' attachment to the English Crown. The choices made in that year continue to be of vital relevance because they are at the origin of two key themes in the history of the islands, loyalty and autonomy.

What will 1940–1945 stand for? Surviving under the prevailing conditions certainly was an incredible boost to self-confidence in the islands which that great leveller war turned from oldy-worldy places into modern polities. All of a sudden islanders were swept into the maelstrom of global politics and modern war, they had to grapple with the complexities of international law, face dilemmas of various kinds and redefine the meaning of loyalty in a modern sense, things the rather straight-laced and antiquated fabric of island society had never made allowance for. The cleavages left by the Occupation, together with the post-war return of the now more politicised island evacuees from the mainland, challenged the old consensual culture and spelt the arrival of adversarial politics. In the space of five years the Channel Islands had grown up. One always remembers one's teenage years with some fondness. Perhaps this is the reason why the memory of these years is so fiercely and tenaciously defended.

Sources

I ARCHIVAL SOURCES

Archives Nationales de France (AN)

AJ 40/543. Description des fonctionnaires

AJ 40/547. FK 515

AJ 40 821A. Mbf in Frankreich. Abt. Wi V/2 Währung, Kredit, Versicherung

AJ 40 1105. DSK Paris

F 60 1009. Commission Interministérielle pour la repression du marché noir

F9/5572. Amicale des Anciens déportés politiques de l'île anglo-normande d'Aurigny (M Azoulay) to Ministre des Victimes Civiles de la Guerre, rapport sur l'île d'Aurigny, 3 April 1946

Bank of England Archives (BoE)

C40. Chief Cashiers Policy Files

OV173. Liberation of Occupied Territories

Bundesarchiv (BA)

1 Military Archives (MA), Freiburg

RH 26/319. 7th Army High Command

RW 4/624 and 625. OKW/Wehrmacht HQ

RW 5/243. OKW/Foreign Section/Abwehr

RW 35/537. Military Government in France (Militärbefehlshaber in Frankreich)

RW 36/257. Military Government in Belgium and North France (Militärbefehlshaber in Belgien und Nordfrankreich)

RW 49/97. Abwehr Command France (F/IIIc)

2 Reich Documents Section (R), Berlin

R 22/1341 and 1342. Reich Ministry of Justice

NS/47/48. Lebensborn.

3 Zentrale Nachweistelle (ZNS), Aachen

W 11/104 to 107. Court Martials-General Correspondence

Z 726. Court of the 319th Infantry Division

Imperial War Museum (IWM)

IWM Misc. 2826 189/2.

Interviews

Bates, Marion
Blampied, John
De Sainte Croix, Eddie
Falla, Raymond
Ginns, Michael
Grau, Herr

Green, Mabel Vera
Grosslopp, Werner
Harmsen, Judge
Howard, J. (Home Office)
Hühnegarth and Kassens

Killman (Luftwaffe)
Le Brocq, Norman
Le Maistre, Vernon
Mansell, Tom
Mière, Joe
Misiewiec, Ted
Perkins, Stella

Prigent, Gordon
Sinel, Leslie
Unnamed German Soldier

Private Papers and Diaries

Aitken, Mrs. D.O.
Andrew, Comm. O.M.
Attenborough, G.
Bazeley, C.G.
Bullen, Mrs. I.
Coles, Mrs. J.

Fletcher, R.E.H.
Girard, P.
Hamel, E.
Lainé, Miss A. Le M.
Le Cocq, W.
Miller, T.J.

Moon, Miss G.
Querée, Mr.
Strong, H.E.
Woodall, F.G.

Foreign Documents

EDS series: Historical studies on German Armed Forces operations by the Cabinet Office
Historical Section

Guernsey Nebenstelle Files (FK 515)

Papers belonging to Captain J.R. Dening
Item 2640. Legal Staff, Force 135

Jersey Archive (JAS)

A   Records of the Lieutenant Governor of Jersey
B/A/L   Bailiff's Chambers: Liberation Files
B/A/W   Bailiff's Chambers: Occupation Files
C/C/L   Occupation and Liberation Committee 1984-1996
D/AP   Various States Greffe / States Committee Correspondence files and other papers
D/AU   Treasury Records
D/Z   Law Officers' Department
L/C/20   Vivienne Mylne Collection
L/C/24   Joe Mière Collection
L/C/144   Copy of the Occupation Diary of the Reverend R. Douglas Ord
L/D/25   Channel Islands Occupation Society (Jersey) Collection
L/F/54   Bonhams and Langlois Collection
L/F/64   Perkins Collection
M/19   Correspondence of Dr W Casper and Mr V Musso
R/03   Jersey Sound Archive
R/05   Philip Gurdon Sound Archive
A5   List of political prisoners in the Channel Islands, 1940-1945

States Greffe, Jersey

Protocole of 174th meeting of the Finance Committee, 6 December 1946
Letter received from the Home Office on the subject of financial settlement for Jersey

Institut für Zeitgeschichte, Munich (IfZ)

Microfilms
MA 544. Einsatzstab Reichsleiter Rosenberg

Island Archives Service, Guernsey

FK 1/11. FK 515 Nebenstelle Guernsey Feldgendarmerie an Nebenstelle (Mil. Führung), 26
Jul 1941
FK 4/8. GFP Gru 131, Aussenkommando Steinberger. Bericht über Straftaten/
Eigentumsvergehen, die in den Monaten Oktober 41 bis Januar 1942 zur Anzeige kamen,
und in denen als Täter deutsche Wehrmachtsangehörige genannt wurden, 18 January 1942

FK 5-6. 'Bericht über Studienreise nach den britischen Kanalinseln vom 10. bis 25. September 1941', by Professor Karl Heinz Pfeffer

FK 5-11. Leutnant Seyferth, Aussenstelle Jersey der Propagandastaffel Nordwest, 'Historische, staatsrechtliche und bevölkerungspolitische Betrachtungen ueber die britischen Kanalinseln unter besonderer Berücksichtigung der Verhältnisse auf Jersey', n.d.

FK 13/4. Feldkriegsgericht des Kommandeurs der 13. Flakdivision. Feldurteil in der Strafsache gegen den Oberleutnant Otto Feld, 29 September 1943

FK 23-3. Feldkommandantur papers

FK 29-6. Letter of Feldkommandantur to Nebenstelle Guernsey, 1 Apr 1943

Minutes of the Controlling Committee, June 1940-June 1945

Minutes of the Finance Committee, February 1945-November 1946

Diary of Ken Lewis

National Archives – Public Record Office, London (PRO)

Home Office (HO)
45   Registered Papers
144   Registered Papers, Supplementary
222   Police Research and Planning Branch and successors: Police Research Bulletin

War Office (WO)
11   German Occupation of the Channel Islands: death and ill-treatment of slave labourers and transportation of civilians to Germany
32   Registered Files (General Series)
106   Directorate of Military Operations and Military Intelligence and predecessors: Correspondence and Papers
192   Channel Islands: deportation and ill-treatment of civilians
199   Home Forces: Military Headquarters Papers, Second World War
205   21 Army Group: Military Headquarters Papers, Second World War
208   Directorate of Military Operations and Intelligence, and Directorate of Military Intelligence: Ministry of Defence, Defence Intelligence Staff: Files
212   Orders of Battle and Organisation Tables, Second World War
219   Supreme Headquarters Allied Expeditionary Force: Military Headquarters Papers, Second World War
227   Officer of the Engineer-in-Chief: Papers
235   Judge Advocate General's Office: War Crimes Case Files, Second World War
258   Department of the Permanent Under-Secretary of State: Private Office Papers
309   Judge Advocate General's Office, British Army of the Rhine War Crimes Group (North-West Europe) and predecessors: Registered Files
311   Judge Advocate General's Office, Military Deputy's Department, and War Office, Directories of Army Legal Services and Personnel Services: War Crimes Files
365   Department of the Adjutant General, Statistics Branch: Published Statistical Papers
677   War crimes in the Channel Islands: evidence and investigations

Treasury (T)
160   Finance Department: Registered Files
161   Supply Department: Registered Files
231   Exchange Control Division: Registered Files

Agriculture, Fisheries and Food Departments (MAF)
83   Ministry of Food: Supply Department: Supply Secretariat
103   Ministry of Food: Services Department: Services Secretariat
150   Ministry of Food: Legal Department: Registered Files

Government Communications Headquarters (HW)
1   Government Code and Cypher Schools: Signals Intelligence passed to the Prime Minister, Messages and Correspondence
5   Government Code and Cypher Schools: German Section: Reports of German Army and Air Force High Grade Machine Decrypts
13   Government Code and Cypher Schools: Second World War Intelligence Summaries

Cabinet Office (CAB)
84   War Cabinet and Cabinet: Joint Planning Committee, later Joint Planning Staff, and Sub-Committees: Minutes and Memoranda
120   Ministry of Defence Secretariat: Records
121   Special Secret Information Centre: Files

Foreign Office (FO)
95   Political and other departments: Miscellanea, Series I
96   Political and other departments: Miscellanea, Series II
371   Political Departments: General Correspondence from 1906
898   Political Warfare Executive and Foreign Office, Political Intelligence Department: Papers
916   Consular (War) Department, later Prisoners of War Department
950   Claims Department: Correspondence and Claims Files
1052 Control Office for Germany and Austria and Foreign Office: Control Commission for Germany (British Element), Prisoners of War/Displaced Persons Division: Registered Files
1057 Control Office for Germany and Austria and Foreign Office: Control Commission for Germany (British Element), Reparations, Deliveries and Restitutions Division: Registered Files and Reports
1060 Control Office for Germany and Austria and Foreign Office: Control Commission for Germany (British Element), Legal Division, and UK High Commission, Legal Division: Correspondence, Case Files and Court Registers
1063 Control Office for Germany and Austria and Foreign Office: Control Commission for Germany (British Element), Liaison Allied Contingent Branch: Registered Files

Treasury Solicitor (TS)
26   War Crimes Papers

Air Ministry, Royal Air Force and related bodies (AIR)
9   Directorate of Operations and Intelligence and Directorate of Plans: Registered Files
37   Allied Expeditionary Air Force, later Supreme Headquarters Allied Expeditionary Force (Air), and 2nd Tactical Air Force: Registered Files and Reports

National Savings Committee, Post Office Savings Department and Department for National Savings (NSC)
11   Post Office Savings Department: Savings Certificate Office: Correspondence and Papers
21   Post Office Savings Bank and Post Office Savings Department: Departmental Policy Files

Central Office of Information (INF)
9   The Dixon Scott Collection

Dominions Office, Commonwealth Relations Office, and Foreign and Commonwealth Office (DO)
35   Dominions Office and Commonwealth Relations Office: Original Correspondence

Ministry of Defence (DEFE)
2   Combined Operations Headquarters: Records

Colonial Office, Commonwealth and Foreign Office, Commonwealth Office and Empire Marketing Board (CO)
323   Colonies, General: Original Correspondence
968   Colonial Office and Commonwealth Office: Defence Department and successors: Original Correspondence

Security Service (KV)
2   Personal Files
4   Policy Files

Prime Minister's Office (PREM)
3   Operational Correspondence and Papers

Captured Records of the German, Italian and Japanese Governments (GFM)
33   German Foreign Ministry Archives: Photostat Copies

Lord Chancellor's Office and various legal commissions and committees (LCO)
6   Crown Office: Registered Files
57   Chancery and Lord Chancellor's Department: Extinct Hereditary Peerages and Deceased Life Peers Case Files

Privy Council and other records collected by the Privy Council Office (PC)
8   Original Correspondence

Admiralty, Naval Forces, Royal Marines, Coastguard and related bodies (ADM)
1   Admiralty, and Ministry of Defence, Navy Department: Correspondence and Papers
116   Admiralty: Record Office: Cases
179   Admiralty: Portsmouth Station: Correspondence
199   Admiralty: War History Cases and Papers, Second World War

General Register Office, Government Social Security Department and Office of Population Censuses and Surveys (RG)
28   National Registration: Correspondence and Papers

Transport Department and related bodies, and London Passenger Transport Board (MT)
59   Shipping Control and Operation: Correspondence and Papers

Ministry of Health and successors, Local Government Boards, and related bodies (MH)
76   Emergency Medical Services and related bodies: Registered Files, Circulars and Second World War Medical History Papers

Ministry of Supply and successors, Ordnance Board and related bodies (SUPP)
14   Ministry of Supply Files

Special Operations Executive (HS)
6   Western Europe: Registered Files
451   Channel Islands

Société Jersiaise Library, Jersey

Occupation Boxes

Box No. 1 (Evacuation and Escape):
Item 10: 'A narrative prepared from a verbal account given by Denis Vibert'.
Item 11: 'Jersey Under German Occupation: A verbal account of Denis Vibert's escape'

Box No. 3 (Prisoners):
Item 8: Various papers produced by Lieutenant Haas, Lucie Schwob and Susanne Malherbe
Items 9 and 14: Various articles on Pete Bogatenko
Item 11: Various articles on Feodor Buryi

Box No. 10 (Diaries):
Item 10: 'Wartime Banking', a diary belonging to Mr Phillips
Item 16: 'Beyond the Rocks', a screenplay written by C.I. A'Court
Item 27: Diary belonging to Mrs. C.C.F. Monkton
Item 32: Letters from Mrs. Emma Huchet to a Mrs Dean
Item 36: Letters from Dr R.N. McKinstry to his wife
Item 42: Letter written by Muriel Smith

Box No. 14:
Letters addressed to C.T. Le Quesne from Ralph Vibert, Denis Vibert and an individual
    identified as 'Jack'
Anonymous report on conditions in Jersey
Anonymous letter received by one Mr Podger

State Archives of Hessen, Wiesbaden

46/18893   Prosecutor's Office at District Court Frankfurt
409/4   Preungesheim prison records

State Archives of Saxony-Anhalt, Merseburg

Rep. C 131 II.   Naumburg Death Register

State Prosecutor's Office, Hamburg

Verfahren gegen Klebeck, Hartwig und Rometsch

Russian State Archives, Moscow

Report on crimes committed in the Alderney camps from 1942 to 1945, by Captain
    Pantcheff, 23 June 1945

Wannsee Villa, Berlin

Testimonies of the Holocaust:
Major Hoffman and other persons
Maximilan List

II ORAL SOURCES

Interviews with:

Dieter Ballauf	Michael Ginns	Bob Le Sueur
Sir Peter Crill	Kurt Hälker	Alf Vibert
Don Filleul	Michelle Irving	

Bibliography

1 PUBLISHED WORKS

Adler, H.G., *Des verwaltete Mensch. Studien zur Deportation der Juden aus Deutschland*, Tübingen, 1974.

Allen, Michael Thad, *The business of genocide: the SS, slave labour, and the concentration camps*, London, 2002.

Aubin, H.E., *The Occupation bicycle park*, Jersey, 1992.

Auerbach, Hans, *Die Kanalinseln, Jersey, Guernsey und Sark*, Paris, 1943.

Aufsess, Baron Von, Casper, Wilhelm, *In the eye of the hurricane, Remembrances from the Channel Islands 1941-1943*, Jersey, 1991.

Aufsess, Baron Von, *The von Aufsess occupation diary*, edited and translated by Kathleen J. Nowlan, Worcester, 1995.

Bachmann, K.M., *The prey of an eagle*, Guernsey, 1985 (reprint).

Balleine, G.R., *Balleine's History of Jersey*, revised and enlarged by Margaret Syvret and Joan Stevens, Chichester, 1981.

Beecken, Olaf, *Dokumente von den Kanalinseln zur Festungszeit: August 1944-Mai 1945: Ein Beitrag zur Geschichte der Endphase der deutschen Besatzung* (3 vols), Hamburg, 1999.

Beecken, Olaf, *Guernsey, Jersey, Alderney, Sark: A postal history of the German prisoners of war 1945-1947*, Hamburg, 1998.

Bell, William M., *The commando who came home to spy*, Guernsey, 1998.

Bell, William M., *Guernsey. Occupied but never conquered*, Guernsey, 2002.

Bennett, Rab, *Under the shadow of the Swastika: the moral dilemmas of resistance and collaboration in Hitler's Europe*, Basingstoke, 1999.

Benvenisti, Eyal, *The international law of occupation*, Princeton, 1993.

Bertrand, L.E., *A record of the work of the Guernsey Active Secret Press 1940-1945*, Guernsey (published by the Guernsey Gazette and Star), 1945.

Bessenrodt, Hauptmann, *Die Insel Alderney. Aufsätze und Bilder*, Guernsey 1943.

Binding, Tim, *Island madness*, London, 1998.

Boelcke, Willi A., *Des Schwarzmarkt 1945-1948. Vom Überleben nach dem Kriege*, Braunschweig, 1986.

Bois, F. de L., *A constitutional history of Jersey*, Jersey, 1970.

Bonnard, Brian, *Alderney at War 1939-1949*, Stroud, 1993.

Braudel, Fernand, *La Méditerranée et le monde méditerranéen à l'époque de Philippe II, vol. I: La part du milieu*, Paris, 1990.

Briggs, Asa, *The Channel Islands. Occupation and Liberation 1940-1945*, London, 1995.

Briggs, Asa, *The war of words: The history of broadcasting in the United Kingdom, Vol. 3*, Oxford, 1995.

Broszat, Martin, Elke Fröhlich and Falk Wiesemann, eds., *Alltag und Widerstand: Bayern im Nationalsozialismus*, Munich, 1987, 6 vols.

Brown, Rupert, *Group processes. Dynamics within and between groups*, Oxford, 2000 (reprint).

Bunting, Madeleine, *The Model Occupation: The Channel Islands under German rule 1940-1945*, London, 1995.

Cahun, Claude, *Écrits*, Paris, 2002. Edited by François Leperlier.

Cohen, Frederick, *The Jews in the Channel Islands during the German Occupation 1940-1945*, Jersey Heritage Trust (in association with the Institute of Contemporary History and Wiener Library), 2000.

Cortier, Daniel, *Jean Moulin: l'inconnu du Panthéon*, Paris, 1993.

Cortvriend, V.V., *Isolated Island. A history and personal reminiscences of the German Occupation of the island of Guernsey June 1940-May 1945*, Guernsey, 1947.

Cruickshank, Charles, *The German Occupation of the Channel Islands*, London, 1975.

Davies, Peter, *Dangerous Liaisons: Hitler, collaboration and World War Two*, London, 2004.

De Carteret, Basil, Mary Deslandes and Mary Robin, *An island trilogy. Memories of Jersey and the Occupation*, Jersey, n.d.

Elias, Norbert, *Studien über die Deutschen. Machtkämpfe und Habitusentwicklung im 19 und 20 Jahrhundert*, Frankfurt-am-Main, 1989.

Eriksen, Thomas, *Small places, large issues. An introduction to social and cultural anthropology*, London, 2001 (reprint).

Falla, Francis, *The silent war. The inside story of the Channel Islands under the Nazi jackboot*, Guernsey, 1994 (reprint).

Falle, Audrey, *Slaves of the Third Reich*, Jersey, 1994.

Febvre, Lucien, *A geographical introduction to history. An introduction to human geography*, London, 1999 (reprint).

Foot, M.R.D., *Resistance. An analysis of European resistance to Nazism 1940-1945*, London, 1976.

Forty, George, *Channel Islands at war: A German perspective*, Surrey, 1999.

Fraser, David, *The Jews of the Channel Islands and the Rule of Law 1940-1945 – 'Quite contrary to the principles of British justice'*, Brighton / Portland, 2000.

Freeman-Keel, Tom, *From Auschwitz to Alderney*, Craven Arms (Shropshire), 1993.

Garnier, Val, *Medical history of the Jersey hospitals and nursing homes during the Occupation 1940-1945*, London, 2002.

Gellately, Robert, *The Gestapo and German society. Enforcing racial policy 1933-1945*, Oxford, 1990.

Gibson, Robert, *Studies in French fiction in honour of Vivienne Mylne*, London, 1988.

Ginns, Michael, *German tunnels of the Channel Islands*, Jersey, 1993.

Ginns, Michael, *The Organisation Todt and the Fortress Engineers in the Channel Islands*, Jersey, 1994.

Hachmeister, Lutz, *Der Gegnerforscher: die Karriere des SS-Führers Franz Alfred Six*, München, 1998.

Haestrup, Jørgen, *European Resistance Movements, 1939-1945. A complete history*, Westport, London, 1981.

Harris, Roger E., *Islanders deported. Part 1: The complete history of those British subjects who were deported from the Channel Islands during the German Occupation of 1940-45 and imprisoned in Europe*, Illford, 1980.

Harvey, Winfred, *The battle of Newlands: The wartime diaries of Winifred Harvey*, edited by Rosemary Booth, Guernsey, 1995.

Hathaway, Sibyl, *Dame of Sark: An autobiography*, Jersey, 1986 (reprint).

Hawes, Stephen and Ralph White, eds., *Resistance in Europe 1939-1945* (based on the proceedings of a symposium held at the University of Salford, March 1973), London, 1975.

Hazéra, Jean-Claude, Renaud Rochebrunne, (de), *Les patrons sous l'occupation*, Paris, 1995.

Hensle, Michael, *Rundfunkverbrechen. Das Hören von 'Feindsendern' im Nationalsozialismus*, Berlin, 2003.

Hillsdon, Sonia, *Jersey – Occupation remembered*, Norwich, 1986.

Hirschfeld, Gerhard and Patrick Marsh, eds., *Collaboration in France. Politics and culture during the Nazi occupation 1940-1944*, Oxford, 1989.

Housden, Martyn, *Resistance and conformity in the Third Reich*, London, 1997.

Jackson, Julian, *France – The dark years 1940-1945*, Oxford, 2001.

Jackson, Julian, *The Fall of France. The Nazi Invasion of 1940*, New York, 2003.

Journeaux, Donald, *Raise the white flag – A Life in occupied Jersey*, Leatherhead (Surrey), 1995.

Kaufmann, J.E., *Fortress Third Reich. German fortifications and defence systems in World War II*, London, 2003.

Keiller, Frank, *Prison without bars: Living in Jersey under the German Occupation 1940-45*, Bradford-on-Avon, 2000.

King, Peter, *The Channel Islands War 1940-45*, London, 1991.

Klarsfeld, Serge, *Le calendrier de la persécution*, Paris, 1994.

Kogon, Eugen, Hermann Langbein and Adalbert Rückerl, et al, *Nationalsozialistiche Massentötungen durch Giftgas*, Frankfurt, 1983.

Kommittee zur Untersuchung der Verhältnisse an westdeutschen Universitäten (ed.), *Die wissenschaftliche und politische Karriere des Dr. phil. Habil. Karl Heinz Pfeffer, Professor für Soziologie der Entwicklungsländer an der Universität Münster. Eine Dokumentation*, Leipzig, 1963;

Kondakov, Georgi, *The island of dread in the Channel. The story of Georgi Ivanovitch Kondakov*, edited by Brian Bonnard, Stroud, 1991.

Kosthorst, Erich and Bernd Walter, *Konzentrations-und Strafgefangenenlager im Dritten Reich. Beispiel Emsland. Dokumentation und Analyse zum Verhältnis von NS-Regime und Justiz*, Düsseldorf, 1983.

Lean, Tangye, *Voices in the darkness. The story of the European radio war*, London, 1943.

Le Brocq, Edward, *Memoirs of Edward Le Brocq 1877-1964*, Bradford-on-Avon, 2000.

Lemprière, Raoul, *History of the Channel Islands*, London, 1980.

Le Quesne, Edward, *The Occupation of Jersey day by day*, Jersey, 1999.

Le Ruez, Nan, *Jersey occupation diary*, Bradford-on-Avon, 2003 (reprint).

Le Sueur, Francis, *Shadow of the swastika: Could it all happen again?*, Guernsey, 1990.

Lewis, Dr John, *A doctor's occupation*, London, 1982.

Liesner, Thelma (compiler), *One hundred years of economic statistics: United Kingdom, United States of America, Australia, Canada, France, Germany, Italy, Japan, Sweden*, London, 1989.

Machon, Nick, *Liberation: The Story of Guernsey in captivity and the long road to freedom*, Guernsey, 1985.

Mahy, Miriam M. *There is an occupation…*, Guernsey, 1992.

Mallmann, Klaus-Michael and Gerhard Paul, eds., *Die Gestapo – Mythos und Realität*, Darmstadt, 1995.

Marshall, Michael, *Hitler invaded Sark. The full story of the German occupation of Sark*, Guernsey, 1967 (reprint).

Martinière, Joseph (de la), *Le décret et la procédure 'Nacht und Nebel' ('Nuit et Brouillard')*, Orleans, 1981.

Maugham, R.C.F., *The island of Jersey today. Its scenery, history, people, administration and residential potentialities*, London, 1938.

Maugham, R.C.F., *Jersey under the jackboot*, London, 1980 (reprint).

Mière, Joe, *Never to be forgotten*, Jersey, 2004.

Mollet, Ralph, *Jersey under the swastika. An account of the Occupation of the island of Jersey by the German forces, 1st July 1940 to 12th May 1945*, London, 1945.

Moore, Bob, ed., *Resistance in Western Europe*, New York, 2000.

Morris, Lillie Aubin, *A collection of occupation recipes*, Jersey, 1994.

Nebel, Gerhard, *Bei den nördlichen Hesperiden*, Wuppertal, 1948.

Newman, Leonard S. and Ralph Erber, eds., *Understanding genocide. The social psychology of the Holocaust*, Oxford University Press, 2002.

Packe, Michael St. J., and Maurice Dreyfus, *The Alderney Story 1939-1949*, Alderney, 1971.

Pantcheff, T.X.H., *Alderney fortress island. The Germans in Alderney, 1940-1945*, Chichester, 1981.

Partridge, Colin, *Hitler's Atlantic Wall*, Guernsey, 1976.

Paxton, Robert, *Vichy France: Old Guard and New Order*, New York, 2001 (reprint).

Perrin, Dennis, *The Occupation and Jersey freemasonry*, Jersey, 1995

Pfeffer, Karl Heinz, *England – Vormacht der bürgerlichen Welt*, Hamburg, 1940.

Pocock, H.R.S. (compiler), *Memoirs of Lord Coutanche*, Chichester, 1975.

Reimann, G., *The black market, inevitable child of statism*, Hindsdale, 1948.

Rings, Werner, *Life with the enemy: collaboration and resistance in Hitler's Europe 1939-1945*, London, 1982.

Rivett, Peter J., *A tiny act of defiance*, Paignton, 2001.

Royle, Stephen A., *A geography of islands: small island insularity*, London, 2001.

Sanders, Paul, *Histoire du marché noir 1940-1946*, Paris, 2001.

Sanders, Paul, *The ultimate sacrifice*, Jersey, 2004 (reprint).

Saunders, Anthony, *Hitler's Atlantic Wall*, Stroud, 2001.

Sauvary, J.C., *Diary of the German Occupation 1940-1945*, Upton-upon-Severn (Worcestershire), 1990.

Schwarz, Gudrun, *Nationalsozialistische Lager*, Frankfurt, 1991.

Seidler, Franz W., *Die Organisation Todt. Bauen für Staat und Wehrmacht 1938-1945*, Bonn, 2 vols.,1998.

Semelin, Jacques, *Unarmed against Hitler. Civilian resistance in Europe 1939-1943*, Westport / London, 1993.

Sinel, Leslie, *The German Occupation of Jersey: A complete diary of events, June 1940-June1945*, Jersey, 1984 (reprint).

Steckoll, Solomon H., *The Alderney death camp*, London, 1982.

Stoney, Barbara, *Sybil, Dame of Sark*, London, 1978.

Streit, Christian, *Keine Kameraden. Die Wehrmacht und die sowjetischen Kriegsgefangenen 1941-1945*, Stuttgart, 1978.

Strobl, Gerwin, *The Germanic isle: Nazi perceptions of Britain*, Cambridge, 2000.

Stroobant, Frank, *One man's war. The dramatic true story of life in the Channel Islands under the jackboot of German occupation*, Guernsey, 1984 (reprint).

Tessin, George, *Verbände und Truppen der deutschen Wehrmacht und Waffen-SS im Zweiten Weltkrieg 1939-1945*, Osnabruck, 1974.

Thomas, Jürgen, *Wehrmachtsjustiz und Widerstandsbekämpfung: das Wirken des ordentlichen deutschen Militärjustiz in den besetzten Westgebieten 1940-45 unter rechtshistorischen Aspekten*, Baden-Baden, 1990.

Thomas, Roy, *Lest we forget. Escapes and attempted escapes from Jersey during the German occupation 1940-1945*, Jersey, 1992.

Tillion, Germaine, *Ravensbrück*, Paris, 1988.

Tolstoy, Nikolai, *Victims of Yalta*, London, 1979 (reprint).

Toms, Carel, *Hitler's fortress islands – Germany's occupation of the Channel Islands*, London, 1967.

Torode, Annette, *George d'la Forge. Guardian of the Jersey – Norman heritage. A study of the life and writings of George Francis Le Feuvre 1891-1984*, Jersey, 2003.

Tremayne, Julia, *War on Sark: The secret letters of Julia Tremayne*, Exeter, 1981.

Trevor-Roper, Hugh, ed., *Hitler's table talk, 1941-1944: his private conversation*, London, 2000 (reprint).

Van Grieken, Gilbert, *Destination 'Gustav': A wartime journey*, Guernsey, 1992.

Van Holk, Lambertus Jacobus, *Foreign occupation as an ethnical problem*, London, 1946.

Vibert, Ralph, *Memoirs of a Jerseyman*, Jersey, 1991.

Virgili, Fabrice, *Shorn women – Gender and punishment in Liberation France*, Oxford, 2002.

Vilatte, Sylvie, *L'insularité dans la pensée grecque*, Paris, 1991.

Wachsmann, Nikolaus, *Hitler's prisons: Legal terror in Nazi Germany*, London, 2004.

Warmbrunn, Werner, *The German occupation of Belgium 1940-1944*, New York, 1993.

Weinmann, Martin, ed., *Das nationalsozialistische Lagersystem*, Frankfurt, 1990.

Weithley, Richard, *So it was. One man's Story of the German occupation from boyhood to manhood 1940-1945*, Jersey, 2001.

Wood, Alan, and Mary Wood, *Islands in danger. The story of German Occupation of the Channel Islands*, London, 1955.

2 UNPUBLISHED MATERIAL

Chardine, Albert, 'Recollections' (a typed transcript of his recollections, custody of the Société Jersiaise).

De Gruchy, Dorothy, 'Jersey, personal diary'.

Gardner, W.G.A., 'The story of a group of British war-resisters who fell into enemy hands in the German occupied Channel Islands in World War 2', unpublished history, 1991 (custody of the Société Jersiaise).

Garland, Garfield, 'A brief history of the Guernsey deportees to Germany, September 1942 to June 1945'

L'Amy, J.H., 'The German occupation of Jersey', unpublished memoirs, n.d. (custody of the Société Jersiaise).

Stocker, W.A., personal diary (custody of the Société Jersiaise).

On-Line resources

Bunting, Madeleine, 'Our part in the Holocaust: One Channel Island at least is owning up to its wartime shame', *Guardian Online*, <http://www.guardian.co.uk/comment/story/0.3604.1130.153.00.html>

'The Channel Islands Birth Cohort Study', <http://www.lsbu.ac.uk/health/research_exfunded.shtml>

'Documents of the Holocaust, Part III, Evidence by Blobel on the burning of bodies and obliterating the traces of bodies of Jews killed by the Einsatzguppen', <www1.yadvashem.org/about_holocaust/documents/part3/doc212.html>

Fremdherrschaft und Kollaboration: Erscheinungsformen in Nordosteuropa 1900-1950, Nordost-Institut in Lüneberg, Germany, 13-16 November 2003,<www.ikgn.de/veranstaltungen.kollaboration.htm >

Hämäläinen, Unto, 'More than just eight deportations to Nazi Germany. New book reveals 3,000 foreigners handed over during World War II', *Helsingin Sanomat International Edition*, 4 November 2003, <www.helsinki-hs.net/news.asp?id=20031104IE14>

Hassall, Peter, *Night and fog prisoners*, memoirs published online, <www.jerseyheritage trust.org/occupation_memorial/pdfs/hassallbookcomplete.pdf>

Jakobson, Max, 'Wartime refugees made pawns in cruel diplomatic game. Elina Sana book describes history of refugees extradited from Finland to Nazi Germany', *Helsingin Sanomat International Edition*, 4 November 2003, <http://www.helsinki-hs.net/news.asp?id=20031104IE7>

Straede, Therkel, *Oktober 1943. Die dänischen Juden-Rettung vor der Vernichtung*, <www.um.dk/publikationer/um/deutsch/oktober/oktober.doc>

Theses and Dissertations

Constantakopoulou, Christy, 'The dance of the islands: perceptions of insularity in classical Greece', Ph. D. Thesis, Oxford, 2002.

Evans, A., 'The language of occupation: Guernsey, 1940-1945', MA dissertation, Warwick, 2002.

Forrester, J.M., 'Nearer to France, closer to home: tourism and the Jersey way of life', Ph. D., Queen's University, Belfast, 1996.

Jones, Priscilla Dale, 'British policy towards 'minor' Nazi War criminals', *1939-1958*, Ph D. dissertation, Cambridge, 1990

Kelleher, J.D., 'The rural community nineteenth-century Jersey', Ph. D., Warwick, 1991.

Le Herissier, Roy, 'The development of the government of Jersey 1771-1969', Ph. D., Kent, 1971-2.

Le Rendu, Luke, 'The positive management of dependency: Jersey's survival as a microstate in the modern world', D. Phil., Oxford, 1999.

Ochsen, Kristine (von), 'Claude Cahun-Published / Unpublished. The textual identities of Lucy Schwob 1914-1944', University of East Anglia, 2003.

Ralphs, Christopher Philip, 'The Atlantic Wall, testament to the Third Reich – A study of the German defences of the Atlantic Coast during 1941-44', BA dissertation, University of Glasgow, 1994.

3 PERIODICALS, NEWSPAPER ARTICLES, BROCHURES

'Banking in Jersey under German Occupation', in: *Journal of the Institute of Bankers*, October 1946, 208 pp.

Banks, A. Leslie, 'Effects of enemy occupation on the state of health and nutrition in the Channel Islands', in: *Monthly Bulletin of the Ministry of Health and the Emergency Public Health Laboratory Service*, 4 (1945), 184-195.

Bell, William, 'Escape from Alderney', in: *Channel Islands Occupation Review*, 26 (2000), 5-15.

Bloxham, David, 'The Jews of the Channel Islands and the Rule of Law 1940-1945 by David Fraser', in: *English Historical Review*, CXVII, 470 (February 2002), 226-227.

Coutanche, Lord Alexander, 'The Government of Jersey during the German Occupation', in: *Société Jersiaise Bulletin*.

Crill, Peter, 'The story of an escape from Jersey', in: *Société Jersiaise Bulletin*, 21 (1973-1976), 107-112.

Ellison, George et al., 'How did the Occupation affect the health of Channel Islanders? A rationale for the 'Channel Islands Birth Cohort Study', in: *Channel Islands Occupation Review*, 26 (1998), 39-43.

Frowd, Michael et al., 'A Russian in hiding – Feodor ('Bill') Burriy', in: *Channel Islands Occupation Review*, 27 (1999), 59-70.

Ginns, Margaret J., 'Karl Greier-Reluctant soldier' in: *Channel Islands Occupation Review 1981*, 46-67.

Ginns, Margaret, 'French North-African prisoners of war in Jersey', in: *Channel Islands Occupation Review 1985*, 50-70.

Ginns, Michael, 'The Commandant', in: *Channel Islands Occupation Review 1981*, 6-11.

Ginns, Michael, 'The 319 Infantry Division in the Channel Islands', in: *Channel Islands Occupation Review*, 19 (1991), 40-68.

Grove, Jenny Chamier, 'Jail and escape under the jackboot', in: *Channel Islands Occupation Review*, 29 (2001), 29-43.

Heaume, Richard, 'Marie Ozanne', in: *Channel Islands Occupation Review*, 23 (1995), 79-82.

Holmes, D.C., 'The story of the Palace Hotel explosion, March 1945', in: *Channel Islands Occupation Review 1980*, 25-28

Hull, Mark M., 'Accidental tourists: Germany, the Channel Islands and espionage 1940-1945', in: *Channel Islands Occupation Review*, 29 (2001), 10-28.

Le Brocq, Norman, 'Clandestine activities', in: *Channel Islands Occupation Review*, 27 (1999), 39-58.

Mayne, Richard, 'People who escaped from Jersey during the Occupation', in: *Channel Islands Occupation Review 1975*, 22-24

Mayne, Richard, 'Forgotten islanders', in: *Channel Islands Occupation Review 1974*, 15-18

Perrin, Dennis G., 'Jersey freemasonry during the Occupation', in: *Channel Islands Occupation Review*, 23 (1995), 83-87.

Powell, Colin, 'Occupation and Liberation: A financial perspective', in: *Société Jersiaise Bulletin*, 26 (1993-1996), 363-380.

Rose, Dr. Alistair, 'Impressions of the Occupation of Guernsey', in: *Channel Islands Occupation Review*, 28 (2001), 6-28.

Srebnik, Henry, 'Small island nations and democratic values', in: *World Development*, 32 (2004), 329-341.

SPD Preungesheim, *8. Mai 1945-8. Mai 1985. Preungesheim '40 Jarhe danach – Erinnern oder vergessen?'*, 1985.

White, Herbert, 'Methodism Occupied', in: *Channel Islands Occupation Review*, 22 (1997), 51-60.

Willmot, Louise, 'The goodness of strangers: Help to escaped Russian slave labourers in occupied Jersey 1942-1945', in: *Contemporary European History*, II, 2 (2002), 211-227.

Willmot, Louisa, 'Noel McKinstry', in: *Channel Islands Occupation Review*, 31 (2003), 25-30.

Facsimile of an order from Himmler to List in: *Channel Islands Occupation Review*, 34 (2004), 20.

Jersey Evening Post
March 1940-December 1947, September 1963, March 1966, February 1995, November-December 1996, July 1997

Guernsey Star
June 1940-December 1945

Guernsey Express
June 1940-December 1945

Daily Telegraph
'Appeal of sleeping with the enemy – John Keegan finds a new history too fair to live up to its own hype', 21 January 1995.

Die Neue Ordnung
'Abstecher nach den Kanalinseln', 16 August 1942

Magdeburger Zeitung
'Im kleinsten Feudalstaat der Welt', 3 April 1939.

Sunday Telegraph
'A little bit of Nazi Britain', 29 January 1995.

The Times
'Finance in the Channel Islands', 8 May 1945.
'Obituary: Lord Coutanche Former Bailiff of Jersey', 19 December 1973.
'Islands struggle to keep us occupied', 18 July 2004.

Index

216th Infantry Division (ID) 174
319th Infantry Division (ID) 124, 174, 176, 177, 183, 198, 208
999 Brigade 205–6

Ackermann, Leo 195, 197–8
'Administration of the Channel Islands under the German Occupation, The' 240–1
agricultural workers 153–4
agriculture 6–7
    Alderney 201–2, 227
    black market 39–40
    dairy herds 5, 96, 105, 147
    Guernsey 6–8
    Jersey 6, 8, 9n
    potatoes 8, 9n, 153
    pre-war 3
    sheep 202
    vegetables and fruit 6, 7, 8, 9n, 23
    wheat 5, 6, 8, 34, 201–2
alcohol 10, 35, 36
Alderney
    agriculture 201–2, 227
    barter trade 34
    black market 34, 208, 214
    British civilians 192, 201, 202–3, 217
    corruption 208–9, 212–16, 228
    deaths 199–200, 206, 207, 209–10, 213, 215, 218–21
    eliminatory prejudice 206–7, 209, 212
    escapes 199, 200, 217
    Feldkommandantur 184, 201
    food 204, 208, 209–10, 213, 215, 217, 228
    forced workers 193, 205, 218
    fortifications 192, 212
    French Jews 194, 227
    Germans 204–7, 212, 217, 218
    health 204, 214
    labour camps 193–5, 194, 216
    lack of civilians 227–8
    liberalisation 215
    looting 192
    mismanagement 184, 212–17
    Occupation 191, 192, 201
    officers 204
    'Ostarbeiters' 193
    OT 191, 194, 195–6, 197–8, 200, 201–2, 203, 206, 208, 210, 211, 213, 214, 215, 217, 221
    OT partner firms 195–6
    penal colony 203
    prisoner transports 220–1

prostitution 214–15
Resistance workers 195
Russians 193–4, 196, 197, 203, 206, 207, 212, 218, 220
slave labour 191, 206–11, 216, 218
SS 184, 191, 196–9, 200, 206, 208–9, 210–11, 215–16, 221
survival 215, 216–18
violence 191–2, 206–11
volunteers 193
workforce 194, 218
Allied air raids 19, 57, 109, 111, 115, 161, 178, 184
Amicale d'Aurigny 219, 221
anonymous letters 43, 51–2, 66, 106; *see also* denunciations
anti-Semitism 59, 75, 141, 184
    Europe 57–8, 62
    France 132
    Germany 162, 187
    Jersey 79, 94
    see also Jews
Attenborough, G 31, 34, 35, 40, 42, 78, 156
Attlee, Clement 247
Audrain, Dennis 110
Auerbach, Sonderführer Hans 204

Bailiffs 61
    Guernsey *see* Carey, Victor; Sherwill, Ambrose
    Jersey *see* Coutanche, Alexander
    post-war assessment 240, 247–8
Bake (CID) 244
Bandelow, Major 183
banking 21–5, 26–9, 45, 48–9, 54–5
bankruptcy 53
barber and hairdresser shops 36, 37
Barclays Bank 21–2, 23, 27
barter trade 30, 31, 32, 34, 38, 40, 41
Bates, Marion 221
Baudains, Mrs 252–3
Bedane, Albert 131
Belgians 222, 224
Belgium 12
Benes, Edvard 102, 103
'benign occupation' 183
Bercu, Hedwig 131, 138, 142n
Berger, Dr 128
Bergman, Ingmar 58
Bertram, W J 100, 239n
Bertrand, L E 112–14
Best, Dr Werner 184
Billot, George 239n

birth rates 155
    illegitimate births 168–9, 172
black market 14, 30–41
    agriculture 39–40
    Alderney 34, 208, 214
    auction sales 30, 41
    barter trade 30, 31, 32, 34, 38, 40, 41
    currency 24, 25
    double standards 31–2
    Europe 39, 96
    formation 30–1
    French imports 38, 96
    German involvement 37–9, 40, 126, 214
    grievances 232
    grocers 37
    Guernsey 34, 37–8, 40
    Jersey 34–5, 38
    law enforcement 42–3, 138
    looted goods 41
    luxury goods 40–1
    morality 31, 33, 85
    Organization Todt 38
    prices 35, 36–7, 37t, 40
    Purchasing Commission 18–20, 21
    stages 34–5
    types 34
blackout regulations 82
Blackwenn, Dr 123
Blampied, Edmund 141–2
Blampied, John 34, 173
Blampied, Marianne 141–2
Bloch, Dr 197
Blücher, Countess 182
Bode (GFP) 126
Bödeker, Heinrich 162
Bogatenko, Peter 107
Bogrand, Raphael 33
Bois & Bois 99
Boots the Chemist 19, 28, 30, 149–50
Bormann, Martin 140
Bosland & DeWolf 196, 215–16
Bracken, Brendan 102
Braun (Baubrigade) 196
Brichta, Julia 138
Bridges, Sir Edward 240
Britain 14, 59, 61, 170, 251
British army personnel 75, 77, 140; see also
    commando raids
British civilians 192, 201, 202–3, 217
British Intelligence 127, 237, 249–50
'Britton, Colonel' 101, 105
Brock, Maria 217, 224
Brooks, T J 102
Brosch, Dr 89
Brown, Mary and Constance 229
Brown's Café, Jersey 229
Budny, Antoni 216
Bunting, Madeleine 59, 131, 140, 167–8, 171, 216,
    221, 258–9

Burbach, Johann 217–18
Burckhardt (Red Cross) 184
Buryi, Feodor (Bill) 106, 130
Busse, Kurt 210, 213
Butterworth, Mr A 19, 150, 152–3
Büttmann, Bauleiter 195, 212, 214

cable sabotage 83–5
Caesar, Hans-Joachim 28
'Cahun, Claude' see Schwob, Lucie
Cardinal (OT) 197, 198
Carey, Victor 23, 61, 83, 84, 86, 87–8, 141, 236, 240,
    241–2, 243, 247
Casper, Dr Wilhelm 18, 139, 176, 184–5
Channel Islands
    conformity 71, 104
    continuity 67–9
    German perception of 185–9
    insularity 1, 141, 252
    population 1, 2
    relationship with Germany 67–8, 158–9
    wealth 1, 3, 55
    see also Hague Convention
Channel Islands Monthly Review 184
Channel Islands Occupation Birth Cohort Study
    154–5
Channel Islands societies 102
'Channel Islands under German Occupation, The'
    243
children 151, 156, 223, 226
CID (Criminal Investigation Department, UK) 237,
    249
Clark, Ernest 202
clergy 117, 134
Clift (Petrol Controller) 231n
clothing 9, 10, 19, 43
Cohen, Frederick 131, 143n
Cohu, Rev Clifford 115–17, 130
collaboration 58–9, 74, 97–8
    Britain 59, 61, 251
    classification 238
    co-operation 61–7
    collaborationism 59–60
    conspiracy of silence 52
    definitions 57, 59–60, 251
    Denmark 67
    Eastern Europe 57
    economic collaboration 58
    France 60, 61, 68, 74, 95, 144
    Germany 57
    Greece 68
    Guernsey 80–4, 85–9, 90–1, 236
    and Hague Convention 92–3
    heart-and-soul collaboration 67, 74–5, 97, 202
    'horizontal collaboration' 167–72, 232, 235, 252
    Jersey 84–5, 89, 236
    local authorities 61–7, 69–74, 75–8, 79, 80, 95–6,
    231
    margins of action 72–3

Netherlands 61
police 78–9
post-war view 233–53
posturing 93–5
'restraint and influence' 77
'River Kwai' syndrome 78
shield philosophy 67, 95, 97
state collaboration 59, 60, 68
submission 67, 97
Sweden 58
Switzerland 58
tactical collaboration 67, 75–9, 80, 97
types 67
see also anonymous letters; denunciations; resistance
commando raids 90–1, 134
communications 1, 2
compensation 52–3
concentration camps 74, 107, 134, 135, 210–11
    Auschwitz 57, 133
    Buchenwald 199
    Sachsenhausen 196, 199
Constantakopoulou, Christy 1
Cooper, Fred 100
Cornish (butcher) 38
corruption
    Alderney 208–9, 212–16, 228
    Germans 10, 25–6, 39, 43, 208–9
    see also black market
Cortvriend, V V 151
Coutanche, Alexander 31, 35, 54, 64, 73, 77, 84–5,
        88, 93–4, 123, 124, 132, 136, 173, 177, 189,
        201, 228, 236, 239, 241, 242n, 243, 245, 247
Coutanche, Centenier 238n
Creron, Thomas 202–3
Cresley (food controller) 100
Crill, Constable Sydney 239n
Crill, Sir Peter 97
Cruickshank, Charles 34, 84
culture 174, 182
currency
    control 44–5
    Purchasing Commission 21–4
    speculation 24–7, 39, 45
    withdrawal of RM 47
Customs controls 14
Czechs 102–3, 174, 179, 224

Daily Sketch (Guernsey) 40, 51
Davey, James 63
Davidson, Nathan 142n
Davies, Peter 60, 67, 97
DAWI *see* German Institute for Foreign Studies
De Beauvoir, Simone 91
De Gaulle, Charles 103
De Gruchy, Dorothy 173
De Sainte Croix, Eddie 93
deaths 151, 152–3, 154, 155
    Alderney 199–200, 206, 207, 209–10, 213, 215,
        218–21

Guernsey 3, 150, 152–3, 154, 226
    Jersey 150, 154, 226, 227
debt 53–4
Dening, Captain J R 103, 237, 240, 244
Denmark 67, 94, 132, 184–5, 191
denunciations 39, 76, 128–9
    anonymous letters 43, 51–2, 66, 106
    Guernsey 88, 114, 126
    Jersey 63, 66
    post-war 236
Département de la Manche 17
deportations 42, 75, 93, 233
    Alderney 220–1
    categories 134
    Freemasons 134, 141
    GFP 126
    Jersey 64, 93, 158, 223–4
    Jews 133, 134, 136n, 139, 141–2
    post-war 245, 247, 252–3
Deslandes, Mary 158
Deubau (Düsseldorf) 195, 198
Dökel, OT-Truppführer 224
Dorey, Jurat Edgar 7, 100, 241
Dorothea Weber 221
Du Parq, Lord Justice 88, 233
Duquemin, Cyril 114
Duret Aubin, Charles 43, 48, 63–5, 66, 73, 86, 88,
        89, 124, 166, 231n, 246
Dutch citizens 50, 131, 196, 214, 215, 224, 229

Ebersbach, Dr 161
Ebert (Sylt) 207
economics
    compensation 52–3
    Guernsey 4, 24, 47, 49, 53, 55, 90
    import controls 14
    Jersey 4, 47, 48–9, 53–4, 55
    law enforcement 12–14, 31–2, 42–4, 72
    normalisation 45–6
    Occupation costs 4–5, 21, 24, 44, 92
    pre-war 3, 13
    price control 9–13, 42–3, 147
    quality and distribution control 9
    rationing 8–9, 147
    securities trading 29–30
    subsidies 5, 15
    wage control 14–15
    war economies 2–3
    war profits 46, 47–50
    see also banking; black market; currency; employ-
        ment; supplies
Ede, Chuter 242, 247–8
Eichmann, Adolf 186, 254
Einart (GFP) 37, 111, 127, 128
Einsatzstab Reichsleiter Rosenberg (ERR) 128,
        140
electricity 6, 11, 12, 113, 114
Emma C 38, 85
employment 4, 5, 7, 14–16

escapes and escapees
    Alderney 199, 200, 217
    debriefings 99, 102, 111, 178–9, 231–2
    forced and slave labour 105–8, 123, 125, 129–30
    Guernsey 82, 100, 108, 110, 178, 185
    help given to 71, 99–100, 105–10, 130
    Jersey 71, 99–100, 105–8, 110, 178
Europa Seminar 187
evacuations 2, 41–2, 92, 151, 176
Evening Press (Guernsey) 88
evictions of civilians 3, 90, 153, 163–4

Falla, Frank 114–15
Falla, Raymond 3n, 17, 18, 19, 72–3
Feldkommandantur (FK) 73, 110, 175–7
    Alderney 184, 201
    Chartres 80
    Guernsey 7, 8, 89
    Jersey 14, 28, 29, 66, 73, 76, 89, 124
    Nebenstelle 89, 182
    shipping 18, 73
    St Lô 17
Ferrers (British Consul) 125–6
Filleul, Don 167
Financial & Trust Company Ltd 28
Finkelstein, John 134–5
Finland 144–5, 181
fishing 82, 112, 148
FK *see* Feldkommandantur
Fletcher, R E H 9, 13, 159–60, 222
food
    Alderney 204, 208, 209–10, 213, 215, 217, 228
    barter trade 34
    bread 5, 147
    cooking 148–9
    diet 76, 151–2
    ersatz ingredients 148
    fish 82, 148
    from France 18–19
    Guernsey 90, 147, 228
    Jersey 147, 151–2, 224, 228
    meat 19, 20–1, 39–40, 42, 147
    potatoes 9n, 148
    pre-war 3
    prisons 76
    rationing 8–9, 151
    salt 6, 148
    scarcity 8, 9, 95, 148–9, 151, 152–3, 154, 155, 160, 178–9, 181
    vegetables 9, 148
    see also agriculture; milk; supplies: prices
Force 135 46, 47, 91, 236–7, 240, 251
forced workers
    Alderney 193, 205, 218
    escapees 105–8
    Guernsey 222
    Jersey 222, 225
    see also slave labour
Ford Motor Company 58

Forster, Ivy 107
fortifications 156, 158, 176, 177, 181
    Alderney 192, 212
    Guernsey 6, 222
    Jersey 222–3
France
    anti-Jewish measures 132
    armistice 68
    black market 96
    collaboration 60, 61, 68, 74, 95, 144
    food 18–19, 153
    fortresses 181
    illegitimate births 172
    prostitution in Paris 171
    resistance 79–80, 103, 109
    supplies from 2, 3, 16–20, 38, 96
Frank (Alderney) 214
Franka 220
Fraser, David 94, 139–40, 141–2
Free French 103
Freeman-Keel, Tom 221
Freemasonry 73, 75, 77, 128, 134, 140–1
French, Brigadier 46, 237, 243
Frowd, Mike 252
fuel 5, 12, 17, 19, 114, 148–9

Gallichan, Walter 203
Garden, Centenier 63–5, 100
GASP (Guernsey Active Secret Press) 112
Geheime Feldpolizei (GFP) 124–5
    Guernsey 38, 127–8
    Jersey 66, 120, 121, 125–7
German Institute for Foreign Studies (DAWI) 186, 187
Germans *see* Occupation troops
Germany 14, 57, 162, 171, 187
Gestapo 124–5, 126, 134, 135, 144
GFP *see* Geheime Feldpolizei
Gilbert, Charles 248
Gill, A A 255
Gillingham, Joseph 114
Ginns, Michael 68
Glasshouse Utilisation Board (GUB) 4, 6, 7, 9n, 165
Goebbels, Josef 120
Goebel, Dr 126
Goedhardt, Bauleiter 195
Goettmann (German official) 126
gold and jewellery 30, 39, 40
Goldhagen, Daniel Jonah 57
Göring, Hermann 94, 120, 140
Gould, Louisa 106–7, 130
Gould, Maurice 110
Granville raid 181
Grasset, Sir Arthur 245
Grau, Herr 167
Greece 68
Gregory, Adrian 257n
Grosskurth, Heinrich 181
Grünfeld, Marianne 133, 243

Gruschke, Bronislaw 209
Guardian 59
GUB *see* Glasshouse Utilisation Board
Guernsey
    agriculture 6–8
    and Alderney 201
    billeting 89, 159
    births 169
    black market 34, 37–8, 40
    children 151
    collaboration 80–4, 85–9, 90–1, 236
    Committee for the Control of Essential
            Commodities 18, 50
    deaths 3, 150, 152–3, 154, 226
    denunciations 88, 114, 126
    escapes and escapees 82, 100, 108, 110, 178, 185
    evictions 90
    Farm Produce Board 9n
    Feldkommandantur (FK) 7, 8, 89
    finance 4, 24, 47, 49, 53, 55, 90
    fishing 148
    food 90, 147, 228
    forced workers 222
    fortifications 6, 222
    GFP 38, 127–8
    glasshouses 4, 6, 7, 9n, 165
    health 123, 149, 150, 151, 171–2, 227
    Jews 133, 136, 138, 139, 143, 243
    Labour Bureau 15
    labour camps 222
    law enforcement 124
    Nebenstelle 89, 182
    Occupation 191
    Organization Todt (OT) 209
    OT partner firms 222
    police 91
    post-war assessment 241–2, 243, 252
    Potato Board 4, 9n
    prostitution 171–2
    RAF raid 109
    resistance 81, 82, 88, 104, 105, 108, 111, 112–15,
            118–19
    slave labour 222, 226
    SS 139
    unemployment 5, 7
Guernsey Active Secret Press (GASP) 112
Guernsey Underground News Service (GUNS) 113,
        114
Guernsey Zeitung 205
guide books and brochures 166, 205
Gunkel, Herman 90, 161–2, 164

Hacquoil, Dora 107
Hacquoil, George de la Perrelle 239n
Hagen, Herbert 186
Hague Convention
    banking 29
    Channel Islands reliance on 69–70, 72, 189
    'correct relations' 73–4

German view of 70, 89, 92–3
    interpretation of 92, 201
    labour 15, 16, 92
    legal 'black holes' 70
    occupation costs 92
    'radio offences' 65, 78
    services and supplies 18, 92
Hälker, Kurt 109
Hall (Jersey purchaser) 19–20
Hans Grimich 222
Harmsen, Judge 157
Harrison, Arthur 228
Hassall, Edmund 38, 85
Hassall, Peter 32, 50, 110
Hathaway, Sybil, Dame of Sark 182–3
Haushofer, Professor Albrecht 187
Hay, First Lieutenant 207
health 150–1, 153
    Alderney 204, 214
    diet 76, 151–2
    Guernsey 123, 149, 150, 151, 171–2, 227
    Jersey 123, 149, 150, 151, 171
    medicine 6, 19, 149
    occupation troops 150, 166, 171–2, 174, 181, 204,
            214
    VD 171–2, 214
Heider, Kommandant 129
Heilmann & Littmann 222, 224
Helling (OT) 208, 214
Hemmen, Hans-Richard 22
Heydrich, Reinhard 102, 184, 186, 187
high society 181–3, 185
Hill, Catherine (née Jacobs) 138
Himmler, Heinrich 120, 198, 211, 215
Hind, General 251–2
Hirschfeld, Gerhard 60
Hitler, Adolf 59, 120, 127
Hoffman, Johann 212, 213
Hoffman, Major Karl 192, 212–13, 214, 219
Hoffman, Stanley 59, 60
Holocaust 254
Home Office 46, 48, 50, 54, 86–7, 151, 158, 233–4,
        238, 239, 244, 245, 246, 247, 250
Huelin, Les 108
Hüffmeyer, Admiral 177, 181
humour 173
Huyssen affair 75–6, 142

IBM 58
Information and Records Branch 99, 157
insularity 1, 141, 252
interdependence 158–9
internment camps 19, 31, 133n, 134, 137, 141, 193
Irish citizens 233, 235, 246, 252, 253
'Island At War' (TV series) 183, 255
Italians 134, 174, 222, 245, 252

Jakobson, Max 144
Jassner, Inspector 127

Jean Langlois & Co, Rennes 19
Jersey
  agriculture 6, 8, 9n
  billeting 89, 159
  births 168–9
  black market 34–5, 38
  children 151
  collaboration 84–5, 89, 236
  deaths 150, 154, 226, 227
  defiance 229–30
  denunciations 63, 66
  Department of Agriculture 9n, 13
  Department of Essential Commodities 13
  Department of Transport and Communications
     9n
  deportations 64, 93, 158, 223–4
  escapes and escapees 71, 99–100, 105–8, 110, 178
  Feldkommandantur (FK) 14, 28, 29, 66, 73, 76,
     89, 124
  finance 4, 47, 48–9, 53–4, 55
  food 147, 151–2, 224, 228
  Food Control Office 9n
  forced workers 222, 225
  foreign workers 223, 224
  fortifications 222–3
  General Hospital 230
  GFP 66, 120, 121, 125–7
  health 123, 149, 150, 151, 171
  Jews 79, 94, 132, 134, 136, 137–9, 143, 243
  labour camps 222
  law enforcement 124
  liberalisation 227
  Occupation 191
  OT 158, 224, 226–7, 229–30
  OT partner firms 222–3, 224
  police 38, 63–6, 78–9, 91, 124
  post-war assessment 236–7, 238, 239, 241, 243,
     245–7, 252–3
  prostitution 171
  resistance 84, 99–100, 104, 105–9, 115–18, 119–24
  Russians 158, 223, 224, 225, 226, 227, 228, 229
  slave labour 124, 222–6
  subsidies 5
  unemployment 5
  violence 224, 225, 226, 227, 229
Jersey Communist Party 108
Jersey Democratic Party 108, 238, 246
Jersey Evening Post 84, 226, 228, 252
Jersey Loyalists 238, 241, 245, 246
Jews
  administrative discrimination 75, 76–7, 79, 93–4,
     135–40, 141–5
  Alderney 194, 227
  anti-Jewish measures 131–3, 135–9
  aryanisations 136n, 137
  civilian residents 133–4
  deportations 133, 134, 136n, 139, 141–2
  Europe 57–8, 62, 136–7, 144–5
  Guernsey 133, 136, 138, 139, 144, 243

  Holocaust 254
  Jersey 79, 94, 132, 134, 136, 137–9, 144, 243
  'U-boats' 131
  yellow stars 139
  see also anti-Semitism
Jodl, General 92
Jouault, Jean Louis 17, 20

Kaiser, Josef 220
Kamprad, Ingvar 58
Karl Ploetner 222
Kassens, Herr 158
Keegan, John 258
Kehl & Co 224
Keynes, John Maynard 2–3
Kibble, Ernest 203
Killer, Frank 226
Klebeck (Baubrigade) 196, 200
Knackfuss, Colonel 15, 89, 123, 129, 183, 227, 229
Knott, Lady 100
Kondakov, Georgi 197, 216, 218, 219
Konnertz, Frontführer 198
Koslov, Grigori 107
Krause 19
Kricsbach, Clemens 205–6
Krüger (Alderney) 214
Kugler, Oberleutnant 171

labour requisition 15–16
Lainé, Jurat Sir Abraham 133
Lainé, Miss A 222
Lambert (French consul) 108
Lanz, Major Albrecht 82n, 86, 89, 104, 183
Laval, Pierre 68
law enforcement 70–1
  black market 42–3, 138
  differential treatment 77
  economic regulation 12–14, 31–2, 42–4, 72
  German courts 124
  'greater good' 63–5, 77–8, 129, 144
  Guernsey 124
  Jersey 124
  legal traditions 71
  looting 41
  offences 105, 114, 125–6, 142
  'radio offences' 63–6, 78, 105, 110–11, 115–16,
     117–18, 203, 204
  'restraint and influence' 77
  Royal Courts 12, 14, 50, 105, 137
  Sark 104, 126
  sentences 104, 107, 114, 121–2
  see also concentration camps; Hague
     Convention; internment camps; police;
     prisons
Le Brocq, Norman 108–9, 227
Le Brun, Centenier 238n
Le Brun (Vale resident) 52
Le Cocq (Alderney) 203
Le Druillenec, Harold 107, 130

Le Feuvre, Deputy Philip 239n
Le Feuvre, Jurat Francis 241
Le Gresley (solicitor) 99–100
Le Maistre, Vernon 72
Le Marinel, Very Rev Matthew 31
Le Masurier, Major 100, 231n
Le Quesne, Edward 16, 64, 79, 124, 225, 232
Le Quesne, John 227
Le Riche's grocery, Guernsey 81
Le Sueur, Bob 31, 90, 100, 106, 107, 130
Leach, Mollie 118n
Leale, John 7–8, 16, 22, 33, 54, 69, 81, 83, 86, 87,
        88, 89, 92, 97, 164–5, 236, 240, 242
Legg, Ernest 114
Liberation Day 257
Linke, Frontführer 212, 214
List, Maximilian 196, 197–8, 200, 215
Lloyd, Esther Pauline 137, 138–9, 142n
Lloyds Bank 21, 26
local authorities
        administrative discrimination 75, 76–7, 79, 93–4,
                135–40, 141–5, 231
        'collaboration' 61–7, 69–74, 75–8, 79, 80, 95–6,
                231
        disempowerment 177
        finance 42–3, 44
        post-war view 233, 234, 235
        see also law enforcement; Purchasing
                Commission
looting 41, 90, 163–4, 191, 192, 225–6
Luce, Frank 223
Luftwaffe 179

Maas, Dr 183
Machon, Charles 114
Magdeburger Zeitung 185
Maggs, Violet 230
Maison Saint Louis, Jersey 117
Maison Victor Hugo, Jersey 171
Malherbe, Suzanne 41, 119–22
'Malzan' demolition party 181
Manley, Major 100, 238n
Mansell, Tom 39
Markbreiter, Charles 46, 100
Martel, Basil 162
'Martin, Basil' 129–30
Massmann, Captain 197
Mathews, Sir Theobald 238, 239–40, 243, 245–6,
        247
Maxwell, Sir Alexander 87, 234, 242
McKinstry, Dr R N 76, 106, 122–4, 149, 151, 241
mechanisation 5–6
Mental Hospital, Jersey 123
Mental Institution, Guernsey 123
Messervey (Department of Transport) 231n
MI5 103, 240, 243, 244, 247, 249
MI19 99
Michel (grower) 238n
Mière, Joe 78, 104, 167

milk 5, 15, 43, 96, 105, 147
Minotaure 221
Minshull-Ford, Maj-Gen J R 41
Misiewiec, Ted 215, 216–17, 219
'model occupation' 74, 81–2, 86
'Moore, Marcel' see Malherbe, Suzanne
Morrison, Herbert 233, 234, 235–6n, 247, 250
Moulin, Jean 79–80
Moullin (bicycle shopowner) 112
Mourant (assistant food controller) 100
Moyse, George 32, 126
Mühlbach, Paul 108–9
Müller, Major General Erich 73, 177, 180, 183, 213
Mussert, Anton 97
Mylne, Reverend 117, 148

Naumburg-on-Saale prison 116
Nazism 127, 162, 186, 191, 207, 211, 213
Nebel, Gerhard 204
Nebenstelle 89, 182
Netherlands 61, 62, 96–7, 154, 155, 191
news
        dissemination 115, 129, 189
        newssheets and leaflets 108, 110, 112, 114, 178–9
        post-war 233
        radio 63, 83, 111, 112–13, 160, 161, 162, 163, 189,
                203, 204
Newsam, Sir Frank 233–4
Nicolle, John 116
Nicolle-Symes affair 83, 86, 87, 91
Niemöller, Pastor Martin 162
Norman, Jurat 231n
North Africans 194, 205, 223, 224–5
Norway 181, 191

Oates, Major Reginald 33
Occupation costs 4–5, 21, 24, 44, 92
Occupation memory 235, 255–9
Occupation troops
        Alderney 204–7, 212, 217, 218
        aristocracy 181–3, 224
        BBC news 112
        billeting 4, 13, 21, 32, 41, 54, 89, 159
        black market 37–9, 40, 126, 214
        commando training 181
        consumerism 9
        corruption 10, 25–6, 39, 43, 208–9
        culture of obedience 72, 125, 162–3, 177–8
        Czech draftees 174, 179, 224
        food shortages 178–9, 181
        Georgians 174, 179
        'good Kommandant' 183
        health 150, 166, 171–2, 174, 181, 204, 214
        inferiority complex 164
        islanders' names for 173
        Italian auxiliaries 174
        leisure pursuits 165, 166, 167, 205
        letters to 157n
        loneliness 167

Occupation troops (*cont.*):
  looting 90, 163–4
  morale 110, 111, 128, 177–81, 204–5, 212
  naïveté 113, 125, 162, 177–8
  numbers 89, 104, 159
  officers 179–80, 204
  Polish draftees 174, 179, 224
  political paranoia 177
  pride 97
  respect for British 128, 165
  Russian battalions 157, 174, 179
  self-assertion 7–8, 164–5
  see also 216th Infantry Division; 319th Infantry
        Division; Feldkommandantur (FK);
        Geheime Feldpolizei (GFP); relationship
        between Germans and islanders
Oettingen, Prince 88, 181, 182, 185
Office des Changes, France 22
Olbricht 222
Oltsch & Co 222
Orange, Clifford 79, 131, 136, 137–8, 142–4
Ord, Reverend Douglas 3, 90, 125, 129, 152, 159,
        160–4, 169
Order for the Protection of the Occupying
        Authorities 63, 76, 129
Ordner, Julius 211
Organization Todt (OT) 18, 38, 158, 176, 195
    Alderney 191, 194, 195–6, 197–8, 200, 201–2,
        203, 206, 208, 210, 211, 213, 214, 215,
        217, 221
    Guernsey 209
    Jersey 158, 224, 226–7, 229–30
Oselton, Frank 202
Ozanne, Marie 118–19

Paehlicke (Alderney) 207
Page, Frederick 63–4, 78, 136
Pannier, Mr (Donville) 20
Pantcheff, Theodore 191–2, 196, 214, 215, 218, 220,
        221, 252
Panzer, Dr 195, 197, 198
Parker, Captain John 86
Parsenow, Captain 197
patronage 141
Paxton, Robert 74, 95
Peace Pledge Union 248
Pearl Assurance Co Ltd, Jersey 32
Perkins, Stella 106, 107–8, 125, 130, 174, 258
Pétain, Marshal Henri Philippe 59, 68, 95
Pfarr, Jacob 205–6
Pfeffer, Karl Heinz 92, 93–4, 132, 185–6, 187–9
Picot, Alexander 239n
Pike, Albert 202
Pinel, John 207
Pitolet, Berthe 107
Poehlke, Hermann 209
Polacek, Przemysl 117
Poles 174, 179, 224
police 13, 61

Guernsey 91
Jersey 38, 63–6, 78–9, 91, 124
  see also Geheime Feldpolizei (GFP)
Pontac 178
Poole, Captain 238n
Pope family 202
Portelet 148
Post Office Savings 27, 55
post-war assessment 233–54
  compensation 52–3
  deportations 245, 247, 252–3
  Europe 253–4
  Guernsey 241–2, 243, 252
  historiography 253–4
  intelligence 249–50
  Jersey 236–7, 238, 239, 241, 243, 245–7, 252–3
  oral history 254
  practicalities 252
  trials 248–9
posturing 93–5
Power, Colonel 236, 242, 249
Preungesheim prison 114–15, 116
price control 9–13, 42–3, 147
Prigent, Gordon 203, 206
prisoners-of-war 38, 88, 224–5
prisons 76, 104, 107, 114–15, 116, 124
profiteers 45, 48, 50–1, 231, 238, 243, 252
propaganda 68, 82, 101, 160–1, 163, 185, 188, 225,
        228
prostitution 171–2, 214–15
psychological pressure 149, 151, 152, 153, 163
public houses 35, 36
Purchasing Commission 3, 4, 17, 18–21, 23, 44; *see
        also* supplies

'Radio Sunshine' 52
radios
  batteries 113, 114
  BBC Editors 'Survey of the Week' 112
  confiscation 78, 110, 111, 115, 126, 158, 161, 163,
        176
  crystal sets 111, 114, 117–18
  direct messages to Channel Islands 102
  German raids 113
  listening parties 111
  news 63, 83, 111, 112–13, 160, 161, 162, 163, 189,
        203, 204
  'radio offences' 63–6, 78, 105, 110–11, 115–16,
        117–18, 203, 204
  time signals 117
Radziwill, Countess 182
Ramsbotham, Dr 191
rationing 8–9, 147, 151
Raymond J 128
Rebling (agricultural expert) 201
Red Cross 124, 152, 184, 225
Reffler, Dr 88, 118
Rehabilitation Committee 52
Reich Security Main Office 186

relationship between Germans and islanders 156–72, 256–7
  Deslandes' comments 158
  Fletcher's comments 159–60
  Leale's comments 164–5
  Ord's comments 159, 160–4, 169
  religion 118
  between the sexes 167–72, 214–15, 232, 235
  von Aufsess' comments 165–6
  Woodall's comments 166–7
resistance 71–2, 79–80, 97, 98, 99
  administrative resistance 122–4, 129–30, 135–7
  discretion 129, 130–1
  Europe 71, 79–80, 100, 102–4, 109
  futility of 103–4, 251–2
  Guernsey 81, 82, 88, 104, 105, 108, 111, 112–15, 118–19
  Jersey 84, 99–100, 104, 105–9, 115–18, 119–24
  passive resistance 105
  policy 100–2, 104
  sabotage 83–5, 105
  sheltering 71, 99–100, 105–10, 130
Rey, Charles 117–18, 118n
Rhône Poulenc, Paris 19
Richardson, Advocate 100
Richardson, Mary 131
Richardson, Philip 239n
Riches, A R 26
Richter, Sonderführer 202, 203–4
Riedel, Hans 204
Riegner, Hubert 206
Riley, Major Robin 253
Riley, Yvonne, Dame de Rozel 182, 253
Rings, Werner 60, 67
Ritchie, Douglas see 'Britton, Colonel'
'River Kwai' syndrome 78
RKKs (Reich credit cashier bills) 21–3, 24, 25, 26–7, 33–4
Romania 134–5
Romeril (farmer) 253
Rosenberg, Alfred 140
Rossi (father and son) 134
Royal Courts 12, 14, 50, 105, 137
Rozel Manor 253
rumours 31, 35, 163, 233
Russian battalions 157, 174, 179
Russian slaves
  Alderney 193–4, 196, 197, 203, 206, 207, 212, 218, 220
  escapees 105–8, 123, 125, 129–30
  Jersey 158, 223, 224, 225, 226, 227, 228, 229

Saarbrücken prison 114, 116
Salvation Army 118
Samares Manor 100
Sark 104, 126, 134, 158, 182–3, 185
Sarre, Alfred 100
Sarre, William 107
scavenging 41, 90, 148

Scavenius 94
Schmidt, Alfred 157
Schuster, Frontführer Helmuth 224
Schwalm, Lieutenant Colonel 214–15
Schwob, Lucie 41, 119–22
Scriven, Arthur James 226
Sculpher, Inspector W R 81, 118, 136, 138, 142
second-hand trade 2, 34, 43
Secret Field Police see Geheime Feldpolizei (GFP)
securities trading 29–30
Security Service (SD) 186, 187
Seger, Judge 66
Service du contrôle économique 19–20
Shawcross, Sir Hartley 52
Sherwill, Ambrose 49, 81–2, 85, 86–7, 183
shipping 1, 17, 18, 73
Sinel, Leslie 31, 42
Singer Sewing Machines Ltd, Jersey 28
Six, Franz 186–7
slave labour 68, 75, 205, 222
  Alderney 191, 206–11, 216, 218
  atrocities 191–2, 206–11, 224, 225, 226, 227, 229, 233
  economic collaboration 58
  escapees 105–8, 123
  Guernsey 222, 226
  Jersey 124, 222–6
sleep 149
Snow, Brigadier 234, 237, 239, 242, 243–4
social conformism 71, 104
Société Générale 21
'Soldier without name, The' 120
Spaniards 205
  Alderney 193, 194
  Guernsey 209
  Jersey 108, 222, 223, 224, 225, 229
Special Operations Executive (SOE) 102–3
Speer, Albert 58
Spehr, Otto 200
Spitz, Auguste 133, 243
Spohr (GFP) 127–8
SS (Schutzstaffel) 58, 184, 186, 187
  Alderney 191, 194, 196–9, 200, 206, 208–9, 210–11, 215–16, 221
  Guernsey 139
St Aubin 223, 225, 229
St Brelade 119, 120, 223, 225, 229
St Clement 108, 226
St Helier 124, 151, 178
St Lô 17, 20, 174
St Martin 149, 161
St Nazaire 158
St Ouen 106, 225
St Peter Port 108, 148, 179
St Sampson 118, 148
St Saviour 63–5, 115, 117
Standop (OT) 208, 214
Steinberger (GFP) 125–6
Steiner, Therese 133, 243

Stopford, Major 240, 243, 244–5
Suominen, Elina 144–5
supplies
    from France 2, 3, 16–20, 38, 96
    Germans 9–10, 13–14
    prices 17–18, 35, 36t, 39
    scarcity 9, 10, 34
    shipping 17, 18
    see also black market
Sweden 14, 58
Switzerland 14, 58
Szulc, Jan 215, 216

taxation 48–50, 54
Tierney, Joseph 116
Tietz (Alderney) 214
Times, The 102
Timmer, Gerrit 50–1, 252
Timmer Ltd 7, 50
tobacco 10, 13, 14, 34, 150
trade 2, 29–30, 35; see also black market
transport 2, 5–6, 95
Trautvetter, Werner 207
Treason and Treachery Act 236, 238, 240
    trials 248–9
Treasury Solicitor 234
Tregear (wholesaler) 238n
Troubil (shoemaker) 108
Troy (Jersey Evening Post editor) 238n
Turpin, Bernard 129

unemployment 4, 5, 7

V-sign campaign 101, 103, 126, 241, 243
Van Amelin, Ivan 219
Vasili (Russian prisoner) 107
Verdaguer, Jaime 209
Vibert, Alf 177
Vibert, Dennis 79, 110, 231
violence
    Alderney 191–2, 206–11
    Jersey 224, 225, 226, 227, 229

voluntary workers 193, 205, 222
Von Aufsess, Baron 85, 86, 90, 100, 165–6, 167, 168,
    170, 181, 182, 184, 228
Von Grienbacher, Freiherr Rupert 224
Von Helldorf, Lt Colonel Hans 73, 89, 165, 168,
    180, 181
Von Schmettow, Oberst Rudolf von Graf 73, 85,
    89, 100, 124, 177, 179, 180, 181, 183–4, 214,
    225–6, 228
Von Unruh, General 227

wage control 14–15
Waldeck, Prince 181
war culture 257
War Office 46, 48
war profits 46, 47–50
War Profits Levy (Jersey) Law 48
'Watchman' 148, 149
water supply 17
Weber, Dorothea 131
'Wehrmacht exhibition' (1998) 57
West, Oberbefehlshaber 73, 174, 176
Westdeutsche Steinindustrie (Saarbrücken) 222–3
White, Miss 100
Wickings, John 229 30
Willmot, Louise 105, 124, 255
wirelesses see radios
Wölfle, Karl-Heinz 32, 38, 126–7, 215–16
women 149, 167–72, 214–15, 232, 235, 252
Wood, Alan and Mary Seaton 87, 184, 236n
Woodall, F G 30, 166–7, 258
work education camps, Germany 116–17
work schemes 14–15
'World at War, The' (documentary) 62, 96
Wranowksy, Annie 139

Xaver Dorsch 220
xenophobia 143

Zachmann, Reinhold 162
Zuske, Inselkommandant 214–15, 217